Lieutenant Joseph Finkle
Redwood City, California

JUVENILE DELINQUENCY

JUVENILE DELINQUENCY

EDITED BY

Joseph S. Roucek
University of Bridgeport

10/17/60   10.00

PHILOSOPHICAL LIBRARY

Printed in the United States of America

TABLE OF CONTENTS

Preface
  Joseph S. Roucek, *University of Bridgeport*

PREFACE

Young criminals were spotlighted in the latest (1957) report from the Federal Bureau of Investigation on crime in the United States. Juvenile delinquency has increased to the point where more than half of all major crimes—robberies, burglaries, larcenies, etc.—are committed by persons under 21. Boys and girls under eighteen account for nearly 46 percent of all the arrests for serious crimes. J. Edgar Hoover, Director of the FBI, believed that young people who commit such crimes as murder "deserve notoriety." He was urging that in such cases the names of juvenile delinquents—and the names of their parents— be made public.

In May of the same year, the Senate Subcommittee to Investigate Juvenile Delinquency discarded many traditional "causes" of child crime. Lack of organized recreation, poor housing and low economic status were tossed out as real factors in the rise of delinquency. The group blamed instead weak family life and lack of psychiatrists, social workers, and other therapeutic forces to prevent or cure the personality problems arising from family and social strains at all economic levels. The Subcommittee repeatedly urged more research in the social sciences. The report said that many areas of special problems, including vandalism, never had been researched. And if the delinquency rate continues upward at the 1948 through 1955 pace, the report warned, then 1,000,000 children will appear before the courts in 1965.

However, the Subcommittee said that it had not relied completely on a projection of the census and crime statistics in predicting future trends. It expressed the view that an increasing awareness of the problem plus preventive and treatment measures taken by Federal, state and local governments might affect the current trends.

The greatest cause of crime is public indifference, Erle Stanley Gardner, the writer of detective stories, who is also a lawyer and criminologist, said on July 14, 1957, in his opening address to the institute, sponsored by the National, Western, and Colorado Probation and Parole Association, meeting in Denver.

These three spot-lighted reports are just a few selected ones of the many publications, pamphlets, and pleas continuously impressing the American public that something should be done about the ever-growing problem of juvenile delinquency. The subsequent chapters in this volume make it abundantly clear that there is apparently hardly any agreement of the many and numerous causes of this phenomenon, but that there must be a more adequate, scientific approach to it and that this approach is hindered by many popular misconceptions remaining in the folklore and common sense approach to the problem. (Probably the most prevalent misunderstanding is that juvenile delinquency can be cured by passing more laws and by appointing more police officers!).

The very flood of studies and publications covering the various aspects of juvenile delinquency indicates another need: to digest and to systematize the widely scattered available knowledge pertaining to this field, so that more effective measures for prevention (based on comparative aspects) can be taken, and that the law enforcing agencies, the administration of justice, and the maintenance of penal, correction and "re-educational" institutions, can discharge their functions more effectively. The following chapters suggest that the adequate understanding of criminal behavior is based on the theory of multiple causation, that it is always a combination of causes which produces juvenile delinquency, and that this combination varies from one case to another. This approach of this book conduces to a realistic appraisal of the many factors at work in the generation of juvenile delinquency, and cautions against the easy type of overgeneralization frequently found among those who attribute crime to a single cause, such as "The parents are to blame," "Slum conditions are the cause of crime," or "The lack of educational facilities is the cause of all troubles."

Juvenile delinquency is especially an important field to study in that it provides a source of recruits for adult crime. Organized delinquency is a cumulative social process, in the sense that each successive stage leads to more serious offense, and the longer the individual is caught up in such a pattern the more difficult it is for him to extricate himself from it.

There are as many attempted solutions offered by various social agencies to handle juvenile delinquency as there are the real or alleged causes. These need also be surveyed and known to the serious student of this problem area in order to discard the useless methods and to try out the more effective experiments. Two fundamentally opposed views clash in the treatment of the juvenile delinquent. On the one hand is the view that the delinquent must be punished because of the act he had committed against society and in order to deter him and others from further acts of delinquency. The other is the view that the goal of treatment should be the protection of society and the rehabilitation of the juvenile delinquent into normal law-abiding activities. Other factors, such as the legal definition of the juvenile delinquent, the extraordinary powers of individual discretion granted the prosecuting authorities, the whole system of juvenile courts, complicate the procedure. But the very seriousness of the whole problem has resulted in recent years in the trends emphasizing rehabilitation and the return of the criminal to society as soon as there is some assurance that he will be able to confine himself to lawful behavior. Above all, the following chapters stress that juvenile delinquency touches upon so many aspects of society that an adequate prevention program involves a vast number of interrelated activities. Although basic limitations are imposed on all preventive programs so long as there are slums and poverty, so long as the school does not effectively challenge pupils with varying needs and abilities, or so long as families are centres of personality conflict, it is also evident that much can be done within the broad limits set by the institutional structure. Thus schools can try more effectively to meet the different personality needs of their pupils, and better housing conditions, reducing congestion and assuring more adequate recreational facilities, can be sought for; or youth councils can work more effectively in coordinating community resources for youth.

Finally, these systematic surveys by specialists in their respective fields are concluded by a consideration of the international trends in juvenile delinquency—a field which is seldom and always insufficiently considered in the growing number of routine textbooks dealing with the *American* aspects of crime and juvenile delinquency.

JOSEPH S. ROUCEK

JUVENILE DELINQUENCY

Part I

The Framework

CHAPTER 1.

DIMENSIONS OF THE PROBLEM

DANIEL GLASER
University of Illinois

Defining "Delinquency"

Much controversy arising in discussions on the extent and causation of delinquency would be eliminated if the discussants all referred to the same thing when using the term "delinquency." Unfortunately, this word generally is not used in the same way by different persons, nor is it used consistently by single individuals.

The various assortments of behavior which have been called "delinquency" do not differ completely; they vary mainly in their range. The broader conceptions of delinquency generally encompass that which is involved in narrower definitions, but include other forms of behavior as well. However, all current definitions are vaguely phrased, and are inconsistently interpreted.

Legal Definitions

The first legal distinction of "delinquency" from "crime" generally is credited to the pioneer juvenile court legislation of the State of Illinois, promulgated in 1899. The definition employed at that time still is the law in Illinois, and served as the model for many other states and several foreign countries. It reads:

The words 'delinquent child' shall mean any male child who while under the age of seventeen years or any female child who while under the age of eighteen years, violates any law of this state; or is incorrigible, or knowingly associates with thieves, vicious or immoral persons; or without just cause and without the consent of its parents, guardians or custodian absents itself from its home or place or abode, or is growing up in idleness or crime; or knowingly frequents a house of ill-repute; or knowingly frequents any policy shop or place where any gaming device is operated; or frequents any saloon or dram shop where intoxicating liquors are sold; or patronizes or visits any public pool room or bucket shop; or wanders about the streets in the night without being on any lawful business or lawful occupation; or habitually wanders about any railroad yards or tracks or jumps or attempts to jump onto any moving train; or enters any car or engine without lawful authority; or uses vile, obscene, vulgar, profane or indecent language in any public place or about any school house; or is guilty of indecent or lascivious conduct; any child committing any of these acts herein mentioned shall be deemed a delinquent child. . . .[1]

The first sentence of the Illinois law indicates what lawyers generally think of as delinquency, and what constitutes delinquency in British Common Law. It is any act committed by a child which, if committed by an adult, would be a crime. This confines delinquent behavior to violations of criminal law. Although criminal law varies from state to state, these laws have considerable uniformity and specificity in their definitions of felonies (major crimes), such as burglary, larceny, robbery, and rape. They are much less specific in their definitions of misdemeanors (lesser offenses), like disorderly conduct and vagrancy. But this is only the beginning of the non-specificity involved in defining juvenile delinquency.

Returning to the first sentence of the Illinois law, we see that, in effect, it defines a child as a male under 17 years of age or a female who has not yet had her 18th birthday. This age borderline between childhood and adulthood varies from state to state. In a majority of states both boys and girls are considered juveniles if under 18, while in California one may be a juvenile until one's 21st birthday, and in Georgia and several other states one ceases to be a juvenile after one's 16th birthday. But in most states this borderline is not clear-cut: for more serious crimes one may be prosecuted as an adult criminal even at ages below the upper-limit of juvenile status. Thus, in Illinois one may be tried as an adult criminal after one's tenth birthday; the youngest person committed to an adult penitentiary sentence was thirteen. An age range in which there is jurisdiction of both adult criminal law and juvenile delinquency law exists in all but three states (New Hampshire, Oklahoma, and Virginia). The duration of this period of dual jurisdiction varies. For example, it is 16 to 18 in Indiana and Wisconsin, and 18 to 21 in California. In many states, like New York, there are differing ranges of dual jurisdiction for different types of offense, the adult courts having the greatest range of jurisdiction for the most serious offenses. Several states give adult courts exclusive jurisdiction in murder cases.

Perhaps the main differences between the legal conceptions of "delinquency" and "crime" are those indicated after the first semi-colon in our quotation from Illinois law. A juvenile can be classified as "delinquent" if he is "incorrigible" (which may mean almost anything), if he associates with "vicious or immoral persons," if he is absent from home without just cause or consent, or if he is "growing up in idleness." These types of behavior are delinquency but not crime. A boy or girl can only be arrested and placed in confinement or under court supervision for such behavior if it occurred when he or she had not yet reached the birthday which terminates juvenile status. After that birthday they may leave home, be incorrigible or grow up in idleness as much as they like, as long as they do not violate any adult criminal laws.

The derivations and ramifications of the legal treatment of delinquency in the law will be elaborated in the next chapter. Our main point here is that "delinquency" in the law is a much broader concept than "crime," although the two terms are often used interchangeably in popular discourse as well as in scientific writings on the causes of each. "Delinquency" includes all acts committed by a child which would be "crime" if committed by an adult, but it also includes a large variety of loosely defined behavior which legislators thought might be conducive to crime.

The law on delinquency is designed to prevent juveniles from developing into adult criminals as well as to deal with crimes committed by juveniles.

Psychoanalytic Definitions

Psychoanalysis has had a tremendous influence on psychiatry and clinical psychology, and has affected the treatment of delinquency through its influence on social work. Psychiatric social work has had outstanding prestige in the profession of social work, and this profession has been the source of the principal modification and supplementation of the legal profession's supervision of the treatment of delinquents in our society. This relationship between these several professions has been particularly prominent during and since the second quarter of the twentieth century.

In the early evolution of juvenile courts, during the first quarter of the twentieth century, the distinction of delinquency from crime in the law was rationalized by a simple type of behavioristic psychology. Crime, insofar as it was not explained by heredity, was seen as developing in the adult in consequence of economic deprivations and lack of moral training in childhood. The courts, therefore, were interested in correcting deficiencies in child rearing by providing shelter, supervision, and religious and vocational training.

Psychoanalytic psychology complicated earlier thinking by bringing in notions of emotional disturbances and conflicts of the unconscious mind in childhood as causes of adult criminal mentalities. The preventive interest in the treatment of delinquency thereby became much broader than that of merely dealing with dangerous acts of children and correcting neglect in formal training. August Aichhorn, the pioneer in psychoanalytic treatment of delinquents, asserted that delinquent, dissocial, "so-called problem children" and "others suffering from neurotic symptoms" could not readily be delineated because "they tend to merge into each other." This is because the basic disturbance was seen as unconscious, or "latent" delinquency, rather than visible or "manifest" delinquency. From this standpoint, treatment would be misguided if it were prompted by overt misbehavior only.[2]

Later psychoanalytic writings frequently distinguished between the delinquent and the neurotic, the former being described as one who directs his aggression outward, and the latter as one who directs his aggression inward. On the basis of this distinction, delinquents are often described as *alloplastic* personalities while neurotics are designated *autoplastic*.[3]

However, some psychatric literature refers to delinquents and criminals as "acting-out neurotics," as distinguished from other neurotics who are portrayed as more inhibited and anxiety-ridden.[4] At any rate, despite variety and inconsistency in terminology, psychoanalytic influences in thinking about delinquency have led to a broader conception of what constitutes delinquency than that characterizing purely legal thinking. From the psychoanalytic standpoint, any disturbed emotional development leading to hostility and aggressive impulses towards other persons or objects, or any other mental processes which involve violation of conventional moral values, constitutes delinquency regardless of whether or not these mental phenomena are expressed in overt acts of an aggressive or immoral nature. As Aichhorn indicated, any child who has any problem of adjustment to others in any normal situation—in the family, the school, or the community, for example—is likely to be included in the study of delinquency by psychoanalytically oriented persons.

Operational Definition: The Sociological Perspective

Sociologists studying delinquency have focussed their attention primarily on those youth who have been designated as delinquents officially by the actions of police and courts. This would suggest that sociological usage of the term "delinquent" corresponds to legal usage. Actually, such correspondence does not occur, in part because legislation on delinquency is phrased so as to be capable of highly flexible interpretation, and in part because influences other than the statutes affect an official's conception of his duties in dealing with delinquents. One of many interests of sociologists in studying delinquency has been that of determining what these additional influences are by studying just how certain children come to be selected out for official designation as delinquents.

The factors which sociological studies suggest determine the actual designation of a youth as delinquent are somewhat complex, and tend to be interrelated, but for convenience they may be classified into five main headings, as follows:[5]

a. *Tolerance Level of the Community.* It is well established that some communities will tolerate much more deviation from conventional standards of "respectable behavior" than is permitted in other communities. In general, large cities grant youth more license than small towns allow. This difference in tolerance is especially apparent with respect to such activity as creating public disorder, roaming about without supervision, and being sexually promiscuous. However, such lesser tolerance does not characterize all small towns and villages. In addition, within the larger cities, there is much variation in the tolerance of deviant behavior from one neighborhood to the next; behavior which would be overlooked in the slum areas is not condoned in the upper class residential areas. Finally, tolerance levels frequently fluctuate within any community. After a wave of certain types of delinquency, or at least, after much publicity is given to juvenile misbehavior, there is likely to be an official "crackdown" during which behavior which might previously have been overlooked will lead to arrest and the designation of those involved as delinquents.

b. *Visibility of the Misbehavior.* Some of the legislation on delinquency, as we have seen, specifies that certain misbehavior, like use of obscene language, is forbidden in public places. In general, official action is much more likely to be taken against deviant conduct if it occurs in a public place like a crowded street or a schoolroom than if it occurs in a back alley or a private home. Not only is the more public behavior more readily detected by the police, but it comes to the attention of a larger number of other citizens and hence cannot so readily be overlooked by authorities. Thus the visibility of a youth's act, in a particular instance, may be a major factor in determining whether he will be treated as a delinquent.

c. *Status of the Complainant.* Somewhat related to the visibility of misbehavior in determining what official action it will provoke is the status level of the persons who are offended by the behavior. Usually, complaints from higher status persons such as public officials or prominent business men will result in more vigorous police and judicial action than complaints from persons of low status in the community. This is particularly true with respect to petty thefts, vandalism, and disorderly conduct. Members of low status minority groups, such as poorer Negroes and Mexicans, are reported to have found that police response to their complaints is highly uncertain, and they often do not call in authorities when they are the victims of crime and delinquency. Youths, therefore, can commit offenses against them with much less risk of being officially designated "delinquent" than would be the case were they to commit offenses against more prominent persons, even in the same neighborhood.

d. *Status of the Misbehaving Youth.* It has been well established that official agencies take a more punitive attitude towards misbehavior by low status youth than towards the same behavior in higher status youth.[6] The son of a highly respected family who is caught stealing or in less serious misbehavior often is merely reprimanded or taken to his parents by the victim, or even by police, where similar activity by a youth from "across the tracks" would lead to official arrest and classification as a delinquent. In general, where the social status of the youth and his family is lower than that of the complainant, the greater the difference between their statuses, the more likely it is that the youth's activities will be called "delinquency." Furthermore, once a youth has acquired a "bad reputation" through prior infractions or being found in the company of known delinquents, the police are more likely to be called in and are more likely to take official action than they would if the same misbehavior were committed by a youth of "good reputation." Thus the prior behavior and associations of a youth may be a factor in determining whether his activity at a given time is officially treated as delinquency.

e. *Idiosyncratic Characteristics of Officials.* In addition to the aforementioned factors, innumerable variations in the thinking of law enforcement and judicial officials affect the actual designation of specific behavior as delinquency. Some judges are highly legalistic in their orientation towards juvenile behavior and refuse to hear complaints regarding acts which would not clearly be crimes if committed by an adult. Others have acquired more of a psychiatric social work orientation toward youth and are concerned with all major emotional disturbances and conflicts which a child experiences, even where no serious threat to others is manifested. Most juvenile court and police officials are somewhere between these extremes in their point of

view, but in addition, each has some distinctive personal prejudices or tolerance towards specific types of behavior, and few
are completely consistent in these matters.

We may conclude that the operational definition of delinquency, the actual designation of certain acts as "delinquency"
in the day to day work of official agencies, is a function of
innumerable social and personal variations on diverse legally
and psychoanalytically derived themes.

Measuring Delinquency

It should be obvious that anything as indefinitely defined as
delinquency cannot be measured very adequately. Nevertheless, compilations of statistics on delinquency are carried out
on a national, state and local basis. Much care should be taken
in appraising their significance.

When we talk of the quantity of delinquency in a given
area for a given period of time, we can mean several things.
First of all, we may mean the number of youth, say 10 to 17
years old, who violate certain standards of behavior (which
may or may not be precisely defined). Secondly, we may refer
to the number of such youth who are detected in such behavior.
Thirdly, we may mean the number of cases who were actually
dealt with by official agencies. Fourthly, we may mean the
cases formally heard by a juvenile court and adjudged delinquent.

Each of the successive categories above is likely to be somewhat smaller than the preceding categories. We shall discuss the
narrowest category first, and work back to the broader ones.
We should note, however, that for each of these categories we
may refer to the number of incidents of delinquency or the
number of boys involved. The latter figure is the larger of the
two on any single day, since most delinquent incidents involve
two or more perpetrators. Further difficulties arise from the
fact that if one tabulated the amount of delinquency in a
longer period of time, such as a year, one might add the youth
who was involved in delinquency several times during the
period with the youth who was involved only once, or one
might count each time a given youth was involved in delinquency as a separate case. It should be clear from all of the
foregoing that comparison of statistics on delinquency for

different areas or different periods requires detailed knowledge of how each set of statistics were gathered.

The most widely cited statistics on delinquency in the United States refer to the narrowest category of delinquents which we have distinguished, the court cases. These statistics are contained in *Juvenile Court Statistics*, published annually by the Children's Bureau of the U.S. Department of Health, Education and Welfare. This compilation was started in 1923, was altered drastically in form and title in 1927 and 1946, and received minor revisions in other years. It reports the number of youths adjudicated delinquent and is based on a tabulation of separate case judgments in a given year.

The *Juvenile Court Statistics* report issued late in 1956 reported a total of 324,369 juvenile delinquency cases disposed of during the year 1955 in 1,549 courts located in 41 states. The areas in which these courts have jurisdiction contain only 66 percent of the child population of the Unted States, but this is a more complete coverage than that of any previous issue of these statistics. It is estimated that there are over 2000 juvenile courts in the United States, but most of these do not operate on a full-time basis; their staff and facilities are used most of the time in adult civil and criminal cases.

It may occur to many that one could account for the 34 percent of the U.S. population not covered in the *Juvenile Court Statistics* for 1955 by adding approximately 50 percent to the published figures. This procedure would be questionable for many reasons, but especially, because most of the courts not reporting are from areas of low population concentration. From reports which are received it seems likely that large urban areas have much more delinquency in proportion to population than smaller communities. At present the Children's Bureau is attempting to obtain a complete tabulation of statistics from 502 courts so selected as to cover a representative sample of American communities. This sample was so chosen that the child population of the area over which the 502 courts have jurisdiction would be nearly identical with the total child population of the United States in its geographical distribution, division into different size communities, economic area distribution and racial composition. When this undertaking is completed it will be possible to make an estimate of delinquency trends in the United States by adding appropriate proportions to the data for the 502 courts representative sample. Such an estimate will merit more confidence than any estimate which may be made by expanding the figures from the larger but less representative group of courts covered in current reports.

One difficulty with the early juvenile court statistics collected by the Children's Bureau was that some courts reported a youth as a delinquent only when a judge or referee had processed a written petition, complaint or other legal paper and had formally ruled that the person complained of was a juvenile delinquent, while other courts included cases where complaints were received informally and were settled by oral agreements or orders after conferences and investigations, without the filing of legal documents. This difficulty has been resolved in part by the Children's Bureau solicitation of separate totals on "official" and "unofficial" cases from each court. Over half (51 percent) of cases reported for 1955 were handled "unofficially." It is likely that the completeness with which cases handled unofficially are reported varies sharply from court to court, depending on their record-keeping practices as well as other procedures. In the publication for 1955 the percentage of total cases which were reported as handled unofficially varied from less than 18 percent for Rhode Island to 67 percent for Ohio, and the proportions for individual cities varied even more markedly.

A second major source of statistics on delinquency in the United States is the data on arrests of persons under 18 years of age reported in *Uniform Crime Reports,* a compilation of police statistics published by the Federal Bureau of Investigation. The report issued in 1956, for the year 1955, covered 1,477 cities, each over 2,500 in population and altogether containing about one-fourth of the United States population. (See Table 2, this chapter) This is the most complete coverage yet achieved in this compilation which, in its present form, dates only from 1952. The difficulties in estimating total delinquency arrests in the United States from these figures are analogous to those arising in estimating total adjudications of delinquency from Children's Bureau statistics. There is no basis for knowing that the one-quarter of the population covered is a representative sample, and indeed, the fact that small towns and rural areas are omitted suggests that the sample is not representative. An additional major problem in use of police arrest statistics is extreme variation and fluctuation in police record-keeping, although the F.B.I. is making continuous progress in promoting standardized high quality procedures in our more than forty thousand local police systems.[7]

The tabulation of all instances of delinquency handled officially, including those handled by agencies other than the juvenile courts and the police, has never been carried out continuously for any prolonged period of time nor for any major segment of the country. However, there have been some limited surveys involving this type of tabulation, notably a pioneering experiment in our nation's capitol. For a 12-month period from June 1943 through May 1944 the U.S. Children's Bureau and the Council of Social Agencies of the District of Columbia operated a central registry which received reports on every instance of alleged delinquency handled by several different agencies representing the police, courts, social work and the school system. This study received reports on 15,223 cases of alleged delinquency involving 7,828 different children. Of the total cases, 27 percent were reported by the Juvenile Court, 13 percent by the Metropolitan Police Department, 15 percent by Public Welfare agencies and 45 percent by the Board of Education. Of the separate children involved, only 43 percent had any recorded dealings with the juvenile court during the year of this survey. It is noteworthy also that many children were referred to the juvenile court without the police being brought into their cases, although other surveys suggest that the police are the major source of court referrals and generally dispose of many cases without referring them to the court or even formally booking them.[8]

In connection with a long run study in which intensive counselling was given to presumably delinquency-prone youth, an analysis has been made of the relationship between violations of law known to the counsellors and violations recorded in the Juvenile Court for 114 boys counselled continuously from age 11 to age 16. Only 13 of the 114 boys had not broken any law, to the counsellors' knowledge, but only 40 of them had been registered in the Juvenile Court at least once in the five-year period. Of 6,416 separate infractions of law by the boys known to the counsellors, only 95 had become the basis for court complaint. There were no complaints on 1,400 violations of city ordinances, only 27 complaints (0.6 percent) on 4,400 minor offenses, and 68 complaints (11 percent) on 616 serious felony-type offenses. Incidentally, the proportion of offenses known to the court to offenses known to the counsellors was about the same for boys of every intelligence level, which contradicts a popular notion that only stupid delinquents get caught.[9]

The total number of delinquent acts committed is likely never to be known. Probably almost every youth at one time or another engages in behavior which would be considered "delinquent" by most definitions of the term. It is also probable that the majority of the less serious acts, and perhaps even a majority of the acts which would be pronounced felonies if an adult were caught at them, never are handled by any official agency. Part of this stems from an inability to detect the perpetrators of the offenses, and part of it comes from a reluctance to call in official agencies to deal with them. Specific factors affecting whether or not offenders are processed by official agencies were indicated in our discussion of the "operational" definition of delinquency.

Several investigators have attempted to estimate the relative proportions of detected and undetected delinquency by asking presumably law-abiding persons to fill out anonymous questionnaires regarding their past misconduct. Such studies have resulted in impressively frequent admissions of serious larceny, burglary, malicious mischief, falsification or fraud and other offenses by most respondents.[10] However, a survey by Professor James F. Short, Jr., of Washington State College, in which delinquents in state training schools and youth of similar age in high school were compared, suggests that those officially designated delinquent commit misconduct much more frequently than those who are not so designated. Also, the official delinquents admit more serious offenses. For example, 61 percent of high school boys and 92 percent of training school boys in a western state sample admitted stealing things worth two dollars or less, but only 5 percent of the high school boys as against 80 percent of the training schools admitted stealing things worth fifty dollars or more. Furthermore, only two percent of the high school boys admitted stealing things worth fifty dollars or more "more than once or twice," but this frequency was admitted by 48 percent of the training school boys.[11]

Estimated U.S. Delinquency

As we have seen, all routinely collected statistics on delinquency are more or less incomplete tabulations of what we have called "operationally defined" delinquency, that is, misbehavior which has come to the attention of official agencies. Absolute figures on the total amount of misbehavior occurring, including that which is not reported to official agencies, cannot possibly be obtained, nor can this total even be very meaningfully estimated. Nevertheless, by assuming that fluctuations and divisions of unreported delinquency are proportionate to fluctuations and divisions of reported delinquency, assertions frequently are made that American youth are becoming increasingly delinquent, or that certain components of the juvenile population are more delinquent than other components.

On the basis of fluctuations in juvenile court statistics, prevailing opinion holds that American youth reached a new peak of delinquency during World War II, became less delinquent during the immediate post-war years, then became increasingly delinquent from 1948 on, surpassing the wartime peak after 1952. This trend in juvenile delinquency is summarized in the first four columns of Table 1.

Arrests of juveniles were tabulated by the F.B.I. prior to 1952 on the basis of separate fingerprints submited by police agencies making arrests. These totals, in Column 5 of Table 1, reached peaks and low points in the same years as the court cases, but did not rise proportionately as high as the court cases during the war, and were particularly low during the post-war years. The latter decline generally is assumed to have been caused by the increasing practice of not fingerprinting juveniles. Accordingly, since 1952, the arrest totals have been tallied by the separate police forces from their operation logs, using standard forms and procedures recommended by the F.B.I. The *Uniform Crime Reports* have been prepared by the F.B.I. by totalling these tabulations of separate police forces rather than by counting separate fingerprint reports. When this new system was introduced the number of juvenile arrests reported immediately more than doubled, even though most of the United States population was not covered by such reports at first (see Table 2). However, the trend in these figures since

1951 still parallels the trend in juvenile court cases for the same years.

TABLE 1
Indices of Juvenile Delinquency in Relation to U.S. Child Population 10-17 Years of Age and Number of Police Employees per 1000 City Inhabitants, 1940-1955
(1940=100)

Year	U.S. child popu- lation 10-17 yrs. of age	Juvenile court delin- quency cases	Ratio of column 3 to column 2	No. of finger- prints of arrested persons under 18 submitted to F.B.I.	Police employees per 1000 city inhabitants	
					All cities	Cities over 250,000 pop.
(1)	(2)	(3)	(4)	(5)	(6)	(7)
1940	100	100	1.00	100	100	100
1941	99	112	1.13	105	—	—
1942	97	125	1.29	107	114	100
1943	96	172	1.80	135	110	98
1944	93	165	1.77	132	107	95
1945	92	172	1.87	140	104	92
1946	91	148	1.63	107	104	101
1947	91	131	1.44	97	109	105
1948	90	127	1.41	90	114	110
1949	91	136	1.49	93	117	114
1950	91	140	1.54	98	121	115
1951	93	149	1.60	106	106	103
1952	95	166	1.75	—	109	104
1953	99	187	1.89	—	111	105
1954	102	198	1.94	—	115	108
1955	105	216	2.06	—	120	114

Columns 2, 3 and 4 are based on U. S. Children's Bureau Statistical Series, Report No. 37, *Juvenile Court Statistics 1955* (Washington: 1956), Table 4; Columns 5, 6 and 7 are based on Federal Bureau of Investigation, *Uniform Crime Reports,* for the years indicated. See Table 2, and text, regarding police arrests after 1951. Data on police employees were not published for 1941.

One occasionally hears speculation that, despite the juvenile court and juvenile arrest trends, we are not at a new peak of juvenile delinquency. To assume that we are is to assume a constant rate in police and court efficiency, that is, that the delinquent behavior which comes to police and court attention constitutes a constant proportion of the total delinquent behavior occurring in our country. It is not unreasonable to assume, however, that manpower shortages and extra wartime duties made the efficiency of the police and courts low during World War II, so that the wartime peak of delinquent behavior may have been relatively higher than Table 1 suggests.

TABLE 2

Analysis of Arrests of Persons Under 18, 1952-1956

Year	Arrests of persons under 18 (in thousands)	Total population of cities reporting data for Column 1 (in millions)	No. of persons under 18 arrested per thousand total population (ratio of Column 1 to Column 2)
	(1)	(2)	(3)
1952	86	23	3.7
1953	150	37	4.1
1954	164	39	4.2
1955	196	42	4.7
1956	234	41	5.7

Based on Uniform Crime Reports for the year indicated.

Conversely, expansion of police and court staffs since the war could have resulted in an increase in the number of juvenile arrests and juvenile court cases without an increase occurring in the actual amount of delinquent behavior by American youth. Partial support for this interpretation is provided by Columns 6 and 7 of Table 1, which show some decrease in policing during the war years, especially in large cities. But the post-war decline in court cases coincided with an increase in policing, while the increase in juvenile delinquency during the Korean War coincided with a decrease in policing. Statistics on trends in juvenile court personnel are not available. It is apparent that, while we cannot be absolutely certain about the accuracy of prevailing notions that delinquency has been climbing to unprecedented heights since 1952, the validity of specific counterclaims remains undemonstrated.

The significance of urbanization for delinquency is suggested by *Juvenile Court Statistics* for 1955 which reported 35.1 cases of delinquency per 1000 population 10-17 years of age for courts serving areas of 100,000 population and over, and only 5.5 cases per 1000 population 10-17 years of age for courts serving areas of under 5000 population. These figures include both "official" and "unofficial" cases. The direct relationship between the population of a court area and its delinquency rates is fairly consistent for all sized communities. Part of the reason for this differential may well be that the courts in smaller communities operate with a narrower legalistic definition of delinquency, since these courts are staffed primarily by part-time employees among whom social work or clinical psychology training is a rarity. However, from the relationship of delinquency to the anomie and social disorganization of urban life, which is discussed elsewhere in this volume, one would expect less delinquency in smaller communities. When this is considered together with the fact that more of our population than ever before is concentrating in and around large cities, and that modern means of communication and transportation permit the rural population to live and think much like urbanites, it seems reasonable to believe that delinquency, like urbanism, may be at an all time high for the country as a whole.

Within large cities there is considerable variation in delinquency rates. For example, for the city of Chicago it is estimated that 5.7 percent of the boys 10 to 16 years old were named in juvenile court petitions alleging delinquency during 1945-1951, but the proportions for different community areas within Chicago varied from a low of 0.3 percent to a high of 16.9 percent. The corresponding figure for girls 11 to 17 years old in the city as a whole was 2.0 percent, with a low of zero and a high of 11.8 percent for different community areas within the city. Since almost all youth named in such petitions in Illinois fall within these seven year age ranges and the period covered in this survey was seven years, it is believed that these figures are close to life time probabilities of being named a delinquent for the youth of Chicago.[12] Incidentally, this probability has been close to 5 percent for the boys in Chicago throughout a period of nearly fifty years for which Shaw and McKay have investigated court records.[13] It should be noted that these are "official" delinquent cases only. However, around

90 percent of all cases reported by Cook County Juvenile Court (Chicago) have been "official" cases.

For the country as a whole, boys outnumber girls in juvenile court delinquency cases by a ratio of about 5 to 1. Recent Children's Bureau tabulations do not indicate the specific charges for delinquency complaints, but the 1945 tabulation by the Bureau named "stealing" as the complaint in 42 percent of boys' cases, followed by "act of carelessness or mischief" 19 percent, "traffic violation" 10 percent, "truancy" 7 percent, "running away" 6 percent, "being ungovernable" 6 percent, "sex offenses" 3 percent, "injury to person" 3 percent and "other reasons" 4 percent. For girls, "being ungovernable" was the principal complaint and covered 22 percent of the cases, with "running away" 19 percent, "sex offenses" 18 percent and "truancy" 13 percent. Examination of the actual misbehavior involved suggests that most of these complaints, or nearly three-quarters of girls' cases, involve conflict between the parents and the girl over the girl's activities with members of the opposite sex. In addition, "stealing" accounted for 12 percent of girls' cases, "act of carelessness or mischief" 8 percent, "injury to person" 2 percent, "traffic violation" 1 percent and "other reasons" 5 percent. It is alleged that many of these complaints also involve parent-daughter controversies over the daughter's affairs with boys. As a rule, girls' cases seem to come closer to boys' cases, both in frequency and in type of complaint, as one moves from smaller to larger communities. Complaints against girls also become closer in frequency to complaints against boys as one moves from the younger ages to the upper limits of the juvenile age range.

International Statistics

Statistics on official delinquency issued by the governments of foreign countries generally cover their respective countries more completely than any figures compiled by the United States government. This is because most countries have all courts supervised by a national Ministry of Justice. Many countries also have a national police administration, in contrast to our independent municipal police forces. Such central control is alien to the traditional American political principle of maintaining a check on the possibility of a police state which could subvert democratic government and prevent free national elections. However, the collection of uniform and complete statistics is easier in many other countries simply because national officials can prescribe standard statistical reports and can insist that these be submitted to the national government by all local courts and police offices. No U. S. governmental agency has such authority.

Nevertheless, it is almost impossible to compile any meaningful international statistics on delinquency. This is because the figures issued by any one government rarely are comparable with those issued by another national government. This results mainly from differences in the legal conception of delinquency, including its age range, and differences in court procedures required for designating a child delinquent. Additional difficulties arise from differences in the decisions by national statisticians as to when to count a youth delinquent: at arrest, hearing, adjudication, conviction or sentencing. Some of these terms do not even apply to delinquents everywhere. Furthermore, no statistics which we have encountered from foreign lands have anything comparable to the U. S. Children's Bureau tabulation of cases handled unofficially by court agencies.

Post-war trends in juvenile delinquency in different countries vary greatly, as is shown by Table 3. However, no major country for which statistics are available seems to have had as marked and continuous an increase as that experienced by the United States. One can speculate on the reasons for this difference, but no explanation can be proven valid by adequate and incontrovertible data. Our opinion, stated briefly, is that delinquency has risen more rapidly in the United States than elsewhere because: (1) The U. S. population has experienced more economic and geographic mobility than any other national population in recent years, thus weakening the cohesion of communities, which ordinarily are able to regulate the behavior of their members by informal censure and approbation; (2) The period of adolescence, when both the rights and the responsibilities of a person are ambiguously and divergently defined, seems to have become markedly longer in post-war United States, due to changes in vocational opportunities and in training required for vocational success. This ambiguity is compounded by uncertainty regarding the date and duration of military service obligations.

TABLE 3
Post-War Delinquency Reported by Selected Countries

Year	England & Wales	Japan	West Germany	Finland	Sweden	Switzerland	Belgium
	(1)	(2)	(3)	(4)	(5)	(6)	(7)
1946	62,355	204,236	—	310	601	714	4,751
1947	58,243	205,547	—	256	496	725	3,537
1948	71,998	266,418	—	107	441	779	3,351
1949	65,660	267,494	—	166	443	753	2,605
1950	69,591	291,545	—	139	455	699	2,572
1951	75,857	303,185	30,495	118	469	682	2,370
1952	72,834	274,238	30,000	122	470	795	2,499
1953	63,770	258,227	29,670	134	448	664	2,172
1954	59,992	—	29,219	120	372	713	2,379
1955	60,666	—	—	—	—	686	—

Notes on numbered columns:
(1) Juveniles found guilty of offenses (under 17 years). *Annual Abstract of Statistics, 1956,* Table 69, p. 68.
(2) Juvenile Arrests (under 25 years). *Japan Statistical Yearbook, 1954,* Table 293, p. 516.
(3) Felony and Misdemeanor Convictions (14 and over but under 18), *Statistisches Jahrbuch fuer die Bundesrepublik Deutschland, 1956,* p. 104. (Note that the West German Republic was not established until the latter part of 1949 and annual statistics were not collected until 1951.)
(4) Juvenile offenders sentenced, including suspended sentences (15-17 years). *Statistical Yearbook of Finland, 1956,* Table 347, p. 315.
(5) Persons convicted in courts of first instance (15-17 years). *Statistical Abstract of Sweden, 1956,* Table 329, p. 277.
(6) Sentenced (under 18). *Statistisches Jahrbuch der Schweiz, 1955,* p. 540.
(7) Judgments of Minors, *Annuaire Statistique de la Belgique et du Congo Belge,* Annee 1955, p. 166.

Types of Delinquents

A leading American sociologist, Robert K. Merton, has asserted: . . . the concept "juvenile delinquency" belongs to the family of blanket concepts which obscure rather than clarify our understanding of human behavior. . . .

As with any other class of human behavior, a designating tag or label has been introduced. In the course of assigning a class name, however, there develops a tendency to attend primarily to the similarities, consequential or not, between the items which are encompassed in that class . . . the term recurs time without end, and there develops a presupposition that this is in some sense a thing, an entity. . . . Yet, can we accept the presumption that this wide array of behaviors or the individuals engaging in one or another of these behaviors are of substantially like kind? For all salient purposes, is a "delinquent" who periodically engages in petty theft the same kind of individual and member of his group as one who periodically engages in violent attacks on others? . . . Just as grouping enormously varied conditions and processes under the one rubric of disease led some zealous medical systematists to believe that it was their task to evolve a single over-arching theory of disease, so it seems that the established convention of idiom, both vernacular and social scientific, of referring to "juvenile delinquency" as though it were an entity, leads many to believe that there must be a basic theory of "it's" causation.[14]

The notion that delinquency is diverse, and that treatment to cure or prevent it is handicapped when delinquency is conceived as a single type of phenomenon, has been set forth many times. Nevertheless, efforts to differentiate delinquents into clearly distinguishable categories have not resulted in any widely accepted typology. Perhaps the most commonly adopted differentiation is between youth whose misbehavior is believed to be an individual expression of personality disturbances, on the one hand, and youth who are believed to misbehave not so much because of personality defects as because their primary loyalty is to a group of boys among whom delinquency is considered normal. The first type, or personality disturbance delinquent, generally is subdivided into other types according to the alleged nature of their disturbance, such as the "psychopath" or the "egocentric wayward", the "anxiety ridden" or "borderline neurotic", and the "acting-out neurotic." No set of subtype categories has become standard. The second major classification of delinquent is variously called the "normal delinquent", the "gang delinquent", the "cultural delinquent", the "socialized delinquent", or the "delinquent superego type."

Detailed theories on the causes of these types of delinquency and their treatment will be discussed in later chapters. We are concerned at this point only with efforts which have been made to estimate the relative frequency of the different types. One general observation is noteworthy: like the several blind men whom legend reports got different conceptions of an elephant by feeling different parts of it, those who disagree on the relative prevalence of different types of delinquent generally have worked with different selections of delinquents, or have been predisposed by prior training to see only certain features of the delinquents whom they encountered. Sociologists have regarded the "gang" type as the typical delinquent, and they stress the fact that most youth officially committed as delinquents by the courts perpetrate their offenses in groups of two or more, while most of the remaining "lone" delinquents are encouraged by approval from other delinquents. Psychologically oriented persons dismiss this by such aphorisms as "birds of a feather flock together." Almost all delinquents are referred to them individually, and psychologists by training are disposed to seek and find personality difficulties in every such case. The sociologist then asks: How many people are there, delinquent or non-delinquent, youthful or adult, in whom one cannot find some personality conflicts and disturbances, if one is disposed to seek and to find such phenomena? The social or personality causation-type controversy only is clearly resolved if delinquency itself is seen as a personality trait, and if all of the social relationships of the youth are taken into account in explaining the initiation and nurture of this trait.

Probably the most systematic research on the relative frequency of different types of delinquent was that undertaken by Lester E. Hewitt. This study was based on a three category typology of delinquents developed from clinical observations by the psychiatrist Richard L. Jenkins. These types, and their identifying traits, are:

1. *Unsocialized Aggressive:* assaultive tendencies, initiatory fighting, cruelty, defiance of authority, malicious mischief, inadequate guilt feelings.
2. *Socialized Delinquency:* bad companions, gang activities, co-operative stealing, furtive stealing, habitual school truancy, truancy from home, staying out late nights.
3. *Overinhibited:* seclusiveness, shyness, apathy, worrying, sensitiveness, submissiveness.

Case files on 500 boys referred as delinquents or problem children to the Michigan Child Guidance Center were checked for the above traits. Any youth found to have at least three of the traits of one type was classified as of that type. By this procedure, 44 cases (8.8 percent) were classified Unsocialized Aggressive, 57 cases (11.4 percent) were classified Socialized Delinquent and 68 cases (13.6 percent) were classified Overinhibited. In addition, eight cases had the traits of both Unsocialized Aggressive and Socialized Delinquent, while five cases had the traits of both Overinhibited and Socialized Delinquent. But the remaining 318 cases (63.6 percent) could not be classified into any single one of these types.[15]

The Hewitt and Jenkins study methodology may be criticized, and the cases of a state child guidance center may not be considered typical of all delinquents. But case study observation in institutions and agencies for delinquents suggests that any typology which differentiates delinquents on the basis of the acts for which they first come to official attention is likely to lose utility steadily thereafter. This is because youth of diverse background and personality gain much in common by virtue of being placed in a position where they all feel themselves alienated from or in conflict with the representatives of conventional law-abiding society, and they find strong and immediately available social acceptance and support from each other. Through what Tannenbaum has called "the dramatization of evil" and "the hardening process", the diverse youth who have in common only that they are regarded as juvenile delinquents, acquire a sub-culture which gives them common traits as juvenile delinquents.[16]

Thus the blanket use of the term "juvenile delinquent", of which Prof. Merton complains, may perhaps create conditions which merit its blanket use, for the term may constitute what Prof. Merton elsewhere labels a "self-fulfilling prophecy."[17]

The most persistent and significant factors differentiating delinquents into types are those features which have major significance in differentiating all of us. Sex and race provide the major social cleavages in their world, as in ours, and to a lesser extent age and social-economic home background divide them. But common treatment by others and common problems make for remarkable unity and similarity among youth who are dealt with as delinquents for long. So perhaps the most important typology of delinquents for any practical purpose would be one based on some arbitrary division along the gradient of delinquent experience. Such a gradient has as one extreme the youth first dealt with as having done "something bad," and near the other extreme the youth who is the product of eight or ten years of continuous conflict with anti-delinquent parents, teachers, police or other "respectable" people. Most youth are between these extremes and inconsistent in their values and identifications.[18]

But the remainder of this volume will tell more of this, and will discuss racial, economic and other criteria which have been used for differentiating delinquent and non-delinquent youth into types that are of some academic value for analytic purposes in connection with various investigations of specific factors in delinquency.

Summary

"Delinquency" is an ambiguously and inconsistently used term. It refers to crimes committed by persons of juvenile age (most frequently defined as under 18), but it also refers to many non-criminal acts alleged to be conducive to crime (e.g., undue absence from home, idleness). In addition, whether a youth is officially designated delinquent by police or courts is a function of the visibility of his behavior, his status in the community, and the status of the complainant, as well as the nature of his actual behavior.

Delinquency statistics for different areas, or reported by different agencies from the same area, generally are not highly comparable. This is partly because of variations in what is defined as delinquency, and partly due to variations in the completeness with which those acts defined as delinquency are reported to the official agencies which compile statistics. While journalistic estimates of the number of persons appearing in U. S. juvenile courts as alleged delinquents run as high as a million per year, official tabulations as of the mid-1950's totalled only about one-third of a million. This represented a new high. The last previous peak occurred during World War II, after which there was a decline to a low point in 1948. No foreign country for which statistics are available seems to have experienced as marked and persistent an increase in delinquency as that reported for the United States since 1948.

Efforts to classify delinquents into distinct types have not resulted in any widely accepted uniform categories. Although a great diversity of behavior by children comes to be labelled "delinquency," initially distinct types seem to merge into each other, perhaps because delinquents increasingly develop common sub-cultural traits the more they are exposed to identical treatment by non-criminal society and its official agencies.

Selected Bibliography

Sidney Axelrad, "Negro and White Institutionalized Delinquents," *American Journal of Sociology* LVII (1952), 569-574. Presents statistics showing that Negroes are committed to state training schools at a younger age than Whites, and on the basis of less serious misbehavior.

Daniel Bell, "What Crime Wave?", *Fortune* (January 1955), 96-99, 154-156. Discusses spuriousness in crime statistics due to changes in statistics tabulation practices.

Albert K. Cohen, *Delinquent Boys* (Glencoe, Ill.; Free Press, 1955). The outstanding statement on how and why young males handicapped in meeting conventional society's standards develop a sub-culture which provides a different and more easily satisfied set of behavior standards.

Federal Bureau of Investigation, *Uniform Crime Reports* (Washington, D.C.). Published semi-annually. This is the official tabulation of arrests and crimes reported to police in the U.S.

Lester E. Hewitt, & Richard L. Jenkins, *Fundamental Patterns of Maladjustment* (Springfield, Ill., 1946). A highly original and systematic effort to establish the validity of a typology for classification of delinquents.

Solomon Kobrin, "The Conflict of Values in Delinquency Areas," *American Sociological Review* XVI (October, 1951), 653-61. A superior statement on the differentiation of delinquents from non-delinquents.

Fred J. Murphy, Mary M. Shirley, & Helen L. Witmer, "The Incidence of Hidden Delinquency," *American Journal of Orthopsychiatry*, XVI, (October, 1946), 686-696. Compares delinquency known by counsellors with that recorded by official agencies.

Edward E. Schwartz, "A Community Experiment in the Measurement of Juvenile Delinquency," *Yearbook of the National Probation Association 1945* (New York, 1946), 157-182. Describes an intensive check on the amount of delinquency not reported to the police or the courts, but recorded by school and social work agencies.

Edward E. Schwartz, "Statistics of Juvenile Delinquency in the United States," *The Annals*, CCLXI (January, 1949), 9-20. An excellent summary of this field, though slightly dated now.

Thorsten Sellin, *The Criminality of Youth* (Philadelphia, 1940). A notable survey of international statistical sources, many of them not available in the United States. Most of the figures are quite old.

United Nations, *Comparative Survey on Juvenile Delinquency*. In five parts, each published separately, as follows: Part I, North America (in English) (1952); Part II, Europe (in French) (1952); Part III, Latin America (in Spanish) (1952); Part IV, Asia and the Far East (in English) (1953); Part V, Middle East (in English) (1953). This includes a systematic comparison of the legal definition of delinquency and its differentiation from adult crime throughout the world. Only Parts I and III contain an appreciable amount of statistical data.

U. S. Children's Bureau, *Juvenile Court Statistics* (Washington, D.C.). Published annually. This is the official tabulation of statistics from juvenile courts throughout the U. S.

James S. Wallerstein, & Clement J. Wyle, "Our Law-Abiding Law-Breakers," *Probation*, XXV (April, 1947), 107-112. A summary of crimes admitted by persons not generally regarded as criminals.

Helen L. Witmer, & Ruth Kotinsky, *New Perspectives for Research on Juvenile Delinquency*, U.S. Children's Bureau Publication No. 356 (Washington, 1956). An edited transcript of a conference of outstanding sociologists, psychoanalysts, social workers and other specialists concerned with developing a more scientifically adequate understanding of delinquency.

Daniel Glaser is Associate Professor of Sociology at the University of Illinois where he has taught since 1954; was employed by the Illinois Parole and Pardon Board as Sociologist-Actuary at the Joliet-Stateville and Pontiac prisons from 1950 to 1954 and was a Prisons Officer with U. S. Office of Military Government in Germany from 1946 to 1949. He received a Ph.D. from the University of Chicago and is the author of numerous articles in sociological, criminological and correctional journals.

CHAPTER 2.

LEGAL ASPECTS OF JUVENILE DELINQUENCY

Donald J. Newman
St. Lawrence University

Conflicting Meaning of Delinquency

Juvenile delinquency represents many things to many people. To the police, delinquents may merely be underage criminals; to school authorities, the truant and the boy who smokes in the washroom may epitomize delinquency. To some parents, other people's ungovernable children and to some store-keepers, the gangs loitering on the corner may be their ideas of delinquents. Even experts who study and work with young offenders lack consensus on the limits of the concept. Some authorities discuss delinquency as "emotionally disturbed" behavior, others talk of "persistently anti-social behavior" and at least one researcher has defined delinquency as "behavior disappointing beyond reasonable expectation."[1]

The confusion concerning the meaning of delinquency is not a question of whose definition is more nearly correct but rather it is a problem naturally growing out of any attempt to define satisfactorily, in a few descriptive sentences, a form of social problem which is neither a legal nor a behavioral entity. Any definition which is functional to the agency, the school or for that matter, the neighborhood, is as correct, in its own context, as any other definition. However, while functionally, a boy whom the neighbors do not like may be considered a delinquent *in that neighborhood*, the meaning of juvenile delinquency finds its ultimate basis in law.

It should be added, parenthetically perhaps, that the law

does little to settle differences in definitions. Variations in delinquency statutes, vagueness in regard to the types of behavior included, disagreements as to the maximum ages involved and variations in court practices all contribute to what Tappan has called "legal nihilism" rather than precision and clarity."[2]

Nevertheless, tradition as well as the existence of special legislation, special courts and officials, and distinct provisions for the rehabilitation of youthful violators makes it inevitable to seek the foundation of delinquency as a concept in the law, even before considering the clinic or the school.

Differential Treatment of Children in Penal Law

The legal basis of juvenile delinquency extends back to the very earliest times and is explicitly related to the development of the legal philosophy that excused children from guilt for criminal acts. The idea of juvenile courts and separate custody for young law violators is a relatively new development but the distinction between child and adult responsibility is old. In Roman law, children under seven years of age were deemed incapable of committing crimes and this magic "age of reason" has extended to the present day. The ancient Hebrews felt that a child was incapable of sin prior to his thirteenth birthday, at which time he achieved religious maturity. Ancient Saxon law excused children under twelve from murder.

Throughout the development of common law in England and criminal law in the United States "childhood", variably defined, has been a defense to criminal liability on the assumption that a child is incapable of *mens rea*, culpable intent based on the ability to judge one's acts in terms of right or wrong.

The Romans, and later the English, further distinguished the culpability of children between seven and puberty, the assumption being that children in this category were also incapable of crimes unless there was evidence that they did, in fact, understand the wrongness of their deeds. An early New York statute, following this policy, stated:

I. A child under the age of seven years is not capable of committing a crime.

II. A child of seven years and under the age of twelve is presumed to be incapable of crime, but the presumption may be removed by proof that he had sufficient capacity to understand the act or neglect charged against him and to know its wrongfulness.[3]

A few years later the upper limit of this statute was extended to fourteen and still later to sixteen years of age. Today all states have increased their maximum age limits of a child beyond puberty and have likewise raised their minimum limits under which no crime (excepting capital offenses, certain serious crimes, and, of all things, traffic violations in some states) can be committed. The most common age limit of childhood is eighteen (twenty-seven states, the District of Columbia, Alaska, Hawaii, and the Federal Juvenile Delinquency Act), followed by sixteen (seven states), and seventeen (six states), then twenty-one in two states. The remaining states provide different age limits for various types of delinquency and some states make distinctions in the delinquency ages of sexes. Not all states set seven years as the lower limit for delinquency, although this is the usual barrier below which no crime can be committed. However, not being able to convict a child of a crime because of his age does not preclude adjudicating him delinquent.[4]

About forty states provide a certain amount of flexibility in the upper age limit so that at the discretion of the court or prosecuting attorney, an adolescent a year or two under the maximum delinquency age may be tried for a crime. In other words, the criminal court is given concurrent jurisdiction with the juvenile court in certain types of offenses or where other conditions, such as a previous record of delinquency, might lead the juvenile court to waive jurisdiction.[5]

Some states maintain an intervening period between childhood and adulthood during which time adolescent law breakers are considered neither delinquents nor on a par with adult criminals. New York is a case in point. In this state, the maximum age of delinquency is sixteen, with concurrent criminal court jurisdiction after the fifteenth birthday. Between sixteen and twenty-one, however, law violators may be found "wayward minors" or "youthful offenders" under two separate but overlapping laws, rather than criminals.

Interestingly, with the exception of concurrent jurisdiction, childhood is measured chronologically, rather than by some other test of maturity. This in spite of Blackstone's comment that "one lad of eleven years old may have as much cunning as another of fourteen; in these cases our maxim is that *'malitia supplet aetaten'* (malice provides age)."[6]

In *Commonwealth v. Trippi,* defense for the twenty-two year old defendant, convicted of first degree murder, appealed the decision by claiming, and establishing that he had a "mental age" of only thirteen years. The conviction was upheld however, the court saying, "when a man reaches manhood the presumption is that he possesses the ordinary mental capacity normally pertaining to his age. . . . The presumption of the lack of power of thought and capacity in favor of the child is due more to the number of years he has lived than to the character and development of his mind."[7] Low mental age may, of course, excuse a person from criminal liability if it negates his ability to distinguish the wrongness of his acts.

While children, therefore, cannot commit crimes it is abundantly obvious that some of them violate the criminal code and must be culturally dealt with some way, most likely as a separate category. Herein is at least part of the basis of juvenile delinquency laws. The various state statutes first of all define who is a "child" or "juvenile" and then go on to list those acts or conditions which are considered "delinquent." Part of this list includes those acts which, if performed by adults, would be considered crimes. The list by no means ends here, as we shall see, for the scope of delinquency is much broader than the criminal code.

Equity and the Doctrine "Parens Patriae"

It is a mistake to think of delinquents as merely under-age criminals or to conceive of the juvenile court as simply a more informal criminal court. While some delinquents do violate criminal laws, many children do not but are nevertheless adjudicated delinquent. And the Juvenile court as presently conceived, has different origins and far different methods and procedures than criminal courts of record.

The modern juvenile court can trace its beginnings directly to the philosophy underlying courts of chancery, or equity, in English law. Beginning about the thirteenth century, Britain developed courts of chancery as a reaction against the rigid doctrines and procedures of the common law courts. These new courts were very much more informal than the old hearings and less bound by the rituals and procedural mandates. They were designed to be fairer, or more equitable, than other courts and hence were concerned more with the unique facets of each case than with precedent and legal pomp. They heard cases of people who had failed to find succor or relief in other legal channels. Particularly, the chancery was the refuge of orphans, widows, "lunatics" and others in need of special aid.

In regard to minors, courts of equity acted under a common law doctrine of *parens patriae* which, making the king the father of his country, thereby entrusts him with ultimate guardianship over children and others in need of responsible guidance. This principle, substituting state for king, is the basic philosophy of juvenile courts today. The English courts of chancery dealt solely with children who were "neglected," "dependent" or "destitute" and did not extend to delinquency, as such, until much later. In fact, Pound has stated that the extension of the chancery philosophy to delinquents came about chiefly through the initiative of a "few socially minded judges" whose consciences revolted "from the legal rules that required trial of children over seven as criminals and sentence of children who were over fourteen to penalties provided for adult offenders."[8]

Regardless of which came first, the adaptation of equity principles to delinquency and the doctrine of *parens patriae* form the basis of modern special courts for children. An interesting question about *parens patriae* arises in a country such as ours in which the sanctity and freedom of the individual family is an honored tradition. In such a value framework, can the state, through the juvenile court authorities, assume control of a child in opposition to parental wishes?

One theoretical position is taken by those who contend, on the basis of certain common law inferences, that the parent is entitled to the control, education, and management of his child against all other institutions. On the other hand, *parens patriae* is based on the position that the status of childhood is a creation of the state, either through common law or statutory enactment, and that parental control is merely a privilege and duty conferred on the parent by the state. As Herbert Lou explains it:

In theory, all persons in the status of infancy are wards of
the public, and the public has delegated the power of raising
and caring for them, in sacred trust, to their parents. The
parents, representing the state and having custody of the
children in trust, owe a duty to the public to act as guardians
of infant citizens for the state. The state can enforce that duty
by deposing them as guardians and by putting the infants at
the common guardianship of the community, if public good
requires.[9]

In general, children's courts concur with this viewpoint and
while in cases in which neglect rather than delinquency is alleged
it is necessary to show that the parents are incompetent or have
failed to provide for the child, in delinquent actions, it is sufficient to demonstrate a condition of delinquency without alleging or proving parental failure, for the court to assume control
of the child.

The Development of the Juvenile Court

The first juvenile court in the United States, or for that matter,
in the world, was established in Cook County (Chicago), Illinois
in 1899. The law on which it was based, defining itself as the
"act to regulate the treatment and control of dependent, neglected and delinquent children," provided for a circuit court
judge to hear juvenile cases in a separate court-room and to keep
separate records. Its most significant feature was the embodiment
of the concept that a child who broke the law was not to be
regarded as a criminal but as a ward of the state. To this effect,
delinquents were placed in the same category as dependent and
neglected children and were to receive the same care, custody
and discipline as these children, which would be approximately
that which should have been given by their parents. The law
also substituted for the criminal procedure of arrest, magistrate's
hearing, bail, trial-by-jury and conviction the more informal
methods of petition, investigation, summons, an informal hearing
and adjudication. Equity practices replaced criminal procedure.
Colorado followed the lead of Illinois and, largely through
the efforts of Judge Ben Lindsey, a juvenile court law was
passed in 1903. By the next year, ten other states had passed
similar laws but at this early date the coverage of juvenile hear-

ings was usually limited to only the largest cities in these states. Eventually all states and possessions adopted delinquency legislation and most Western countries had established juvenile courts by 1925.

The Legal Characteristics of Juvenile Court

The juvenile court differs markedly from the criminal court in both philosophy and procedure. It is true that the two are often associated in popular thinking and that many individuals, including some police, judges and custodial personnel refer to delinquency as if it were crime. Nevertheless, the juvenile court is not a criminal court; a hearing is held, not a trial, delinquents are adjudicated, not convicted. It is not the state *versus* John Doe, but the State *in the interest* of Johnny Doe that dominates juvenile hearings.

One of the most important distinctions between these courts has to do with the manner in which cases are handled from inception of termination. Criminal defendants are arrested on the basis of warrants (or "on view" if a policeman sees them committing the crime), are indicted by a grand jury, are given a hearing before a magistrate who may set bail, are arraigned (at which time they enter a plea), are tried before a jury, if they wish, and, if they are convicted "beyond all reasonable doubt," they are sentenced to prison. Juvenile procedures are much different from this. Minors are not arrested on warrants, rather they are "referred" to the juvenile court by petitions. From here on in, the entire court activity is designed to diagnose, as accurately as possible, the reason the child is before the court and to determine what course of action will be in the child's best interest and, of course, the best interests of the community in which he lives. Some of the major procedural distinctions of the juvenile court will be discussed in some detail:

A. *The Social Investigation by the Court.* Because the purpose of the juvenile court hearing is to act in the best interests of the child before it, an investigation is made of all conceivable aspects of the case. Unlike an investigation in a criminal case, the purpose is not to gather evidence of guilt or innocence of the acts alleged, but to discover as much relevant social data as can be helpful to the court in handling the particular case. Of course, if a delinquent act is alleged and the child denies it, one purpose of the investigation is to evaluate the accuracy of the allegations. As the Connecticut juvenile court said: "Where a child has denied his delinquent act there should clearly be an adjudication of innocence or guilt before a widespread invasion of his personal privacy and that of his family is undertaken."[10]

The investigation for the juvenile court is ordinarily carried out by trained probation officers who are full-time officials of the court. The court may also call upon various authorities (such as psychologists, psychiatrists, physicians, and officials) to contribute their special brand of knowledge to the case. Basically all aspects of the investigation are diagnostic. Kahn lists a dozen different areas which should, ideally be always read by the investigator before he summarizes the case and gives his recommendations to the judge. Among these, in addition to facts surrounding the alleged delinquent act or condition are: (1) family history; (2) conditions of home and neighborhood; (3) school record and activities; (4) religious activities; (5) leisure time activities and special interests; (6) mental and physical condition; (7) the child's version of his delinquency and his attitudes; and (8) parent attitudes.[11]

The emphasis is on the total personality of the child before the court and not only on the alleged offense. Unfortunately, the actual picture of such social investigations is a far-cry from their theoretical significance. Many courts are understaffed while in others investigations become so stereotyped that records all read alike and fail to accurately diagnose the individual child. Many reports contain a vast amount of irrelevant and useless information and, depending upon the orientation of the case workers involved, are filled with remarkably similar check lists on breast-feeding, toilet-training and other superficial, quasi-psychiatric data.

B. *The Informal, Non-Criminal, Nature of Hearings.* Most state laws require children's cases to be held separately from trials of adults and exclude the general public from attendance. Likewise the laws explicitly state that the juvenile hearing is, and should be, free from the technical rules of evidence which govern criminal trials, and that the hearing be held in an informal manner. The child himself, and his parents, should be freed from the notion that he is being tried for a crime. The combative aura of the trial, with its cross-examination of witnesses, formal statements for the defense and so on, is absent.

It is clear in the law that a juvenile court hearing is not a trial. The Pennsylvania Supreme Court, answering a charge that a child's liberty of right of trial by jury was abrogated by a juvenile hearing, answered "The fallacy exists in presuming that the child is tried for any crime" (and since) "the child is not tried for any offense, hence there is no abrogation of rights."[12] Because the child is not tried, therefore, the usual protection given the criminal defendant is absent in juvenile hearings. Unless otherwise provided in the juvenile court statutes, the youth has no right of jury trial, no right to counsel, no right to cross-examine witnesses, hearsay evidence may be used and so on. At the same time, the court is instructed to arrive at the truth of the matter and to maintain fairness in dealing with all parties. Although procedures may be informal, it is still a court and has legal limitations.

In cases involving delinquent acts which, if committed by an adult, would be violations of the criminal code, the proceedings may be more formal. It is generally understood that when issues of fact in such cases are to be determined, rules of evidence should not be disregarded. The New York Court of Appeals said, "The customary rules of evidence shown by long experience as essential to getting at the truth with reasonable certainty in civil trials must be adhered to. The finding of fact must rest on the preponderance of evidence adduced under those rules. Hearsay, opinion, trends of hostile neighborhood feeling, the hopes and fears of social workers are all sources of error and have no more place in children's courts than in any other court."[13]

The youth who is adjudicated delinquent while deprived of any value of rigid procedures benefits from the noncriminal nature of the proceedings since his adjudication does not amount to a criminal conviction and he does not, therefore, accumulate a criminal record nor suffer the loss of certain civil rights and privileges that follow conviction for a crime.

Some authorities feel that the distinctions between criminal trials and juvenile hearings are more theoretical than actual. As Tappan points out, while juvenile hearings are held separately from criminal cases, the judge in many instances is only a part-time juvenile authority spending most of his effort hearing criminal, civil or probate cases in another court.[14] He cannot fail to bring his dedication to these more rigid procedures and to these conceptions of justice with him to the juvenile court. Even in those metropolitan areas which boast a specializing juvenile judge, his training and experience often fit him more ably for the formalized benches of other courts.

C. *The Privacy of the Juvenile Court.* All state laws are rigorous in their insistence that any records of juvenile proceedings be kept separately from criminal records. Most laws, too, provide that such records are not for public reading, freedom to inspect them being limited to court officials, the parents of children involved and certain other parties, perhaps the police or research workers, whom the court feels have legitimate purposes for inspection. This privacy of records extends, in most instances, to newspapers and other forms of mass media. The Standard Juvenile Court Act proposes that the reproduction of the name or picture of any child under the jurisdiction of the juvenile court be made a misdemeanor carrying a fine and/or a year's imprisonment. The purpose of the emphasis on privacy is "to prevent the humiliation and demoralizing effect which follow on publicity of children's cases, making it more difficult for the juvenile court to utilize the child's feeling of self-respect in effective rehabilitation."[15]

Not everyone accepts this rationale without criticism. The non-public nature of juvenile hearings has been negatively compared to "star-chamber" proceedings. And newspapers, particularly, have criticized the "closed door" policy of the courts, basing their criticism rather vaguely on allegations of censorship or denial of freedom of the press. This may be a debatable subject, but it is doubtful if "freedom of the press" is the basic issue. No court should be a star chamber, to be sure, but other methods of review of cases are available. It is likely that newspapers are more interested in sensational or unusual cases than in accurate reporting of the court's activities. A survey of editors, judges, lawyers and criminologists in respect to a related issue of allowing newsmen to photograph criminal proceedings, substantiates this.[16] However, should juvenile courts become more "legal" and less "social" than they now are, the sixth amendment guarantee of a "public" trial will have to be weighed against the limitations on "freedom of the press."

D. *The Right to Appeal Juvenile Court Decisions.* Since the juvenile court *is* a court although children are not "tried" before it, its decisions may be appealed to higher courts. Most states make special provision for this in their juvenile laws and in instances where the laws are silent, courts have generally held that delinquents have the same right to appeal as misdemeanants and felons. It is because of this right that the juvenile court must establish delinquency on facts rather than merely by jurisdiction. Failure to prove alleged delinquency by sufficient facts and not more conclusions, and absence of these facts reported in the record of the hearing is usually grounds for reversal of the juvenile court's decision.[17]

An appellate court may reverse the decision of a juvenile court *in toto* or may confirm the finding that the child is delinquent but modify the disposition. Usually appeals are sought in cases which have resulted in the commitment of the child to a juvenile institution. The parents or advisors of the child ask a reversal of the commitment seeking probation as an alternative and appellate courts can grant, on their estimate of facts in the case, such a partial reversal.

The right of appeal is probably used less in juvenile than in criminal cases because, first of all, juvenile dispositions are ordinarily less severe than criminal sentences. If a child is remanded to the custody of his parents, or placed on probation he is less likely than a man sent to prison to appeal the decision, particularly since there is no publicity surrounding the case, even if he feels innocent of the alleged delinquency. Of course if he is sent to an institution, this is another matter, and appeals occur most frequently in such cases.[18] Then too, appeals are expensive and, after all, children are involved in delinquency hearings and generally poor children at that. Furthermore, many children and their parents do not know that juvenile court decisions can be appealed for in many states the judge is not obligated to inform them of this right and delinquents rarely are represented by counsel.

It should be noted that appeals from the juvenile court are quite often successful, as far as the appellant is concerned, particularly in cases involving institutional commitment. As Lou explains it: "The decision of the juvenile court is often changed from the commitment to probation, not because its decision has any better basis than that of the juvenile court, but because the district attorney, who is overloaded with work, generally agrees to such a reduction if the offense or the amount of damages seem to him to be trivial."[19]

Perhaps the right to appeal seems legally and philosophically inconsistent with the fact that juvenile courts supposedly act in the best interests of the child and do not seek to convict or punish him. The original hearing is conducted in such an informal, non-rigid manner and yet appeals are based upon a rather formal examination of "facts." This, in turn, necessarily leads the juvenile court to act as a quasi-criminal hearing or, in the other direction, leads judges to dismiss cases on evidential bases rather than "in the interest of" the youngsters. On the other hand, while juvenile courts may advocate equity, the plain fact is that some children are deprived of their liberty, although technically not "sentenced" to a correctional school, and there must be some recourse from any arbitrary action on the part of a judge. It may be argued that the juvenile judge, being closer to the case, knows wherein the best interests of the child lie whereas the appellate court, distant and unconcerned with personalities, cannot possibly evaluate the case accurately from a "behavioral" standpoint. Even if juvenile judges were trained behavioral scientists, which most of them are not, evaluating the best interests of any child on the basis of one or two meetings and a more or less stereotyped social workers' report, would seem ridiculously presumptuous. Any judgment involving a child's reputation or freedom, regardless of the phraseology in which it is couched, must be subject to review. And since the adjudication is made by a court, it seems evident that a higher court must be available to examine it.

E. *Dispositions and Informal Adjustments of Cases.* The child coming before the juvenile court must face the fact that his very presence there means something will happen to him, if nothing more than an investigation and a reprimand. As Tappan says of many urban children's courts, "The child enters with what is in effect a presumption of his delinquency and, under the conditions of today's 'chancery' procedure there, it is almost impossible for him to rebut that presumption, once a probation officer has found a personal problem in his history to work on. Who is to save the child from his saviors?"[20]

The petition which refers him to the court, whether it originates with the police, the school or from other sources, is based upon someone's belief that the child needs court supervision. The court investigates this and, since the very existence of referral is a "problem," makes some decision in the interest of the child.

Informally, the court may not accept the case, but refer it to another agency. Or "non-official" meetings may be held with the child and "non-official" advice, or warnings, given him. In some instances a sort of voluntary, informal probation is worked out enabling the probation officials to "treat" the problem without any official adjudication of delinquency. Reports of the United States Children's Bureau indicate that about half the cases coming before the courts in any one year are handled unofficially. While the legal definitions of delinquent behavior are extremely vague in themselves as we shall see, the extension of court functions to unofficial cases broadens the jurisdiction of the court, in fact if not in theory, to include considerable non-delinquent but "problem" cases. "Delinquency" is a broad enough concept; "children with problems" is limitless.

Official dispositions of the court following adjudication of delinquent status include (1) dismissal (usually with reprimand) or continuance, a form of holding the case without official probation, to enable the court to investigate further or to collect restitution or reparation for damages, (2) commitment to the custody of parents, pastor, or some other responsible adult for perhaps an indefinite period of time, (3) referral to a special agency for psychiatric or medical help, (4) probation, involving supervision by one of the probation officers attached to the court, (5) foster-home placement or (6) commitment to an industrial or training school. Many state laws provide, and the standard juvenile court act recommends, that any commitment be for an indeterminate period of time but not beyond the child's twenty-first birthday, release on parole before this date to be determined by institutional authorities or some other body comparable to an adult parole board.

About 10 per cent of delinquency dispositions involve commitment to a state, religious or private institution or agency, from a quarter to a third of all cases are placed on official probation but most cases are dismissed with reprimand, and qualifications of restitution or reparation.

Theoretically the juvenile judge disposes of cases in the manner best suited to reform, rehabilitate, protect, or to otherwise further the "best interests" of the child before him. Consequently he should consider all legal facts and the social history and diagnostic records of the child and, in the light of his knowledge of the case and available facilities for dealing with it, make a sound and just disposition. There is some evidence, however, that in the flexible aura of the juvenile court even more than in criminal courts, personal and professional biases, conflicting personalities and other non-legal irrelevancies enter into the choice of disposition. Judges and caseworkers generally come from a somewhat higher social class background than the children before them and, of course, reflect their class ideas of propriety, attractiveness, suitableness of home life, attitudes toward lower class religions, ethnic groups, races and so on. Irrelevant factors such as a child's appearance, his skin color, or even his father's occupation or reputation, may be the deciding issue that deprives him of his liberty, euphorically couched in a disposition designed for his "best interests." Reckless, in discussing "categoric risks" of adjudication and commitment, points to the differential treatment before the court of girls and boys, different races, differing economic groups and similar categories.[21]

F. *Miscellaneous Legal Problems of the Court: Jurisdiction and Delinquency of Parents.*

In most states, the juvenile court has jurisdiction over dependent and neglected children as well as delinquents. In some states, mentally defective and some physically handicapped children are wards of the court and other courts include in their jurisdiction marriage annulments of minors, adoption procedures, issues arising from illegitimacy and similar "domestic relations" problems of teen-agers. Dependent and neglected cases alone may take half or more of the court's time in some areas.

One of the most debatable issues of jurisdiction has to do with the amount of control the court has over parents, guardians and other adults who may contribute to the delinquency of a child. Some jurists have called for punishing the parent rather than the child and newspapers have spread the slogan: "There is no such thing as a delinquent child; there are only delinquent parents!"

All states have criminal legislation forbidding "contributing to the delinquency of a minor" or similar wordage, non-support and desertion, and specific offenses by adults against minors. In many states, the juvenile court is given concurrent jurisdiction with the criminal court in some, or all, of these matters. Now, non-support and specific offenses, particularly sex violations against minors, are more or less clear-cut legal issues, depending upon the evidence and facts of the case. "Contributing to the delinquency of a minor" however is a somewhat different matter and the law is less clear on exactly what is involved. In the first place, "contributing" can obviously be by omission as well as commission and in general this is what the issue of punishing parents hinges on. It is clear enough should a Fagin-like parent teach his child to steal that he has violated the law. Likewise if the parents desert the child and he resorts to theft or idleness, cause lies against them. On the other hand, if the parent fails to adequately teach the child a sense of right or wrong, is he criminally liable? If so, how can this be proved?

Some states have answered this by adopting statutes which presume the parents' guilt if a child is adjudicated for delinquency more than once. Other than this however, the limits of contributing are not clear. In a well-known California case a man was convicted for contributing because he had had adulterous relations with the mother of the children involved, causing her to neglect them. The California Supreme Court reversed this conviction however, stating that the effect of his actions had only a "possible" effect on the children, not an "inevitable" one which would be necessary to establish his liability.[22]

On the other hand, courts have generally held that it is not necessary for the child to actually be adjudicated delinquent in order to establish liability for contributing.[23] This position is

predicated on the hope that "contributing" legislation will prevent delinquency from occurring and, of course, if the court must
wait for it to happen before acting on the contributing causes,
then, the prevention feature is defeated. It is a difficult matter,
however, to prove contributing to the delinquency of a minor
if in fact the minor is not delinquent. Ordinarily cases actually
decided in this category involve such things as sexual advances,
indecent exposure and similar cases in which the child is innocent but the adult's action endangers his morals, or frightens
him or has "some effect" on him.

It is rare that a case of contributing by omission is established against a parent except for neglect, absence from home
and spending time in bars, non-support or some similar "neglect"
category. Failure to properly train the child, but not actually
teaching him impropriety, is a debatable ground for liability in
the first place and, even if allowed in some statutes, is a difficult
association to prove. "Failure to protect" the child from delinquency however, may lead to liability in some instances.[24]

It makes little difference in contributing statutes that the
child may be already delinquent at the time of the adult's action.
If the defendant's behavior causes the "continuation" of delinquency, it is enough for contributing.[25]

"Contributing" statutes have generally been upheld by higher
courts and while they have been on the books in most states for
many years, they have been resorted to only sporadically. In some
jurisdictions they are almost never enforced, in others, they are
used more frequently depending on the whim of the judge or the
fad of the times. Recently there has been some upsurge in interest in parental guilt which has been debated in technical journals,
in women's magazines and exhorted from some pulpits. In general, however, enforcement of such provisions has not been widespread and even where used, has not had the desirable effect
hoped for by advocates of the procedure. Nevertheless, parental
lack of supervision probably remains the after-dinner speaker's
chief theory of delinquency causation and this sentiment may
cause an increment in parental delinquency cases.

The Legal Content of Delinquency

The procedures for handling alleged delinquents are so flexible, as we have seen, that practically any child with a "prob-

lem" can come under the jurisdiction, official or otherwise, of the juvenile court. Laws defining the content of delinquency are likewise so broad and so flexibly interpreted that almost any behavior or condition, especially the home conditions and environmental settings of poor children, can constitute delinquency, if the court so interprets it.

All states and the Federal Act agree, however, that violations of the substantive criminal code of any state, district, or municipality by a person in the juvenile age category shall constitute delinquent acts. Interestingly, and inconsistently, about one third of the states except murder, capital (or life imprisonment) offenses or certain other serious felonies from this rule, holding instead that these acts are crimes if committed at any age above the usual seven-year-old minimum. Why this is done is not clear. On the one hand, youngsters are theoretically unable to know the nature of their actions and therefore cannot commit crimes which involve culpable intent in any form. Yet, the offenses excepted from this holding are those very crimes in which the mental state, or intent, of the actor is of the utmost legal importance. Furthermore, in delinquency rationale, children should not suffer the retribution of revenge underlying the punishment meted the criminal. Certainly, however, the offenses excepted are those carrying the most severe punishment that the state can give.

With these exceptions then, there is general consensus that acts of children which violate the criminal law are *ipso facto* delinquencies. Here at least there should be clarity on the limitations of this form of delinquency for the criminal code is specific, precise and rigidly construed. It is based on substantive norms that spell out the concise *actions* (or omissions), the nature of the required *intent* and the necessary *consequences* for behavior to be considered a crime. The state must offer appropriate evidence on all of these levels to prove "beyond a reasonable doubt" the guilt of the accused adult. Presumably, then in the case of a boy petitioned for some such violation as stealing, let us say, the juvenile court would adjudicate him delinquent on the basis of the sections of the criminal code appropriate to the condition of his theft. However, since the procedural norms of the juvenile court are not designed to "try" the boy, since the hearing is informal, since no "conviction" results, the criminal code can be given merely a passing glance. It is not necessary for the court to "prove beyond a reasonable doubt" that the boy's intentions, actions and the consequences of his actions did actually constitute theft as defined in the substantive code. The court will of course, examine and possibly investigate the petition but generally if there is *any* evidence of theft, will adjudicate delinquency. Of course, the boy may appeal the decision but, as mentioned earlier, appeals are more often made from the type of disposition given by the court than from the adjudication of delinquency itself.

All this means that when a law states that delinquency is "any act which if performed by an adult would be a crime" it does not imply that the substantive code is applied to minors in the same way as it is to adults. The rigid procedures, the rules of evidence and the requirements of intent and so forth do not carry over. What is borrowed, rather, are general categories, "breaking and entering", "auto theft" or "robbery while armed", without the explicit, and many times very subtly determining, meanings of these terms provided in the adult code. Consequently, even on this level, which at first glance is based on precise norms, the legal meaning of delinquency remains broad and more or less subjectively determined by the opinion of the judge in conjunction with other officials of the juvenile court.

Delinquency is by no means limited to violations of the criminal code. In fact, it is probable that over half of the children brought before the juvenile court have not broken any penal law but are petitioned for a number of other acts and conditions listed in special juvenile legislation.[26] Delinquency legislation varies from state to state but a partial list of offenses or conditions constituting the law's definition of delinquency would include: Truancy, growing up in idleness, incorrigibility or being ungovernable, associating with vicious or immoral companions, smoking, drinking alcoholic beverages, loitering (especially in pool rooms and railroad yards), using vile or obscene language, wandering the streets at night (or where provided, breaking curfew), immoral or indecent conduct (usually sex-related as in pornography, masturbation, fornication but may include other behavior, "necking" etc. at the discretion of the court), begging, running away from home, operating motor vehicle dangerously, acts of mischief, and many

other categories. Statutes sometimes end the list with a catch-all
phrase such as "so deports himself as to injure himself or endanger others" or "any other act or condition not in the best
interests of the child." Some states modify their list by including
the word "habitually" before the act described. Not all legislation includes all of the above categories and some states add
others, often quaintly worded e.g. "patronizes dram house."[27]

Obviously, such lists do little to clarify the legal limits of delinquency and in conjunction with quasi-chancery procedures,
extend the coverage of the juvenile court far beyond the "young
criminals" concept of delinquency.

The Standard Juvenile Court Act of the National Probation Association, recognizing that definitions of delinquency
have little substantive meaning, does not attempt to define
delinquency but enumerates certain conditions and actions, that
may give the juvenile court jurisdiction over the child. In effect
it is saying that a delinquent is any child over whom a juvenile
court exercises jurisdiction. Bloch and Flynn point to this as
analogous with the old dilemma of the psychologists who defined intelligence as that which intelligence tests measured.[28]

The Legal Dilemma of Delinquency

The legal position of juvenile delinquency today has jurists
gnashing their teeth, social workers on the defensive, researchers confused, and the public, alarmed, clamoring for decisive
action. The legal-oriented seek more rigid legal meaning; the
treatment-oriented seek greater flexibility of definitions in the
direction of social and psychiatric conceptions. Students of delinquency cannot even accurately measure its extent because of
the shifting-sand nature of laws, interpretations and enforcement. And the man-on-the-street maintains his own private definition of delinquency which is just as correct as the next fellow's, for under various conditions practically any behavior is
delinquency to some court, somewhere.

The legal dilemma of delinquency is this: How is it possible
for a court of law, dedicated in all sincerity to the humane value
of acting in the best interest of a child as a substitute parent, to
in fact remain a court, bound by procedures and based upon
substantive, codified norms of conduct, and affording its charges
all the hard-earned protections that the law gives adults? As

we have seen, the chief emphasis in most courts has been on equity, on treatment, and presumably on "humaneness" rather than on legal precision. This has resulted, however, in a legal wasteland. The extended jurisdiction of the juvenile court, the incoherence of delinquency definitions, all have led to accusations of unfairness, arbitrariness rather than equity. Are such laws and procedures humane? Some think not. Tappan says that, "however benign in motive" they are "not only inappropriate to a court but may be harmful, because the tribunal may thus do positive injury to children who do not in fact require authoritative manipulation by an agency that is unspecialized for subtle diagnosis or therapy."[29] Law is law evidently, and clinical diagnosis of individuals is something else again.

It is generally admitted that even under ideal conditions in elaborate settings with trained social scientists acting cooperatively, delinquency in individual cases cannot be predicted much better than by chance hunches, nor can it be treated or prevented in the majority of cases. How then can a court in the brief period allotted the average case determine with any degree of scientific precision the "best interests" of the child before it? Do the juvenile laws pertaining to procedures and definitions actually do the job they are designed for? Do the courts, operating under these laws, actually prevent delinquency from occurring or stop it where it has occurred? The evidence of growing delinquency rates would seem to say "no" and the moot argument that rates would be even higher if there were no courts gives little satisfaction. Tappan, speaking of the lack of due process in juvenile laws, says of the children involved, "they are incarcerated. They become adult criminals, too, in thankless disregard of the state's good intentions as *parens patriae*."[30]

On the other side of the argument are ranged all those values pertaining to our cultural conceptions of childhood. We recognize, in the law and elsewhere, that children are not adults and cannot take adult responsibilities. We do not wish to subject our young people to jails, prisons nor to the impersonal, authoritative combat of criminal trials. Yet we are faced with children neglected and children who, in their behavior if not in their awareness, are as vicious and destructive as any adult law-breaker. Sticking to our guns, like the movie chaplain who has "never known a bad boy", we seek to "understand" youth and to rehabilitate young offenders rather than accepting the more fatalistic and certainly no more effective philosophy of repression and punishment used in criminal cases. To this end we have established child guidance clinics, parental education programs, settlement houses in the slums and, of course, the juvenile court. Must we, however, become so dedicated to treatment and prevention that we ignore matters of guilt or innocence and neglect basic procedural safeguards of liberty, reputation and indeed happiness?

Fortunately, perhaps, nothing is static and our legal treatment of delinquency is subject to experiment and change. Hopefully we can arrive at a solution that effectively reaches a compromise between the views of legal and social work extremists and operates factually for the best interests of neglected and delinquent minors.

A major development in this respect is seen in the Youth Correction Authority Act drafted as model legislation by the American Law Institute in 1940. This act, with certain revisions, has been adopted by a few states but has reached its maximum development in California with the establishment of the Youth Authority program. The jurisdiction of the act extends to all delinquents under 21, referral to the authority coming from criminal as well as youth courts.

It is not our purpose here to debate the relative merits of the youth authority in action. Suffice it to say that this act contributes two things to the possible solution of the juvenile court dilemma. First, the more or less arbitrary disposition of cases is taken out of the hands of the judge and given instead to the authority which is composed of a body of experts (psychiatrists, psychologists, lawyers, sociologists and so forth) who have at their disposal diagnostic facilities far beyond those of the juvenile court. The Authority determines as accurately as possible the personality and/or social factors contributing to the delinquency of the child and recommends the use of specific facilities to effect his rehabilitation. While diagnosis in delinquency is far from a settled scientific reality, the Authority would have available the best possible facilities, and very importantly, the necessary time, to make as accurate a diagnosis and to direct as effective a rehabilitative program as possible. The various juvenile clinics, reception facilities, institutions and probation and parole services would be integrated under one central diagnostic, treatment, and yes, even preventive, program.

Secondly, the Youth Corrections Act provides for increased legal protection for the delinquent by giving him right of counsel, right to have witnesses in his behalf rather than only against him, and the right to appeal, on the basis of evidence, any decision of the Authority not only to courts, but to review by the directors of the Authority itself. It limits the maximum length of his incarceration and provides for periodic review of his case during his disposition to the authority.[31]

On the other hand, the proposed law has added some fuel to the confusion of already existing ideas of delinquency. By extending the age limit of coverage to twenty-one years, the law has gone beyond the maximum age of delinquents provided in most state laws and has lumped together conceptions of delinquency with what other states refer to as "youthful offenders" e.g. the age range between sixteen or eighteen and twenty-one. Furthermore, the model law has placed most of its emphasis on treatment after adjudication but has done little to improve substantive definitions of delinquent acts or the procedures which lead to adjudication. These remain as major stumbling blocks to legal realism in this area.

Some jurists have opposed the act for a number of reasons in addition to its failure to be more substantively oriented. The transferring of dispositions to the Authority and the provisions for the "indeterminate time" of the Authority's jurisdiction have caused some concern over the reduction of the judge's importance by removing his "sentencing power." It seems to me that such an argument is based more on the injured self-esteem of judges than on objective evidence of skill in making successful dispositions of cases. The great case load and subsequent shortage of time, the lack of diagnostic skills and facilities, and other limitations on judges' decisions make it evident that the best interests of adjudicated delinquents can better be determined by special diagnostic and treatment staffs, governed, of course, by suitable legal checks, than by a judge sitting alone.

The Youth Correction Authority Act is not the only form of legislation designed to improve treatment of delinquents. It has never been adopted completely by any state, although California comes close, and, like all model laws, must be

adapted to any unique conditions wherever it is tried. Some
states, like New York and New Jersey, have developed programs
of their own including reception centers, diagnostic clinics, youth
camps and other specialized institutions, but, as in the Federal
Youth Corrections Act (1950), retain distinctions between juvenile delinquency and later adolescent youthful offenders.

While change is occurring in delinquent and adolescent legislation, the lack of legal conciseness and clarity remains a pall
over the entire problem. As much research and attention should
be given to legal aspects of delinquency as to its many other
facets.

Proposals for Legal Reform in Delinquency Legislation

To answer the legitimate criticisms of those who challenge
the actual, as distinct from the theoretical, equity of juvenile
courts, a number of legal changes must be made in delinquency
legislation. It is here proposed that the following changes be
made in the typical laws and procedures of most states:

1. The jurisdiction of juvenile courts should be limited to
delinquency cases and not to other problems, such as neglect
or dependency. This means that there must be available
other agencies, and if necessary, other courts, to handle
these cases. This may seem an expensive proposal, but in
the light of increasing delinquency rates, the case loads of
most courts are increasing to the point of diminishing returns in terms of being effectively able to handle the numbers
of children who come before them. Undoubtedly an effective
court is less costly in the long run than an inefficient one.
2. The concept "delinquency" must be based upon substantive norms of behavior. Statutory definitions should include
categories listing the serious, *overt* behavior that is to be
considered delinquency. Vague conditions ("growing up in
idleness"), catch-all phrases and other terms open to loose,
even discriminatory, interpretation should be eliminated or
markedly clarified so that objective tests of their existence
can be made.
3. Adjudication of delinquency should follow legal proof that
the child violated a clause of existing delinquency laws. The
rules of evidence followed by other courts should be rigidly

adhered to in juvenile courts as well. The opinions of teachers, ministers, social workers and other interested parties should remain opinions, not proofs. Hearsay evidence and speculative judgments, should not be used to influence the court to deprive a youth of his liberty any more than such things are used to incarcerate adults.

4. The court should have jurisdiction in official cases only. Unofficial hearings, "voluntary" probation, and informal "treatments" have no place in a court, regardless of the possible kindness motivating them. Should cases come to the attention of the judge that are not in his bailiwick but that he feels need attention, he should be so familiar with the resources of his community that he can refer them to non-legal agencies. The court should deal with delinquents, not all children who have problems.

5. Social investigations of the child should be made following adjudication of delinquency rather than before, as are pre-sentence investigations of adults. This will save the court considerable time and money for in cases which are dismissed, no lengthy investigations need be made. Furthermore, if the condition of delinquency is established on the basis of facts surrounding specific actions of the child, a broad social investigation is irrelevant to adjudication. Investigate the facts first, causes only after the facts have established delinquency.

6. The procedures and conditions of the hearing should be revised to give maximum legal protection to the child accused of delinquency. He should not only have right of counsel, but this right should be carefully explained to him and counsel provided if his family is indigent. He should be clearly informed of the nature of the delinquent acts alleged against him. He should be able to cross examine hostile witnesses and to produce witnesses in his own behalf. He should be heard before a jury if he wishes. He should be able to challenge irrelevant evidence and be free from self-incrimination. His right to appeal decisions of the court should be clearly understood. Furthermore, the procedures of the court should be consistent from one hearing to the next.

7. Delinquency legislation should include in its substantive

context all violations of the criminal code, including murder and other serious felonies. Any exceptions would be inconsistent with the entire legal philosophy that exempts children from criminal liability. It is a horrible fact that children can kill, but to expose them to the repressive measures of penal law merely because their behavior is horrible, accomplishes nothing and destroys much.

8. Dispositions should be made by, or at least on the advice of, panels of experts similar to those proposed in the model Youth Corrections Authority Act. The court should have the function of adjudicating or dismissing the case and within the age limits provided by law, committing the adjudicated children to some central body which has a diagnostic and treatment function. This panel should, after careful study and observation, decide how and where and for how long the children should remain in its care. Decisions made by this panel would include, in addition to institutional or camp placement, cases to be placed on probation, in foster homes, or in the care of medical, psychiatric or other specialized agencies. Appeals to higher courts from the dispositions given by these panels would, of course, be permitted.

Now lest all this sound as if the juvenile court is merely being turned into a junior criminal court, let it be emphatically recommended that many present distinctions between these courts be retained. The privacy of the hearings and the confidence of records of the juvenile court should be rigidly adhered to. Hearings should be as informal as is consistent with the protection of rights. The hearing room should of course be distinct from the criminal court and the wig-and-gown ritualism of the trial dispensed with. Adjudication as a delinquent should not amount to a criminal conviction with attendant loss of certain privileges. Furthermore, the equity philosophy of the court should remain its underlying principle. Careful procedures and substantive norms need not destroy fairness, but they should, if excessive, hair-splitting formalism is avoided, contribute to it. The establishment of such norms and procedures is not to provide "loopholes" through which delinquents may escape justice but rather to implement our

legal assumption of innocence of all people before all courts
and to hold the doctrine of *parens patriae* within just and humane limits.

Adjudications still should not be convictions any more than
dispositions should be sentences. Perhaps it would be feasible
to exempt the court from finding delinquency "beyond reasonable doubt" and establish adjudication on some lesser basis,
the "weight of evidence," but still on the foundation of testable
facts. Perhaps, too, the juvenile court in keeping with its equity
philosophy, should be less bound by the principle *stare decisis*
(deciding a case on the basis of how similar cases have been
decided), than other courts. This does not mean that the court
can be completely inconsistent in its decisions but only that it
should not be so hide-bound to precedent that its findings work
at odds with its goal of acting in the "best interests" of its charges.

Juvenile delinquency does not end with the court and
any changes in laws and procedures will not "cure" it, at least
not by themselves. But while delinquency does not end in the
law, in a very real sense, it begins here. Basically, juvenile delinquency is a legal concept and delinquents are law-breakers
even if not criminals. We owe it to our young people to be as
careful in planning the laws governing their behavior and the
procedures by which these laws are implemented, as we are in
drafting any legislation. Something must be done about delinquency, to be sure, but in doing this something we must
not become so carried away by plans of reform and rehabilitation that we become careless in selecting those we wish to rehabilitate. We need to give delinquency clarity and substantive
meaning in law before we can even define the problem we are
attacking. And, if the civil rights of children are injured in our
attack, then the cure is worse than the disease.

Selected Bibliography

Herbert A. Bloch & Frank T. Flynn, *Delinquency: The
Juvenile Offender in America Today* (New York: Random
House, 1956). An up-to-date text in the field of delinquency that
contains a number of pertinent chapters on the philosophy and
workings of the juvenile court and juvenile court laws.

S. P. Breckinridge, "Legal Problems of the Juvenile Court,"
The Social Service Review, XVII, No. 1, (March, 1943), 12-14.

A brief article which discusses some of the important legal cases which have been instrumental in determining the legal limitations of the juvenile court.

Gilbert Cosulich, *Juvenile Court Laws of the United States,* 20. Ed. (New York: National Probation Association, 1939). A comprehensive collection of juvenile laws prior to the changes brought by World War II and the post-war adjustments.

John R. Ellingston, *Protecting Our Children from Criminal Careers* (New York: Prentice Hall, 1948). A discussion of the Youth Correction Authority Act as implemented in California.

Mabel A. Elliott, *Conflicting Penal Theories in Statutory Criminal Law* (University of Chicago Press, 1931). An excellent discussion of legal philosophies with three chapters devoted to legal issues in juvenile delinquency.

Alfred J. Kahn, *A Court For Children: A Study of the New York City Children's Court* (New York: Columbia University Press, 1953). An excellent study that demonstrates the many difficulties faced by juvenile courts in operation. This study of New York's juvenile courts indicates particularly the tremendous case-loads and understaffing found in courts in operation versus courts in theory.

Herbert H. Lou, *Juvenile Courts in the United States* (Chapel Hill: University of North Carolina Press, 1927). A definitive work in the area of legal aspects of delinquency, while not a recent book, it gives comprehensive treatment to all legal phases of delinquency including procedures, variations in definitions, conduct of hearings, appeals and dispositions.

Jerome Michael & Herbert Wechsler, *Criminal Law and Its Administration* (Chicago: The Foundation Press, 1940). This standard work on criminal law contains valuable sections on immaturity as a legal concept including important legal decisions and a discussion of the legal meaning of delinquency.

Roscoe Pound, "The Juvenile Court and the Law," *National Probation and Parole Association Yearbook,* 1942. One of the best known, legal theorists speaks of the problems involved in juvenile court laws.

Sol Rubin, "The Legal Character of Juvenile Delinquency," *The Annals,* 261, (January, 1949). A well-known writer in the field of legal phases of delinquency discusses the vagueness and variability of laws defining delinquency.

A Standard Juvenile Court Act (New York: National Probation and Parole Association, 1949). Legislation proposed by a committee of experts designed to make delinquency a uniform concept in all states. This work is based on a survey of delinquency legislation and attempts to meet some of the problems of existing delinquency laws.

Standards for Specialized Courts Dealing with Children, Children's Bureau. Publication 346 (Washington, D.C.: U.S. Department of Health, Education and Welfare, 1954). Implementing the Standard Juvenile Court Act, this publication was developed with the cooperation of the National Council of Juvenile Court Judges. It proposed to clarify and to make more uniform many juvenile court procedures.

Frederick B. Sussman, *Law of Juvenile Delinquency; The Laws of the Forty-Eight States,* (New York: Oceana Publications, 1950). A brief but comprehensive discussion of variations in legal aspects of delinquency. This work contains a state by state analysis of juvenile jurisdiction and a succinct discussion of issues involved in defining and processing delinquents.

Paul W. Tappan, *Comparative Survey on Juvenile Delinquency, Part I: North America.* (New York: United Nations Division of Social Welfare, 1952). A comparative analysis of the limitations and problems of juvenile delinquency.

Paul W. Tappan, *Juvenile Delinquency* (New York: McGraw-Hill, 1949). A standard text in the field that contains probably the most comprehensive and enlightened analysis of various legal aspects of delinquency.

Negley K. Teeters, and John Otto Reineman, *The Challenge of Delinquency* (New York: Prentice Hall, 1950). A text that contains excellent discussions of the origins of the social jurisprudence underlying our legal treatment of delinquents.

Donald J. Newman, Ph.D., Assistant Professor of Sociology at St. Lawrence University (Canton, New York), has taught at the University of Wisconsin and has been a Fellow of the American Bar Association, participating in their nation-wide "Survey of Criminal Law and Litigation;" is the author of various research articles in the field of criminology and delinquency and for the past three summers has been a lecturer at the Frederick A. Moran Memorial Institute on Delinquency and Crime; is also a member of the sub-committee on Relationships Among Academic Departments of the Committee on Corrections of the Council on Social Work Education.

Part II

The Search for Causes

CHAPTER 3

THE BIOLOGICAL BASIS OF JUVENILE DELINQUENCY

WILLIAM McCORD
Harvard University

In recent years, "The Bad Seed" received considerable acclaim both on Broadway and in the movies. The play told the story of an "angelic" little girl who killed one of her playmates and several other people. So clever was the girl in dispatching those who annoyed her that she escaped detection until, by accident, the child's mother discovered a medal which had belonged to one of the victims. As played on the stage, the monster's mother was a loving, average, middle-class woman. How could a murderer arise from such a perfect environment? The mother found the answer when she discovered that her own mother had been a hatchet murderer. Equipped with this piece of information, everything became clear: the "bad seed" planted by the grandmother had emerged in the child.

This play may have been good melodrama, but it is not good science. Unfortunately, it typifies the attitude often held by laymen toward the causation of crime.

In this article, we shall review briefly the evidence for asserting that criminality is innate, biological, or constitutional—due to a "bad seed."

Age, Sex, and Race in the Causation of Delinquency

Let us begin with certain obvious, "biological" facts concerning criminals:

Many more men than women commit crimes. In 1951, four times as many boys as girls were referred to juvenile courts. In 1952, eight times as many men as women appeared before adult courts in America. The male-female ratio increases when one examines the more "daring" crimes: in 1952, for every *one* woman, 10.3 men were arrested for assault; 22.6 for robbery, 40.5 for burglary, and 43.2 for auto theft.

Most criminals are young. In 1952, 23 percent of all the criminals arrested in America were under 25, and an additional 38 percent were under 40.

Proportionately, Negroes more often commit crimes than do whites. Negro children appear in juvenile courts three to four times more often than white children.

Sex, age, and race are all biologically determined and all bear a statistical relationship to criminality. Does this mean, then, that these three variables are independent causal factors or are they simply reflections of other environmental causes? It is difficult to answer this question in a definitive manner. Let us examine each variable separately.

There is no proof that the biological difference between men and women leads men to commit more crimes. Men are better equipped by nature for those crimes which require strength, dexterity, and speed; yet, this fact explains only why men are better *able* to commit crimes, not why they actually *do* become criminal.

Cultural, as well as biological factors contribute to the difference in criminal behavior. The role expectations of American culture accentuate the biological differences. Our culture rewards men who exhibit the "masculine" traits of courage, adventuresomeness, strength, daring, and leadership—traits which are encouraged in the delinquent gang. Women, on the other hand, cannot achieve prestige or recognition through participating in "masculine" activities; the "manly" woman is derided. Since the fundamental motive underlying delinquency is a search for recognition or "status," it is clear that men can achieve prestige through the masculine activities involved in delinquency. Women who have an inordinate need for prestige must, on the other hand, turn to other channels for satisfaction. Thus, it would appear that the male-female difference in criminality is only partially a biological phenomenon.

The age difference in crime, too, seems to be closely linked to the environment. Numerous studies have shown that a high proportion of delinquents "reform" as they enter adult life.[1] Is this reformation due to biological maturation or is it rather an environmentally caused change?

Younger men, it is true, have more strength and agility than older men; but this fact by itself hardly explains the contrast. Here again, the explanation revolves around the expectations of American culture. Young men in our society must pass through an adolescent period of "stress and strain." As anthropologists have demonstrated, in other cultures, this adolescent tension does not exist. The major problem for adolescents in all societies is establishing their manhood. Our society, unlike others, does not conduct specified "puberty rites" which signify the distinct transition between boyhood and manhood. Our children, unsure of their masculinity, must create their own "puberty rites." This they do through a variety of expedients: ownership of a car, army service, membership in a fraternity, or through participation in delinquent activities. Membership in a gang, wearing of gang emblems, and testing one's strength represent ways of establishing a masculine identity.

After proving themselves, gang members can gain new status through marriage, jobs, or army service. When they become wage earners, husbands, and fathers, the responsibilities inherent in these roles cannot be jibed with the adventuresome activities of youth. Consequently, having passed through adolescence successfully and having assumed new adult roles, they no longer have the same pressing need to "prove themselves."

For a variety of deep psychological reasons, a small group of the "unreformed" continue their delinquency into adulthood. They are slightly augmented by another group of men (like drunkards or sexual perverts) who, typically, become criminal only later in life. Even so, this group of older criminals is smaller than the large number of delinquents who pass through their "puberty rites" and reform.

There is no evidence that the contrast between Negro and white crime rates is due to a physiological difference between ethnic groups. Negroes, as a group, are more often subjected to influences which are known to produce delinquency: residence in a slum neighborhood, low socio-economic status, and other social disabilities. In addition, Negroes must carry the burden of racial bias, so prevalent in America (a bias which is naturally reflected in the arrests made by white police of Negro criminals). The continual frustration caused by discrimination undoubtedly leads to more aggression. The Negro seldom responds directly in an aggressive manner toward the source of bias. Studies of Negro students in the South show that although their first reaction in encountering overt prejudice is a desire to "fight back," most often, the discrimination is accepted peacefully. Aggression is often displaced toward other objects. Most crimes of violence committed by Negroes are directed against members of their own race—although, in all justice, they should be directed against the whites. As another result of discrimination and frustration, the Negro family seems to be more disorganized than the average white family: this influence, too, leads to a higher rate of crime.

At this stage of our knowledge, therefore, it seems most reasonable to presume that differences in crime rate which are related to age, sex, and race are side-products of deeper environmental causes.

Heredity

In many sections of Europe and South America, the "bad seed" theory of crime is still the most popular. Certainly, if it could be proved that crime was due to hereditary "taint," the task of controlling crime would be immensely simplified. Sterilization of the "unfit" would presumably be an effective counterattack upon criminality. Indeed, certain distinguished investigators have enthusiastically advocated sterilization programs. In Denmark, for example, a rather high proportion of criminals, particularly sexual criminals, are being sterilized. Unfortunately for the proponents of this approach, there is very little evidence to support their contentions.

During the 19th century, the accepted explanation of crime was the theory which pinned the blame on hereditary or constitutional factors. Under the general influence of social Darwinism and the specific influence of Cesare Lombroso, investigators during this century tabbed the criminal as an atavism— a throw-back to a more primitive period in the evolution of man. The famous "Jukes" and "Kallikaks" research gave wide credence to this belief.

In 1877, Richard Dugdale, a social investigator of prisons, published "The Jukes," a study of a family of paupers and criminals.[2] Dugdale traced the progeny of "Max Juke," a New York settler, born between the years of 1720 and 1740. By 1874, "Max" had 709 descendants, of whom 180 were paupers, 140 were criminals, and 50 were prostitutes. Although the validity of Dugdale's information was questioned, his study was hailed by hereditarians as proof of the biological causation of crime.

In 1912, a second study, "The Kallikaks" was published by Henry H. Goddard and appeared to support the hereditarian theory.[3] Goddard examined the family tree of a Revolutionary War soldier who married a supposedly feeble-minded girl. Of their 480 descendants, Goddard claimed that 143 were feeble-minded and only 46 were mentally normal. Feeble-mindedness, Goddard believed, was the fertile ground from which criminality grew. As proof, Goddard cited the fact that the soldier had married a normal woman, too, and their descendants had all been honest and distinguished citizens.

In later years, other investigators (particularly German scientists) have attempted to trace the familial background of known criminals. These investigators have consistently found a higher proportion of criminal parentage in the background of the criminals than could be found in control groups of non-criminals. Most recently, Mohr, a Swiss investigator, found that 68 percent of a sample of Swiss criminals had criminal parents; in America, Partridge found an incidence of 50 percent, and Glueck, an incidence of 60 percent.[4] These figures create a difficult problem of interpretation, for it is impossible to separate the influence of heredity from that of environment. Criminal parents may turn out criminal sons because the sons follow their example or because they transmit to the sons some sort of biological predisposition to crime. Were criminal tendencies the result of the parents' influence or of their genes? These studies cannot tell us.

One possible way of separating these influences is through the examination of twins. A number of studies have compared the life histories of fraternal and identical twins. Presumably, if there is a greater resemblance in criminal activity between identical twins, then an hereditary basis for criminality would be established. Studies in "crimino-biology" have been conducted primarily by German scientists. Lange, in 1929, compared the life histories of 13 identical twins with the lives of 17 fraternal twins.[5] He noted that 10 of the identical twins had "concordant" lives; that is, either both boys were criminal or both were non-criminal. On the other hand, only 2 of the 17 pairs of fraternal twins had concordant lives. Other German studies by Legras in 1932, Kranz in 1936 and Stumpfl in 1936 analyzed other samples of twins and confirmed Lange's results.[6] In America, a research team headed by A. J. Rosanoff discovered that twenty-five of thirty-seven identical twins as opposed to only five of twenty-eight fraternal twins had led concordant lives.[7] Taken together, these five studies investigated 104 identical twins, finding that 67.3 percent had led concordant lives. In contrast, only 33 percent of the 112 pairs of fraternal twins had similar lives.

In 1943, Rosanoff analyzed the largest sample of twins yet compiled: four hundred pairs. In this extensive research, Rosanoff once again found that identical twins more often resembled each other. The similarity in criminal histories of identical twins was 1.4 times that of fraternal twins.[8]

One conclusion from this research is that criminal tendencies are, at least to some degree, inherited. Nevertheless, social scientists have been extremely wary of accepting such a conclusion. Critics have questioned the reliability of the studies, particularly their criterion for establishing "monozygocity" (that twins came from one egg) and the validity of their social investigation of criminal histories. Then, too, other studies have contradicted the original findings. Kallman, for example, demonstrated that the children of "psychopathic" criminals have a higher incidence of criminality than do siblings of psychopathic criminals.[9] If this study is valid, the incidence does *not* follow the closest lines of blood kinship.

Kallman's research indicates that an hereditary theory of crime would be in contradiction to current genetical theory. Even if the results of the twin studies are accepted, many scientists would hesitate to ascribe the greater behavioral similarities of identical twins to heredity. Identical twins are treated in a more similar manner; they tend to be closer companions; and more often, they are comrades in the same activities. This environmentally-imposed similarity may account for resemblance in their criminal histories. Consequently, the general opinion among criminologists is that twin studies, while provocative, have failed to establish the existence of an inherited predisposition to crime.

A subsidiary issue, the relation between intelligence and crime, has atracted great attention. Intelligence, while affected by many environmental influences, appears to be largely determined by heredity. At the turn of the century, it was widely believed that stupidity led to crime. The "Jukes" and "Kallikaks" research added weight to this view. The work of H. H. Goddard and Charles Goring gave substance to the opinion. In 1914, Goddard reviewed the evidence and came to the conclusion that 50 percent of all adult criminals were feeble-minded. He bolstered this position by citing studies of reformatory inmates in Illinois, New York, Massachusetts, and New Jersey; the studies concluded that at least 70 percent of the convicts were "feeble-minded."[10]

In England, Charles Goring, a distinguished student of "criminal biology," concluded that the feeble-minded formed a disproportionately large quota of British criminals.[11]

By the 1920's, however, further research based on larger samples and more refined instruments cast serious doubt upon the contention. Edwin Sutherland, for example, reviewed 350 studies concerning intelligence and crime. He noted that the proportion of criminals diagnosed as feeble-minded decreased from 50 percent in the period 1910 to 1914 to 20 percent in the period 1925 to 1928.[12] A recent study at Harvard traced the criminal records of a group of 253 children who had received treatment from the Cambridge-Somerville project during the 1930's. When the children were, on the average, ten years old, their intelligence was measured by the Stanford-Binet test; these scores were compared to their criminal records in the 1940's and 1950's. Approximately equal proportions of children at each level of intelligence were later convicted of a major crime:[13]

Intelligence		Percent Convicted of Crimes
Superior (Over 110)	(N: 23)	26
Average (91-110)	(N:111)	46
Dull Average (81-90)	(N: 59)	44
Sub-Normal (Below 81)	(N: 46)	35

To the best of our knowledge, there is no direct relationship between intelligence and crime.

In passing, it should be mentioned that some scientists entertain an enthusiastic belief that endocrinological disorders—perhaps caused by heredity—underly all criminal behavior. Aside from a few isolated cases, there is no substantial evidence for this view.

Physique

One popular approach to the establishment of a biological basis of crime has been through the examination of the bodily constitution of delinquents. The assumption underlying this approach is that physique is relatively constant and, probably, inherited. Therefore, if it were discovered that criminals had constitutions which differed from non-criminals, a fundamental biological difference would be proved.

The "constitutional school" was initiated by Cesare Lombroso, an Italian physician who believed that criminals possessed a distinct body type. In the 1880s, Lombroso was struck by the contrast in tattoos which he observed on the bodies of soldiers. The tougher soldiers wore "indecent" tattoos, while the more dependable men had quieter tattoos. From this, Lombroso moved on to a study of other physical "stigmata." He observed a large number of criminals in Italian prisons and came to the opinion that criminals, as a group, were characterized by low brows, long ear lobes, lack of chins, either extreme hairiness or an extreme lack of hair, and other physical signs. In addition, he carried out several autopsies, one on the famous outlaw "Vilella." The outlaw's brain, in Lombroso's judgment, resembled that of lower vertebrates. Lombroso concluded that the criminal was a biological regression to a primitive, ape-like stage of evolution.[14] Lombroso's opinions gained wide circulation, and a school of "criminal anthropology" developed around his doctrine.

Lombroso's position came under devastating attack, however, by Charles Goring and Karl Pearson in 1913. In *The English Convict*, the two scientists reported their findings after an investigation of the physical characteristics of three thousand British prisoners. They found no evidence of a consistency in the physical traits of the criminals and no reason for accepting Lombroso's generalizations.

While Lombroso's specific theories have fallen into disrepute, other investigators have continued his line of research into modern times. In America, the most famous studies in criminal anthropology have been conducted by Ernst Hooten, William Sheldon, and Sheldon and Eleanor Glueck.

In 1939, Ernst Hooten stirred a controversy with the publication of *Crime and the Man,* an impassioned defense of the belief in physical determinism. Hooten made 107 anthropometric measurements of 14,477 convicts and compared the measurements to those of a non-criminal control group of 3,203. He concluded that the criminals gave evidence of distinct physical inferiority. His research was widely attacked, for Hooten's control group was far from representative. It included, among others, swimmers at a bathing beach, firemen, and militia men —all of whom could be considered as physically superior to the normal population.[15] Other critics pointed out the biased nature of Hooten's conclusions (e.g. that physical inferiority is evidence of "degeneracy" and degeneracy is defined as criminality) and the manner in which Hooten overlooked certain environmental causes (like poor nutrition) of physical inferiority. Consequently, Hooten's conclusions, that criminals are physically inferior and should be sterilized, fell on deaf ears.

Other scientists, like Sheldon and the Gluecks, have reached the conclusion that delinquents are actually physically *superior* to the normal population; if one defines superiority as being muscled, tightly knit, and physically solid. Sheldon, for example, made a series of comparisons between boys incarcerated in an institution for homeless children.[16] The delinquents, he found, tended to be "mesomorphic"; they were characterized by the relative dominance of muscles, and a heavy, hard body outline. Non-delinquents, on the other hand, were either "endomorphic" (soft and fat) or "ectomorphic" (thin, fragile, and linear). Sheldon, like Hooten, concluded his report with a panegyria on sterilization. Social scientists have been cautious about accepting Sheldon's research since it is based on measurements taken only *after* a boy had become delinquent. Critics point out that delinquency is a muscular affair which, through the nature of its activities, could be expected to build up the physical strength and hardness of its participants. Therefore they ask, how does Sheldon know that the "mesomorphy" of the delinquents preceded their delinquency? Unless one assumes that physique is entirely constitutional and cannot be affected by the environment, then it may be that "mesomorphy" is a result rather than a cause of delinquency.

The most careful attempt to relate physique to delinquency has been the work of Sheldon and Eleanor Glueck, for it is based on a comparison of five hundred delinquents meticulously matched to five hundred non-delinquents. The Gluecks' research into the relation between constitution and delinquency has been reported in two volumes, *Unraveling Juvenile Delinquency* and, most recently, *Physique and Delinquency*.[17]

Over a number of years, the Gluecks' anthropological staff photographed, analyzed, and categorized the somatypes of the one thousand children. The results showed that the delinquents, as a group, were primarily mesomorphic. They were stronger, more muscular, heavier, and more tightly knit.

In 1956, the Gluecks published a more detailed report, which especially concentrated on the differential reaction of the various body types to environmental conditions. In addition, the Gluecks attempted to establish the relative incidence of different personality traits (as measured by the Rorschach test and by psychiatric interviews) in the different body types. The Gluecks constantly emphasized the continuity between the organism and its environment. These were their major conclusions:

A variety of personality traits, like hostility, suspiciousness, defensiveness, vivacity, and adventuresomeness were characteristic of the delinquents as a group. Regardless of their physique, the delinquents possessed these traits in common. In addition, a number of sociocultural factors were typical of the delinquents' background and appeared to exert an equally criminogenic impact on all the physique types. These influences included such factors as delinquency or alcoholism in the father, emotional disturbance in the mother, lack of attachment between the child and his parents, and unsuitable discipline.

Aside from this "common ground of criminogenesis," the Gluecks found certain variations between different physiques. The "mesomorphs," who comprised 60 percent of the five hundred delinquents, were strong, muscular individuals. Among non-delinquents, the mesomorphs significantly differed from the other types in being "less sensitive, less aesthetic, and less sensuous," in lacking a tendency to phantasy and lacking feelings of inadequacy. The delinquent mesomorphs, on the other hand, had a number of traits which differentiated them from other delinquents who had different physiques. Such traits were: greater feelings of inadequacy, more emotional instability, more emotional conflicts, and greater destructiveness.

One striking contrast between the physique types was that mesomorphs tended to "under-react" to adverse familial conditions (for example, a smaller proportion of mesomorphic delinquents than of other types of delinquents came from broken homes). Ectomorphs "over-reacted" to poor familiar conditions. Of those ectomorphs who became delinquent, higher proportions had been reared in broken homes or by incompatible parents or had lived in families with hostility among the siblings and in which cohesiveness was generally lacking. In personality, the non-delinquent ectomorphs differed from the other non-delinquents in being more sensitive, less emotionally stable, and more aesthetic.

Endomorphs, the Gluecks concluded, had a series of traits which made them relatively immune to delinquency. As compared to mesomorphs and ectomorphs, the endomorphs were more submissive to authority, more sensuous, more conventional, and more inhibited.

A fourth or "balanced" type of physique included, in equal measure, characteristics from the other three types. Perhaps because they possessed physical traits in such equal proportions, the "balanced" type, as a group, differed from other non-delinquent boys only in that they were less fearful of failure and defeat. Few of them became delinquent, but the reasons for their immunity did not emerge from the Gluecks' analysis.

This provocative study by the Gluecks reached two major conclusions: mesomorphs tend to react with action towards environmental frustration; when they possess personality traits which are not "compatible" with the "constitutional host," they are most likely to become delinquent. Ectomorphs, on the other hand, are strikingly more receptive to adverse familial conditions.

If the Gluecks have succeeded in establishing a constitutional basis for delinquency, their work would be of revolutionary importance. Nevertheless, many social scientists hesitate to accept this evidence. The Gluecks' research has been subjected to two major criticisms: First, as with Sheldon's work, critics question the "retrospective" nature of the research; it may be, they argue, that delinquent activities create a stronger body build as well as a more aggressive temperament. Since the Gluecks studied children after they had become delinquent, this criticism, for the present, must remain unanswered. Second, critics attack the Glueck's dependence upon low levels of statistical significance in the conclusions which they draw. Generalizations are based upon statistical relationships which are significant only at the .10 level (that is, there is one possibility out of ten that the result could have been due to chance). The Gluecks' reply that the "procrustean bed" of statistics should not cause the abandonment of findings that "are both clinically relevant and highly suggestive of fruitful hypotheses."[18]

Thus, in the present controversial state of our knowledge, hypotheses concerning the relations between physical constitution and crime appear suggestive, but inconclusive. It is a field of research which, in the future, may prove fruitful.

Brain Structure

Another promising approach in this search for the "bad seed" of criminality is through the examination of man's (inherited or acquired) brain structure. The crude beginnings of the attempt to relate criminality to brain activity can be detected in the "science" of phrenology.

Phrenology was invented by Franz Joseph Gall, a Viennese physician. In the late 18th century, Gall hypothesized that man's psychological faculties could be directly related to the contour of his brain and skull. Bumps, inequalities, or abnormal configurations of the skull indicated equivalent malformations of a man's character. Gall spent his life examining the skulls of convicts, the insane, and normal people. Gall's disciple, a publicist named Johann Christoph Spurzheim, advertised the "discoveries" of phrenology until it became, in the nineteenth century, a popular and dignified science. Prison administrators became infected with the fad and classified their convicts on the basis of skull configurations. The rise of psychology and scientific neurology dampened the public's enthusiasm for phrenology, for it soon demonstrated that man's mind was not divided into separate "faculties."

As neurology replaced phrenology, it became apparent that

damage to the brain could result in marked changes in personality—sometimes in an "anti-social" direction. Brain injuries
inflicted at birth or by accidents often cause a decrease in inhibition and an increase in aggression. As early as 1848, physicians
noted that workers injured in industrial accidents could turn
overnight from law-abiding citizens to criminals. Boxers, who
sustain repeated head injuries, often exhibit erratic, aggressive,
pseudo-criminal behavior.

Brain injuries only rarely produce criminal tendencies; nevertheless, every criminologist can report certain exceptional cases
where brain damage played a major role. I will mention only
two cases from my own experience: "John," a young soldier
during the Second World War, came from an upper-middle class
home in the Midwest. His social-cultural environment was entirely normal. During adolescence, John attended a private
school and went on to college. At no time, did he participate
in criminal activities. During the war, however, he received
a serious bullet wound in the cortical area of his brain. After
months of hospitalization, he survived the wound and returned
to his home with an honorable discharge. His parents noticed
that his character had absolutely changed. He became irritable,
extremely tense, and highly aggressive. He fought bitterly with
former friends and, several times, caused barroom brawls. One
night his mother discovered that he kept a knife and a pistol
under his pillow. When she mentioned it the next morning, John
threatened her with the gun. John was committed to a private
mental hospital where his aggression continued. Treatment
has been of no avail.

"Herby," the second case, was reared in a New York slum.
When he was three, Herby fell from his bed and suffered a
severe concussion. He survived the injury, but it soon became
obvious that his intelligence had been severely impaired. Although he had been a mild-mannered baby, his childhood was
characterized by a hair-trigger temper. Herby developed a fas-
cination for fires. After he had been involved in several explosive
attacks on other children as well as several incidents of arson,
he was committed to a progressive reform school. In the school,
long-term psychological treatment made certain modifications
in his behavior, but today Herby remains in a state school for
retarded and delinquent children.

John and Herby form only a tiny fraction of the criminal

population. Extensive studies of the medical histories of criminals have failed to uncover brain damage in any significant number of cases.

Certain diseases, particularly encephalitis, and epilepsy, can sometimes result in criminal behavior. These diseases undoubtedly have a destructive effect upon the brain, but their results are varied and subtle. In a minority of cases, they can result in anti-social behavior, but the specific reasons for this effect are unknown. A history of encephalitis or epilepsy has been detected in only a minority of the criminal population. Cases where brain tumors, birth injuries, or lobotomies have led to criminal behavior can also be found in the literature of crime. But again, such cases are extremely rare.

Today, no criminologist would claim that easily detectable injuries to the brain underlie all criminal behavior. Some scientists do, however, believe that subtle neurological disorders may play an important role. Although neurology is still young, it has been fairly well established that the cortex and the hypothalamus have a distinct influence upon inhibition. Certain areas of the medula appear to have a strong relation to aggression. Consequently, it is possible to hypothesize that injury (or perhaps abnormal stimulation) of these areas is related to criminal behavior. Nevertheless, the hypothesis remains just that, for we have no definitive evidence for such a generalization.

One approach towards detecting subtle disorders within the brain is through the use of the electro-encephalogram—an instrument which measures the electrical activity within the brain. Extensive use of the E.E.G. has established certain standards of "normal" waves. When the E.E.G. waves of an individual pass out of this range of normality, there is indirect evidence of disfunction within the brain. About 15 percent of the "normal" (non-criminal, non-psychotic) population exhibit abnormal waves. If a higher proportion of criminals have abnormal waves, a neurological basis of crime might be indicated. A number of studies, some more reliable than others, have concentrated upon the brain waves of criminals.[19] Probably the most dependable and extensive research was conducted by Ostrow and Ostrow.[20] In 1946, these scientists measured the brain waves of 440 convicts at a Federal prison. They compared the patterns found in homosexuals, epileptics, schizophrenics, and psychopaths (impulsive, loveless, guiltless criminals). An extremely high proportion of each of these groups exhibited abnormal waves. Fifty percent of the psychopaths, fifty-six percent of the homosexuals, eighty percent of the schizophrenics, and ninety-eight percent of the epileptics had abnormal patterns. But strangely, a high proportion, sixty-five percent, of imprisoned conscientious objectors also had abnormal waves. By the standards of society, conscientious objectors cannot be considered in the same class as the other criminals. Perhaps the most significant result of this study is that it hints that all social deviants, regardless of the particular form of their deviance, have abnormal waves. If this discovery is confirmed by other studies, several interpretations would be possible. One might argue that some vaguely defined neurological "predisposition" underlies deviance; but one could also argue that the deviance itself creates the abnormal patterns. It has been well established that changes in the environment and changes in personality can result in alterations in the E.E.G. pattern. Is the deviance due to brain disorder or is the "disorder" due to the deviance? At this point, we do not know.

Another indication of neural disorder is the presence of physical "signs"—tics, tremors, irregular reflexes. Some scientists have investigated criminals in a search for these marks of neural disfunction. Their results have been contradictory. In Britain, Sessions-Hodges examined seventy criminal "psychopaths" and compared them to fifty non-criminals. He found that seventy-six percent of the criminals as compared to ten percent of the control group gave evidence of neural disorder; many had an equivocal plantar response.[21] In contrast, Sheldon and Eleanor Glueck failed to confirm Sessions-Hodges' findings; instead, they found that non-delinquents give more evidence of neurological disorder. In the Gluecks' comparative study of one thousand individuals, they noted that there was no significant difference between the delinquents and the non-delinquents in the proportions with irregular reflexes or functional deviations (stuttering, lisping). In terms of specific disabilities, the Gluecks discovered that a significantly higher proportion of non-delinquents had dermographia, marked tics, extreme nail-biting, and ambidexterity.[22] Thus, the evidence is highly contradictory: Sessions-Hodges (and others) assert that delinquents possess more neurological "signs" while the Gluecks' evidence indicates the exact opposite.

Our knowledge concerning the relation between crime and brain structure is sketchy. Tentatively, we can conclude that, in some cases, brain disorder in the inhibitory area may play some role in crime. Neurology is still in its infancy and its future development may have great relevance to the understanding of crime.

The Biological Basis of Delinquent Types

American criminology, long dominated by sociology, has often failed to make distinctions between the different psychological types of delinquents. Consequently, social science has not progressed very far in the understanding of particular kinds of deviance. If proper psychological distinctions are drawn, we may discover that certain kinds of criminals are "biologically predisposed" to their crime, while other types are entirely determined by the environment. Our present knowledge hints that a biological basis may exist for four types of delinquents: the psychopath, the homosexual, the alcoholic, and the psychotic.

Contemporary evidence indicates that psychopathy results from a combination of neurological and social influences. A variety of studies indicate that the psychopathic delinquent— a highly impulsive, aggressive, guiltless, and loveless individual—always undergoes parental rejection. Nevertheless, all rejected children do not become psychopathic. On the other hand, evidence drawn from E.E.G. studies, medical histories, and physical examinations, show that a high proportion of psychopaths suffer from neurological disorder (probably in the cortical or the hypothalamic areas). Therefore, a "neuro-social" theory of psychopathy has been proposed: psychopathy results either from severe parental rejection or from a combination of neural inhibitory weakness and mild parental rejection.[23]

Homosexuality, too, may have a biological source. Evidence concerning this form of deviance is vague. Psychologically, the disorder appears to stem from a familial background characterized by a highly indulgent mother and a dominating father. Given this environment, a child sometimes rejects the male ideal and identifies with his mother through the acceptance of the female role. Some evidence indicates that this particular choice may be prompted partially by an excess of estrogen over androgen hormones in the individual. This hormonic basis for the disorder is far from proved, but perhaps it may play a part.

Alcoholism is another form of "criminal" deviance which may have some relation to the individual's physiology. A number of social-psychological studies have firmly established a cultural and familial basis for alcoholism. Nevertheless, there is also some indication that the sugar level of the blood or the activity of the adrenal cortex may be related to the disorder. Like so many forms of deviance, it is difficult to disentangle the *effects* of alcoholism on the organism from possible causative relationships. Although without firm proof, there are some suggestions that alcoholism may derive from a physiological predisposition.

Psychotic criminals make up only a small part of the total criminal population. Yet it is their crimes which often draw the most public attention. Most psychotics never become involved in criminal activities, but those few who do can be very troublesome to society. Increasingly today, psychiatry is uncovering evidence concerning the biological basis of psychoses: twin studies have delineated an hereditary predisposition to the disease and a variety of bio-chemical studies are beginning to specify the causal connections.

Summary

Given our contemporary state of knowledge, these generalizations seem justified:

Crime rate variations linked to age, sex, and race appear to be largely environmentally, rather than biologically, determined.

There is no direct evidence for a hereditary predisposition to crime. Studies of ancestral histories and comparative research on the life history of twins have failed to differentiate satisfactorily between nature and nurture.

There is no direct evidence of a relationship between intelligence and crime nor between the functioning of the endocrine glands and crime.

The relation between criminality and physique is still in a controversial stage. The Gluecks' research, the most dependable of its kind, has suggested that more delinquents have a mesomorphic body structure and that psychological traits as well as reactions to environmental influences vary with physique. If the statistical basis of this research is accepted, the finding is subject to two interpretations. First, one might conclude that some inherent factor determined physical constitution and with it, the individual's basic temperament. Second, one might conclude that the correlation between mesomorphy and delinquency is due to the activities in which the delinquent participates.

The actions of a small portion of criminals seem causally linked to brain injuries caused by birth traumas, tumors, accidents, or brain diseases. While obvious neural disorders are absent, E.E.G. studies tentatively indicate that subtle neural disorders may be present in a relatively high proportion of criminals. A specific neurological source of criminality has yet to be proved.

Certain types of criminality—psychopathy, homosexuality, alcoholism, and psychotic criminality—may have a physiological or neurological background.

Our knowledge about the biological nature of crime is an ill-defined and uncertain state. Perhaps the only way in which the situation can be clarified is through the introduction of longitudinal studies. Ideally, children should be examined at birth and at various other points in their life. A full record of their genetical, biochemical, anthropological, and neurological characteristics should be kept. After a passage of years, the subjects' social adjustment could be traced. Equipped with the knowledge which would emerge from such research, we could solve many of the controversies which surround the subject of the biological origins of crime.

Even if we assume that future research will uncover a "bad seed" of crime, considerable attention will need to be devoted to the specific relation between the organism and its environment. Social-psychological research has amassed a fund of information concerning the environmental correlates of crime. To cite just a few well-known examples: delinquency concentrates in non-cohesive families; certain urban areas are centers of delinquency; the homicide rate of America is nearly ten times that of England. It is impossible to subsume these facts entirely under a biological explanation of crime. It would be absurd, for example, to explain America's high crime rate as due to biological differences between Americans and Englishmen. Consequently, researchers must, at all times, keep in mind the interaction between the environment and the individual's constitution. Assuming that there is such a thing as a bad seed (and there is little evidence for such an assumption), environment determines its growth.

Selected Bibliography

Harry Elmer Barnes & Negley K. Teeters, *New Horizons in Criminology* (New York: Prentice-Hall, first edition, 1943). Chapter VIII is a comprehensive survey of the evidence, slightly tinged with a sociological bias.

Sheldon & Eleanor Glueck, *Unraveling Juvenile Delinquency* (Cambridge: Harvard University Press, 1950), Chapters XIV and XV. An important comparative study of 500 delinquents and 500 non-delinquents.

Sheldon and Eleanor Glueck, *Physique and Delinquency* (New York: Harpers, 1956). A further investigation of physical constitution; the definitive work of its kind.

Henry H. Goddard, *The Kallikaks* (New York: Macmillan, 1912). A classic study of a "degenerate" family.

E. A. Hooten, *Crime and the Man* (Cambridge: Harvard University Press, 1939). An enthusiastically written, but highly criticized study of the relation between physique and crime.

Johannes Lange, *Crime and Destiny* (New York: C. C. Boni, 1930). An investigation of the hereditarian basis of crime.

Cesare Lombroso, *Crime: Its Causes and Remedies* (Boston: Little, Brown and Co., 1911). A classic work.

William McCord and Joan McCord, *Psychopathy and Delinquency* (New York: Grune & Stratton, 1956), Chapter IV. Proposes a neuro-social theory of the causation of psychopathy.

M. F. Ashley Montague, "The Biologist Looks at Crime," *The Annals of the American Academy of Political and Social Science*, (September, 1941), 46-57. A review of the hereditarian approach.

A. J. Rosanoff, "Criminality and Delinquency in Twins," *Journal of Criminal Law and Criminology*, (Jan.-Feb., 1934), 923-934. The most important of the twin studies.

William B. Tucker, "Is there Evidence of a Physical Basis for Criminal Behavior," *Journal of Criminal Law and Criminology*, (Nov.-Dec., 1940), 427-437. An over-view of the problem.

William Maxwell McCord, Ph.D., an Instructor in Social Psychology and General Education at Harvard University; he was a teacher and counselor at San Quentin Prison in 1950. Between 1952 and 1955, directed an evaluation of the effects of treatment at the Wittwyck School; in 1956, he was a group therapist at Norfolk Prison in Massachusetts. Along with his wife, Joan McCord, is the author of *Psychopathy and Delinquency* and several articles. With Joan McCord and Irving Zola, he will soon publish *The Genesis of Crime,* a follow-up study of the Cambridge-Somerville Experiment. After holding a Woodrow Wilson fellowship, Dr. McCord received his Ph.D. in Social Science from Harvard University in 1955; has been a consultant on delinquency to several community projects and a psychological consultant to the Office of Scientific Research, U.S. Air Force. Currently, he is conducting research on the social psychological origins of alcoholism and is developing a theory concerning the nature of conscience.

CHAPTER 4.

A CRITIQUE OF THE PSYCHIATRIC APPROACH

MICHAEL HAKEEM
University of Wisconsin

The psychiatric approach is emerging as the most popular approach to the problem of juvenile delinquency. It is gaining ascendancy over all other approaches. Legislation is being much influenced by it. Institutions and agencies established to deal with delinquency are increasingly incorporating psychiatric understandings and procedures into their operations. Disposition of delinquents is more and more based on psychiatric considerations. Psychiatrists and psychiatrically oriented personnel are much sought after for help in the handling of delinquents. Indeed, one of the most critical questions professional workers can ask about a program of research, treatment, or prevention in the field of juvenile delinquency has become: "Is there a psychiatrist on the staff?" Many behavior specialists and many laymen, too, have come to believe that the psychiatrist is *the* authority on delinquency. As a result, the contributions of psychiatry and the views of psychiatrists on matters both of theory and of practice have attained tremendous prestige in this field. This accounts, in part, for the fact that this trend has been subjected to little scrutiny and to even less criticism.

Social workers have identified almost completely with the psychiatric approach. Some of the clinical psychologists are hardly distinguishable from the psychiatrists. Some sociologists, particularly those working in criminology and corrections, have been prone to go along with it, though to a far lesser extent than the groups just mentioned. Recently, to illustrate how far afield it is possible to drift from one's profession, a sociologist, just by reading a book for review in a professional journal, could tell that some of the illustrative cases "appeared to be in need of psychiatric help." He also wonders how group living could resolve "inner conflicts."[1]

Ideology of the Psychiatric Approach

The psychiatric approach proceeds on the basis of, and is interested in fostering, a certain ideology regarding juvenile delinquency. This can be referred to as the clinical ideology, and its theories and methods are analogous to those of clinical medicine.[2] The major tenets of this ideology are that delinquency is a disease and the delinquent is a sick person. Even the language of medicine is used. The delinquent is called a "patient." Such terms as "pathology," "diagnosis," "prognosis," "treatment," "symptom," "recovery," and "relapse" occur in abundance in the psychiatric literature on the handling of delinquents. An excellent example is provided in the following passage by a psychoanalyst:

"Using medical terms delinquency can be described as a very widespread illness, affecting mainly young people and causing gross symptoms in perhaps 5-8 per cent of the male and 0.5-1 per cent of the female population under 21. The total incidence is certainly much higher as mild cases usually are treated at home, not necessitating public expense. The most dangerous age is just before (boys) and just after (girls) puberty. The illness, on the whole, is benign. The later in age gross symptoms appear, the greater the complete recovery rate. Unfortunately in about 50 per cent of the young, in 30 per cent of the adolescent, and in about 10 per cent of the adult men and women it is followed by relapses. The illness then takes a prolonged course but even then in most cases heals off. There are, however, some cases which—despite all sorts of treatment —remain chronic."[3]

Numerous psychiatrists and social workers have explicitly expressed their adherence to the medical ideology and its tenets in their approach to delinquency. For example, Abrahamsen, a psychiatrist, says "In all my experience I have not been able to find one single offender who did not show some mental pathology. . . . The 'normal' offender is a myth."[4] Karpman, who is Chief Psychotherapist at St. Elizabeth's Hospital, recently launched a journal on psychiatric criminology whose purpose, he avowed, is to "fight for the recognition of the criminal as a very sick person, much sicker than either psychosis or neurosis. . . ."[5] Psychiatrists often refer to delinquency as a "medical problem."[6] The medical orientation to the treatment of delinquents is emphasized in the following statement by a psychiatrist: "When a patient goes to the hospital with a physical illness, he receives medication and therapy directed specifically to his ailment. . . . We send our children to correctional institutions to be treated for an illness. . . ."[7] Another psychiatrist expresses the ideology by holding that "delinquency and criminality lie within the domain of psychopathology."[8] Young, a social worker, refers to juvenile delinquents as "sick children."[9] Alt and Grossbard, two social workers, whose primary function, one would have supposed, is to concern themselves with the impact of social factors and the culture on behavior, have concluded that "delinquency appears to be primarily a psychological problem and is to a large extent independent of any given culture."[10] In addition, these writers have decided that delinquency is "one form of emotional disturbance."[11] And finally, leaving no scintilla of doubt as to where they stand on the matter, they assert that "treatment has to be primarily directed on an individual level and through a psychological approach."[12]

This sampling of statements should be sufficient to illustrate the point. However it is put, they all mean to convey the same basic theme: Delinquency is a disease and the delinquent is a mentally or emotionally sick person.

One interesting feature of much of the psychiatric and social work literature which advocates this ideology is its propagandistic flavor. Often, there is highly emotionalized insistence on the correctness of the position, shrill claims as to its merits, powerful remonstrance with dissenters, and clamorous demands for its implementation. Very frequently, pronouncements having far-reaching effects are made and acted on in the complete absence of supporting evidence or with total disregard for contradictory evidence.

On the other hand, it should not be supposed that psychiatry presents a united front regarding its views on delinquency. A few psychiatrists have rejected the position under discussion and have insisted that the overwhelming majority of delinquents are normal. Others have gone further and have even cautioned against the expansion of psychiatry into a field like delinquency.[13] Time and again, some psychiatrists have warned their colleagues that "psychiatry has been grossly oversold to the general public."[14] One psychiatrist has even expressed gratitude to sociologists for having investigated delinquency so "thoroughly and scientifically" that, according to him, it is one problem that can be removed from the realm of medical (psychiatric) concern.[15] However that may be, the advocates of psychiatric expansionism have been successful in pressing their claims and seem to have prevailed.

The extent to which the proponents of the psychiatric approach have been successful in getting their views adopted can be seen in one of its most dramatic implementations. This is the rise and rapid spread of medically oriented establishments in the form of diagnostic and treatment centers, clinics, and psychiatric units of various types designed for the care of delinquents and children with other behavior problems. The popularity of these facilities and the relatively trivial nature of the vast bulk of the problems referred to them are clearly shown by a recent study of the Los Angeles Child Guidance Clinic. It was determined in this study that only about 21 per cent of 500 cases referred to the clinic could unequivocally be said to require its ministrations.[16]

These facilities are staffed by various combinations of physicians, psychiatrists, nurses, psychologists, social workers, and others committed to the medical ideology. They are equipped as medical establishments. Sometimes the personnel, particularly the psychiatrists and nurses, actually dress in white, just as they would in a general hospital. The public is encouraged to look upon these establishments as medical facilities, the inmates as "patients," and the activities carried on there as being comparable to the activities of any other medical facility. The general orientation is that the delinquent's body, nervous system, brain, brain waves, and mind must be looked into to understand the causes of his delinquency and to treat him.

Although the social history is gathered and this is looked into also, it is mainly interpreted in terms of the frame of reference provided by the psychiatric approach. Social factors and social relationships are not viewed and interpreted sociologically. They are not regarded as factors which, in their own right, can explain behavior but merely as the raw material for incorporation into psychiatric, particularly psychoanalytic, formulations. The psychiatrist, of course, is not competent to apply the sociological frame of reference because he has not had training in sociology. For the same reason, the social worker is equally incompetent in this respect. Yet, only rarely are sociologists part of the team of workers in these establishments.[17]

Diversity of Views

While the ideology described above is widely shared, and there is general uniformity in its basic dogma and beliefs, quite a different situation is encountered when it comes to the more specific issues relating to the causation, treatment, and prevention of delinquency. Here, the views of psychiatrists show no more consensus than do those of the proverbial man on the street. They show, in fact, enormous diversity. There is an endless array of varying, very often completely contradictory, emphases, opinions, and theories.

This grows out of the fact, not sufficiently recognized, that, more frequently than not, what psychiatrists say about the problem is simply personal opinion, guesswork, or speculation and does not constitute special knowledge founded on a solid core of evidence yielded by research. But even psychiatric research on delinquency very often results in widely varying and discrepant conclusions. An additional difficulty is that, most of the time, the psychiatrist is almost totally ignorant of, or chooses to disregard, the vast body of knowledge regarding behavior in particular, accumulated by sociology, anthropology, social psychology, and psychology.[18]

This is neatly shown in an astounding confession of ignorance made by a psychiatrist who has long worked in the field of juvenile delinquency. First, it should be pointed out that for well over one hundred years ecological studies have been made showing the differential distribution of social problems, including crime and delinquency. This approach was systematized and given great impetus by sociologists in a long series of ecological studies published in the twenties and thirties. The classic study, *Delinquency Areas,* published by Clifford R. Shaw and his associates in 1929, proved that delinquency is concentrated in certain areas. It also systematized, substantiated, and underscored what had long been recognized and publicized by sociologists and others, namely, that delinquency is, in large measure, a product of certain traditions, social situations, and modes of life of certain groups. Since then, there has been a very large literature extending and elaborating these views. Despite all this, the following statement can still be made by a psychiatrist:

"Some of us have *begun to suspect* that some of the patterns that have been assumed to be part of acting-out pathology are in reality not at all uncharacteristic of the mode of operation of certain socio-economic segments of the community's youth. *As yet, however, there are but few definitive studies that provide any systematic exploration of these questions.*"[19] [Italics mine.]

Some of the diversity in the viewpoints manifested by psychiatrists can be gleaned from the next section which deals with the problem of diagnosis of the personality and mental condition of delinquents.

Diagnosis of Delinquents

Psychiatrists, in their approach to delinquency, have from the very beginning taken it for granted that the mental condition and personality of delinquents *must* deviate from the normal. It has been seen that this view is at the very foundation of their ideological position. This also accounts for the fact that so many psychiatric facilities for delinquents never diagnose a single "patient" as "normal."[20]

That delinquents deviate from the normal in personality traits or mental condition, or that there are certain personality traits or constellations of traits which mark them off from nondelinquents has not been scientifically established. Much of the effort of researchers on delinquency has gone into attempts to determine the validity of this hypothesis, but the question has not yet been satisfactorily answered.[21] Examining 113 researches which, through the use of objective tests, attempted to differentiate offenders from nonoffenders on the basis of personality traits, Schuessler and Cressey came to the general conclusion that such differentiation had not been demonstrated.[22] A series of studies made subsequent to this survey attempted to differentiate delinquents from nondelinquents and to predict delinquency on the basis of the Minnesota Multiphasic Personality Inventory, a widely used personality test.[23] The investigators concluded that this is possible. It is very doubtful if either objective has been accomplished, however.[24]

The search for evidence to substantiate or negate the hypothetical differences between delinquents and nondelinquents has been handicapped by the lack of a scientific conception of what constitutes normality in personality and in mental functioning. The search is also handicapped by the fact that there have not been developed scientifically standardized, reliable, and valid means of measuring personality traits and their deviations.[25] Despite this, as has been seen, some psychiatrists have decided that all delinquents are abnormal. Others, like Bender, complicate matters by insisting that "there is no such thing as a normal child."[26] In the meantime, most psychiatrists working with delinquents proceed as if scientifically validated personality categories had already been established, the conception of normality had been agreed upon, and the deviation of delinquents from normality had been proved. They have been willing to diagnose personality on the basis of the highly prized "clinical" method which is notoriously unreliable and which has mainly resulted in arbitrary and subjective judgments and decisions.

Some psychiatrists are quite aware of this state of affairs and have been frank in discussing it.[27] In reviewing the present status of child psychiatry, Ackerman, for example, says:

"Much confusion has reigned in the field of diagnosis in child psychiatry. It has literally been a "Tower of Babel." A variety of diagnostic systems have been employed. Diagnostic terms have been used loosely and ambiguously. Scientific communication between different psychiatric institutions working with children has been difficult because of a lack of common language. What is diagnosed primary behavior disorder in one child center is diagnosed psychoneurosis in another. Within a single child clinic, the same diagnostic terms may be used differently by different psychiatrists."[28]

The same point is made in the following statement by another psychiatrist:

> The personality and biases of the psychiatrist may also influence his choice of a diagnostic label. It has been an observation of mine, in staff meetings and seminar groups, that most of us have a consistent tendency to look for particular features in the primary data and emphasize these in drawing inferential conclusions.[29]

There have been attempts to escape this dilemma which has been so great a source of embarrassment to the pretensions of psychiatry to being a medical specialty on a par with any other. This has most often taken the form of minimizing the importance of diagnosis. Sometimes there has been substituted for the diagnosis a descriptive summary of the personality of the subject. However, this apparently has solved nothing, for such a description is, according to Ackerman, "too largely determined by subjective emphases in a particular examiner's mind."[30] He insists, as probably most clinicians would, that diagnosis must be retained and that diagnosis comes first and therapy second.[31] Anyway, the official publication of the American Psychiatric Association has gone on record with the statement that "in psychiatry, as well as in all medical disciplines, accurate diagnosis is the keystone of appropriate treatment and competent prognosis."[32]

Striking evidence of the unscientific and arbitrary nature of the diagnosis of the personality and mental condition of delinquents is provided by a comparison of the results of psychiatric examinations given to various groups of them by different psychiatrists. For this purpose, three tables giving the psychiatric diagnoses of delinquents in a juvenile court, in a psychiatric clinic attached to a probation bureau of an adolescents' court, and in a correctional institution will be set forth. All diagnoses of mental deficiency have been excluded.

Examination of these three tables yields some interesting observations. First to be noted is the wide diversity of diagnostic categories used. Most of the designations appearing in any one of the tables are completely absent from the others. The diagnostic categories of the institutionalized cases are so different from those of the other two groups that it is hard to imagine that the examiners were engaged in the same kind of activity— rendering psychiatric (that is, medical) diagnoses—and that they share the same universe of discourse. It should also be pointed out that the diagnostic terms used are subject to highly variable definitions, overlap tremendously, and have not been objectified. Every day, parents, teachers, employers, judges, clergymen, college deans, policemen, friends, colleagues, and others must make judgments of the type represented in most of these diagnostic categories. There is no evidence that their judgments regarding such traits are less reliable or valid than those of psychiatrists and social workers.

ADOLESCENTS' COURT CASES[33]

Diagnosis	No.	Per cent
Psychosis	54	14.9
Psycho-neurosis	21	5.8
Neurotic character disturbance	141	39.0
Psychopathic personality	70	19.3
Organic	5	1.4
Pathologic personality	48	13.3
Situational maladjustment	21	5.8
Exuberant adolescence	2	.6
Total	362*	

* A total of 63 cases without a diagnosis were excluded.

JUVENILE COURT CASES[34]

Diagnosis	No.	Per cent
Psychoneurosis	97	36.9
Conduct disorders	81	30.8
Immaturity	38	14.4
Character disorder (inc. psychopathic personality)	17	6.5
Mental conflict	11	4.2
Latent schizophrenia	7	
Schizophrenia	5	4.9
Early paranoid schizophrenia	1	
Grand mal epilepsy	1	.4
No psychopathology	5	1.9
	263	

INSTITUTIONALIZED CASES[35]

Diagnosis	No.*	Per cent
Adequate	74	14.9
Dynamic	139	28.0
Aggressive	75	15.1
Adventurous	275	55.3
Extroverted in action	282	56.7
Extroverted in affect	190	38.2
Emotionally stable	90	18.1
Suggestible	297	59.8
Stubborn	206	41.4
Sensitive	158	31.8

* Based on 497 cases. A case can have more than one diagnosis.

As a matter of fact, a recent, comprehensive review of the experimental and other research done on the ability to judge people's emotions, abilities, personality traits, action tendencies, and motives concludes that there is a fairly consistent lack of correlation between training in psychology and the ability to judge people correctly. In fact, laymen often make more accurate judgments than do psychologists and other clinicians. In one of the studies cited, it was shown that physical scientists are superior to psychologists, social workers, and psychiatrists in making judgments of people. Although there is some conflicting evidence, the general conclusion is that laymen are better judges of people than are clinicians in the behavior sciences.[36] At the very least, it certainly has not been proved that the clinicians are consistently better judges of people than are laymen.

Another obvious conclusion to be derived from a comparison of the three tables is the great divergencies in the proportions of cases falling under the few categories that are comparable. For example, whereas almost 15 per cent of the adolescents' court cases were found to have a psychosis, only 4.9 per cent of the juvenile court cases were given this diagnosis, this high a percentage being secured by adding the 7 cases of latent schizophrenia to the 6 cases of schizophrenia. On the other hand, the psychiatrist apparently did not find a single psychotic among the institutionalized cases. Again, while about 37 per cent of the juvenile court cases were given a diagnosis of psychoneurosis, only 5.8 per cent of the adolescents' court cases, and none of the institutionalized cases fell in that category. Psychopathic personality was the diagnosis in 19.3 per cent of the adolescents' court group, in only about one-third as many of the juvenile court group, and in none of the institutionalized group. No less than 39 per cent of the adolescents' court cases were diagnosed "neurotic character disturbance." Yet, this category is not even listed in the tables of the other two groups.

Although the three groups of cases are not exactly comparable as to age and sex and are from different geographic locations and correctional agencies, it is extremely unlikely that these are the variations which are correlated with the diagnostic variations. It is far more likely that the diagnostic variations are correlated with the variations in the personalities, emotional conditions, and preconceptions of the examining psychiatrists.

Further illustration of the diversity of viewpoints and of the reasoning and procedures underlying the psychiatric approach to delinquency will be seen in the following review of three selected theories on causation. The three views on causation to be presented are, of course, a negligible fraction of the numerous views, systematic and unsystematic, which are available. Such a small number, regardless of the specific selections, would always be subject to criticism as being nonrepresentative or for omitting views which are preferred by some practitioners or giving views which are rejected by some. The views were selected because they are well-known and are widely applied. They also give an idea of the wide diversity of approaches. Furthermore, they are "psychological" theories in the strict sense. They do not involve organic factors, and the focus is not on social factors, sociologically interpreted. These views are not presented as being representative of the entire range of views in existence. They do illustrate the kinds of reasoning and procedures which underlie the psychiatric approach. Any other psychiatric theory of causation that could have been reviewed would have illustrated the same problems and would have been subjected to the same kinds of criticism which will be leveled at the views presented.[37]

Emotional Disturbance

One viewpoint on the causation of delinquency which has been widely accepted by psychiatrists, social workers, and others hinges on the postulation of certain "needs," "drives," or "wishes," the gratification of which is sometimes blocked.

This viewpoint recalls the proposition of Dollard and others that frustration begets aggression, one form of which is crime or delinquency.[38] It is even more reminiscent of the theory of W. I. Thomas, a sociologist, who attempted to show that delinquency emerges from the frustration of the four fundamental wishes which he posited—security, recognition, response, and new experience.[39]

Be that as it may, this view of delinquency causation is most commonly associated with a study by Healy and Bronner in which they compared 105 delinquents with a control group of 105 nondelinquent siblings who were matched, in as many cases as possible, for sex and for age proximity.[40]

The subjects, both delinquents and nondelinquents, were studied by psychiatrists, psychologists, and social workers who used the general orientation and procedures customarily followed by such teams in child guidance clinics. Comprehensive information was secured about each child. Since, rightly, the family rather than just the child was regarded as the unit of study, such information was also secured about the family. Analyses of the data were made, and judgments regarding personality and the roots of adjustment or maladjustment were arrived at. The delinquents and nondelinquents were then compared, and this resulted in a conclusion which Healy and Bronner call "amazing." This was the central conclusion to emerge from their study, and it is stated by the authors as follows:

> It finally appears that no less than *91 per cent of the delinquents* gave clear evidence of being or having been very unhappy and discontented in their life circumstances or extremely disturbed because of emotion-provoking situations or experiences. In great contradistinction we found similar evidences of inner stresses at the most in *only 13 per cent of the controls.*[41]

In short, the delinquents, in contrast to the nondelinquents, were suffering from profound emotional disturbances. These took the form of feeling unloved, having thwarted impulses, feeling inferior, experiencing discomfort about family disharmonies or parental derelictions, being jealous, being unhappy due to mental conflicts, and having a sense of guilt.[42] Typically, a child had more than one type of disturbance.

On the basis of this major finding, Healy and Bronner developed their theory of causation which can be summarized as follows: The child has "great driving forces which have strong emotional concomitants." These are the powerful and deep-rooted motivations of behavior. Examples of these are the urges or wishes for security, acceptance, recognition, affection, adequacy, satisfying accomplishments, adventure, ownership of possessions, and, in the words of the authors, "for having, seeing, or doing." Interference with the fulfillment of these makes the child feel thwarted, deprived, frustrated. When this happens, the child, mostly unconsciously, seeks substitutive satisfactions, one form of which is delinquency. Through delinquency, the child is able to secure gratification for impulses which he could not satisfy legitimately. Gang membership can bestow status; various depredations can satisfy adventurousness; sexual favors can elicit reactions that are mistaken for affection.

The sources from which the child acquires ideas of delinquent behavior are not hard to find—they are plentiful in the society. But since these are also accessible to the child who does not act on them, a question is raised as to why the delinquent had not developed inhibitions or barriers against the acceptance of this alternate route to the satisfaction of frustrated impulses. The reason is that "there had been no strong tie-up to anyone who presented a pattern of satisfactory social behavior." Lack of an affectional relationship between the child and a parent whom he could admire created a barrier to the acceptance of attitudes that would have insulated him against acting on delinquent ideas. On the other hand, the nondelinquents did have such tie-ups, which demonstrates how vastly different the parent-child relationship can be in the cases of different siblings living in the same family. These tie-ups, along with the fact that the nondelinquents were not tormented by profound emotional disturbances, enabled them to get satisfaction for their needs and wishes in socially acceptable ways. Delinquency, in short, represents a flight from intolerable emotional disturbances and a means of satisfying powerful urges and wishes whose satisfaction in acceptable ways is being blocked.[43]

As has been mentioned, this study has been frequently cited and the theory it propounds has had widespread influence on professional persons dealing with delinquency. One book even refers to it as "one of the finest, if not the best, studies in the

entire field of delinquency causation."[44] It has been concluded
by some that the study has provided irrefutable evidence of the
paramount role of emotional disturbance in the causation of delinquency. However, close scrutiny of the study reveals that it
falls far short of having scientifically validated such a view. Some
of its shortcomings have been set forth in the following excerpt
by Sutherland who was one of the very few to look at it in a
critical way.

First, the difference between the delinquents and their
non-delinquent siblings is probably exaggerated. The staff
in these clinics was composed almost entirely of psychiatrists
and psychiatric social workers, who have been predisposed
to an interpretation of delinquency in terms of emotional
disturbance. Since the tests of emotional disturbance are
not standardized, these staff members cannot easily check
on their preconceptions. Also, the staff became much better
acquainted with the delinquents than with the non-delinquents, since they carried on three-year treatment programs
for delinquents and on that account would be more likely
to discover the emotional disturbances of the delinquents.
The inadequacy of the investigations of the non-delinquents
is revealed by the report that only 21 percent of them were
"even mildly delinquent." In a sample of university students
in classes in criminology over a ten-year period at least 98
percent report that they were at least "mildly delinquent"
in childhood. Second, the emotional disturbance, even if not
exaggerated, is not demonstrated to be the cause of the
delinquent behavior; the delinquent behavior may cause the
emotional disturbance. No organized effort was made in this
study to determine whether the emotional disturbance preceded the delinquent behavior. Third, the process by which
emotional disturbance produces delinquent behavior is not
adequately investigated. The argument is: a child is emotionally disturbed, so he commits a delinquent act. Emotional disturbance, however, does not in itself explain delinquent behavior, as is shown by the 13 percent of the
non-delinquents who were emotionally disturbed, and by
the fact that there is no correlation between the frequency
of emotional instability among school children and delinquency rates of school districts.[45]

In further criticism of the study, it can be said that it does not fulfill one of the most imperative dictates of scientific methodology, namely, the presentation of the research data and operations in such a way that the study could be replicated by other investigators. In view of this, acceptance of this study must have been based on faith and on a strong will to believe. It is not even known, for example, what questions were asked of the subjects by the examiners, whether they asked the same questions of the delinquents and nondelinquents, whether they asked the same questions in the same way of each subject, and whether the examiners' verbal and facial reactions to the subjects' responses were controlled and identical in all instances. It is not known what weight was assigned to each factor considered and what means were used to insure that the factors would be weighted consistently in all cases. Nothing is said about the methods followed in making judgments as to the presence, kind, degree, duration, and meaning of the emotional disturbances. It is not even indicated who made the final judgments. Was it the clinical team as a whole? Was it the decision of one psychiatrist or of a majority? Was there 100 per cent agreement among the personnel in all cases? This is hardly likely, and yet nothing is said about cases on which there were disagreements.[46] Suppose, for example, that the social worker and psychiatrist differed on the emotional mechanisms operating in a particular case. Or, suppose that the social worker insisted that in a given case the subject, by an entirely normal process of learning, was adopting the patterns of delinquent behavior available in the home and no emotional disturbance was involved, and the psychiatrist was equally insistent that profound emotional disturbances were the key factor in the case. How was the difference resolved? In those cases, did the psychiatrist's judgment yield to the social worker's, or did the psychiatrist's decision prevail? Nothing is mentioned regarding these problems. Yet, replication would have to be guided by a detailed account of the procedures followed in the original study.

To elaborate a point touched on indirectly by Sutherland, it should be noted that, as in most studies exploring the relationship between personality and delinquency, the psychiatrists and others who made the judgments about emotional disturbances knew which subjects were in the experimental group and which in the control group. Given the well-known inclination of some psychiatrists and other clinicians to see emotional disturbance wherever they see delinquency, and for some even to equate the two, there is an objectifying procedure which it is incumbent upon them to introduce into their studies, namely, the concealment of the identity of the subject as far as his delinquency status is concerned.[47] To give one final shortcoming among many others that could be mentioned, the study lacks a test of reliability. Healy and Bronner assert that they rechecked their findings three times. A far more scientifically sophisticated procedure would have been to have others independently check the findings.

Insofar as Healy and Bronner's views on delinquency causation are made to rest on the research reviewed here, they must be rejected because of the defects already related. Their views must be further rejected on the grounds of additional logical considerations. The contention that juvenile delinquency constitutes an escape from, and a substitutive satisfaction for, frustrated needs or wishes is appealing but not convincing. The fact of the matter is that the motivation of all activities and all behavior can be and has been traced to the urge to satisfy the identical needs, frustrated or not, which Healy and Bronner posit as the fertile soil from which delinquent behavior springs.

Indeed, psychiatrists, more than any other group, have been indefatigable and superbly imaginative in their attempts to trace all behavior—from sinfulness to saintliness—to the operation of the same mechanism of the satisfaction of various personality needs. To illustrate, psychiatrists and psychoanalysts have time and again insisted that the choice and pursuit of a medical career or one of the medical specialties is motivated by the personality needs and the emotional condition of medical students and doctors. Even the emergence of new psychoanalytic theories which deviate from those of Freud has been attributed by Ernest Jones, the famed psychoanalyst, to the operation of unconscious motivations in the authors of such theories. And, according to Jones, it does no good to appeal to reason in these matters. Since the source of the new theories is "on an unconscious level it follows that controversy on a purely conscious scientific level is foredoomed to failure."[48]

In short, if this theory explains all behavior, as it is often made to do, then it is so broad and so general that it is useless in explaining specific behavior. Thus, in the present context, the central question—why do some individuals turn to delinquency to satisfy emotional needs and others turn to other pursuits, such as a medical career or the development of a new psychoanalytic theory, to satisfy identical needs?—remains unanswered.

Maternal Deprivation

Another psychiatric theory attributes delinquency to "maternal deprivation." Bowlby, an English child psychiatrist, is the staunchest advocate of this view. Maternal deprivation occurs, according to him, when a child lacks a "warm, intimate, and continuous relationship with his mother (or permanent mothersubstitute) in which both find satisfaction and enjoyment."[49] Separation of the mother from the child for any reason, hospitalization or institutionalization of the child, change from one mother-substitute to another, and lack of loving care by the mother or permanent mother-substitute even when with the child are all forms of maternal deprivation.

Bowlby and others have taken the position that the effects of maternal deprivation are utterly disastrous to the child. It is said to lead to physical and mental illnesses, grave personality defects, intellectual and other developmental retardation, emotional disorders, and juvenile delinquency. Bender says that there is "failure or retardation in all aspects (or facets) of the personality development. . . ."[50] Ribble, whose writings have been very influential in creating concern about deprivation, claims that not many years ago more than half of the deaths of infants under one were due to lack of mother love, which is, of course, not true.[51] The effects of maternal deprivation are depicted as being truly gruesome. Bowlby, seeking reasons why this phenomenon has not received more attention until recently, says, "So painful, indeed, are the agonies which these children suffer on separation that it may well be that those who have their care shut their eyes in self-protection."[52]

There are varying opinions on the age of vulnerability to the baleful effects of maternal deprivation. Bowlby, summarizing the evidence, concludes that "deprivation occurring in the second half of the first year of life is agreed by all students of the subject to be of great significance and . . . many believe this to be true also of deprivation occurring in the first half, especially from three to six months."[53] Bowlby himself maintains that all children under three years of age and a very large proportion between three and five are vulnerable to damage from deprivation.[54] He and others further state that psychopathic character can result from deprivation for at least three months and probably more than six during the first three or four years of life.[55] The degree of damage is said to vary with the degree of deprivation. To show the effects even of a very brief separation, Bowlby has recently reported the case of a girl two years and five months old who was hospitalized for eight days. Her parents prepared her psychologically for the event. They also visited her in the hospital. Bowlby argues, not convincingly, that the girl suffered long-lasting and distressful reactions as a result of the brief separation from her mother.[56]

Under certain conditions, the harm done by deprivation is somewhat reversible. In the main, however, the effects are lifelong and the prognosis is grim. Bowlby cites Spitz and Wolf who say that after three months of deprivation recovery is rarely, if ever, complete.[57] He also cites Goldfarb who holds that mothering given after the age of two and one-half years as a corrective for previous deprivation is useless.[58] Bowlby himself sets one year as the upper age limit beyond which, in most cases, the harm cannot be undone.[59] Bender takes the view that in cases of psychopathy growing out of deprivation the future is practically hopeless. She recommends that such children be institutionalized, no attempts at correction be made, and their dependency on the institution or some person be fostered.[60]

Bowlby made a study of 44 juvenile thieves, most of them persistent offenders, referred to a child guidance clinic. He compared them with a control group of 44 juveniles referred to the same clinic for problems other than thievery.[61] Only 2 of the thieves, and these only reluctantly, were regarded by Bowlby as psychologically normal. In the 42 others he found psychological abnormalities of various types. The group of the abnormal which mainly captured Bowlby's interest were those in the category he designated "affectionless character." Fourteen thieves and none in the control group fell in this category. In 12 of the 14 there was a history of maternal deprivation. Seventeen of the thieves and only 2 of the controls had undergone separation from their mothers or foster-mothers for six months or longer during their first five years.

On the basis of a history of such separation in 17, or about 38 per cent, of 44 cases, Bowlby came to the sweeping conclusion that "prolonged separation of a child from his mother (or mother-substitute) during the first five years of life stands foremost among the causes of delinquent character development and persistent misbehaviour."[62]

The contention that maternal deprivation and the psychological disturbances which allegedly result from it are important in the production of delinquency cannot be accepted seriously, and the conclusions arrived at by Bowlby are not warranted. The reason is that, to date, the work on which this assumption rests falls far short of meeting the criteria of scientific creditability. Bowlby's work particularly is characterized by gross naïveté regarding the methodological requirements for testing the hypothetical relationship between maternal deprivation and delinquency.

Bowlby's etiological generalization is based on the fact that 14 of the 44 thieves were found to be "affectionless characters" and that 12 of these 14, plus 5 others—17 in all—had a history of separation from the mother or mother-substitute. Yet, a great many more thieves, 27 in number, did not have such a history; and more than twice as many thieves were not diagnosed "affectionless character" as were—30 in contrast to 14. Furthermore, 13 of the thieves, almost exactly the same number diagnosed as "affectionless characters," were diagnosed as "hyperthymic characters." From Bowlby's data, there is no more justification for connecting delinquency with the former category of abnormality than with the latter. The diagnoses of personality which are used in this study, incidentally, are highly arbitrary, subjective, overlapping, and loosely defined.

Another shortcoming of Bowlby's methods is that he knew which subjects were thieves and which were not before he made his judgments of personality. He also had access to the history of maternal deprivation before making the diagnosis of "affectionless character." The better procedure would have been to determine whether an examiner can pick out cases of maternal deprivation on the basis of an examination of the mental and physical traits of the subjects, without the benefit of information from the case history or from other sources that such deprivation had occurred. Furthermore, Bowlby did not subject his judgments to a reliability check by having other examiners make independent diagnoses of the cases.

In fact, Bowlby's entire diagnostic procedure is open to serious objections. He says that the least valuable basis for making a judgment about the mental status of his subjects was the psychiatric and psychological examinations. He further asserts that he habitually ignored his psychiatric interviews when they revealed the subject to be normal, which was true in half of the cases in his sample. In those instances, he admits, he turned to the reports of the mother and teacher as the basis for his diagnoses.[63] This is an important admission, for it means that when his own psychiatric examination failed to reveal any abnormality in the personality, he looked elsewhere for information which could get the subject under some category of abnormality. When the psychiatric examination revealed abnormality, he apparently did not look elsewhere for information which might have shunted the subject into the normal classification. It is not surprising that Bowlby found virtually 100 per cent of his cases abnormal.

Bowlby's gross innocence of scientific method is shown in still another way. Being much impressed with the fact that a number of studies have come to the same conclusions that he has, he says, "What each individual piece of work lacks in thoroughness, *scientific reliability*, or precision is largely made good by the concordance of the whole. Nothing in scientific method carries more weight than this."[64] [Italics mine.] This, of course, is not so. Consensus of investigators is, indeed, an important criterion of reliability, but only if the studies themselves are scientifically sound. That a series of studies, no matter how numerous, come to the same conclusions does not make up for the lack of scientific reliability of the individual studies.

As a matter of fact, the studies by Spitz, which are cited at length by Bowlby in support of his position, have been subjected to devastating criticism by Pinneau.[65] Bowlby also cites Ribble's work on deprivation as supporting evidence. It happens that Pinneau has also checked Ribble's observations and conclusions against "the most representative, and controlled physiological, anatomical, and psychological experiments, observations, and studies." This review led to the conclusion that almost every point made by Ribble was refuted by the evidence.[66]

In the meantime, another psychiatrist, Lewis, has reported a conclusion diametrically opposed to that of Bowlby. On the basis of an elaborate study of maternal deprivation, she states, "The figures as a whole, while too small to permit a clear inference, fail to confirm the belief that a characteristic form of delinquent personality, recognizable on psychiatric examination, commonly ensues upon a child's separation from his mother in his early years."[67]

Bowlby himself, after having presented his findings with frenetic insistence as to their certainty, after having issued impassioned pleas for legislative and other action, after having made the most incautious and sweeping statements, after having unduly excited the social workers, after having aroused the grim concern of a few national and international organizations, and after having gone so far as to suggest that the matter was a closed issue,[68] has, in a recent study, changed his mind. He now admits that the case for the effects of deprivation was overstated. He concedes that the conclusion that deprivation "commonly" results in psychopathy or "affectionless character" was a mistake.[69]

The Theory of "Superego Lacunae"

Some psychiatrists have developed an etiological formulation which holds that a child's delinquency is sanctioned, permitted, or encouraged by the parent, usually the mother but sometimes the father.[70] It is contended that this observation has been verified in every case in which the parent could be psychiatrically studied. The formulation is said to be invariably true—given delinquency, there must be a sanctioning parent; given a sanctioning parent, delinquency has to eventuate.[71] Most often the parent is acting unconsciously, but sometimes, consciously.

This theory has it that the parent uses his child as a pawn whose delinquencies serve to vicariously gratify the parent's own forbidden impulses to commit the very derelictions which he induces in his offspring. The term "superego lacunae" has been applied to the breach in the character formation of the child which makes possible the delinquent acts. The defects in the child's superego have their counterpart in like defects in the parents who, in turn, derived them from their parents.[72] Often one child in the family is singled out for the role of the scapegoat. It may be an unwanted child, an adopted child, or a child who resembles a relative toward whom the parent feels aversion. It may be any child who for one reason or another is in disfavor.

Examples abound in the literature which expounds this view. A parent may say to his child, "Fires are dangerous, but if you must get it out of your system, then we'll set some in the yard."[73] The point is that such a parent is permitting and encouraging fire-setting in his child. The exhibition of aggression and brutal force in the media of mass communication is society's way of inviting children to be violent and destructive. A mother's undue concern about the possibility of a daughter's misbehavior on dates expresses a veiled desire to actually have her daughter misbehave. Thereby, the mother's own powerful longings for promiscuity would be satisfied. When a parent dismisses a child's trifling offense with the comment that he will "outgrow it," he means to sanction and encourage the continuation of delinquency. Sexual misbehavior and even sex crimes can be accounted for by the same subtle process by which the child is corrupted into serving the imperious impulses of the parents. In this instance, blame is fixed on the current tendency of families to "accept or even encourage varying degrees of nudity, including the complete variety, with conversion of the bathroom and its gamut of functions into something resembling a family Grand Central Station."[74]

In further elaboration of this theory, Johnson has suggested that the child's delinquency not only provides vicarious gratification to the parent but also serves as a means for the parent's expression of destructive, hostile urges felt toward the child.[75] Pushing the theory still further, Eissler maintains that parents, in addition to seducing their child into delinquency, present obstacles to his rehabilitation.[76] A child may be undergoing psychiatric treatment for delinquency. The parent uses every pretext to disrupt the treatment and to interfere with its progress whenever it promises to be successful. For example, the case of a child who was under psychiatric treatment for stealing and other delinquencies is cited. Whenever improvement was being made, "his mother's purse lay on the table, or money was left lying about, or a cabinet, which contained valuables was not locked."[77] The mother was tempting him to steal. She could not bear to see the delinquent rehabilitated because his delinquencies were serving her unconscious needs.

More than this, society itself does not want delinquents rehabilitated. It finds them useful as scapegoats. Society's persecution of the criminal acts as an "outlet for aggression, which can be rationalized on the basis of morality and which can provide the desired relief by externalizing inner conflicts without creating conscious guilt feelings."[78] The sensational presentation of crime news, the retention of slums, the vindictiveness toward offenders, the reluctance to apply psychiatric treatment to offenders, the maintenance of punitive correctional institutions all point to society's insistence that delinquency and crime be nourished and perpetuated.

The very agencies and institutions established to rehabilitate the delinquent are enmeshed in the same hidden motivations to keep delinquency flourishing, according to Eissler. She illustrates this by saying that the personnel of correctional institutions and agencies may welcome a psychiatrist as a consultant. He may be led to believe that the personnel are sincere in seeking his help. When he proposes changes which promise real success, however, the staff resists them. As a further example of the extremes to which society will go in fostering the criminality which gratifies the nefarious motives that lurk in people's unconscious, Eissler tells about a superintendent of a correctional institution for juveniles who held office several decades ago. He instituted progressive measures. Despite this, he was dismissed from his position. "Apparently the community could not tolerate a future without criminality."[79] Even some psychiatrists, she contends, are impelled by the same motivations "to interfere with any future rational attitude toward criminals and crime prevention."[80]

This formulation of causation cannot be accepted as valid. No experimentally controlled studies have been undertaken to test it, and no scientifically deduced evidence has been put forth in support of it. A critical test to which the theory has not been subjected, and to which it has to be subjected, is a predictive test. To meet this test, psychiatrists would be required to examine a large series of matched parents, some of whom have delinquent children and some of whom do not. The psychiatrists could elicit any information needed. They would be barred, however, from any information which would reveal the identity of the parents as far as the delinquency status of their children is concerned. And they would be barred from information as to the delinquency of the children. The test is whether, under these conditions, the examiners can designate the parents who have superego lacunae, and, therefore, have delinquent children. The further test is whether they can match the superego lacunae of the parents with those of their children, and, therefore, designate what delinquencies the children had committed. There are also other requirements which the formulation has to meet before it can be accepted as something other than speculation.

The point is that the theory, as it is, issues from procedures which violate some of the most elementary canons of scientific methodology. It depends heavily on anecdotal recitation and untested clinical hunches presented in the guise of data. Central to the theory are such concepts as "the unconscious" and "superego," which, as used in it, are metaphysical and not scientific.[81] The theory, therefore, should not be made the basis of actual decisions in dealing with delinquents and should not be entertained as an established principle in deliberations involving their disposition.

It should be noted, finally, that practically all of the behavior and utterances of parents for which they are now being so roundly rebuked and which are given such sinister interpretation in this theory constitute exactly what numberless psychiatrists have espoused and have urged on parents as making for good mental health. Take the example referred to above regarding nudity and common use of the bathroom as being inducements to sexual misbehavior and sex crimes. For the past several decades and up to the present, psychiatrists have been zealously urging parents to be more "natural" in these matters in order that their children will not suffer sexual repression and trauma and will develop normal personalities. A bit of typical advice of this sort is given by a renowned child psychiatrist. He tells parents that it is well to give the child "plenty of opportunity to watch the toilet habits of the adults in the family, rather than excluding him from the bathroom when they are using it."[82] Take the example in which the parent proposes to his child that they set fires in the yard. Allowing the child to participate in setting fires is precisely the advice given by some psychiatric experts.[83] One psychiatrist even commends the wisdom of a mother who allows her infant daughter to play with fire, to put her hand in it, and to burn her fingers by lighting matches.[84] Take, finally, the example which has it that society is encouraging criminality by allowing depiction of violence and brutality. One of the most widely read experts on child rearing advises that a child who bangs another on the head, who plays at shooting, and who enjoys blood-and-thunder comic books is thereby undergoing training which will make of him a worthwhile citizen.[85]

Psychiatric Treatment

A psychoanalyst recently wrote, "It is a commonplace in medicine that if for any illness there are many methods of treatment none of them is worth much."[86] This is precisely the situation in the psychiatric treatment of delinquents. The same confusion, the same conflicting claims, the same lack of scientific caution, the same absence of methodological know-how, the same propagandistic effusions are found in this phase of the psychiatric approach as have been demonstrated to exist in other phases.

In treatment, as in other connections, the consensus among psychiatrists lies mainly in their adherence to the ideology of the psychiatric approach and in their insistence on the unsupported contentions that delinquency calls for psychiatric treatment and that the psychiatrist is the expert in the treatment of delinquents. When it comes to concrete and specific issues in the psychiatric treatment of delinquents, there is vast disagreement. A few illustrations, from among hundreds, will make this clear. One writer claims that it has been proved that "individual therapy is not the method of success" in serious delinquency. The best results, he contends, have been achieved almost exclusively through group therapy.[87] Another, on the other hand, maintains, "Psychoanalysis, I can say with confidence, shapes up to be the most significant tool for research and treatment of the psychosocial disease called crime." She goes on to say that it is particularly effective at the delinquency age span.[88] But a third says that it is precisely one of the shortcomings of the psychotherapeutic approach to delinquents that they are at

"an age which is not well suited to treatment."[89] In the meantime, a fourth takes a different tack and advises that successful
treatment of an offender by psychiatry is "exquisitely rare."[90] To
cite another set of contradictions, one psychiatrist cautions the
therapist working with a delinquent against acting out with
him.[91] But, according to another, the very key to the therapeutic approach to a delinquent is the therapist's acting out
with him just enough for the delinquent to see that the therapist "has enough aggressiveness, vigor, and even combativeness
to subdue the delinquent at any time."[92]

It should be pointed out that the term treatment or therapy
is used very loosely in the psychiatric approach to delinquency.
Practically everything the psychiatrist does is regarded as
treatment. For example, if the psychiatrist recommends placement of the child in a foster home, this is regarded as treatment.
If the psychiatrist recommends a change of job, of school, of
residence, or similar "environmental manipulation," to use the
social work term, this is regarded as treatment. The position
has been taken that even this kind of "treatment" should not
be administered by persons having no medical training, except
under psychiatric supervision.[93]

Actually, there is no specific medical or psychiatric treatment
for delinquency. Only a negligible fraction of all that the psychiatrist does in his work with delinquents calls for medical
training. Little more of it requires psychiatric training. Practically all of it calls for sociological, psychological, and social psychological training which the psychiatrist does not have.

Although psychiatric proposals for treatment of delinquents
are numerous and varied, the procedure most commonly associated with the psychiatric approach is psychotherapy. A brief
review of this type of treatment will throw additional light on
some of the problems and defects of the psychiatric approach.

Psychotherapy

It is difficult to define psychotherapy because the psychiatrists
themselves are not sure what it is. Over fifty definitions of psychotherapy were deemed necessary to accommodate the variety
of viewpoints voiced by participants in a professional conference.[94] One source lists twenty-six different types and schools
of thought of individual therapy.[95] There is much conflict even

among Freudians as to what Freudianism is, as can be seen by the fact that "in many cities there are two or more psycho-analytic groups professing the Freudian orthodox theories."[96]

The essential point in psychotherapy is that the psychiatrist explores and tries to unravel those emotions, thoughts, and complexes of the subject which are regarded as being the main-spring of his difficulties. These difficulties are said to be largely unconscious. Psychotherapy is a psychological kind of treat-ment. It is generally agreed that the number of therapeutic failures or successes is the same irrespective of the school of thought to which the therapist has allegiance. It is not only psychiatrists who do psychotherapy. Psychologists, social work-ers, clergymen, and others do also. Probably most psychiatrists insist, however, that only a medically trained practitioner can or should do psychotherapy. Sometimes it is admitted that nonmedically trained social workers and psychologists, given training in psychotherapy, can carry out that function as well as the psychiatrist can.[97]

Probably the most realistic approach to psychotherapy and one which comes nearest to describing what it ultimately con-stitutes is the view that regards it as professional friendship and the psychiatrist as a "professional friend."[98] Medical train-ing is certainly not needed for this. Many people have a knack of reaching others, having a constructive impact on them, instilling new values and attitudes in them, helping to resolve their difficulties, and getting them to accept new and more effective ways of making required adjustments. More people could be trained to perform this function for professional pur-poses. Contrary to prevailing views, it is highly doubtful if such training needs to be medical training, and it is equally doubtful if it needs to be elaborate and lengthy training in social work.

Some psychiatrists have maintained that psychotherapy of the delinquent child is not enough. It is urged that the parent or parents must also be treated. Johnson even says that if the parent cannot be treated, or if the child cannot be removed from the home during treatment, the child should not be treated because he would become worse. Sometimes two, three, or more psychiatrists, or a combination of psychiatrists and social work-ers, may be needed to treat the case of one delinquent child, each therapist working on a different member of the family.

Three psychiatrists who warn that the task of treating a delinquent "is prodigious," cite a case of a delinquent girl under their treatment. She and her parents were getting a minimum of twelve hours of treatment a week, "and this for months and years."[99]

This reasoning is based on an unfounded generalization, espoused by psychiatrists and social workers, that not only is the delinquent himself a sick child; his parents are sick, too. Therefore, they need treatment as well as the child. A social worker and a psychiatrist, writing jointly, have contended, for example, that many of the parents of delinquents have "character disorders." They classify these parents into the following categories: oral erotic, oral sadistic, anal erotic, and anal sadistic. However, the writers give no evidence that would dispel any suspicion that their classificatory scheme and their procedures in categorizing the parents might be arbitrary, subjective, unreliable, and invalid.[100]

Results of Treatment

One of the most vital and yet most neglected areas of research in delinquency is the testing of the comparative merits of different treatment approaches. At the present time, the assumption that psychiatry offers the most successful and the most scientific treatment is based more on faith than on demonstrable effectiveness. There is no evidence to support the alleged superiority of the psychiatric approach over other available approaches. Most of the evidence that is available shows the psychiatric approach to delinquency to be a failure, if recidivism is taken as the criterion. This does not mean that there has been conclusive evidence to this effect. Nor does it mean that further research, particularly experimentation, with various approaches is not needed before final judgment can be made regarding the exact contribution that psychiatry can make. But in such research, it is not only the different procedures within the psychiatric approach that need to be compared and assessed. There is also a need to compare the psychiatric approach with non-psychiatric approaches, the effectiveness of trained personnel, such as social workers, with personnel who are not trained professionally; and the effectiveness of personnel with various types of training and with different degrees of training. The point is that the best approach to treatment must be experimentally determined. And the point is that, at present, advocacy of one or another form of treatment is dictated more by passionate conviction than by scientific evidence.

A number of studies have been undertaken to determine the efficacy of treatment which embodies the psychiatric approach or its various tenets. A review of the more adequate ones is instructive. Some years ago, the Gluecks made a thorough study of the outcome of 1,000 boys who had been handled both by a juvenile court and by what would be regarded as one of the most advanced children's psychiatric clinics operating at the time of the study.[101] Out of 923 cases on which there was sufficient information, it was found that 88.2 per cent had committed crimes during a five-year period following treatment. The Gluecks concluded that the clinic and court had not been accomplishing their major purpose.[102]

One study sought to determine whether the increasing professional services and the greater application of the psychiatric orientation in a juvenile court over a period of twenty years was accompanied by a decrease in recidivism on the part of delinquents adjudicated by the court.[103] The supposition was that cases dealt with more in accordance with the newer ideology regarding the treatment of delinquents should show a lower rate of involvement in adult crime than those dealt with in an earlier period when such an ideology held less sway. Such an expectation did not materialize, for the percentage of juvenile delinquents who each year eventually became adult offenders remained relatively constant throughout the period studied.

In another study, delinquents who had received psychiatric treatment in a court-affiliated clinic were compared with a group not receiving such treatment to determine whether there was a difference between the two groups in criminality subsequent to treatment or non-treatment.[104] The two groups were found to have almost identical outcomes. There was some evidence, however, that those who received more intensive treatment engaged in crime to a lesser extent than those whose treatment was not equally intensive. The investigators attributed the general failure of psychiatric treatment to the possibility that those receiving treatment were the most confirmed delinquents and may have been the cases with "real personality and emotional difficulties."[105] However, this reservation overlooks one of the most persistently urged tenets in the psychiatric ideology. The psychiatrists urge that it is particularly the cases with "real personality and emotional difficulties" that should be reserved for their attention and that can be helped by them.

Another important research is one which did not follow up treated delinquents but checked on the results of an attempt to prevent delinquency.[106] The question was whether boys who were regarded as most likely to become delinquent could be prevented from doing so. An experimental group of 325 such boys was matched with a control group of 325 equally vulnerable boys. The experimental group was given the benefit of what can best be called social work treatment. This was withheld from the control group. The boys in the treatment group were assigned to counselors who established a warm, sympathetic, friendly, helpful relationship with them. They were helped with educational problems, were given guidance, were referred to various agencies for needed services, and so forth. The majority of the counselors had social work training. For the greater part of the treatment period casework supervision was available to the counselors, and there was a definite psychiatric slant in the approach.[107]

The results of this study showed that there was little difference in outcome between the two groups. They became delinquent to about the same extent. There was some evidence, however, that delinquents who had been in the treatment group were less persistent offenders than delinquents who had been in the group not receiving treatment. Interestingly, the most successful counselor was a nurse who had no formal training in social work. Her approach was authoritarian and resembled that of the social worker of a bygone era.[108] Her work with her charges would doubtlessly be severely frowned upon by modern, professionally trained social workers.

Conclusion

The psychiatric approach to juvenile delinquency has been powerfully influential and has been accorded a paramount place in attempts to deal with the problem. That such influence is completely out of line with the minimal contributions which psychiatry has made to the understanding and control of delinquency should be clear from the evidence adduced above. The psychiatric approach is ardently fostered by its adherents as a scientifically designed and validated solution to the problem of delinquency. However, that its main weakness is its lack of scientific sophistication and its willingness to make claims and advocate programs in the absence of scientific evidence has also been demonstrated. The psychiatric approach must be recognized as being mainly a value-laden position as to how delinquents should be viewed and dealt with. It cannot be looked upon as representing a scientifically founded set of understandings and skills specifically applicable to the treatment of delinquents. Psychiatry, as it operates in the field of delinquency, certainly cannot be looked upon as a branch of medicine, putting into practice knowledge and techniques in keeping with the traditions, methods, and competencies of the medical profession.

In view of these strictures, it may be wondered how the psychiatrist has attained his position of prominence in the field of delinquency. To understand this, it must be remembered that the medical man enjoys terrific status in our society. As a physician, he is certainly deserving of laudation. However, the physician has always been looked to not only for advice on medical matters but also for advice on all sorts of problems, even those lying far outside the field of medicine. The doctor used to be viewed as a source of wisdom on economic matters, family affairs, and community problems. He still plays that role to some extent, even after the rise of a host of disciplines dealing with all sorts of nonmedical matters upon which the physician was formerly regarded as an expert. Psychiatry has persisted in the old role more than has any other branch of medicine.

The psychiatrist, as has been shown, is highly inadequate when it comes to scientific methodology. There is much evidence, too, that he is handicapped by being largely unsophisticated and poorly informed about scientific knowledge of human behavior. The social worker, though somewhat better schooled than he in these respects, is still inadequate. Most of the general public and most legislators and administrators cannot be expected to have the technical knowledge necessary for making expert evaluation of the claims of psychiatry. They have something else: an abiding respect for and a faith in the medical man. They accept what he says. They feel confident that what the doctor advises and prescribes must be tested and true. It is not so in the psychiatric approach to juvenile delinquency.

Selected Bibliography

August Aichhorn, *Wayward Youth* (New York: Viking, 1935). First published in Vienna in 1925. Something of a gospel of the psychoanalytic approach to the treatment of delinquents. A relatively simple application of Freudian principles to delinquency. Has some good sociological insights, but they are not recognized as such.

Ralph Banay, *Youth in Despair* (New York: Coward-McCann, 1948). Consists largely of a psychiatrist's highly eclectic, uncritical, and mostly unscientific ruminations on delinquency.

Lewis Diana, "The Rights of Juvenile Delinquents: An Appraisal of Juvenile Court Procedures," *Journal of Criminal Law, Criminology, and Police Science,* VLVII (January-February, 1957), 561-569. A sociologist takes a critical look at the ideology of social work which underlies the modern juvenile court. Raises serious question about this ideology, especially insofar as it deprives the child of certain traditional rights.

H. Warren Dunham, "The Schizophrene and Criminal Behavior," *American Sociological Review,* IV (June, 1939), 352-361. An excellent study of the relationship between schizophrenia and crime, including delinquency. The relationship is negligible.

K. R. Eissler, ed., *Searchlights on Delinquency: New Psychoanalytic Studies* (New York: International Universities Press, 1949). An excellent source from which to get a picture of how diverse, speculative, methodologically naive, and farfetched the psychoanalytic approaches to delinquency can be. Contributions by numerous writers.

Kate Friedlander, *The Psycho-analytical Approach to Juvenile Delinquency* (New York: International Universities Press, 1947). A thoughtful and logical statement of one psychoanalytical view of delinquency. Explains delinquency in terms of antisocial character development resulting from early interpersonal relationships.

Sheldon and Eleanor Glueck, *Unraveling Juvenile Delinquency* (New York: The Commonwealth Fund, 1950). A very important study comparing delinquents and nondelinquents. The Gluecks misinterpet their findings in favor of an emphasis on psychological factors in causation. Social factors actually turned out to be the most significant ones.

William Healy, *The Individual Delinquent* (Boston: Little, Brown, 1915). A pioneer work in the psychiatric approach to delinquency. Gave impetus to the case-study method.

Lester Eugene Hewitt and Richard L. Jenkins, *Fundamental Patterns of Maladjustment: The Dynamics of Their Origin* (Springfield, Ill.: State of Illinois, [1946]). An interesting report of an attempt to come to grips with the problem of typology in delinquency. Does not see all delinquents as "sick."

William McCord and Joan McCord, *Psychopathy and Delinquency* (New York: Grune & Stratton, 1956). Useful for its comprehensive review of the material on psychopathy. The authors miss the most important lesson to be deduced from their review: Psychopathy is a useless concept.

Maud A. Merrill, *Problems of Child Delinquency* (Boston: Houghton Mifflin, 1947). A comparative study of juvenile court subjects and a group of nondelinquents. Heavy emphasis on psychological test differences.

Edwin Powers and Helen Witmer, *An Experiment in the Prevention of Delinquency: The Cambridge-Somerville Study* (New York: Columbia University Press, 1951). The soundest attempt to date to assess the effectiveness of a psychiatrically slanted approach to the prevention of delinquency.

Fritz Redl and David Wineman, *The Aggressive Child* (Glencoe, Ill.: The Free Press, 1957). Two books, *Children Who Hate* and *Controls from Within*, in a one-volume edition. Description of a psychiatrically oriented residential treatment program for delinquent and emotionally disturbed children. Inspired by August Aichhorn's work.

Fredric Wertham, *The Circle of Guilt* (New York: Rinehart, 1956). A novelized account of a noted psychiatrist's work in preparing for the trial of an actual juvenile murderer. Again, a good example of loose thinking, illogical procedures, shifting frames of reference, and a strong proclivity toward glamorization.

Leontine R. Young, "We Call Them Delinquents," *Federal Probation*, XV (December, 1951), 8-12. A journalistic, emotional, and almost poetic article on delinquency by a professor of social work. Illustrates the absence of an interest in scientific considerations.

Michael Hakeem, Ph.D., is Associate Professor of Sociology and Social Work at the University of Wisconsin. He is a member of the staffs both of the Department of Sociology and Anthropology, and the School of Social Work. He has also taught at the State University of Iowa and the Ohio State University. At Wisconsin, he is responsible for the Curriculum in Correctional Administration and teaches courses and seminars in juvenile delinquency, correctional institutions, and probation and parole. He was a sociologist for five years in the Division of the Criminologist of the Illinois State Prison. He has done research and has published on the prediction of parole outcome. He is now engaged in further examination of the psychiatric approach to juvenile delinquency and criminality. Another major concern which the author is exploring is the applicability of sociological principles to correctional practice.

CHAPTER 5.

SOCIOLOGICAL PROCESSES

AND FACTORS IN JUVENILE DELINQUENCY

S. Kirson Weinberg
Roosevelt University

From the sociological viewpoint, juvenile delinquency is regarded as deviant behavior which is learned predominantly from association with delinquent peers. The processes by which the juvenile selects and conforms to his delinquent associates and acquires their orientations, values, and practises, are prime interests for sociological study. In this chapter our concern is with delinquency as a peer group experience; then with the respective influences of 1) the urban community 2) ethnic groups 3) social class and 4) the home and family, upon delinquent behavior.

Delinquency As A Peer Group Experience

Delinquency consists of a variety of activities which violate the law. The persistent forms of delinquency, such as stealing, vandalism, and gang fights, are group experiences which the individual delinquent learns from his associates. This phenomenon is reflected in the fact that the overwhelming majority of delinquents are arrested in groups, usually in pairs or triads and that in one series over eighty-five percent were arrested in groups of two or more. The child may begin innocently enough in playful pranks with other boys; pranks lead to truancy from school and malicious mischief. But as the child grows into adolescence, his deviant activities become more complicated, more sinister, and more concerted. His mischievous play turns into aggressive behavior, from destroying property, stealing, to fighting with other gangs, usually of another ethnic group; or, from simple, impulsive pilfering, to planned thefts. The child who moves into a high-rate delinquency area has the necessary alternative of accepting or rejecting participation in the wayward group. Sometimes he is molested by the gang because he is a stranger. He has to come to terms or strive to avoid them.[1] Inadvertently he comes into contact with the ideology of stealing. To fulfill his desire for companionship, to be accepted, he participates with the gang, and from this association acquires loyalties to them as well as codes of behavior, an argot, and a general manner.

The gang frequently becomes the basis of the boy's social identity; intensified by conflict, the gang becomes the basis for his protection as well as participation:

> "Inclusion in the gang was absolute, and human relations outside it were cut to a minimum. Even its territory was staked with minute precision. When two Brownsville kids who were strangers had some contact, the first question was 'What's your block?', and the answer fully established identity."

The establishment of this territory as the area of protection became as much a source of identity as it would be in a nonliterate society.[2]

Because the peer group is an in-group with which he identifies, he views his social world from their perspective. Delinquency becomes one strand in a way of life and a prospective source of livelihood. Consistently influenced by his delinquent associates, he increasingly regards stealing as proper, and recognizes that as a group participant in this law-breaking activity, he is compelled to abide by their codes as surely as the conventional person abides by the norms of conventional society. In this sense the juvenile becomes a sub-cultural type who identifies himself in a specific way as a delinquent. He finds the direction to his behavior outside of formal and conventional agencies and from the unconventional influences of the informal relations on the street and street-corner. He learns of the power of criminal groups which has become traditional in the area. As a member of a group which consists of older boys as well as younger boys, he becomes a link in a traditional chain which he perpetuates by his identification with the delinquent way of life.

In these areas the prevalence of delinquents is so marked that the normal individual child may become delinquent in the process of development.[3] But in areas where delinquency is less prevalent, the juvenile has a choice between delinquent and non-delinquent groups. The delinquent becomes attracted to the delinquent companions, while the non-delinquent selects non-delinquent associates. Non-delinquent brothers of delinquents have indicated why they did not associate with delinquents or resort to delinquent activities:

"I had the courage to refuse to go with bad boys."
"It's the friends you make. I couldn't break away from good ones anymore than my brother could break away from bad ones."[4]
"I played with the same boys as my brother. But they couldn't talk me into taking things. I knew stealing was wrong. I didn't want to get into trouble. So I just stayed away when they went out for trouble."[5]

The delinquents, on the other hand, by their association with delinquents, acquired a different conception of themselves, and had different likes and dislikes. They participated in the delinquent group because they were influenced by other groups, including the community at large, the ethnic group, social class, and most important, the family. Specifically, then, how do these groups contribute to the juvenile's acquisition of delinquent behavior and to his selection and acceptance of delinquent associates?

Delinquents Predominate In Poverty-Ridden Deteriorated Areas

Delinquents are scattered unevenly in the urban community. Their residential distribution in many large cities reveals that the highest rates of delinquency are concentrated in the poverty-ridden deteriorated urban areas frequently adjacent to the center of the city, and that, except for factory areas, these rates tend to decline towards the city's edge. This residential pattern of the families with delinquents conforms to the ecologi-

cal distribution of other types of social disorganization. The
rates of delinquency vary so that in some areas every fourth
or fifth boy is an arrested delinquent, while in other areas no
boy is an arrested delinquent. The areas with high rates of male
juvenile court cases also have high rates of child truancy, high
rates for adult crimes, and frequently high rates for girl delinquents.[6]

These high rates of delinquency persist despite the change
of ethnic composition in the area. In some areas the succession
of a different ethnic group may increase the delinquent patterns,
and hence the increased rates of delinquency. The highest rates
of delinquency predominate among the children of the recent
migrants to the city.[7] These rates of delinquency are based upon
the official statistics which measure the arrests and court appear-
ances of juveniles; these statistics do not, of course, include all
the delinquents who commit offenses. Thus one argument is
that since many middle-class children are not arrested, the official rates are biased and exaggerate the delinquency of the
lower classes.[8] Another argument is that certain ethnic groups
have private agencies to care for behavior-problem children
who otherwise would be handled by the police.[9] Despite these
qualifications, delinquency still prevails in the lower classes,
and the rates in these areas seem to accurately represent the
residential distribution of delinquency.

On the basis of a five-zone subdivision of the city, delinquency rates decline progressively from the highest rates in
the first zone adjacent to the center of the city, to the lowest
rates in the fifth zone most removed from the city's center
and towards the city's edge. This has been demonstrated for
Chicago, Cleveland, Philadelphia, Richmond, Denver, Birming-
ham, Seattle, and many other cities.

The flight of so many people to the suburbs has created a
somewhat similar problem to the initial flow of migrants to the
less attractive areas around the center of the city. Both are
forms of improvised settlement in the city. The difference is,
however, that the suburbs comprise an aggregate of people without any concerted organization. The extension of this form of
community living in the suburbs and the relative lack of organization in these areas has facilitated the rise of delinquents.
The suburbs around Chicago at one time had very few delinquents, but, with the centrifugal spread of the people to the

rim of Chicago, these areas jumped to about 2,500 delinquents in 1953-55, which is a considerable increase over former years.

Delinquency and Social Mobility

One interpretation of criminal behavior emphasizes the mobility aspirations of lower class persons. Since this class is limited in its economic climb upward because of the lack of skills, they resort to deviant and criminal behavior. Their rationalization for their behavior would be based upon the means of justifying the end or upon what could be called "a normlessness of means," or a state of anomie.[10] The problem is then to what extent do mobility-aspirations affect delinquent behavior?

One contention is that the parents project their ambitions upon their children, and thus lead them into delinquent activities. But it is evident that the lower-class delinquent boy cannot climb economically by the usual methods of education and vocational advancement. In the lower socio-economic levels he does not have the opportunity nor the interest to acquire the education and vocational skills to climb. In fact, he even repudiates these means to climb socially, although his parents and he are definitely aware of wealth, luxury, and power. Thus the parents in this situation may want their children to get money or monetary gain regardless of the means used.[11] Just as the middle-class norms emphasize a scrupulous respect for property rights, the delinquent defies these norms by misappropriating, destroying, or somehow violating these property rights. "Stealing" institutionalized in the delinquent culture, is more than a way of appropriating objects. It expresses contempt for a way of life by making its opposite a basis for status. Money and valuables are not despised by the delinquent, because delinquent and non-delinquent alike regard money as a most glamorous and efficient means to many ends. But in the delinquent sub-culture, the stolen dollar has an odor of sanctity that does not attach to the dollar saved or the dollar earned.[12] Stealing becomes not only a way of getting money, but also a way of achieving status in the delinquent group and becoming mobile in the criminal world. The role-model for the delinquent is not the bank president nor the professor, but the successful hoodlum and "big-shot" gangster who personify success. "How would you feel toward the King of England or the President of the United

States?" asked one delinquent rhetorically. "Well, the young crook feels the same toward the 'big shot' criminal. The 'big-shot' is the ideal—the ultimate hope of every forward-looking criminal, and is held in awe and respect."

"The 'big shot' is respected by criminals and honored for his power and brains to hold down a big job and have a number of gangsters under him and obeying his commands and orders."[13]

Ethnic Groups and Delinquency

Are boys in some ethnic groups more predisposed to delinquency than boys in other ethnic groups?

In high rate delinquency areas, delinquency patterns of behavior are acquired by many youths of new ethnic groups who come into the areas. In one study of specified areas in Chicago, highest rates of delinquency were found among recently arrived immigrants who resided in these high rate areas. From 1900 to 1950 although composition of the ethnic groups changed in these areas from German and English to Irish, Jewish, Italian, Mexican, and more recently to Negroes, Puerto Ricans and Southern Whites, the rate of delinquency continues to be high. When children of one ethnic group associate with or are influenced by delinquents of another ethnic group, they too will acquire these predatory patterns of behavior.[14] But as ethnic groups move away from these high-rate areas to lower-rate delinquency areas, some times delinquency rates may tend to decline when the group accepts middle-class, conventional values. Delinquency, then, is as much a function of a given urban area as it is of a given ethnic group. On the other hand, some ethnic groups, such as the Italians and Negroes, persist in delinquent behavior despite their length of residence in the urban community. One interpretation of their behavior is that they do not disperse as rapidly from the slum and delinquent areas as do other ethnic groups.

Not all ethnic groups become susceptible to delinquent behavior. Those ethnic groups who remain socially isolated and cohesive, tend to have relatively few delinquents among their children. Thus the Japanese in Seattle, before World War II, exerted intensified controlling influence upon their children, and thus were able to deter them from associating with delinquents from other ethnic groups and also were able to deter them from delinquency. The parents tended to impart a middle-class orientation into their children, and also were able to create the kinds of relationships which enabled them to control them.[15]

But the children of minority groups who are restricted or excluded in their economic and social participation because of language, foreign background, or poverty or race, were deterred from sharing the rewards of middle-class orientation to education and to work. Before 1930 the European immigrant parents were objects of discrimination, and comprised the culturally marginal groups in this country. As wave after wave of immigrants settled in the slum areas of the cities, their first bewildering efforts to adjust to this new environment had many effects. One effect was the high rates of delinquency among their native born children. Before 1930, over fifty percent of the delinquents were native born children of foreign born parentage. By 1950 less than thirty percent of the delinquents were native born children of foreign born parents. But after immigration restrictions, new culturally marginal groups came to the urban community, such as the Negro, the Puerto Rican, the Mexican, and perhaps to a lesser degree, the Southern White and American Indian. With these newly-arrived groups settling into the urban slum areas, their children comprised an increasing proportion of the delinquents. Their lack of community organization, of intense and effective family solidarity, and the declining control of the parents over their children in the urban areas contributes to these conditions.[16]

The Negroes, as the most numerous of newly marginal groups in the urban community, comprise an especially high proportion of delinquents. This condition has resulted both from influences outside the Negro group as well as from intrinsic influences of Negro community and family organization, or the lack of it. These high rates of delinquency do not, however, reflect any inherent racial qualities. First, Negroes are discriminated against because of their recent arrival to the urban community and their racial identity. Second, Negroes are in the lower socio-economic levels, and also have a large proportion of broken homes, which may lead a Negro child to be committed to an institution more readily than a white child. In a comparative study of Negro and white delinquents, it was found that only 18 percent of the Negro delinquents lived with both of their parents, while 46 percent of the whites lived with both of their parents. Many broken homes among the Negroes resulted from desertion and divorce rather than from death of one of the parents. Furthermore, 25 percent of the Negro delinquents were illegitimate. Other higher percentages among Negroes than among whites, indicating absence of the regular parent in the family or discordant relations between parents, were as follows:

> 30 percent of the Negro and 13 percent of the white delinquents were foster children; 33 percent of the Negro and 17 percent of the white delinquents were step-children. Furthermore, the Negro delinquents moved to different home situations to a greater extent than white delinquents.

Third, their community disorganization contributed to high delinquency rates. In one study many Negro delinquents came from all-Negro areas which had very high delinquency rates. Fourth, because Negro adults continue to be discriminated against occupationally, despite slight gains in this direction, they are forced to live in slums longer than other groups. Also a smaller proportion acquire middle class norms than do whites. Hence their children more readily become delinquent. Thus the discrimination and the increasing flow of Negroes to northern urban communities contributes to the high rate of delinquency among Negroes.

In general the differential influence of the ethnic group upon delinquent behavior may be determined, by the following characteristics: 1) The ethnic group may have recently migrated to the urban area of first settlement, which is a high rate delinquency area. 2) The ethnic group may permit its juveniles and youths to associate with the youth of other ethnic groups in the area. 3) The social structure of the particular ethnic group may be loose or disorganized and less likely to resist to delinquent activity than the highly organized group. 4) The ethnic group may tolerate criminal behavior. 5) The ethnic group may continue to reside in high-rate delinquency areas. 6) The adult members of subsequent generations may acquire and impart middle-class norms slowly. By contrast, when a large proportion of a given ethnic group acquire the skills and orientation of the middle-class culture, they will have fewer delinquents in subsequent generations. Thus the English in Chicago have fewer delinquents than the Italians.

Socio-economic Levels And The Orientations
Of Delinquent Families

Although the class position of a boy may affect his getting arrested or going free, the differences between the social classes run deeper and affect the orientation of the general participation of the families. Generally speaking, lower class families are marginal in their participation. But these families are divided into two categories. One category of family tends to have a middle-class orientation, to accept the formal institutions in the community and to orient their children towards improving their social position by conventional means. "After my parents came from the Old Country and settled down, they told me—the boy in the family—to start working hard because this was the promised country and that my relatives were well off and there was no reason why we shouldn't either. They said that I had to do well in school and not fool around and to keep away from the bums who would get me into trouble." By contrast, another family was so disorganized that the parents were just concerned with making a living, and could not concern themselves about the social mobility of the children. In many of the former-type of families who are newly-arrived to the urban environment and hence have not made an adequate adjustment, one of their children may become delinquent. As these families move to middle-class areas, delinquency among their children tends to cease. On the other hand, the latter type of lower-class families who because of disorganized parents continue to reside in high rate delinquency areas in the urban community. Because of the mal-adaptation and neglect of the father and mother, the children feel delinquency is condoned and become averse to middle-class norms of enterprise and adaptability. These types of delinquents are among the emotionally inaccessible types who suspect social agencies and who resist treatment. In New York it was found that one percent of the families on relief comprised 75 percent of the delinquents, and that a large proportion of these families had been persistently on relief. The Gluecks found that 28.6 percent of the families of delinquents were generally dependent, while only 12.0 percent of the families of the non-delinquents were dependent. About twice as many delinquent families as non-delinquent families were receiving financial aid from public or private agencies. Others received aid from relatives and other sources. Not only was there poverty among these families, but also the father and mother were disorganized and could not support their families.[18] Among many delinquent families, the mothers particularly came from disorganized families, and perpetuated by transmitting an indifference to conventional norms to their children which predisposed them to delinquent associates.

One characteristic influence of the family is the consistency of its influences with those of other institutions in the community. When the family encourages suspicion, hostility, or apathy to other agencies in the community, such as the school, the church, or the recreation center, it may alienate the child from the constructive influences of the community and compel him to seek gratification from unsupervised sources, such as the gang and the street-corner hangout or the improvised club.

The "Broken Home" And Delinquency:

The family "broken" by the death of one or both parents, by parental divorce, or by parental separation, inevitably experiences an interval of family disorganization. One parent has to accept the roles of two parents, either by working and caring for the home, or he has to hire a substitute parent figure to assume the other role. How does the "broken home" contribute to delinquency?

Findings tend to differ for this phenomenon. Shidler, in a study in 1918, found that about 25 percent of all American children came from broken homes.[20] Since less than 50 percent of the delinquents come from broken homes, the ratio between delinquents and non-delinquents could not exceed a 2 to 1 ratio. Shaw and McKay found that the ratio for broken homes between non-delinquents and delinquents was 1.18 to 1 for boys, and 1.49 to 1 for girls, which may indicate that the broken home has a greater influence upon girls than upon boys.[21] Slavson, in 1926, found that a sample of delinquents had a significantly higher rate of broken homes than a comparable group of non-delinquents.[22] Cavan compared the broken and intact homes of delinquents in five different studies. The girl delinquents showed a greater discrepancy than the girl non-delinquents, but the boy delinquents and non-delinquents did not differ so markedly. Twenty-five percent of the school girls came from broken homes, but forty-nine per cent of the delinquent girls came from broken homes.[23] In a study of girls from broken homes, Caldwell, in a Spokane study found that 63.5 percent and the Gluecks, in a Massachusetts study, found that 61.8 percent came from broken homes.[24] Similarly 25 percent of the non-delinquent school boys came from broken homes; but, from the aforementioned studies of delinquents, the percentages of broken homes were 34, 37.3, 39.6, and 45.5 respectively. In short, the rates of broken homes for delinquent girls are far higher than for delinquent boys, and the rates for delinquent boys are higher than for those of non-delinquent boys. Although many investigators regard the broken home as a contributing factor in delinquency, its direct or indirect influence upon delinquency must be qualified.

First, the proportion of broken homes among delinquents increases with the age of the delinquents studied. Second, the child from a broken home is more likely to be committed to an institution than a child from a complete home, because officials will find the broken home is a basis for commitment. Hence the ratio of broken homes increases from the initial process of court arraignment to institutional commitments. Third, the frequency of broken homes varies by type of delinquency. Incorrigible children and truants have a higher proportion from broken homes than do property offenders, traffic violators, and misdeameanants.

The mere absence of a parent does not in itself create the social atmosphere which predisposes the child to delinquency. Sometimes the absence of a parent may even deter a child from persisting in his delinquencies. For example, one former delinquent admitted to the writer that he desisted from delinquencies after his father died. His distraught mother confronted him (the oldest child) with the alternative prospects of helping her care for his four siblings or risking jail by his delinquent behavior. His loyalty and attachment to his mother so moved him that from that time (he was 16) he kept out of trouble and was never arrested, despite many temptations. A bereaved family may become more solidified and more organized as a result of a crisis created by the death of a parent. This type of organized family may deter delinquency. On the other hand, the family who experience the desertion of a parent because of marital conflict or parental irresponsibility or negligence, may create the situations which may stimulate the child to delinquent behavior. The child in this situation is also more likely to be arrested for a personal offense or for truanting. But, the boy who is involved in systematic kinds of crime, such as planned stealing with associates, is less likely to be influenced by broken home relations and more likely to be influenced by the gang. Hence, the broken home would have more direct influence upon delinquents who engage in personal offenses and less upon delinquents who engage in systematic crimes.

Fourth, the rates of broken homes vary by ethnic group. Of Negro delinquents, 66.0 percent; of Italians, 27.4 percent; and of the American delinquents, 40 percent came from broken homes. Still, in every ethnic group the percentage of delinquents from broken homes was higher than that of non-delinquents.[25]

Fifth, the broken home tends to have a more perceptible influence upon female than upon male delinquents, and significantly more delinquent girls than delinquent boys come from broken homes. Only one study by Bushard found that more than 56.4 percent of the male sample came from broken homes, but six studies showed that more than 50 percent of the females came from broken homes.[26]

Sixth, the families which become disrupted by the death of one or both parents do not tend to affect the juveniles in the same way as families which become disrupted by desertion or divorce. The bereaved family members may draw closer together; while family members disturbed by parental conflict may have divided loyalties. Cavan found that 18 percent of the non-delinquent boys had been orphaned by the death of one or both parents, but 7 percent had parents who were separated or divorced.[27] On the other hand, 19 percent of the delinquent boys were orphaned by the death of one or both parents; but 15 percent, or double the non-delinquent percentages, came from families torn by separation or divorce.

But more significant than the "broken home" as we have pointed out is the mode of relationships in the family, especially between parents and children as well as between the children themselves.

Culture Conflict and Parent-Child Relations

During the first quarter of the century many delinquents were native-born children of foreign-born parents. These children rejected the stigmatized parental norms as foreign and inferior. Hence they sought role-models outside the family. Some parents tried to restrain their children from deviant behavior so bewildering to them. They became more repressive in their discipline, which merely intensified the rebelliousness of the children.

Parents of contemporary slum families, although not foreign-born, but marginal in their participation, may remain in conflict with their children because of a general emphasis upon "youth culture" which makes parental views and restraints "old fashioned." This emphasis upon "youth," "fun," and play, can coincide with lack of discipline and with wayward behavior. Delinquency then becomes the deviant product by which juveniles accept delinquent behavior in rebelling against the supposedly "inferior culture" of their parents and of authority generally.

The dynamics of mobile and rapidly-changing American society stimulates conflicts between generations and loosens the control over the teen-ager. The inference at one time was that delinquency results between foreign-born parents and native-born children, but the conflict of generations pertains to parents and adolescents generally. The adolescent period is one of separation from parental control and arouses greater reliance upon one's peers for guidance. In the high-rate delinquency areas, these peers are the established delinquents who can exert an intense pressure upon the individual teen-ager to conform to the group. One delinquent admitted that at times he did not want to go with the gang, but that he actually feared the punishment or suspicion that would have resulted. The parents frequently do not understand the pressure upon the adolescent to conform to the gang. Consequently, by hitting, reprimanding, and scolding the boy, they may alienate him further. The difficulty of parental control of the juvenile or adolescent in the delinquency area involves a form of parental influence which will call out an attachment to and an identification with the parents which can resist the existing pressures of the gang.

Parent-Child Relations and Reactions to Delinquency

The family, by influencing the personality formation of the child and by affecting his basic values, predisposes him to select certain associates as well as to have certain orientations to delinquency. First, the family may directly impart delinquent behavior by teaching the younger members to steal, to disobey the law, or to disrespect the law.[28] The Gluecks found that 70 per cent of 1,000 delinquents were reared in families whose parents or siblings had criminal records.[29] In many of these families, one or both parents either had criminal records or had committed offenses for which they could have been arrested. Parents may contribute to the juvenile's delinquency by tolerating his depredations and truancies and by indirectly encouraging his delinquency.

One study of court cases concerning juvenile delinquency found that of 1,127 cases about 500 cases were against the parents themselves. Also the number of parents who were arrested for contributing to delinquency increased from seven in 1937 to one hundred and eighteen in 1946.[30] Some parents unwittingly and even unintentionally influence the child to commit delinquent acts.[31] One investigator observed that one out of several children might unconsciously be singled out by the parents as the scapegoat to act out the parents' poorly integrated and forbidden impulses.[32]

The unstable parent may tacitly sympathize with the child's destructive activities. Or one parent may nullify the other parent's disciplinary efforts and confuse the child by contradicting the commands of the other parent. When the parents reject and estrange the boy, he may seek the company and the approval from accessible delinquent companions. The extent to which the father serves as a role-model for the boy, the extent to which the boy becomes attached to his mother, and the extent to which he feels that both parents are concerned with his welfare, may affect his tendencies to delinquent behavior. The Gluecks found that 52.1 percent of the non-delinquents, but only 17.1 per cent of the delinquents, regarded their fathers as wholly acceptable for emulation.

Sixty-five and six-tenths per cent of the mothers of the non-delinquents, in contrast to 4.2 per cent of the mothers of the delinquents, had firm but kindly relations with the respective subjects; and 55.5 of the fathers of the non-delinquents, in contrast to 5.7 percent of the fathers of the delinquents, related to the subjects in a firm but kindly manner.[33] In brief, the parents of the delinquents, whether by indifference or hostility, hindered

their children from acquiring positive attitudes towards authority. The mothers and fathers of the delinquents were lax, over-
strict, or erratic in about 95 per cent of the cases.[34] The main
result of their relationships was to create the crucial orientation of alienating the delinquents from their parents who, they
felt, were not concerned with their welfare. The delinquents
were hostile to authority, and sought to identify with persons
outside the family. They found ready companionship and acceptance from delinquents of like hostility in the neighborhood.

The important consideration is the family influence upon
personality formation. Parents or siblings may so frustrate the
juvenile that he becomes predisposed to delinquency. Healy and
Bronner found that of 143 delinquents accepted for treatment
at the Judge Baker Foundation, 131 cases, or 92 percent, had
major emotional disturbances from frustrating parental or sibling
relations. The other 12 delinquents were not emotionally disturbed, but became delinquent by compelling group influences.
The delinquents, rejected in their social relations, reacted as
follows: They felt 1) rejected or insecure 2) thwarted in self-
expression, and had other self-dissatisfactions 3) inadequate or
inferior 4) disturbed by family disharmonies or excessive discipline 5) had persistent jealousy or rivalry feelings to siblings
or 6) deep emotional conflicts. In brief, the crucial difference
between the delinquent and non-delinquent subjects was that
the delinquents were more definitely thwarted emotionally in
early life. Hence their personality formations differed accordingly. The delinquents usually sought delinquent associates or
were attracted to delinquent associates with whom they were
able to express their hostility or enhance their conceptions of
themselves. Thus their delinquency had a private meaning which
resulted from their personal frustrating experiences with their
family. But the delinquents also acquired shared meanings from
their participation in the delinquent peer group. The family
may predispose the juvenile to accepting delinquent associates
and their orientations and practices.[35]

The Gluecks, who studied 500 matched delinquents and non-
delinquents from the slum areas, arrived at conclusions which
are consistent with those of Healy and Bonner. They found
that the quality of family life was poorer among delinquents
than non-delinquents; that the family atmosphere was cruder,
the standards of conduct closer, and the families of delinquents

less concerned with self-respect in the community than families of the non-delinquents. The families of the delinquents lacked the cohesion that prevailed among non-delinquent families. In general, the family environments in which the delinquent boys grew up were "less conducive to the wholesome rearing of healthy, happy, and law-abiding children." Seemingly these delinquent families comprised many emotionally inaccessible delinquents who distrust the social agencies and the welfare workers, and hence are less amenable to treatment and rehabilitation.[36]

Sibling Relations

Although the parents exert a basic influence upon the personality formation of the children, the siblings, especially those of the same sex, also can be decisive in their influence towards crime. An older brother can be the tutor of the younger brother. This obtains particularly if the brothers are exposed to similar influences in the same neighborhood and when the brothers associate together. Thus, in *Brothers In Crime,* a study of five brothers who had criminal records, the older brothers influenced and taught the younger brothers to steal, although parental efforts to counteract these influences were slight. On the other hand, the brothers may, in a process of sibling rivalry, select different courses of behavior. One of the brothers may be favored by the parents and acquire a more positive relationship and a different conception of himself than the brother who may be alienated from the family. One brother may conceive of himself as the "good boy," while the rejected brother may regard himself as the "bad boy," and react according to that role. Some non-delinquent brothers of delinquents have remarked why they remained non-delinquent:

> "I want to make something of myself. I want to get an education. I wanted to get ahead in the world."
> "I just felt that I couldn't disobey."
> "I guess something inside me made me want to do right as I see it."
> "I was always afraid to get in trouble."
> "Nobody could talk me into going wrong."

Generally, in these relations, one sibling would become more attached to the parent and would acquire a different conception of his social world than did the delinquent.

On the other hand, the child who is reared with older delinquent siblings, may accept a delinquent orientation and behavior without conflict. In fact, the juvenile, when young enough, may feel proud in accepting the tutelage of his brothers, especially if the parents are too harassed by poverty or personal problems to supervise their children adequately. This form of unhindered tutelage in the ways of delinquency by one brother to another is clearly indicated in the following recollections of a delinquent:

"I was still a youngster when my brother, who was a few years older than me, picked me as one of his companions. He and I and a friend who later became my partner in crime, started going out together and to bum from school. . . . My brother and partner were older than I and more experienced in ways of stealing. At the time I first started stealing pennies from newsstands; my brothers, who were older and a lot more experienced, were already in a different racket. During the time I was stealing with my brother and my partner, I did not take things seriously and it seemed only natural that I was following right in my brother's steps because I was being taught by him and my other buddies."

The brother of this delinquent recalled that his first delinquent act was taught to him by still another brother:

"One of my first experiences in delinquency that I can remember was one morning when I was walking along M with my brother. As it was pretty chilly, we stepped into a department store to warm up. As we were walking through the store (my brother) showed me the candy counter. He walked right up to the candy counter and took some candy from it, and I, seeing how easy he did it, went up and took some too. It seemed so easy to do that, I did not think anything of it and I did it again and again."

Birth Order and Delinquency

Delinquents generally come from larger families than non-delinquents in the general population, because lower class families are larger than middle class families who have lower rates of delinquencies. Still, Burt regarded the "only child" as a definite factor in delinquency. He found that 15.4 per cent of the delinquent boys were only children, but only 2.5 per cent of the non-delinquent group were only children. When the delinquents were not the only child, they frequently were isolated psychologically from the other siblings. Some were the eldest, and emotionally removed from their siblings. Others were youngest among siblings who had grown up.[38] In definite contrast, the Gluecks found that 4.8 per cent of the delinquents, and 8.6 per cent of the non-delinquent controls, were "only children," and that 60 per cent of the delinquents and 47.8 per cent of the nondelinquents, were middle children.[39] Sletto reported that male delinquent only children did not differ in type of offense from children with siblings.[40] Wattenberg maintains that since the meaning of "only child" varies for different ethnic and economic groups, that the status of only child does not have any specific consistency to delinquency.[41] Hart and Axelrad found that only children differed in emotional traits and in type of companions from children who had many siblings. Since the large family correlates highly with group offenders in high-rate delinquency areas, it is not unexpected that the children with siblings would have "undesirable companions."[42]

Sletto found too that delinquency was high for children who had younger siblings of each sex, but low for children who had older siblings of each sex. How the older siblings influence the behavior of younger siblings is hard to determine. Perhaps the oldest sibling position reflects one fact—that their families had recently settled in the city in high rate delinquency areas; when the younger siblings come of age the family move to a non-delinquent area.[43]

Selected Bibliography

Milton L. Barron, *The Juvenile in a Delinquent Society* (New York: Alfred A. Knopf, Inc., 1954). Emphasizes the effect of the total competitive society upon delinquency.

Herbert A. Bloch & Frank Flynn, *Juvenile Delinquency* (New York: Random House, 1956). A well-founded analysis of delinquency emphasizing the sociological approach.

John R. Ellington, *Protecting Our Children from Criminal Careers* (New York: Prentice-Hall, Inc., 1948). Indicates the effects of the gang and group upon delinquency and prevention of delinquency.

Kate Friedlander, *The Psycho-analytic Approach to Juvenile Delinquency* (New York: International Universities Press, 1947). Describes the effects of the family upon delinquency.

Sheldon & Eleanor Glueck, *Unraveling Juvenile Delinquency* (New York: The Commonwealth Fund, 1950). An eclectic or multiple factor approach to an individually matched study of delinquents and non-delinquents in slum areas. A mine of information.

William Healy & Augusta Bronner, *New Light on Delinquency and Its Treatment* (New Haven: Yale University Press, 1936). Matched study of delinquent and non-delinquent subjects.

"Juvenile Delinquency," *Annals of the American Academy of Political and Social Science*, CCLXV (January, 1949). A comprehensive analysis of juvenile delinquency from several viewpoints.

Walter Reckless, *The Etiology of Delinquent and Criminal Behavior* (New York: Social Science Research Council, 1943). Carefully searches for the social processes which contribute to and cause delinquency.

Clifford R. Shaw & Henry D. McKay, "Social Factors in Juvenile Delinquency," *Report on the Causes of Crime* (Washington, D. C., Government Printing Office, 1931). One of the early and careful analyses of the social factors and processes which contribute to delinquency.

S. Kirson Weinberg, *Society and Personality Disorders* (New York: Prentice-Hall, Inc., 1952) Chapter 12. Relates the family and delinquency to several perverse personality types; analyzes the social dynamics of delinquency.

S. Kirson Weinberg, "Theories of Criminality and Problems of Prediction," *Journal of Criminal Law and Criminology*, XLV (1955), 412-24. A critical analysis and integration of group and individual versions of delinquency and the pertinence of theory to the prediction of delinquent behavior.

Dr. S. Kirson Weinberg is Professor of Sociology and Chairman of the Committee on Social Psychology at Roosevelt University. On a research fellowship for the year 1957-58, he formerly taught at the University of Minnesota and Whitman College, Wash., was also Co-Director of Research on Mental Health in a Hospital Inquiry, and Psychologist for the Armed Forces; has made many studies dealing with the application of social psychological and sociological techniques to deviant behavior, the social personality and social relationships, the knowledge of the causes and development of criminal behavior, and has tried to integrate the sociological and psychological or the group and individual versions of delinquency; has studied the informal and formal structure of corrective institutions, such as the prison and mental hospital, the function of deviant cultures upon personality, the changing modes of socially intimate relationships in contemporary society, and the developmental malformation of the disordered persons, especially the schizophrenic, the sex deviate, and the psychopath. He is the author of *Society and Personality Disorders: The Sociology of Personal Stability and Mental Health* (New York: Prentice-Hall, 1952), and of *Incest Behavior: The Universal Crime* (New York: The Citadel Press, 1955), and is a contributing author to the *Criminology: A Book of Readings* Edited by Robert Clark, Clyde Vedder, and Samuel Koenig, to *Mental Health and Mental Disorder* (edited by Arnold M. Rose).

CHAPTER 6.

CULTURAL AND COMMUNITY FACTORS

SIDNEY J. KAPLAN
University of Kentucky

The observation has been made that a society has the kind of criminals it deserves.[1] Such a viewpoint is easily understood. It simply suggests that a society "produces" varieties of behavior, some varieties of which are defined as being normal, and others as being deviant.

While such a view may appear to be an oversimplification since it tends to minimize psychological factors in criminality, it nonetheless focuses attention upon the differences which characterize one society or community as compared to another. There tends, for example, to be a positive correlation between size of community and delinquency. Urban communities differ from rural communities in quality and quantity of delinquency. And within communities there are neighborhoods which exhibit high, moderate, or low rates of delinquency over extended periods of time.

Now even though the recognition that delinquency varies from one community to another is a commonplace, it nevertheless raises a very pertinent question: why is this so?

The answer, is seems evident, is to be found in an exploration of the cultural milieu in which delinquency occurs. Though such an exploration might be general, it would provide a framework of interpretation for making delinquent behavior at least partially understandable.

One cogent illustration of how delinquency is related to a given culture is found in the writings of Robert Merton.[2] As Merton sees it, two very important elements of a society are (1) the goals which most people are taught to seek and (2) the means which are provided to attain these goals. If the means (opportunities) are not provided equally among all segments of the population, some individuals will use deviant means to obtain the very ends which are considered socially desirable. In other words, these individuals accept the socially defined goals, but unable to make use of the socially approved means because of their inequitable distribution, utilize their own illegal means to acquire the goals. This kind of reaction is particularly characteristic of a society where possession of property is a highly valued end. Perhaps the best example of this is to be found in the case of car theft among juveniles. Given the car complex of the United States and the extremely high value which attaches to car possession it is not difficult to understand how juveniles incorporate this value. But since juveniles are often too young to obtain a license, and since many do not have enough money to buy a car (inequitable distribution of means) they simply steal a car.

Juvenile car theft, even though a good many "causes" may apply, can be attributed in part to the "disassociation" or "incompatibility" between ends and means which characterizes the American community. Car theft it may be succinctly put, inheres in the nature of American culture.

This explanation, of course, is quite general. It does not tell us who among juveniles will steal cars, nor does it exhaust the variety of motives which are very likely involved. But it does despite its generality show how delinquency may be a function of a given culture.

A second explanation of delinquency as related to a particular culture is to be found in the problem of *marginality* or *culture conflict*. In the highly heterogenous United States there are standards of behavior which oftentimes make contrary demands. This kind of dilemma is by no means uncommon, but is particularly characteristic of immigrant children, and the children of migrants who have left one part of the country and moved to another. Thus the child of a migrant of Appalachia will be subject to training which may inculcate in him values which are at variance with, say, the values of the northern city in which he is being reared. Consequently the child will find himself in a marginal position between two "cultures," partaking simultaneously of both but partaking of neither wholly.

Strains are set up which discourage the integration of any consistent scheme of personal values. It is this inconsistency of values which may . . . "induce expedient forms of behavior, those most suitable to the individual's needs at a given moment irrespective of the social requirements of the larger community."[3] In short, delinquency in one form or another may result. In the contemporary period the delinquency of marginal juveniles is exhibited in the children of Southern migrants who have gone North, in the children of Puerto Rican "immigrants," and in the children of Mexican immigrants.[4]

The point then is that in a culture with a diversity of values, or in a culture that is characterized by groups that have divergent values, dislocations appear that apparently serve as a seed bed for delinquency. Again it may be said that delinquency may be rooted to a particular culture.

Social Disorganization

Both the "illicit means" and the "culture conflict" explanations of delinquency can be included under the broader concept of social disorganization. This more inclusive term is used very frequently by sociologists to explain deviant behavior of any kind. Very simply, it may be said that a society is disorganized when there is a lack of agreement on what the important social values are, and when the techniques of social control are ineffective. When individuals, groups, and institutions work at cross purposes, when patterns of social expectations are unclear and ill-defined, we have a condition which may be called social disorganization. The extreme or extension of such a state would be chaos or perhaps anarchy. Actually, of course, there is no society which is characterized by complete disorganization. Rather, what may be perceived are varying degrees of disorganization.

In a society, then, which is disorganized the individual may absorb during his socialization definitions of expected behavior which are neither clear nor well defined. Or if they are well defined they may make contradictory demands. Consequently the individual will find it difficult to incorporate a coherent set of values to serve as a guide for personal conduct. In short, doubt, skepticism, or uncertainty, may well characterize the personality of an individual who is socialized in a disorganized society. Unable to make a satisfactory adjustment a juvenile may resolve his conflicts and uncertainties in some deviant manner. This of course is an extreme picture. Were this kind of personality reaction found generally in any society, that society would doubtless not long endure. But it does seem likely that the society which is relatively disorganized will have a commensurate number of personality disorganized individuals whether they be delinquents, drug addicts, alcoholics, neurotics, or just simply those that are maladjusted.

The factors, particularly in modern American society, which contribute to social disorganization are many: sub-cultural variation, rapid technological change, racial differences, a high rate of social mobility, economic competition, increasing internal migration, the increase in urbanization, and general social complexity. All these trends moving with unprecedented velocity make demands of our social system which it is apparently unable to meet effectively. It is, then, the dynamic character of American culture with its inherent strains and dislocations which is reflected in individual deviance.

But societies other than the United States are disorganized. Why in the United States is th erate of juvenile delinquency relatively high? Part of the answer, perhaps, lies in the degree, the intensity of disorganization in America as compared to other societies. Moreover America has its own unique traditions, history, and "character" which are doubtless related to its high rate of delinquency. Mere mention of the "automobile complex" is sufficient testimony to this uniqueness.

Delinquency and American Culture

Among the traits of American culture there are a number which appear significant enough to demand specific exposition if delinquency is to be understood. The special traits to be examined are as follows: (1) Internal Migration, (2) Technological Change, (3) Competition, and (4) Urbanization.

Internal migration: Although the influx of immigrants to the United States has virtually ceased, the problems of migration have by no means ended. Now, however, such social consequences including delinquency that arise from migration appear to be related to internal migration. As Americans have become increasingly mobile, problems of personal and social adjustment have arisen. And this holds true not only for the communities to which migrants go, but also for the communities of origin.[5]

Four types of internal migration are especially important for an understanding of delinquency. These are (1) regional, (2) rural-urban, (3) intercity, and (4) intracity. In each one of those categories the post war trend of high migration has continued bringing about what might be called a constant flux of population. An index of this continual migration are the Bureau of Census figures for the 1954-1955 period.[6] In April of 1955 it was estimated that 19.9% of the population of the country had moved from the house lived in the year previous. Some 13.3% or 21 million people had moved within the same county, and the remainder, 6.6% or 10 million people had moved from one county to another. In other words at least 31 million people had moved from one residence to another in that short period. The descriptive term "population flux" it may be observed is hardly inappropriate.

Needless to say this high rate of mobility is very likely related to the increasingly high rate of delinquency which has characterized the United States since the second world war. That deviant behavior is more than theoretically related to highly mobile families has been documented in sociological research.[7]

Technological Change: One of the more striking aspects of the American scene, particularly from the viewpoint of the foreigner, is the utilization of modern technology. Automobiles, machinery, electronic devices, and mechanical gadgets of all kinds, are part of the overwhelmingly technical face of America. A few short generations ago Americans were limited to a few mechanical aids as they sought to make a living from the earth. Nowadays, however, sheer necessity to tie one's self to the soil no longer exists. Modern technology has swept aside the direction and purpose of the "horse and buggy days" and has replaced them with a multitude of purposes and directions which beckon from every side.

The tremendous rapidity of this technological revolution has brought about sudden shifts in ways of living. Resultant residential changes, occupational changes, class changes, and the like have all been accompanied by problems of adjustment. Man's adaptibility at times has been unequal to the task of coping with these dramatic shifts. The invention and universal use of radio, T.V., automobiles, airplanes, and the increasing trend toward industrial automation have brought problems of adaptation with which Americans have only feebly come to terms.

The rapidity of contemporary technological change and the inadequacy of social response has sometimes been described in terms of "culture lag." This is the tendency for social patterns to lag behind the demands called up by technical progress. Since we are unable to anticipate many of the new social responses a technological change entails, some personal and social maladjustments are probably inevitable. Moreover, by the time man's institutions have caught up with the new changes other changes have come along to complicate the attempts to establish and maintain stability. As the atomic age rushes into the present who can anticipate the social complexities that will no doubt appear? Perhaps part of the price that Americans pay for technical advance is some measure of social instability and its concomitants of personal disorganization.

An interesting theory offered to account for man's instability as it relates to technological advance is to be found in Fromm's *Escape From Freedom*.[8] As Fromm puts it, Western man has been able to free himself from the demands of the earth. His technical genius has permitted him to emancipate himself from the continual day by day quest for bare subsistence which, say, characterizes some primitive societies. Having learned to manipulate his earthly environment with power machines man finds himself free, but without direction. Or putting it in other terms, the direction and purpose which characterized his food hunting and agricultural days no longer exist and now with his food problem solved he finds himself with leisure and freedom he doesn't know how to use. And as a consequence he is prey to various straw-in-the-wind enticements that promise rewards and assurances of all kinds. Similarly, the juvenile can be characterized by this directionless freedom, but only more so.

There is perhaps some truth to the assertion that in the American culture there is no niche for the adolescent, who having no economic obligations, occupies a marginal position between childhood and manhood. He has his freedom, yes, but his society gives him no direction. His "escape from freedom," then, may be in the direction of the "short run hedonism" of delinquency. It is interesting in this connection to note that

Cohen has characterized the delinquent sub-culture as being non-utilitarian and negativistic.[9] Both these traits it may be observed suggest the aimless lack of direction that apparently characterizes juvenile delinquency.

Competition: The description of the American culture as being highly competitive has obvious basis. In America's open class system and expansive capitalistic economy, the opportunities for advancement, success, achievement, and fulfillment are widely available. The ideology of rugged individualism and personal initiative is embraced by the American population generally. And although the acceptance of the American Myth may be qualified with contemporary sociological sophistication, there is little doubt that the attainment of economic and social rewards is possible for increasing numbers of Americans.

Even though the United States of the 50's may be aptly characterized as prosperous, material and social rewards are both highly differentiated and limited. In this context of differentiated and limited accessibility of rewards considerable competition for achievement has developed. Since in the U. S. economic advancement is a major goal which confers not only property but prestige and position upon a person, extreme competition develops which probably encourages illicit activity.[10]

While a good many personal and social advantages doubtless attach to the competitive spirit in America, there are implications for illegal behavior which are undeniable. Merton's analysis of delinquent behavior in terms of the utilization of illicit means to obtain material gain is very compelling.[11] Moreover the continual accounts of crimes against property which characterizes the American Press are eloquent testimony of the pressure of need and greed. Perusal of the Kefauver report of a few years ago more than substantiates the role of competition in American criminal and quasi-criminal activity.[12]

If in the context of competition there are indeed implications for delinquency, it may be expected in America where the apotheosis of competition is to be found, that delinquent motivations will be aroused. And the juvenile, disenfranchised economically as it were, may well expend his energies in seeking out the material goals all "good" Americans are called upon to obtain. To the juvenile whose appetite is whetted by advertisements in newspapers, periodicals, billboards, and on T.V., by the rewarding lives of successful personalities, and by the gleam of passing automobiles, the possibility of theft is by no means remote. And this particularly is true of the juveniles of the lower socio-economic groups whose resources for competition are slim, and whose feelings of deprivation are undoubtedly keen.

TABLE I[13]

Percentage of Population Classified as Urban 1900-1950

Year	Per Cent of Total Population
1900	39.7
1910	45.7
1920	51.2
1930	56.2
1940	56.5
1950	59
1950*	64*

* New Urban Definition

Urbanization: One of the major characteristics of American development over the past several generations has been the amazing shift in residence. At one time the United States was dominated by a rural mode of life. Now, in the middle of the twentieth century the United States is primarily urban. In Table I the changing residential composition of the United States over the past half century is shown.

While these figures are impressive in showing the shift to urban residence, the figures for earlier periods in America's history are doubly impressive. In 1800 and 1850 the percentages of urban population for the U.S. were 6.1 and 15.3 respectively.[14] The change to urban life in the past one hundred and fifty years has been truly revolutionary. But more important are the social consequences which this rapid process of urbanization has entailed.[15]

That urbanization has brought many changes is undeniable. The contrasts between the slow moving, relatively stable life of the rural community and the fast moving, relatively unstable life of the city need no extended commentary. But fundamental to the change and having implications for delinquent behavior is the "new" character of urban social control. In the rural community informal techniques of social control such as gossip, family pressure, and community opinion were effective in controlling behavior. Such apparently is true to a much lesser extent in the urban community. In heavily populated urban communities the pressure and opinions of neighbors may be of minor consequence. The hackneyed observation that many an urban dweller does not know or care anything about his neighbors is not the less true for its being hackneyed. It is no exaggeration to say of urban life that considerable indifference to the approval and disapproval of one's neighbors may exist.

To say, of course, that urban life does not involve intimate contacts in primary groups that serve to control behavior would be an obvious untruth. What is important, however, is that the urban dweller can escape or ignore many of the pressures that would have been unavoidable in the rural community. In other words, the anonymity of the city provides much greater latitude for behavioral variation than does the rural area.

Indeed, America has been described as being a multi-group society. In the American city, interests, loyalties, and sympathies are focused not on general community welfare, but rather upon the affiliations which are made with a wide variety of groups. As a consequence of these varied interests and loyalties, contacts tend to become limited in their duration and intensity. In short, American city life is characterized by social relations which have become increasingly impersonal. In this context of impersonal relations the restraining power of informal social control is diminished and as a consequence there is greater opportunity for deviant and illicit behavior.[16] That this is more than merely conjectural may be inferred from the high rate of crime and delinquency which distinguish urban areas from rural.

Delinquency And Community Influence

It is trite at this stage in the development of the social sciences to insist that delinquency is "caused" by many "factors." Yet despite what would seem to be a contemporary common place there are still many people who see delinquency as arising out of this or that particular cause. That such naivete exists today is difficult to understand.

The appropriateness of a multi-cause approach to delinquency is especially apparent when juvenile delinquency is examined through the framework of the total community. Such community factors as housing, recreational facilities, schools, unemployment, population composition, and media of mass communication among others, are probably all pertinent to an understanding of delinquency. One might simply sum up these varied influences by saying that in a very real sense all the institutions of a city are related to delinquency in one way or another.

Because of this complexity the possibility of appraising delinquency within a framework of the *total community* is limited. The most one can hope for are very broad and general statements of relationships. Modern sociology, let it be said, works most effectively with data of far less ambitious proportions.

And yet despite the generality involved in using a total community approach, it is entirely possible that insights may be obtained that will be of a considerable service in raising problems and focusing research. Such is perhaps true of what is called the ecological approach to delinquency in the community setting.

The Ecology of Delinquency: The ecological method of analysis is concerned with the phenomenon of delinquency and its distribution throughout a given area. A map, for example, which shows the residences of delinquents in a community, or the rate of delinquency as it varies from one part of the city to another, might be utilized in ecological analysis.

This technique is by no means new. Ecological appraisals of social phenomena may be traced back to the earliest social philosophers.[17] But in the modern period ecological investigations may be attributed in large measure to analyses of Chicago made by Park and Burgess in the 1920's.[18] As a result of the impetus of these two theorists a host of research has appeared dealing with the ecology of social phenomena of every kind: psychoses, welfare cases, church attendance, crime, delinquency and so forth.

Perhaps the best known of the ecologists concerned with delinquency are Shaw and McKay, who, in *Delinquency Areas* and *Juvenile Delinquency and Urban Areas* applied the principles of ecological analysis most comprehensively.[19] In their investigations they showed that rates of delinquency varied with the distance from the center of the city. That is, the highest rates of delinquency were found in and around the centers of cities, and as the periphery of a city is approached the rate of delinquency gradually decreases. In short, a gradient of delinquency was found that varied inversely with the distance from the center of the city. What was particularly interesting was that the rates corresponded generally with zones of the city which had been previously differentiated by Burgess.[20]

As Burgess has described the typical city, it has five major areas which form rough concentric circles around the city's center. The Central Zone includes large department stores, specialty shops, the theatre district, and hotels. Adjacent to the central business district is the interstitial area or Zone in Transition. This zone which is being encroached upon by the business district is characterized by cheap boarding houses, small businesses, light manufacturing, warehouses, railroad sidings, and substandard housing. Generally it is an area of physical deterioration. As one proceeds from the area of transition the residential areas become increasingly attractive. Zone number 3, the area of workingmen's homes, providing ready access to the city, is followed by Zone number 4 which contains single family houses and "high-class" apartment buildings. Finally, surrounding the city is to be found the Commuters Zone where the inhabitants of suburbia dwell. These concentric zones it should be pointed out represent abstract or ideal pictures. It was expected that departures from this "ideal" representation would be encountered in empirical research.

As a result of their study of Chicago and other large urban centers, Shaw and McKay were able to delineate what they called "delinquency areas."[21] These areas of high delinquency were found primarily in the Zone in Transition and were characterized by general physical deterioration. In these deteriorated neighborhoods live immigrants, Negroes, migrants from the rural south and other economically and socially underprivileged groups unable to afford better living accommodations. As Calvin Schmid put it so well in his analysis of Minneapolis and St. Paul, characteristics of these areas include (1) the presence of criminal elements, (2) lack of sufficient and constructive recreational facilities, (3) a declining population, (4) overcrowding, (5) poverty, (6) the existence of anti-social traditions and standards, (7) heterogeneous cultural and racial elements, (8) high mobility of population, and (9) substandard housing.[22]

It was Shaw and McKay's conclusion that while physical deterioration was related to delinquency, the more significant point was that the physical deterioration of the delinquency areas were symptomatic of social disorganization. That is, not only were these areas physically deteriorated, but more fundamentally, they were socially deteriorated as well. Characterized by low levels of aspiration, conflicts in social values, feelings of deprivation, residents of these areas were socially demoralized. Out of this "lack of moral order" arise delinquency and other personality disorders.

The roots of considerable delinquency, then, as viewed by Shaw and McKay, are to be found deep in the character of the modern city: its overcrowded slums, its highly mobile population, its conflicts in values, its lack of "character building" facilities, and above all its general state of disorganization.

Although ecological studies of delinquency carried on subsequent to Shaw and McKay's early efforts have generally substantiated their findings, some criticisms are probably appropriate. These criticisms are as follows:

(a) The recognition that a high incidence of delinquency occurs in broken-down areas is a commonplace of which the police of any community are aware.

(b) While disorganization in a delinquency area may "explain" delinquent behavior, there are still many juveniles living in these areas who are not delinquent. How may these non-delinquents be explained?

(c) The gradiant of delinquency may in part be explained by the favoritism which is shown juveniles in the non-delinquent areas due to the wealth and position of their influential parents.

(d) There are delinquents who live outside the delinquency areas. Such delinquency can certainly not be explained by neighborhood deterioration.

(e) Ecological explanations are overly general. A profound understanding of delinquency causes can come only from a detailed study of the biological and psychological traits of the delinquents. Indifference to these traits can lead only to superficiality of explanation. As the Gluecks have suggested, the etiology of delinquency must be traced not only in gross ecological terms, but also in terms of the psychological characteristics of the delinquents.[23]

That these criticisms are pertinent cannot be denied. Yet

in no sense do they detract from the general significance of the ecological conclusions. The fact that a disproportionate incidence of delinquents is produced in the sub-standard areas may be unquestionably accepted. The fact that all juveniles in these areas do not become delinquents in no way suggests that deterioration and disorganization are not involved. Rather, it implies that what is necessary is research on the factors that "select out" those who do become delinquents. In short, what is called for is research on a different level of analysis.

The Delinquent Subculture—A Community Within a Community

Delinquency research has frequently pointed out the tendency for juvenile delinquents to be members of gangs.[24] This fact, of course, may have little significance. It is something of a platitude to note that most children are members of groups that serve to meet a variety of social and psychological needs. If it can be demonstrated however that delinquent gangs meet "special" needs, this would be of obvious value in providing an understanding of delinquent behavior. On the other hand, it may be anticipated that delinquent gangs do not meet "special" needs but as in the case of most juvenile groups, provide companionship, a sense of identity, in-group protection, and a means of passing time satisfactorily. If there is a difference to be found in delinquent groups as compared to non-delinquent groups it may be not so much a difference in "group dynamics" but a difference primarily in the values which are accepted. And these values may be simply a reflection of values of the Zone in Transition where most of these gangs apparently are.

In short, just as the non-delinquent groups in suburbia incorporate suburban middle-class values so also, we may assume, would groups developing in the Zone of Transition take on their own peculiar values. Since in the Zone of Transition there are definitions that support criminal behavior, whatever their source, it may be expected that in the ordinary course of socialization delinquency motivations will be aroused in juvenile groups. Are juvenile gangs, then, psychologically peculiar or are they no more than products of their community surroundings? Or is a choice of these two alternatives realistic? It is not possible that the delinquent gang may have a psychology which is at once peculiar and at the same time be a product of its neighborhood milieu? In other words it may be granted that the delinquent subculture is culturally transmitted, but the more important question, perhaps, is "what is the origin of this subculture and what special functions does it perform for its participants?"

The content of the delinquent subculture has been examined at length by many investigators.[25] One of the most astute theoretical analyses has been offered by Cohen who suggests that the delinquent subculture is *non-utilitarian, malicious and negativistic,* that the breadth of juvenile delinquency, or as Cohen puts it, its *versatility,* is characterized by *short run hedonism,* and that much of the behavior of delinquent gangs seems calculated to preserve and emphasize the importance of group *autonomy.*[26]

If, then, the delinquent subculture can be so described how may it be explained either sociologically or psychologically? According to Cohen the commonly used explanations of "social disorganization," "culture conflict" and "illicit means" are only partially satisfactory.[27] For example, disorganized delinquency areas are actually to some considerable extent organized. There are, contrary to the usually bleak social picture described, evidences of organizations, associations, and even in some degree a "sense of community," which orders behavior. Moreover the theory of disorganization emphasizes the absence of controls. It does not tell us why the peculiar character of delinquent behavior is to be found. As Cohen has suggested, the "social disorganization" approach fails to explain the origin and the particular spirit of the delinquent subculture.[28]

The "culture conflict" theory according to Cohen is also inadequate.[29] Even though there may be variations in social standards within a delinquency area, and even though ethnic groups may have values which are at odds with the overall culture, it may be an exaggeration, however, to maintain that delinquent behavior is positively encouraged. It is probably an exaggeration to suggest that there are racial or ethnic groups that have values which "positively" elicit or encourage the wide variety of illegal behavior which is found in the delinquent subculture.[30] Moreover just as is the case with social disorganization, the fact of cultural marginality doesn't explain why delinquent behavior arises. It simply posits a kind of no man's land of behavior with any number of behavioral possibilities. Any satisfactory theory of delinquent gang behavior must account for the specific direction of that behavior.

Similarly, Merton's theory of "illicit means" is also incomplete.[31] If delinquents use deviant means to obtain socially approved commodities or money, how does this fit in with the aimless non-utilitarian character of juvenile theft? Goods which are stolen by delinquents are often destroyed or discarded. Moreover, the versatility, negativism and the general "spirit" of the delinquent subculture is not explained by this theory.

How, then, does Cohen analyze the origin and function of the delinquent subculture? What theory does he offer to explain the behavior of the delinquent gang?

As Cohen sees the delinquent subculture it arises out of the nature of American society and its class system.[32] Since the delinquent subculture is primarily a "lower class" phenomenon, delinquents, unable to live in accordance with the middle-class standards of the dominant culture because of their disadvantageous social position, adjust by negating the very values which define them as being unworthy. Delinquency, then, represents, in the delinquent subculture at least, a reaction against a low class stigma and an attempt to enhance status. The delinquent gang obtains status both by attacking or demeaning middle class values and by developing group norms which serve to "justify" their delinquencies. A group solution to the problem of status deprivation, suggests Cohen, is an effective solution since it brings with it the sustaining quality of group approval.[33] As Redl has suggested, the delinquent subculture provides "gratifications" without the burden of guilt feelings. Indeed, even moral approval is provided for behavior which the larger community defines as "immoral."[34]

The delinquent subculture, then, is a product of the very nature of the American culture. The values which may serve to encourage good behaviour may simultaneously serve to elicit delinquent behavior. In short, American middle-class values calculated to engender respectability may also serve to "encourage" delinquency.[35]

Agencies of "Moral Risk" in the Community

The theories of delinquency already discussed by no means exhaust the attempt to explain delinquency within the community setting. Other community influences, it may be asserted, also encourage or channelize delinquency. Influences of a very concrete kind can probably be attributed to many of the "agencies" which have accompanied the process of urbanization. For example, poolrooms, penny arcades, bars, juke "joints," cheap theaters, corner hangouts, filling stations, dance halls, and stores selling pornography are probably instrumental not only in transmitting the delinquent subculture but also in giving immediate impetus to criminal behavior.[36]

Even though it is entirely possible that criticism of commercialized recreation may derive from a "moralistic" rejection of what appear to some people to be unsavory establishments, the evidence would seem to indicate that some more than the moralism of do-gooders is involved.

In the Gluecks' study of delinquency in Boston, the delinquent group as compared to the non-delinquent group showed a greater incidence of participation in these kinds of recreation.[37] The comparison demonstrated that in their search for adventure and excitement the delinquents in greater numbers frequented cheap dances, poolrooms, penny arcades and other commercialized recreations of a similar kind.

Even though a relationship between delinquency and "low-grade" recreation seems to exist the matter of causation is problematical. The fact that many youths make use of these commercialized "agencies" without becoming delinquent would suggest only a minor role for these influences in calling up delinquency. Yet it may not be inappropriate to infer that these commercialized establishments make their contribution, however minor or indirect, to delinquent behavior patterns. The fact that police are especially alerted to survey these establishments is probably testimony to their influence. Indeed, in some of our larger urban communities special details are assigned to commercialized recreations to prevent or to deal with delinquent activity as it may arise.

In the final analysis it may be assumed that commercialized recreation is only one of the many factors involved in the etiology of delinquency. The exact role of such "agencies" in contributing to delinquency is yet to be revealed. Yet insofar as these "agencies" are part of the "socialization context" of delinquents, they may well be conducive to delinquency. And this, it may be asserted, is so, despite the fact that many juveniles patronize commercialized recreations without yielding to these ostensible "snares" of delinquency. The fact that both delinquents and non-delinquents have mothers does not rule out the possibility that a specific mother-child relationship may be involved in encouraging delinquency. In short, the fact that studies have shown a high rate of participation in commercialized recreation for delinquents may suggest that such activity is part of the interrelated set of circumstances that elicit delinquency.

Conclusion

An understanding of delinquency in the community setting involves an examination of all the agencies and institutions of the community. Even though the need for a multi-factor approach is generally acknowledged, too often attempts are made to explain delinquency in terms of a single cause.

Among the cultural factors in contemporary America that are relevant to an understanding of delinquency are (1) social disorganization (2) cultural heterogeneity (3) internal migration (4) rapid technological change (5) urbanization and (6) America's "unique" traditions.

Within many American communities are to be found substandard areas characterized by inadequate housing, high mobility, heavy density, and general physical deterioration. Characterizing these deteriorated areas is a condition of social disorganization. Out of this social disorganization or "lack of moral order" arises delinquency. Even though delinquency is scattered throughout a community both geographically and socially, the highest incidence of delinquency appears to be associated with the social disorganization of the areas of deterioration.

Characteristic of these disorganized areas is the delinquent subculture. In part, the delinquency pattern of this subculture can be explained by the theories of "social disorganization," "culture conflict" and "illicit means." In addition to these theories of delinquent behavior it may be suggested that delinquent gangs, usually made up of "lower class" boys, engage in illegal behavior as a kind of "status protest." In order to enhance their feelings of worth in a middle class world that disparages them, they attack and debase middle class values.

Within the community may also be found what are sometimes called "agencies of moral risk." These include poolrooms, bars, cheap dance halls, juke joints, and other contemporary types of commercialized hangouts. Whether these agencies contribute to delinquency or not is problematical. Yet insofar as delinquents participate in "low-grade" recreation, it may be surmised that such recreation may have implications for delinquency.

Selected Bibliography

Harry E. Barnes & Negley K. Teeters, *New Horizons in Criminology* (Englewood Cliffs: Prentice-Hall, 1955). Encyclopedic coverage of problems of criminality; by far the most comprehensive text in the field.

Herbert A. Bloch & Frank T. Flynn, *Delinquency* (New York: Random House, 1956). A recent and comprehensive treatment of the contemporary juvenile offender. Covers the problems of juvenile delinquency from causation to prevention.

Lowell J. Carr, *Delinquency Control* (New York: Harper and Brothers, 1950). A systematic presentation of the context in which delinquency develops coupled with principles of effective prevention and control.

Albert Cohen, *Delinquent Boys* (Glencoe: The Free Press, 1955). A theoretical analysis of the nature of the delinquent sub-culture. Offers not only a description of gang life but seeks to explain it as well.

Mabel Elliot & Francis E. Merril, *Social Disorganization* (New York: Harper and Brothers, 1950). A standard text on problems of American society with an enlightening analysis of the concepts of "organization" and "disorganization."

Benjamin Fine, *1,000,000 Delinquents* (Cleveland and New York: The World Publishing Company, 1955). A study of American delinquency by the education editor of *The New York Times;* an attempt to explain the background of delinquency together with recommendations for its prevention.

Sheldon & Eleanor Glueck, *Unraveling Juvenile Delinquency*

(New York: The Commonwealth Fund, 1950). An eclectic approach to the analysis of the causes of juvenile delinquency. An excellent example of contemporary social investigation.

Saxon Graham, *American Culture* (New York: Harper and Brothers, 1957). An analysis of the development and present characteristics of American society. Contains an excellent treatment of the beliefs and values of the American people.

Rose H. Lee, *The City* (Chicago: J. B. Lippincott Company, 1955). An extensive treatment of urbanization in the world setting. Deals with the process of urbanization as it has affected older patterns of living.

Martin H. Neumyer, *Juvenile Delinquency in Modern Society* (New York: D. Van Nostrand Company, Inc., 1955). A critical appraisal of contemporary juvenile delinquency. Concerned particularly with delinquency in a changing society although other problems of delinquency are handled carefully and completely.

Clifford Shaw & Henry McKay, *Juvenile Delinquency and Urban Areas* (Chicago: The University of Chicago Press, 1942). A study of rates of delinquency in relation to "differential" characteristics of American cities; provides an excellent characterization of "delinquency areas."

Lynn T. Smith & C. A. McMahan, *The Sociology of Urban Life* (New York: The Dryden Press, 1951). A textbook with readings dealing with the nature and development of urban life. Covers both structure and process in urban America.

Donald Taft, *Criminology* (New York: The Macmillan Company, 1950). An elementary treatment of the problems of Criminology. Provides broad perspective for understanding criminal behavior.

Frederick Thrasher, *The Gang* (The University of Chicago Press, 1927). A "classic" study of 1,313 gangs in Chicago; contains a thorough description of Chicago gang life in the 1920's.

William F. Whyte, *Street Corner Society* (The University of Chicago Press, 1955). A provocative description and interpretation of a youthful gang in Boston.

Sidney J. Kaplan, Assistant Professor of Sociology at the University of Kentucky, attended graduate school at Boston University where he took his M.A. in Anthropology and Sociology, and at the State College of Washington receiving the

Ph.D. in 1953; is presently teaching criminology and is actively engaged in legal and delinquency research. His publications include "Criminal Responsibility," *Kentucky Law Journal,* Vol. XLV, Winter 1956-1957, No. 2; "Barriers to the Establishment of a Deterministic Criminal Law," *Kentucky Law Journal,* to be published in the spring of 1958.

CHAPTER 7.

THE SCHOOL AS A FACTOR

P. M. SMITH
Central Michigan College

The school is of growing importance in relation to juvenile delinquency for several reasons. (1) It is the one agency, outside of the home, which is in close contact with most children over the longest period of time. (2) It is responsible for teaching the child how to get along with his fellows, as part of the process of socialization. (3) It is an important means of social control in that it indoctrinates the child in relation to the mores of our culture. (4) It explains the nature of the duties as well as the privileges of citizenship in a democracy. (5) It provides opportunities for recreation and other leisure-time activities under competent supervision. (6) It is in a strategic position to identify children with behavior problems and to refer them to guidance clinics for treatment. (7) It can establish contact with a variety of community agencies designed to contribute to the physical, social, and spiritual welfare of the child whenever such supplementary aid is designated. On the other hand, there is abundant evidence to the effect that the schools themselves are a factor in delinquency causation by reason of their failure to make adequate provision for children who deviate from the norm, whether physically, mentally, emotionally, or socially.

The School as an Agency of Social Control[1]

The American public school especially is believed to be a powerful means of social control because of its traditional teaching functions and its success in reaching most children at a time when they seem most responsive to indoctrination. Parents expect the school to prepare the child for citizenship in a democracy through instruction pertaining to the philosophy, objectives, and practices of our democratic way of life. Parents expect the school to transform the child from a rebellious individualist who manifests little respect for authority at the outset into a socialized conformist who fits into a pattern of regimented behavior which constantly emphasizes the necessity for "law and order." Furthermore, many parents seem convinced that the authoritarian atmosphere of the classroom will prove much more effective in this respect than the comparatively permissive home environment because the child usually stands in awe of persons in positions of authority outside the home who have the right to maintain discipline at all times.

As an agency of social control, the school explains to the child why it is necessary to do things in an orderly manner and in conformity to social custom. By demonstrating the wisdom of sacrificing one's personal interests at times in order to promote the welfare of the larger social group, the school likewise teaches the child a valuable lesson in group loyalty that is essential to effective social control. The child learns in school why "liberty" is ideally interpreted as "obedience to law" and why a democracy requires law-abiding citizens who are motivated by an honest desire to do what is right for its orderly functioning. The school furnishes inducements, through a system of rewards and punishments, which are intended to encourage the child to form behavior patterns and acquire the knowledge and skills that will enable him to become a useful member of society. By bringing the child into association with individuals representing different ethnic, religious, and socioeconomic groups the school has an excellent opportunity to teach the child to respect persons whose backgrounds may be unlike his own, in the spirit of tolerance and understanding. On various special occasions and in a wide variety of ways, the public school likewise can impress upon the child the idea that proper respect for ethical and moral values is basic to the character development of citizens of a democracy.

On the other hand, the sectarian private school, in theory at least, is an even stronger force for social control by reason of its essential religious emphasis. It differs from the public school in its underlying motivation, of course, because it is concerned primarily with the training of adherents of a particular faith, denomination, or sect. The school which is operated under sectarian auspices holds that religion is essential in the life of the child, that religious instruction plays an important role in any sound educational program, and that good citizenship is one of the results of adequate religious training during childhood.

Because of limitations imposed by the principle of separation of church and state under our form of government, the public school may not engage directly in religious indoctrination. Nevertheless, it does apply moral and spiritual teachings in terms of codes of conduct to which both pupils and teachers are expected to conform as rules for right living in the world of which the school is part.

The School as an Agency Contributing to Delinquency

Close observers of the American educational scene are among the first to admit that in some instances the school actually contributes to delinquent behavior on the part of youth.[2] Some of the factors thought to be responsible for this state of affairs are enumerated below. Although our public schools are dedicated in theory to the principle of individualized instruction, in practice the great majority of them are characterized by a high degree of regimentation. Such a situation certainly is not conducive to the kind of atmosphere in which the educative process will be most effective in relation to problem children especially.

Among the factors bringing about conditions contributing to delinquency, directly or indirectly, are the following:

(1) a severe shortage of adequately trained teachers, particularly at the elementary level (and in the near future at the secondary level).

(2) Serious deterioration of physical plant, equipment, and facilities, resulting in the use of obsolete, unsafe, and overcrowded classrooms in many areas.

(3) Inadequate provision for work, study, recitation, and play space to meet the requirements of an expanding school population.

(4) The need for handling large groups of children with a

minimum of disorder so as to conserve the time and energy of teachers and administrative personnel, with little individual attention.

(5) An almost slavish adherence to outmoded conceptions of the meaning of "education," marked by undue emphasis on the value of conformity to custom, irrespective of the individual needs of the child.

(6) The tendency to measure educational progress in terms of the performance of the so-called "average" child, a procedure which places the "deviant"—especially if he be both scholastically retarded and antisocial—at a serious disadvantage because of the harmful effects upon personality of the competitive grading system.[3]

(7) Failure to adapt the curricula to the practical needs of youth in a fast-changing technological age.

(8) "Regressive" rather than "progressive" education in general, with the schools so much concerned about preserving the status quo and the revered traditions of the past that many of them have neither the inclination nor the opportunity to experiment with new ideas.

(9) Racial and religious prejudice and discrimination.

(10) Preferential treatment of children from upper-class families as compared to those who come from the "wrong side of the tracks."

(11) Overemphasis on symbols of status among high school youth, resulting in the formation of cliques and other status groupings based largely upon the occupational and income levels of parents.

(12) False standards of value among school children, based upon money and the things that money can buy, with a tendency to disregard standards based upon personal integrity, fidelity to religious teachings, and respect for human personality.

(13) Unhappy interpersonal and intergroup situations within the schools, which involve discord and strife, such as those stemming from efforts to desegregate the races, or from failure to do so.

(14) Biased teachers who, consciously or unconsciously, reveal their prejudices against minority groups by careless, unwise, and untrue statements in the classroom.[4]

(15) Teachers who lack the moral courage to take a stand

on controversial issues of concern to teen-age youth because
of fear of antagonizing influential persons in the community
who are in a position to bring pressure to bear upon school
board members and school administrators.

(16) Failure of the school system to cooperate in leisure-
time activities for youth by providing trained leaders and
adequate recreational facilities, under an arrangement whereby the school building would function as a community center
at night and supervised playgrounds would be available for
all children of the neighborhood during the summer months.

(17) Lack of professional counseling services for many students who are most in need of them.

(18) Inability of numerous school systems to provide visiting
teacher (school social worker) services.

(19) Relative scarcity of child guidance (behavior) clinics
operated in conjunction with school systems, particularly in
more sparsely settled areas.

(20) Acute shortage of full-time psychologists, psychiatrists,
and psychiatric social workers available for consultation with
children referred to clinics by school authorities.

(21) Inability of the schools to meet the problems of deviant
children in general because of their need to center attention
upon "normal" children who form the bulk of the school
population.

(22) Unsolved adjustment problems of children resulting
from mass migration of families to new industrial communities and from the seasonal migration of agricultural workers.

(23) Critical problems faced by schools located in areas of
unprecedented industrial growth which are so overcrowded
as to deprive the children of the educational and related services to which they are entitled.

(24) Inferior schools in backward rural areas where "education" is definitely a part-time proposition.

(25) Failure to enforce school attendance laws, particularly
in areas most in need of such enforcement from the standpoint of providing equality of educational opportunity for
underprivileged youth.

(26) Inadequate facilities for vocational training.

(27) Lack of satisfactory school health services and of special services in general in many areas for "exceptional" children.

The school contributes to delinquency not only because it provides an environment where large groups of children are thrown together without close supervision but because it creates frustrating situations with which some individuals cannot cope. If persistent truancy be "the kindergarten of crime," then scholastic retardation is the "father of truancy," rather than the reverse. The child who faces constant defeat in the classroom seems destined to seek emotional satisfaction elsewhere. One tragic figure in the school is the retarded child who tries to compensate for scholastic retardation by resorting to anti-social behavior in order to attract attention. In this connection, Neumeyer states that "for many maladjusted and potentially delinquent children going to school is just another frustrating and unhappy experience,"[5] while Carr insists that "a school program unsuited to a child's capacities, or a teacher herself not adjusted, may contribute very definitely to delinquency."[6]

Behavior Problems in the Classroom

Although most children who have behavior problems in the classroom are not classified as "delinquent," it is nevertheless true that those who develop patterns of delinquent conduct reveal symptoms of serious maladjustment at a relatively early age. Thus, the responsibility of the classroom teacher for identifying problem children in the "predelinquent" stage is something that cannot be delegated to anyone else in the school system. For it is in the classroom setting that the observant teacher can detect various symptoms of pupil maladjustment, and her suspicions may be confirmed by repeated observations under controlled conditions. Since all teachers are concerned about the problem of "discipline," any evidence to the effect that a child fails to respond to appeals for obedience because of physical, mental, or emotional abnormalities should be a matter of interest to all staff members. Through the study of various case histories of problem children, teachers can learn how to deal with others who may have similar problems in the future. Especially is this the case where visiting teacher services are available.

During the past few years a great deal of attention has been devoted to discussions of disciplinary problems of the schools. So serious is the situation in many localities that new teachers often designate "discipline" as the problem of greatest concern to them. While it is true that schools of the "blackboard Jungle" type exist chiefly in the minds of fiction writers, doubtless there are enough of them in large urban-industrial areas to create a real problem both for present and future teachers.

According to Elizabeth R. Roby, a former guidance counselor who served in 13 different New York City schools at various times, little can be done with some of the more confirmed trouble-makers of junior high school age. She points out that every public school at the present time has its quota of children who constitute a menace to pupils and teachers alike. Actively and daily interfering with the learning of other children, they are, she maintains, a major source of the breakdown or transfer to other school systems of some of our most capable teachers. They are also, Miss Roby holds, "the cause of delinquency and crime on the part of suggestible and weak-willed boys and girls who, without this influence, could probably manage to keep out of trouble."[7]

The illustrative case cited above may not be typical of conditions in general, but it does call attention to the dilemma in which many classroom teachers find themselves. Compulsory school atendance laws designed for the benefit of children have in some instances resulted in the retention of chronic trouble-makers in classes where they have not the slightest interest in the subject matter studied. As a result, too much of the teacher's time is consumed by futile efforts to maintain discipline, while she is forced to neglect many of her pupils who may be desperately in need of special attention and who would respond to any attempts to help them.

It is significant that various studies of delinquent children are in complete agreement to the effect that a record of habitual truancy from school is one of the factors most often found in the case histories. Personality maladjustment, chronic truancy, scholastic retardation, misbehavior in the classroom, and a later record of juvenile delinquency are interrelated factors. The Gluecks, for example, found that more than nine-tenths of their sample of delinquent boys "seriously or persistently misbehaved in school," in contrast to less than two-tenths of their sample of nondelinquents, and that "truancy was the most uniform manifestation of maladjustment among the 478 delinquents who misbehaved in school."[8] With respect to retardation, they noted that "twice as many delinquents as nondelinquents were two or more years behind the proper grade for their age."[9] From his study at the Passaic Children's Bureau, Kvaraceus concluded that fully one-third of the delinquents referred for treatment had a previous record of truancy, with a truancy rate five times that of the general school population,[10] while they were deficient in scholarship, almost without exception.[11]

Inability of the average teacher to distinguish clearly between the different types of delinquents makes it more difficult for her to understand the true significance of their behavior in the classroom and to take appropriate remedial action. All too often does the busy teacher make the mistake of thinking that the overt misbehavior of the child is the only thing that needs to be corrected. As a matter of fact, such misconduct may be a symptom of deep-seated personality maladjustment whose underlying causes can be found only with the help of a psychiatrist. By confusing what are actually surface symptoms with the real problem itself an untrained person is quite apt to intensify the child's frustrations and thus tempt him to commit other offenses during the process of treatment.

It is noteworthy, in the foregoing connection, that Bertram M. Beck classifies delinquents into "social," "asocial," "neurotic," "organic," and "accidental" types.[12] Doubtless these categories overlap somewhat when applied to certain cases. The social delinquent tends to mingle with the crowd, especially with the "gang," and to engage in aggressive behavior. The asocial delinquent is inclined to keep to himself and he seems incapable of expressing genuine affection or of showing loyalty to the group. The neurotic delinquent, troubled by inner conflicts, is more often found in middle and upper class families which lack warm and satisfying family relationships. The organic delinquent becomes involved in antisocial behavior because of damage to his brain, while the accidental delinquent may be a victim of too rigid disciplinary standards which fail to allow for deviation from the norm, as in the case of sex behavior which children often indulge in for experimental reasons.

Teachers' Attitudes Toward Behavior Problems

In order to learn the views of classroom teachers on such topics as the causes, types, and cures of pupil misbehavior, the

National Education Association made an opinion survey which included a total of 4,270 respondents. The results of the poll show a majority of the teachers holding that, although students' behavior is not so bad as it has been portrayed in the press, movies, and radio, and although their current students are either exceptionally or reasonably well-behaved, there have been rises in impertinence, discourtesy, drinking, stealing, failure to do homework, cheating, and sex offenses during the past decade or two. The average teacher believes, moreover, that one in every ten teachers is likely, before his forty-second birthday, to be struck by a pupil. The specific causes for misbehavior listed by the teachers include: irresponsible parents, unsatisfactory home conditions, lack of parental supervision due to mother working, and lack of training or experience in moral values. "They are primarily social, economic, civic, and moral problems with which the community as a whole must deal," says the report, which in general emphasizes the total community responsibility for the cultural conditions under which our children live.[13]

It is significant that the survey report stressed the importance of the larger social and economic implications of children's behavior problems and that it recognized the responsibility of the whole community for helping to find a constructive solution. Too often do teachers tend to think in terms of the individual alone rather than in terms of the conditioning factors in the environment which may have caused the child to develop antisocial behavior patterns.

The attitudes of the teachers concerning the use of corporal punishment, as revealed by the survey, probably reflect both the influence of time-honored custom and the fears of many persons that they would otherwise be unable to maintain discipline in the classroom. It is noteworthy that 77 per cent of the respondents thought that corporal punishment should be permitted in the elementary schools; 62.5 per cent believed that it should be allowed in the junior high schools; and 37.4 per cent were of the opinion that it should be used in the senior high schools. Although in three-fourths of all the schools contacted, some person, usually the principal, had authority to administer corporal punishment when it was deemed necessary, classroom teachers were generally restricted in this respect. Less than one-third of the urban teachers had such authority, in contrast to the rural teachers of whom almost two-thirds were permitted to use corporal punishment.

Doubtless there have been growing demands for the use of "tough" disciplinary measures to a greater extent than heretofore in some of the more difficult schools in large urban areas. But there is no scientific proof to the effect that corporal punishment will solve behavior problems, in the long run, because it deals with symptoms rather than with underlying causes.

Many teachers are seriously handicapped when dealing with problem children because of failure to understand the relative importance of different types of misconduct. Wickman's study of teachers' attitudes in the schools of Cleveland and Minneapolis indicated that this seemed to be the case. When the judgments of the teachers and of thirty mental hygienists regarding the relative seriousness of 50 behavior problems were compared, it was found that their views in general were far apart.[14] For example, teachers rated the following as the most serious problems: heterosexual activity, stealing, masturbation, obscene notes and talk, untruthfulness, truancy, impertinence and defiance, cruelty and bullying, cheating, and destroying school materials. In marked contrast, the mental hygienists listed as the ten most serious problems unsocialness, suspiciousness, being unhappy and depressed, resentfulness, fearfulness, cruelty and bullying, being easily discouraged, being suggestible, being overcritical of others, and sensitiveness. Whereas "masturbation" was ranked third in importance by the teachers, it was the forty-first item on the mental hygienists' list.

Teachers in general tended to regard the aggressive, defiant, trouble-maker as their biggest problem, while underestimating the difficulties facing the shy, fearful, and suspicious child. Without doubt, teachers' views are greatly influenced by a conviction that any pupil who defies authority in the classroom is guilty of committing a most serious offense because of its disruptive effect in relation to the entire school.

A more recent study of the views of high school teachers, by George A. W. Stouffer, Jr., yielded results much similar to those of Wickman. According to Stouffer, the more extrovertive reactions of pupils, such as impertinence, destroying school material, disobedience, interest in the opposite sex, interrupting, profanity, and inquisitiveness, are the ones felt (by high school teachers) to be the most serious and important. On the other hand, these behaviors, while disturbing to the order and dignity of the classroom, are not considered by clinicians to be of appreciable significance in influencing the future development of the child. Such withdrawing tendencies as unsocialness, fearfulness, shyness, sensitiveness, suspiciousness, and dreaminess, which clinicians view as possibly symptomatic of serious maladjustment, were rated as relatively unimportant by the secondary-school teachers.[15]

Whether or not the clinicians would take a more serious view of the situation if they had to exchange places with the classroom teachers is open to speculation. Certain it is that when the teacher faces a problem situation which requires quick and drastic action, in order to maintain order for the sake of her pupils who are not causing any difficulty, she will be inclined to make use of those resources which are immediately at her command. This means that psychologically approved and clinically tested methods of administering "discipline" may be shelved temporarily in favor of more convenient and less effective short-cuts. In schools where adequate clinical services are available, such problems can be handled through proper channels, with every effort being made to get to the heart of the matter and to adopt measures which will be rehabilitative rather than punitive. But in the typical classroom situation the teacher is responsible for the maintenance of order without the help of other personnel.

The Problem of the Emotionally Maladjusted Teacher

One of the principal sources of trouble in the classroom is the teacher who herself is poorly adjusted to her surroundings. Lack of interest in her work, dislike of children, and frustrations in her private life contribute to the teacher's inability to create the kind of emotional climate in which her pupils can do their best work. Suspicion, prejudice, and hostility seem contagious in that they spread from teacher to pupils and from pupil to pupil. No person is more important in fostering an atmosphere of tolerance, good-will, and sympathetic understanding than the classroom teacher, for she is the key figure in the teaching-learning situation. It is indeed tragic when the teacher is subject to periodic outbursts of anger during which she persists in trying to humiliate any child who has seriously annoyed her. So long as the teacher lacks poise and self-control, it seems unreasonable for her to expect the obedience and cooperation of her students.

In connection with the foregoing, Gilbert J. Rich contends that important limitations are placed upon the effectiveness of the schools in preparing children for life. The poor mental hygiene of teachers, says Rich, is the most noticeable of these limitations. He hastens to point out that he does not mean to imply that teachers are in any great numbers mentally ill, but rather that they do tend to be poorly adjusted. Teachers are often far more concerned with their own dignity than with how their discipline may affect the child. For, they live and work in circumstances rendering them more sensitive to the attitudes of school administrators and school boards than to the emotional well-being of their pupils. Rich also stresses the fact that little effort is being made today to select teachers on the basis of good emotional adjustment.[16]

When one considers the handicaps under which many teachers labor, it is not at all surprising that some of them become more maladjusted the longer they teach. Excessive pupil loads, inadequate salaries, extracurricular duties, family responsibilities, and a wide variety of community pressures upon the school may contribute to the teacher's feeling of insecurity. Because of the nature of her profession, in small communities especially her conduct outside of school is subjected to close scrutiny by the townspeople. She is expected always to be active in the work of community organizations, including religious, civic, and educational groups, so as to help promote better understanding between the school and the constituency that it serves. Faithful in her attendance at P.T.A. meetings, she may become disillusioned when she learns that many parents establish social contacts with the teachers in order to obtain special privileges for their children rather than to help make the work of the teachers easier. In addition to her regular duties, she is often expected to attend conferences, serve on various committees, attend summer school, and find time (and money) for travel. As a result of the many distractions to which she is subjected, the average teacher may find it difficult to maintain a healthy attitude toward her work in the classroom, especially when behavior problems arise.

School boards and school administrators should make every effort, of course, to relieve the classroom teacher of extraneous assignments which interfere with her opportunity to get sufficient rest and relaxation. For teaching today is an emotional strain, and a teacher who is the victim of physical fatigue will find it difficult to enter the classroom in a serene state of mind.

The Emotionally Disturbed Child

It is unfortunate that so many teachers are handicapped in their work by the presence in the classroom of children who suffer from emotional disorders which call for special treatment. If the teacher does not have access to diagnostic and remedial facilities when the need arises, this means that she must do her best to help the child until such aid is finally forthcoming. Meanwhile, she may be forced to neglect other children who need her assistance, in order to prevent the child who is emotionally upset from becoming a chronic behavior problem involving aggressive reactions which threaten the security of others.

The observant teacher can learn to recognize symptoms of maladjustment and to identify children with some types of emotional disturbances. In this way she can play an important role in helping to detect signs of predelinquency. The predelinquent, of course, is a child who will probably become habitually delinquent in his behavior unless he receives corrective treatment. Clinical services for such a child are usually much more effective if treatment is begun before the pattern of antisocial behavior has become well established. Only through the wholehearted cooperation of the classroom teachers can members of the clinical staff, to whom referrals are made, do their best work in relation to the children who are known to be suffering from emotional disturbances.

Darrel J. Mase offers some constructive suggestions in regard to the establishment of special programs designed for the benefit of emotionally insecure and disturbed children, which seem to cover the essential factors: "(1) Early detection and prevention should be the goal of all public school programs. (2) Good mental health programs are good prevention programs. (3) Children will be emotionally insecure and disturbed; the degree of such disturbance should be our concern. (4) The ability to communicate with children is basic to being able to help them. (5) Emotionally disturbed children deserve specialized programs in order to permit them to develop healthy personalities. (6) Specialized personnel must be available to assist teachers and parents. (7) Whenever possible, the program for emotionally disturbed children should be a part of, rather than apart from, the general educational program. (8) Causes for unacceptable behavior patterns must be treated rather than the behavior. (9) Society's treatment of children is generally a contributing factor to severe emotional disturbances."[17]

It is a serious mistake for the teacher to underestimate the importance of children's fears, however trivial they may seem to be at first glance. In many instances, if the nature of these fears is brought to light, a clue to the child's personality disorder may be provided and proper measures can be adopted to effect a solution to his problem without unnecessary delay. The emotionally disturbed child is often a frightened child in need of emotional reassurance, affection, and security. Anything that the teacher can do through casual conversations with him to learn the nature of his fears and to help him to overcome them is bound to be a step in the right direction. Children's worries are real worries to them, and they often need the helping hand of the teacher to give them confidence, especially when their own parents do not understand how to relieve their children's anxieties.

The Problem of Truancy

If it be true that truancy is "the kindergarten of crime," then the school has a golden opportunity to identify future delinquents at an early age and to provide them with adequate preventive and remedial services.[18] Children who have established a pattern of truancy are usually in need of professional help because truancy itself is merely a symptom of personality maladjustment that lies beneath the surface. Many well-intentioned, but unthinking, persons who have a sincere desire to help the truant fail to realize that he has his own reasons for wanting to remain away from school, reasons that to him are quite important. By returning the child to the classroom, against his will, and before the causes of his truancy are known, the school authorities may add to his frustrations and unwittingly encourage him to repeat his action.

Children who are getting along well in school, who make

good progress both scholastically and socially, seldom become truants. It is usually the child who is unhappy in the school situation who finds an escape from his troubles temporarily by becoming a truant. The task of the teacher, the school social worker (visiting teacher), and the clinician is to discover what factors in the child's school environment contributed to his truancy and to try to remedy the situation as soon as possible, particularly if the truant has become involved in delinquent behavior. As has already been noted in this chapter, the great majority of juvenile delinquents have truanted from school repeatedly and their chronic dislike of school was found to be correlated with scholastic retardation.

It is well to note that the problem of the child with a record of truancy must not be confused with that of the child who is involved only in incidental or "accidental" truancy. Certain it is that the great majority of all children have stayed away from school, at one time or another, without the permission of either their parents or their teachers. Younger children sometimes "play hooky" on an experimental basis in their search for new experiences. Occasionally, a sensitive child who is late for school may remain out of class because of fear of censure, ridicule, or punishment for being tardy. The duty of the parents in such cases is to try to view the child's shortcomings in a reasonably objective manner, realizing that the detection of an inclination toward truancy at an early age allows ample time for the application of corrective measures.[19]

In some instances collusion is involved, as when parents request that the child be excused from attending classes—allegedly because of illness—so that he can help with the work at home, run errands, or perform similar tasks. Since the child is aware of his parents' deceit in this respect, he may soon be asking for excuses when he remains away from school on his own accord. When teachers become suspicious regarding the true reasons for repeated absences they can ask that the attendance officer check on the situation, they can consult with the visiting teacher, or they themselves can visit the children's homes. The important fact to remember is that any prolonged absence from school without a satisfactory explanation indicates a breakdown of parental supervision and control which needs to be investigated for the good of the child.

Chronic Absenteeism

A much more serious problem than truancy is that of chronic absenteeism on the part of numerous children who ought to be in school but who are prevented from attending for various reasons. In many instances the education of these children is periodically interrupted for long intervals, and in other cases their attendance is only intermittent at best. Some of them seldom, if ever, have a sustained opportunity to obtain an education under conditions which afford a reasonable degree of continuity. As a result, many thousands of our children are functionally illiterate and incapable of qualifying, later on, for anything other than unskilled and menial types of jobs. The youth with no education has little or no choice of an occupation. When deprived of a chance for employment on that account, it is easy for him to follow the line of least resistance and drift into a career of delinquency and crime.

Some of the factors responsible for this situation are the following: (1) periodic or seasonal migration of many families in their search for employment; (2) child labor; (3) failure to enforce school attendance laws among some families in urban slum areas; (4) failure to enforce attendance laws in some of the more backward and isolated rural areas; (5) non-enforcement of attendance laws among Negroes especially in parts of the rural South; (6) the need for the child's help at home because of a combination of parental illness, unemployment, and extreme poverty. It is perhaps surprising to note that, in a recent typical year, the greatest single cause of children's absences from schools in the city of Detroit was lack of shoes and clothing,[20] an evidence of poverty.

At the secondary-school level the youth who is repeatedly absent usually decides to drop out of school permanently when he reaches the age when his attendance is no longer required. As a matter of fact, however, many teen-agers annually are permitted to quit school, in violation of attendance laws, because the authorities find it impossible to enforce the laws without the cooperation of the parents. In those instances where enforcement officers decide to take drastic action in relation to obstinate parents the results may not be satisfactory because of the resentment which may be aroused. What seems fairly certain in many situations of this type is that disorganized families residing in socially disadvantaged areas often are not particularly interested in seeing that their teen-age children are in school.

High school drop-outs represent an enormous social loss in that numerous young people will never be able to qualify for better-class jobs nor to matriculate at college. Doubtless, many who quit school are getting the wrong kind of education since they must study subjects which do not interest them and which lack practical value. The youth who remains in high school under compulsion, of course, sometimes develops into a serious disciplinary problem in the classroom, thus adding to the teacher's troubles. Unless suitable revisions are made in some of our high school curricula, so as to arouse the interest and meet the needs of more of our youth, we may face an even more serious problem in this respect in the future.

A study of some 31,000 pupils in 441 public high schools outside of Detroit showed that fully one-third of those who enter Michigan high schools fail to finish.[21] The national average is over 12 per cent a year, or about 50 per cent over a four-year period.

Suspension of Pupils for Misbehavior

School administrators are reluctant to suspend pupils for misconduct and generally do so only as a last resort short of summary expulsion. Nevertheless, refusal to admit students to classes for a stated period of time is sometimes an effective disciplinary measure because of the extra work which they must do to catch up with their classmates. As might be expected, the bulk of the suspensions, as well as the expulsions, involve students of high school age. Most of them have previously been guilty of violating school regulations, of breaking various rules, and of creating disorder in the classroom. Some of the expelled pupils may make a fairly good adjustment after being transferred to other schools. Others are sometimes committed to institutions where they can receive special treatment. Yet the very fact that suspensions become necessary is itself an indication that the schools are identifying problem cases too late in some instances to do much good. Whenever the danger exists that an unruly teen-ager will seriously interfere with the school program, it becomes necessary for the school officials to take positive action in this way so as to safeguard the interests both of the classrom teacher and of the other children. The physical punishment of adolescents is not the answer to this problem.

As an indication of the trend in this respect, some figures compiled by the Detroit public schools seem interesting. Between 1950 and 1955-56 pupil suspensions increased by 154 per cent, while school enrollment rose by only 19 per cent.[22] A breakdown of 748 cases of suspension showed the following numerical distribution of reasons for the disciplinary action: (1) chronic misconduct, 190; (2) fighting or injuring other pupils, 126; (3) insolent to teacher, 100; (4) stealing, 61; (5) insubordinate to teacher, 60; (6) threatening other pupils, 35; (7) extortion from other pupils, 32; (8) skipping classes, 31; (9) smoking, 30; (10) striking a teacher, 27; (11) immoral behavior, 27; (12) inability to function in school, 19; (13) carrying dangerous weapons, 10. Herbert D. Sullivan, Detroit school attendance director, stated that in 1950 "striking a teacher" apparently occurred so seldom that it was not listed as a separate category, whereas in 1955-56 a total of 27 suspensions were ascribed to such an offense. Strangely enough, it was reported that suspensions began as early as the kindergarten and that one beginner was actually thrown out of school. Such a case is so exceptional, of course, as to attract considerable attention.

The Mentally Retarded Child

A mentally retarded child who is addicted to antisocial behavior in the school setting always requires treatment of a special type. In the first place, such a child is classified as "exceptional," and it is assumed that special provisions have been made for his benefit so that he may learn what he can at his own particular pace. In the second place, every opportunity must be afforded him to make social contacts under conditions which are as conducive to personality development as those designed for children of normal mentality.

Yet the social environment of the retarded child must be "controlled" for his own protection and peace of mind because he cannot compete on equal terms with children who are much brighter than he. What he needs is a chance to prove that he can successfully perform socially useful tasks and thus win the respect and approval of both his teacher and his fellow students. The tasks assigned him should, of course, be suited to his ability to complete them. But as rapidly as he shows improvement, work of somewhat greater difficulty can be provided to serve as an incentive for greater effort, always with the idea in mind that he is trying to improve on his past performance. Should he be placed in a competitive situation with which he is unable to cope, however, the result might be disastrous because it would only add up to one more failure and thus cause him to lose confidence in himself. According to Ann Miller, "an element common in the lives of all these children is failure, and it is generally conceded that failure underlies much of the antisocial behavior which the mentally retarded exhibit."[23]

Some of the mentally retarded children face peculiar hazards by reason of the fact that brighter children with antisocial tendencies can be expected to try to exploit them or to annoy them. Sometimes they are teased and goaded until they commit some overt act of delinquency. Some are highly suggestible and easily led into situations which may endanger their safety or harm their morals. When one considers how much harder the mentally handicapped child must work to reach the same goal that a normal child can attain with ease, it is understandable why at times he is a pathetic figure in a school world that to him may seem a nightmare. Since he cannot ordinarily be expected to understand the true nature and consequences of certain antisocial acts in which he may become involved, he needs careful supervision by teachers with much patience and understanding.

Social Class Differentials in Pupil Misbehavior

A number of careful studies, such as those by Davis, Warner, Hollingshead, and others, indicate that social class distinctions are quite generally carried over into the school itself.[24] Not only do children from different social classes tend to react in special ways to the school situation but teachers themselves react in special ways to children from different social classes. For example, teachers quite often show favoritism for children from middle and upper class families. Preferential treatment on the basis of social class aggravates the behavior problems of lower class children because they tend to retaliate against the teacher to show their resentment.

A major source of the difficulty is that many teachers have

a conception of the nature and role of the "ideal" pupil which is unrealistic. The standard of "good" behavior which the teacher with a middle class background so often accepts may turn out to be more of a distortion than an accurate representation when applied to lower class children. Goodness or badness depends in large measure upon the social milieu of the particular child because standards of conduct are influenced by the circumstances in which people find themselves and to which they are trying to adjust. In other words, each social class may have motivations, standards, and practices which, in some respects, are peculiar to itself, and the teacher who ignores these differences may be destined for serious trouble.

An interesting study by Howard S. Becker illustrates some of the effects of factors related to social-class upon classroom situations. His investigation was conducted in the city of Chicago, and interviews with classroom teachers were a fruitful source of information concerning the attitudes and habits of children from different social classes. Although teachers in general found middle-class children the easiest to work with and the most responsive to the school program, they did have trouble with some of the upper-class pupils. Pupils of the upper group were considered hard to manage in some respects, and were often designated "spoiled," "overindulged," or "neurotic," for they do not adopt the submissive manner many teachers deem appropriate to the role of child. As one interviewee, speaking of this group, said: ". . . The children are more pampered and, as we say, more inclined to run the school for themselves. . . . The children are not used to taking orders at home and naturally they won't take them at school either. . . ."[25]

Becker found, also, that children from the "better" neighborhoods were regarded as deficient in the important moral traits of politeness and respect for their elders. According to one teacher: "They're not used to doing work at home. . . . They're used to having things done for them. . . . If they drop a piece of cloth on the floor, they'll just let it lay; they wouldn't think of bending over to pick it up. . . ."[26]

But it is the lower-class children who form the biggest problem group because their standards of value and deportment often seem so far out of line when compared with the teachers' middle-class expectations. With regard to slum children, Becker observed that the middle-class teacher was disgusted and depressed by their physical appearance and condition. These children, moreover, are more apt than those of the other groups to get into trouble with law enforcement officials. Their early (by middle-class standards) sexual maturity is quite upsetting to the teacher: ". . . Some of them are not very nice girls. One girl in my class I've had two years now. She makes her money on the side as a prostitute. She's had several children . . . This was a disturbing influence on the rest of the class."[27]

Schools in the underprivileged areas of some of our largest cities usually experience difficulty in attracting and retaining good teachers. Serious disciplinary problems, unpleasant working conditions, and large numbers of slow learners combine to make the teacher's lot in general an unhappy one. Some teachers maintain that many of these children do not realize the value of education, that they lack the desire to improve themselves, and that, consequently, they do not care much about school and schoolwork—which, of course, makes it very difficult to teach them. As one teacher put it: ". . . We have a pretty tough element there, a bunch of bums, I might as well say it. That kind you can't teach at all. They don't want to be there at all, and so you can't do anything with them."[28]

In view of the environmental background of the typical slum child, however, it seems hardly surprising that so many of them regard the school program with indifference. What incentive to learn does the child have when his own parents, in so many cases, take no interest in his academic progress whatever? In families where there is extreme poverty the older children are expected to leave school and find jobs as early as the law allows. As a result, disciplinary problems in the schools where such children attend become more serious than in schools located in middle-class neighborhoods.

Social Class Differences and Scholastic Rewards

Various studies of the grades received by pupils in the public schools in the past have shown that lower-class children, on the average, do work of poorer quality than middle-class and upper-class children. Not only do lower-class children lack the necessary incentives to do their best work, in numerous instances, but they also are the victims of unfair treatment on the part of prejudiced teachers. When children quite consistently receive lower marks than they think they have earned, they tend to become discouraged and to lose interest in their studies. A lower-class child who becomes convinced that the teacher is guilty of favoritism in this respect may express his hostility through acts of aggression both in the classroom and on the playground.

An interesting study by Stephen Abrahamson revealed the existence of statistically significant differentials in students' grades on the basis of social class.[29] His investigation was confined to six schools, one from each of six different communities, including both urban and suburban types. His sample consisted of 705 students in the seventh, eighth, and ninth grades. In order to determine their social status he used Warner's Index of Social Characteristics. While the difficulty of classifying families on the basis of clearly-defined social status groupings must be frankly recognized, it seems reasonable to believe that Abrahamson's categories afford a fair picture of the situation with reference to social class.

After tabulating the grades on the basis of the students' social class backgrounds, Abrahamson made the following observation: The evidence was overwhelming that students in the upper-middle and lower-middle classes received much more than their proportionate share of the high grades and much less than their proportionate share of the low grades. The exact opposite was true for students in the upper-lower and lower-lower classes.[30]

The contrast in distribution of grades, of course, was most striking when comparisons were made for the upper-middle and lower-lower classes. The former received 343 A's and B's and only 19 D's and E's. The latter received 48 A's and B's and 136 D's and E's. It was further noted that "there was a marked tendency for the schools with the greater percentage of upper-middle class students to give out more high grades and fewer low grades than the schools with the smallest percentages of upper-middle class students."

What might be considered a reflection upon the sincerity and integrity of certain teachers are the evidences of partiality which this study brought to light. For, according to the teachers themselves, there existed a tendency for students from the higher social-class backgrounds to be favored. Thus, the teachers indicated that these students were chosen more frequently for the little favors—such as running errands, monitoring, committee chairman, and the like—than were the other children. On the other hand, according to the ratings of the teachers, there was a tendency for students of lower-class backgrounds to receive much more than their share of disciplinary treatment.[31]

Other indications of discrimination against lower-class students may seem even more disturbing from the standpoint of conscientious teachers who are trying hard to find a solution to behavior problems. For example, in three of the six schools the social-class backgrounds of the winners of the much-coveted American Legion Award for the last three years were investigated. Fourteen of the eighteen winners were of upper-middle class background, and the other four were of lower-middle class background. No upper-lower or lower-lower class students were included among the winners.[32] In all of the schools, upper-middle and lower-middle class students held almost all of the offices, while no lower-lower class student held an office.[33]

In regard to the foregoing, it seems probable that the judgments of the teachers, to a considerable extent, determined the results. Even the question of student office-holding is of concern to the teacher, and she can exert subtle pressures to influence the children in their selection of candidates. One might be justified in assuming, however, that most students will resent any overt interference with school elections on the part of the teacher. Yet there are so many ways in which the middle-class teacher can see to it that the bulk of the rewards go to children from middle-class families that the lower-class child is at a great disadvantage in most school situations.

Children who are conscious of being discriminated against, because they belong to the lower social class, may become moody, resentful, and aggressive not only in the presence of the teacher but when in the company of upper-class children whom they sometimes hate as well as envy. As a result, the morale of the school is lowered and conflicts among the children tend to break out when there is little provocation. Certainly the child from the lower-lower class is aware of the meaning of invidious comparisons on the basis of family income and father's occupation.[34] But he has a right to expect fair treatment in the classroom at all times, particularly with reference to the distribution of scholastic rewards.

Prejudice and Discrimination Against Minority Groups

Major factors contributing to deviant behavior are prejudice and discrimination directed against members of minority groups. This is particularly the case in relation to the school as the focal point around which many neighborhood activities revolve. Children of different racial, nationality, ethnic, and religious backgrounds intermingle in the educational and social environment of the public school, which is said to be the "crucible of democracy." If these children discover that the schools are sometimes strongholds of prejudice and discrimination instead of centers for the dissemination of democratic principles and practices, they may become sadly disillusioned and conclude that certain of our claims about the advantages of democracy are nothing less than sheer hypocrisy.

Children identified with minority groups face peculiar problems of adjustment, depending upon the character of their surroundings as determined by such factors as geographical location, composition of the population, and opportunities for employment, housing, and education. When they find themselves virtual social outcasts, as many do, they tend to become more closely integrated in order to offer greater resistance to the encroachments of members of the majority group. Thus, Negro and Mexican-American youths may form their own gangs in the vicinity of the schools where they attend, allegedly for purposes of self-protection. While the gang is a normal sociological phenomenon, it can be a source of much annoyance to teachers and an object of interest to the police when its activities are directed into antisocial channels. Although the incidence of both delinquency and crime is high among Negro youths and Spanish-speaking people, doubtless economic, educational, political, and social class discrimination by the majority group are important factors contributing to lawlessness.

The epoch-making decision of the United States Supreme Court, on May 17, 1954, which declared segregated public schools to be unlawful, paved the way for the establishment of integrated schools in the border states and in many parts of the deep South. The court held that "in the field of public education the doctrine of 'separate but equal' has no place. Separate educational facilities are inherently unequal." Not only were the schools for colored children greatly inferior to those intended for white children exclusively, as a rule, but the practice of segregating the races was clearly based on the unfounded assumption that Negroes are inferior to whites. Thus, in one swift blow, did the Supreme Court demolish the foundation upon which the South had built a dual system of education. Because of strong resistance to desegregation on the part of some Southern states and communities, integration of Negro children and white children in the classroom has proceeded at a slow pace in some areas. Fears that there would be serious disorders, riots, and even armed revolt as an aftermath of the court decision were in general without a factual basis, except perhaps in a few isolated instances.

The outlawing of segregated schools greatly improved the morale of Negro children because it meant that another barrier to equality of opportunity had been removed. To the Negro youth, being deprived of his civil rights meant that the majority (white) group which made the laws in the South was setting an example of lawlessness by defying the edicts of the Supreme Court, in direct violation of the Constitution. Now that the way is open for the association of white and colored students on a basis of social equality in the classrooms everywhere, better understanding between the two races should result and interracial friction in the schools should be reduced to a minimum.

What constitutes a most discouraging aspect of this problem is the "unconscious" bias so often exhibited by white teachers in the North toward their Negro pupils. Many of these teachers may actually think that their attitudes are completely unprejudiced when, as a matter of fact, they reveal unmistakable signs of "disguised" racial antipathy which their Negro pupils recognize without much difficulty. Some white teachers complain about Negro children who seem indifferent, sullen, suspicious, and uncooperative, as if such characteristics were peculiar to the Negro race. What they sometimes fail to realize is that teachers who dislike teaching Negroes cannot conceal their dislike for long and that the complete cooperation of members of this minority group will be more difficult to obtain on that account.

From interviews with white teachers of Negro students in interracial classrooms, and from interviews with Negro college students, the present author is convinced that some white teachers are guilty not only of anti-Negro bias but of flagrant discrimination as well. All too often do they assume a patronizing, obsequious, or condescending attitude, which Negro pupils interpret as sheer hypocrisy because of the failure of these same teachers to accord them equal treatment with whites, scholastically, socially, and in relation to the application of disciplinary measures.

The harmful effects of white-dominated classrooms upon the personalities of many Negro children in some instances can be disastrous. Admitting that the elimination of school segregation is itself a victory for democracy in education, at the same time there is great need of improvement in the treatment of Negroes in schools which are already desegregated, especially if antisocial behavior among members of this minority group is to be discouraged.

Diagnostic, Remedial, and Preventive Services Under School Auspices

So important are the adjustment problems of children believed to be, from the standpoint of their welfare as citizens of the future, that many school systems provide a wide variety of special services for all who can benefit from them. These include health, psychological, psychiatric, and social services, in addition to special teachers for exceptional children. As might be expected, the most complete facilities of a specialized nature are found in the large urban areas where the schools have access to auxiliary services provided by professional personnel associated with various community agencies. But those who think that school social services are in general adequate to meet the needs of problem children usually become sadly disillusioned when they talk with teachers in congested slum areas. It is in such neighborhoods that the need is greatest and the facilities for helping the children often among the poorest to be found anywhere. The same is true of some of the more remote rural areas of the deep South especially. Regardless of whether or not a school system has enough money to provide the services that are required, it occupies a strategic position with reference to the recruiting of trained personnel and the pooling of community resources in the fight against juvenile delinquency.

The School Social Worker

Probably no person is more immediately concerned with the adjustment problems of the children than is the school social worker, otherwise known as the "visiting teacher." It is she who functions in a liaison capacity between the school and the home, and between the school and various social agencies of the community. She is, therefore, a sort of "go-between" in carrying out her role as a "trouble-shooter." To her is committed the task of finding what factors in the child's social background may account for his adjustment problem in school. She is responsible for her assignments both to the school administrator and to the classroom teacher. In large city systems with social service departments she follows procedures which are outlined by the administration. These usually involve periodic visits to different school buildings and regular contacts with teaching personnel. She conducts interviews with "problem" children and their parents, cooperates closely with social welfare agencies, and keeps in touch with law enforcement officers.

When visiting the home, the school social worker is careful not to take sides in any controversy involving the child's parents and his teacher. As a professional person, she is expected to display tact, patience, and understanding in her relationships with all who may be concerned with the problem, and she must not disclose "confidential" information to persons unauthorized to receive it. One of her principal duties is to obtain all the facts which may have a bearing on the child's problem and to write the case history, which will include clinical reports, among other data, that throw light on the nature of his difficulty, together with suggested remedial measures.

Ordinarily, the social worker herself has had some teaching experience as part of her professional training so that she can understand the problems confronting the typical classroom teacher. She is not, as a rule, a "case-finder" because she takes action when cases are referred to her. Nevertheless, she plays an important role in helping to prevent delinquency by notifying the proper authorities concerning home and neighborhood conditions which may endanger the child's health, safety, and morals. By referring children with serious behavior problems to appropriate agencies for diagnosis and treatment she performs an indispensable service for the school. Since a careful "follow-up" of the more difficult cases is essential, the social worker can also make a valuable contribution by helping in this way. All in all, her duties are of such a type as to permit her to hold consultations with staff members, conduct interviews with parents, and place children in contact with social agencies whenever the need arises.

The Child Guidance Clinic

The child guidance clinic was an outgrowth of efforts of the National Committee for Mental Hygiene to develop more effective methods of combatting juvenile delinquency. As part of an experimental program financed by the Commonwealth Fund, the first demonstration clinic was established in St. Louis in 1922, and other clinics were opened in several of the nation's largest cities. Working in conjunction with the schools and with the juvenile courts, these clinics proved their worth from the very start. By providing facilities for the scientific study of children with serious emotional problems, the guidance clinics were able to throw some light on the relation of emotional disturbances to delinquent behavior, and to develop some tests and clinical procedures which have real diagnostic value. Since diagnosis is only a necessary first step in the process of rehabilitation, the clinics devoted a great deal of attention to methods of treatment, using for this purpose a "team" consisting of a psychologist, a psychiatrist, and one or more psychiatric social workers.

One of the chief advantages of the guidance clinic is that it usually reaches the child before delinquent behavior patterns have become firmly established. As a result, suitable corrective measures can be applied at a time when they may prove of greatest benefit.[35] The clinic performs an indispensable service in helping to determine *why* the school child got into serious trouble and in helping to decide *what* should be done about it. After the psychiatric social worker gathers enough background information to compile the case history, any unfavorable factors in the social environment can be identified and treatment of the child's condition can be modified accordingly. It is fallacious to think that an occasional visit to a clinic will be enough to solve the emotional problems of a child who needs a change of environment. Yet such a visit may enable the clinical staff to see what is needed in regard to the home situation and to place the family in touch with some welfare agency which can provide any supplementary services that may be required. The longer the delay in taking action in this respect, the greater may be the probability that the child will fail to respond to clinical treatment.

As an illustration of what is being accomplished in the way of school and community cooperation in relation to child guidance, the "Three Schools Project" in The Bronx, New York City, is outstanding. The New York City Youth Board, in co-operation with the Division of Child Welfare of the Board of Education, established the Project in 1949. According to Frank J. O'Brien, M.D., Associate superintendent, Division of Child Welfare, New York City Board of Education, and Marie Duffin, Consultant on Child Welfare, New York City Youth Board, the Project was originally designed as "a cooperative effort to determine the causes of and methods of correcting juvenile delinquency in two areas of The Bronx."[36] The three schools participating in the Project are Morris High School, Public School No. 37, and Public School No. 42.

The novel feature of this project, according to Mira Talbot, Project Coordinator and Psychiatric Social Worker, is its truly *adequate* provision for treating children who are experiencing difficulties in their personality and emotional adjustments. Within each of three selected schools, fully staffed psychiatric and allied service units have responsibilities limited to their respective school populations. The objectives of the Project were "the demonstration of the need and value of intensive child guidance in these schools, the integration of clinical and educational services, and the utilization of the facilities of the schools to their maximum potential."[37]

A democratic educational philosophy, involving the interchange of opinions among all the professions and at all levels of the professions, is being followed. Thus, following the example of orthodox child guidance teams, originally drafted by the Commonwealth Fund, each psychiatric unit consists of one psychiatrist, two psychologists, three psychiatric social workers, and a supervisor of social work. The roles of each of these disciplines, however, are not defined in strictly orthodox manner. "The delineation is guided more by the modern trend in sound professional practice in which there is less sharply defined segmentation of roles and a greater variation in the pattern of functioning."[38]

Thus, it seems clear that the Project capitalized upon the opportunity to integrate clinical and educational services and to provide a program sufficiently flexible to meet new needs as they arose. Without *adequate* clinical facilities, however, such a Project would seem destined to fail at its very inception, so that the close cooperation between the Youth Board and the Board of Education was essential to its success.

The clinic has maintained an effective relationship with the community. All available community resources, both formal and informal, have been utilized, thereby extending the service of the school-clinic and enabling it to function more broadly and effectively.

Explanations abound for this readiness of the community to work with the new psychiatric service in the school. In the life of the community, the school itself has been a vital factor, serving as the site of parents' meetings, local bazaars, a polling station at election time, and a play school that serves the neighborhood during the summer months. For the children, too, it is more than simply a school, its staff often serving as a family substitute for children from broken homes. As persons close to the situation express it: "Just as the community comes to the school to meet many of its needs, so does the school go out to the community."[39]

There is no necessity today for the school guidance clinic to extend the walls of the school to embrace the community; in the community served by the Project these divisions are already dissolved. Full use is being made of "all the community agencies, facilities, and resources which are necessary to effect an enrichment of the child's experiences and to contribute to the total process of learning and growth."[40]

Numerous other public schools across the nation serve their communities in much the same way as Public School 42, but with at least one important exception: they lack the finances and personnel which are essential for supporting and staffing a school-community guidance clinic. The Bronx experiment, however, illustrates what can be done when capable leaders and sufficient financial aid are available. As in the case of similar experiments, it will probably require many years of careful research to determine the effectiveness of the Three

Schools Project in reducing delinquency within the area which it serves. This much is certain, however: an excellent start has been made, and the project shows promise of greater usefulness to its constituency in the future.

A School Experiment in Predicting Delinquency

An interesting experiment in the prediction of delinquency has been under way in the New York City schools since 1952, under the sponsorship of the Youth Board. The experiment involves an attempt to determine the validity of the prediction table developed by Sheldon and Eleanor Glueck when applied to young children prior to the onset of overt symptoms of delinquency.[41] The validity of the table as a predictive instrument is to be determined by follow-up studies of the children to discover how their later behavior patterns may compare with the predictions made on the basis of the early use of the table. In the event that accurate forecasts of future behavior can be made at a very early age, the Youth Board aims to enlist the cooperation of various social agencies in providing needed services for the future problem children, with the hope of preventing them from becoming delinquents.

In order to measure the efficiency of the table in predicting future delinquent behavior, it was necessary to study children too young to have already engaged in delinquent behavior. Hence, children between five and six and a half years of age who were entering the first grade in New York City public schools were selected for study. In addition, this investigation will include the study of effectiveness of present methods of individual treatment. Plans have been made to provide treatment for one sample of boys with high failure scores (more than a fifty-fifty chance of becoming delinquent), while withholding treatment from a control-group of boys with equally high failure scores. The two samples will be matched for ethnic background. In the words of Ralph W. Whelan, Executive Director of the Youth Board: "The clinical study before and during therapy will make further diagnostic contributions to the understanding of delinquency in its incipient stages."[42]

There is good reason to believe that the study now being made by the Youth Board will set a standard for other cities and their school systems to follow with respect to similar researches in the future. But no research relative to delinquency causation can hope to lead to constructive accomplishment unless the community is willing to provide the social services for children which today are so sorely needed in our large cities.

The New York State Youth Commission has published an interesting report, *Reducing Juvenile Delinquency: What New York State Schools Can Do* (1952), Part I of which is devoted to "The Prediction of Delinquency." The data in the survey were compiled for 4,250 children who attended grades 3 to 8 in 12 different schools. On the basis of a study of 114 cases of known delinquents, the report concluded that "if one asks where one can find the greatest concentration of future delinquents, the answer is: *among the truants.*" In its summary, the report listed the conclusions of the staff regarding what their experiences may indicate for next steps. First, there was an increase of belief in the importance of the school's role in the total program for reducing delinquency. Secondly, it was concluded that the role played by the school can be appreciably more effective in a community situation in which "(a) there is broad planning among all agencies, (b) there is provision for more specialized services than are now available, and (c) there is widespread awareness among citizens for changes of the kind indicated in this study. . . . Delinquency can be markedly reduced, but its reduction requires effort and money."[43]

From various studies of school programs for combatting delinquency, the conclusion seems justified that without the help of other agencies in the community the school itself would face an almost impossible task, but that with the wholehearted support of the whole community a great deal can be accomplished.[44]

Research and Publication

Published materials in the field of juvenile delinquency are today voluminous. The present writer knows of no other topic of a sociological nature which seems of greater interest to the general public than that of children's misbehavior, with the possible exception of marriage adjustment problems. Content analysis of women's magazines especially indicates that a substantial proportion of the articles are devoted to discussions of behavior problems of children, in one form or another.

Educational journals, particularly, are devoting considerable attention to the problem of juvenile misconduct as well as to the matter of "discipline" in the classroom. During the period extending from 1947 to 1956, the *Education Index* listed a total of 270 articles on this topic, including those pertaining to prevention, prognosis, and research. Articles relating to juvenile delinquency appear also in the sociological and psychological journals, often in the form of research reports which are of much more interest to scholars than to the general public. For the busy classroom teacher some of the articles appearing in newspapers and popular magazines supply useful information on short notice. But there is no real substitute for a course in Juvenile Delinquency at the college level which requires the use of a good textbook.

Summary

This chapter has sought to explain the strategic importance of the school in relation to the problem of delinquency. Emphasis was placed upon the role of the teacher in helping to identify children with incipient behavior problems in order that they might be referred to the proper agencies for early treatment. Problems pertaining to mentally retarded and emotionally disturbed children, among others, were discussed in terms of the peculiar character of their difficulties and in relation to the possibility of their becoming delinquent. Such factors as the effects of social class discrimination and racial discrimination upon the behavior of certain students were discussed. Finally, typical diagnostic, remedial, and preventive services under school auspices, designed to aid potential delinquents, were described in some detail. The chapter emphasized that while the school is of major significance as an agency in delinquency prevention it needs the cooperation of other community agencies in order to do its best work in this respect.

Selected Bibliography

Milton L. Barron, *The Juvenile in Delinquent Society* (New York: Alfred A. Knopf, 1954). Chapter X, "Institutional Omissions and Commissions," 165-185, especially "The School and Delinquency," 171-180. This book explains how society is largely responsible for conditions which contribute to juvenile misconduct.

Herbert A. Bloch & Frank T. Flynn, *Delinquency: The Juvenile Offender in America Today* (New York: Random House, 1956), Chapter 8, "The Pressures of the Environment," 177-250, particularly, "The School and Delinquency," 198-202. Gives a thorough treatment of all aspects of the problem of delinquency.

Lowell J. Carr, *Delinquency Control* (New York: Harper & Bros., rev. ed., 1950), Chapter XXIII, "The Functions of the School," 481-497. Describes the problems facing the schools and suggests how they can improve their programs in relation to problem children.

Arthur E. Fink, Everett E. Wilson & Merrill B. Conover, *The Field of Social Work* (New York: Henry Holt and Co., third ed., 1955), Chapter 12, "School Social Work." Presents a helpful picture of the work of the "visiting teacher."

"Juvenile Delinquency: A symposium," *Religious Education,* L, (March-April, 1955), 83-102. An excellent discussion of factors related to children's character development and spiritual growth in terms of their significance for delinquency prevention.

William C. Kvaraceus, *Juvenile Delinquency and the School* (New York: World Book Co., 1945). This particular study was based largely upon the author's experience in connection with the Passaic (N. J.) Children's Bureau which served that city's schools.

Maud A. Merrill, *Child Delinquency* (Boston: Houghton Mifflin Co., 1947), Chapter 4, "Toward School with Heavy Looks." A graphic picture of the school adjustment problems of a sample of 300 California delinquents as compared with a control group of 300 nondelinquents.

Martin H. Neumeyer, *Juvenile Delinquency in Modern Society* (New York: D. Van Nostrand Co., Inc., rev. ed., 1955), Chapter VIII, "Influence of Community Institutions and Agencies," especially 227-241, "Schools, Churches, and Youth-Serving Agencies"; also Chapter XIV, "Social Action and Community Services," particularly 386-390, "The School and Delinquency Prevention."

Florence Poole, "School Social Services," in *Social Work*

Year Book 1957 (New York: National Association of Social Workers, 1957; Russell H. Kurtz, editor), 505-512. A timely discussion of various social services that are available to school children, including those with behavior problems.

Joseph S. Roucek & Associates, *Social Control* (New York: D. Van Nostrand Co., 1947), Chapter IX, "Education," by P. F. Valentine. Explains the role of the school and allied agencies in relation to the formation of behavior patterns especially.

Philip M. Smith, "The Schools and Juvenile Delinquency," *Sociology and Social Research,* XXXVII (November-December, 1952), 85-91. A discussion of "The School as a Factor in Delinquency Causation," "The School as an Agency in Delinquency Prevention," and "Special Problems of School Programs of Delinquency Control."

Philip M. Smith, "Broken Homes and Juvenile Delinquency," *Sociology and Social Research* XXXIX (May-June, 1955), 307-311. Explains why broken homes are often related to other factors which contribute to delinquent behavior.

Negley K. Teeters & John O. Reinemann, *The Challenge of Delinquency* (New York: Prentice-Hall, Inc., 1950), Chapter XV, "Preventive Services," especially "The School's Responsibility for the Prevention of Delinquency," 586-596. A good statement of the duties of the school in regard to delinquency prevention, with a fairly detailed description of typical school services for maladjusted children.

United States Department of Health, Education and Welfare, *Research Relating to Children*, Bulletin No. 4 (Washington, D.C.: 1956); see "Behavior and Personality," 26-82, and "Education," 83-102; also "Delinquency," 70-81. This Report describes current researches which are not yet completed and whose findings are not ready for publication.

United States Department of Health, Education, and Welfare, *A Selected Bibliography on Juvenile Delinquency* (Washington, D.C., 1952). A helpful selection of published materials in this field.

Helen L. Witmer & Edith Tufts, *The Effectiveness of Delinquency Prevention Programs* (Washington, D.C.: United States Department of Health, Education, and Welfare, 1954); Children's Bureau Publication No. 350. See: "The Passaic (New Jersey) Children's Bureau," 41-42, "New York City Youth

Board," 44-47, and "Educational and Therapeutic Programs," 49-50. Includes descriptions and appraisals of outstanding projects and programs for preventing delinquency.

The late Philip M. Smith, Ph.D., was Professor of Sociology at Central Michigan College (1947-1957); was the author of many articles which have appeared in professional journals, as well as of chapters in books. (Dr. Bernard N. Meltzer, Professor of Sociology, Central Michigan College, has been responsible for minor revisions of the original manuscripts for publication).

CHAPTER 8.

RURAL DELINQUENCY

W. P. LENTZ

State Department of Public Welfare, The State of Wisconsin

Dearth of Knowledge on Rural Delinquency

During the last few decades the many studies which have been initiated in the field of delinquency research have, almost without exception, received an urban emphasis. Theories concerning delinquency causation, treatment, and prevention have largely stemmed from studies of urban population. Meanwhile, the rural aspects of delinquency have been neglected. Although there have been a few rural studies, they have been limited in scope and none have ever assumed the proportions of most of the contemporary studies of urban delinquency.

In 1946, when the National Conference on the Prevention and Control of Juvenile Delinquency was held in Washington, D.C., the members of the sub-panel on rural aspects of the problem made note of the lack of information which limited the scope of their deliberations. They went on record as advocating the study of delinquency in various types of communities throughout the country. It was further suggested that regional research centers devoted to rural juvenile delinquency be established and that all possible efforts be made to acquire more knowledge in this field.[1] These recommendations have not been implemented to any great degree. For any definitive analysis of the factors involved in rural juvenile delinquency we must, therefore, rely upon the research efforts of a few individuals.

Since research has received such a strong urban emphasis

the question might well be raised as to whether any of our current explanations of juvenile delinquency may apply to rural areas. The adherents of this point of view are able to cite numerous instances of sociological factors for which rural-urban differences have been demonstrated.[2] For this reason they would appear to be wholly justified in assuming that urban findings are "not proven" for rural areas until similar research has been conducted. An examination of delinquency, especially rural delinquency, throughout the world, tends to lend some support to this idea.

International Aspects of the Problem[3]

For most countries throughout the world, data on rural juvenile delinquency are available only to a limited degree. On the basis of information that is available, it can be concluded that delinquency is more widespread in industrial countries than in those where agricultural pursuits are widely followed. An exception is found in India where some tribes organized along caste lines train their younger members in various types of crimes. Cultural training may include prostitution, minting of false coins, pickpocketing, manufacturing illicit liquor, and other means of obtaining a livelihood outside the law. Also, in some rural areas, the norms of behavior for a sub-cultural group may be in conflict with those of the larger society, thus creating situations which promote deviant behavior.

In countries that have been industrialized for decades delinquency is primarily a problem in the larger urban areas. Rural areas, small towns, and villages are usually not confronted with problems of the same magnitude. Most of Europe and the industrial sections of North America fall into this category.

In other areas of the world, such as parts of Latin America, the Middle East, Asia, and Africa, juvenile delinquency has only recently become a problem. A high incidence of delinquency is reported where there has been considerable disintegration of the traditional way of life concomitant with a growth of urban and industrial centers. Juvenile delinquency is usually a specific phenomenon in such centers and is seldom found in outlying districts.

In some regions the problem of juvenile delinquency is very slight or does not exist at all. This is true of some Pacific islands such as American Samoa, New Hebrides, Gilbert and Ellis Islands; certain scattered territories such as St. Helena, the Aden Protectorate, and a few areas in Africa where outside influences have not yet disrupted the tribal organization nor the close family and community structure. In some of these places, recalcitrant youngsters may be brought before a magistrate, but they are merely reprimanded, returned to their parents, and nothing is reported or recorded. Each family is expected to take care of its own problems; the reprimand is the only type of formal control exercised.

The Extent of Rural Delinquency in the United States

The United States can be included with those industrialized countries that have witnessed the problem of delinquency for several decades. Yet in spite of this familiarity with the phenomenon, the total extent of delinquency is not known because of the absence of nationwide statistics. The number of delinquency cases served is, however, reported to the U. S. Children's Bureau by some juvenile courts. Table I presents some data on the relative number of cases reported according to the size of the population unit served.

TABLE I
Rates of Delinquency Cases by Size of Area Served by Court: 1955[4]

Total Population Served by Court	Population 10-17 Years[a]	Delinquency Cases	Rate per 1,000 population 10-17 Years
100,000 and over (187 courts)	7,060,913	247,908	35.1
50,000 to 99,999 (190 courts)	1,565,747	33,748	21.6
20,000 to 49,999 (499 courts)	2,141,087	31,872	14.9
10,000 to 19,999 (394 courts)	817,359	8,500	10.4
5,000 to 9,999 (192 courts)	207,578	2,116	10.2
Under 5,000 (87 courts	40,651	225	5.5

a.Population figures based on 1950 Census

This table gives data from 987 juvenile courts out of 2,833 such courts in the country. It is estimated that 59.5% of the child population ages 10-17 years of age is covered by these reports. Unfortunately, it is impossible to distinguish the rural areas from the urban in the table, but by taking those areas under 50,000 population it can be seen that 42,713 cases were included. It is apparent that small courts have lower rates and consequently a less intensive problem than that indicated by the reports of larger courts.

Another way to estimate the extent of rural delinquency is through the use of the F.B.I. Uniform Crime Reports. Such an estimate is admittedly crude since these reports are based upon the arbitrary U.S. Census definition of "rural" as places under 2,500 population. The reports for 1955 list a total of 276,374 rural crimes.[5] Ages of offenders are not given for rural sections of the country but if we assume that 10 per cent of them were under 18 years of age (10.5 per cent were under 18 in urban areas) approximately 27,600 crimes could be attributed to this age group. This figure would also have to be increased since only 81 per cent of the rural population is covered by the reports.

These rather crude estimates indicate that the rural problem is less extensive than that of the cities. This may, in part, account for the lack of needed rural studies. It is entirely possible that much more could be learned about juvenile delinquency by focusing attention upon the rural aspects of the problem. Some interest on the part of sociologists has been shown in the past in making rural-urban comparisons, at least of the incidence of delinquency. Before we consider such studies let us first examine the rationale upon which they are based.

Theoretical Basis for Comparing Rural-Urban Delinquency

The comparison of rural and urban types of societies has enjoyed a long tradition in the sociological literature.[6] Distinctions between rural and urban societies have been made largely on the basis of the differences between the two ways of life. Rural life is characterized as traditional and family-centered, with social interaction on an intimate and personal basis. In contrast, urban life offers social contacts which are superficial, impersonal and segmental. Although one can find few, if any, situations where these ideal differences can always be noted, the rural-urban ways of life may be viewed as existing at opposite ends of a continuum.

Clinard has pointed out that the general processes of urbanization are linked to the processes of social disorganization.[7] The urban way of life coupled with rapid cultural change has encouraged the breakdown of traditional social institutions and led to disruption and disorganization in social intercourse. This does not literally mean that all cities show evidence of rampant social disorganization nor does it mean that some rural areas are not being affected by urbanism. It does, however, in some measure make explicit the rationale for comparing rural and urban societies.

Rural-Urban Differences in Social Control

Regardless of whether one fully accepts this approach or not, all must agree that there are some differences in the means of obtaining rural and urban social control. In small towns, villages, and open country, informal means of social control prevail while in the city, particularly the larger metropolitan areas, the more formal means are found.

The value of one's reputation, which is common knowledge in the neighborhood, is highly prized in rural areas. Gossip and ridicule have their effect. One must regulate one's activities in such a way that there will be no occasion for loose talk. Deviant behavior has high social visibility and the limits of group tolerance are common knowledge to everyone.

In the impersonal social interaction of urban life the value of one's reputation is not of paramount importance. One must always depend upon the police or some social agency to handle deviant behavior. It may not be so much a matter of group concern but may be rather a matter of governmental regulation and control.

Let us then turn to some of the comparisons between rural and urban delinquency. Most studies have been concerned with incidence. We shall examine these first and then compare the rural and urban delinquents themselves.

Rural-Urban Incidence

Several studies have demonstrated that higher rates of delinquency are associated with urbanization and that lower rates prevail in non-urban areas. Urban rates may often be two to three times as great as those for other areas. Demographic studies have shown that the rates decrease as one gets farther away from metropolitan areas. The highest rural rates have been associated with "wide-open communities," transitional zones, poverty-stricken sections, and areas where cultural conflict is present.[8]

The existence of rural-urban differences in incidence might be refuted in a number of ways. Incomplete reporting, variations in the toleration of offenses and the lack of handling of cases in an official fashion in rural areas could keep the rates low. Certainly in many rural sections of the country welfare organizations offer only limited services, a fact which must be taken into consideration in analyzing so-called official rural delinquency rates. Perhaps someone might also claim that only those individuals who are likely to evidence deviant behavior migrate to the cities, a selective migration theory.

Whenever careful studies of rural-urban incidence have been made, the usual objections have been overcome. Lunden, for example, asserts that such differences cannot be accounted for in terms of good and bad reporting. He goes on to say that the differences must be explained in terms of the social differences which exist between the two patterns of life.[9] The findings of another study by several psychologists may partially support Lunden's contention. Barker and Wright, in a small midwestern town, followed their subjects closely day after day at home, at school and at play. They found that in this community children were relaxed and healthy, lived in a comfortable tempo with time to explore and master their environment and a great deal of warm encouraging companionship from adults.[10] Such a way of life would tend to minimize the development of delinquent activity.

Rural-Urban Differences in Delinquent Behavior

Aside from the differences in incidence of rural-urban delinquency, are there any other differences which might be noted? Data relating to the deviant behavior itself as well as to the individuals involved would be much more meaningful in attempting to relate rural delinquency to existing theories. Again, there are few studies to draw upon so that our knowledge of the nature of rural delinquency is incomplete. The few studies

which have been made, however, indicate that there are some
real differences between rural and urban delinquent behavior.
There is considerable evidence that the elaboration and processing of deviant values for rural individuals is sufficiently unlike
that for urban individuals and any general theory of delinquency must take this into account.

Our primary concern, therefore, in the following sections
is to consider contrasting types of behavior. What is the offense
picture for rural delinquents? Are the types of offenses they
commit like those of urban boys? Are there differences in the
way their offenses are committed? How do rural and urban
boys compare on the basis of the companionship factor? Is
there differential handling of rural deviants? Is there any evidence of distinctive or unique rural factors? All of these questions will be reviewed and an effort made to indicate some of the
implications for research, treatment and prevention.

The Offense Picture

One study has shown that rural boys committed relatively
simple offenses which tended to be of a less serious nature than
those of their urban counterparts.[11] While it is difficult to cate-
gorize juvenile offenses, even relatively crude classifications indicated such differences. When the number of kinds of specific
deviant acts were tabulated for rural and urban delinquents,
again a significant difference was noted. Rural boys committed
an average of 1.7 types of offenses compared to an average of
three for urban boys. A study in South Carolina also found
that 64 per cent of a group of rural boys committed only one
offense while 70 per cent of those from cities committed two
or more offenses.[12]

In the Wisconsin study differences for specific types of
offenses were also noted. Sex offenses for both groups included
intercourse with teenagers. Rural boys did not participate in
urban type "gang shags" or frequent prostitutes but were, on
the other hand, found guilty of rape. Although the numbers
involved were small it is a curious fact that the latter offense
apparently loomed larger in the value systems of the rural communities, at least to the extent that it served as the primary
reason for commitment to a correctional institution. In committing property offenses rural boys appeared to be far less

concerned with stealing for money but usually did so as a prank or for cigarettes or candy. A preponderance of such boys stole from relatives, particularly when automobiles were involved. Rural boys stole cars as a means of transportation when running away from home or for joy rides; they were not interested in stripping them or selling them as was true for some of the delinquent gangs in large cities.

Some of the rural boys were committed to a correctional institution for offenses which if judged by urban standards would not have been considered as delinquent activities. That is, there was a miscellaneous assortment of misdeeds such as assault, disorderly conduct, and incorrigibility which actually consisted of single offenses such as fighting with a relative, failure to obey parents and similar acts. Rural boys were involved in such activities to a much greater degree than urban boys.

Comparison of Behavior Processing

One significant difference between rural and urban offenders lies in the area of behavior processing. How thoroughly is rural and urban delinquent behavior learned? Information on the knowledges and skills involved in the commission of offenses and the degree of sophistication displayed would provide at least a partial answer to this question.

Clinard, in his study of the careers of young adult offenders in Iowa, found that the rural boys committed relatively simple offenses and displayed little skill and knowledge of criminal techniques.[13] The Wisconsin group, which has been previously discussed, displayed the same characteristics when both rural and urban delinquents were judged according to a specifically devised rating scale.[14] Regardless of whether property or personal offenses were considered, the rural boy in contrast to the urban boy gave the impression of being relatively naive, lacking in specific techniques, and unable to display "know how" in the commission of offenses.

Perhaps the lack of a true criminal culture in the rural area more than any other single factor accounts for this difference. Both organized and professional crime are more likely to be urban phenomena which aid in the perpetuation of a delinquent tradition within certain sections of a city. The process through which this occurs has been amply studied and described by sociologists. There is no indication in rural studies that such a criminal culture has had much effect upon the lives of rural delinquents.

The Companionship Factor

Another urban phenomenon, the delinquent gang, has been shown to be a potent factor in creating delinquency through offering opportunities to participate in deviant values. Do gangs play as great a role in rural delinquent activities? The life histories of rural offenders contain relatively little information concerning gang activities.[15] The Wisconsin study previously mentioned indicated that over 50 per cent of the rural boys were lone offenders. Those who were not in this category were usually not members of a delinquent gang. On the other hand, the urban boys studied were likely to be members of a delinquent gang (86.9 per cent) as well as being apprehended in groups to a much greater degree than the rural boys.[16] Differential association with one or two criminals or delinquents appears to be much more characteristic of delinquents from rural areas and small towns than is true for those from cities.

An interesting historical note on this problem is found in the report of a 1927 study of delinquency in two New York counties.[17] Even at that time it was noted that rural boys and girls were becoming more mobile and were making contacts with deviants in the cities largely because of increased use of automobiles. It was emphasized that there was no problem of professional crime in the country but that there was a scattering of individual cases where delinquent tendencies were noted.

Differential Handling of Rural Delinquents

Some authorities contend that the juvenile courts have never been adapted to serve in the less populous sections of the country. They arose out of and still remain a cultural trait of cities; they do not appear to have been successfully transplanted to rural areas. Carr states that most small (rural) courts have to be substandard.[18] He cites, in support of this contention, the inability of the rural county to support an adequate juvenile court program and suggests that there is some merit in combining several jurisdictions in order to raise standards. Others have suggested that a state-wide system of juvenile courts such as found in Connecticut, Rhode Island, and Utah would help to bolster the rural system of providing justice for juveniles.

It is also true that in many rural counties most welfare facilities for children are lacking. Some counties are so poor and their tax base so overburdened that they have been unable to develop anything comparable to the social services found in cities. Child guidance clinics, group work agencies, and frequently probation services may not be found within the system of rural social welfare.

Lack of rural welfare facilities means more than merely failure to provide certain services; it also means differential handling of rural delinquents. Hathaway and Monachesi have found that there is a tendency for rural boys who are committed to a state correctional institution to evidence less emotional disturbance than boys from metropolitan areas.[19] They conclude, "Rural courts may, therefore, be more prone to send a less disturbed boy to the training school, having little alternative in the community. There may be some preliminary, objective evidence here of the value of adequate rural probation and other social treatment facilities in cutting down the number of youths who are committed."[20]

A recent study in Wisconsin confirms the fact that differential handling does take place. Juvenile courts were classified as to whether they provided broad or limited services. Those providing limited services committed, upon their first appearance, a higher percentage of boys to a correctional school. This was particularly true for non-property offenses, juvenile behavior problems, and violations against persons. Courts with limited services were more frequently found in non-urban areas and such courts committed proportionately more boys to correctional schools regardless of the ages of the offenders.[21]

What evidence of differential handling can be found among rural delinquents themselves after they have been committed to a correctional institution? An earlier study of 420 rural and urban boys committed to the Wisconsin School for Boys described three aspects of the differential handling of boys from small towns and open country.[22]

In answer to the question of how many boys had been placed on probation to a social agency it was found that only 15.4 per cent of the rural boys compared to 70.3 per cent of the urban boys were given this opportunity.

If probation was not extensively used by rural courts, two alternatives in handling the cases seemed probable. Either the court must handle the cases on a non-probation status or relinquish them to some other agency such as the State Department of Public Welfare. The latter alternative was usually followed for the rural group. Rural boys appeared in court an average of only 1.5 ± .53 times while the urban boys averaged 3.5 ± 1.5 times. Approximately 95 per cent of the rural boys were before the judge only once or twice. The urban boys, on the other hand, were in court repeatedly, nearly half of them appearing three or four times and nearly 20 per cent of them from five to eleven times.

There was also evidence that the rural boy was more likely to come from a family which was known for serious deviant behavior. This is in one sense a reflection of the reputation of the family since the rural family which was noted for seriously deviant behavior was usually under surveillance. Nearly 60 per cent of the rural boys and 43 per cent of the urban boys came from such families.[23]

The Implication of Differential Handling

Some practical implications of handling rural cases in a differential manner are clear. The rural boy who committed rather simple offenses, appeared in court once or twice, was usually not granted probation, and was then summarily committed to a correctional institution. The administrators of such an institution were then faced with the problem of providing treatment for such a boy as well as for the relatively crime-wise boys who had also been committed to their care. These problems might well have been avoided if treatment services had been offered earlier.

If commitment to a correctional school is viewed as the first or last step in the rural communities' efforts to work with the delinquent, the net result is the same. The rural boy who is found in such institutions is not as well indoctrinated in the ways of delinquency as his urban counterpart. But does such a boy represent the most recalcitrant delinquents in rural areas? If he does then there are probably also significant differences between rural and urban delinquents "in the open."

When delinquency is looked upon as a status concept there are far deeper implications in the differential handling of delinquents. The labeling of a boy or girl as a "delinquent" brings with it a social situation which may be crucial in determining how the individual conceives of his social role. How does the officially labeled delinquent define his role? Does the early thrusting of this status upon him inhibit or encourage deviant behavior? The delinquent's peers and their attitudes towards him appear to be of prime importance in this situation. If we assert that this labeling process may be a significant etiological aspect of each individual case, then the rural delinquent's development is quite different in this respect from that of the urban boy.

Social Class and Rural Delinquency

While the sociologist has frequently studied the social structure within given communities, the relationship between social class and delinquency has not been fully investigated. Cohen has indicated that urban members of delinquent gangs are likely to be members of what he calls "lower classes."[24] This raises the question as to whether rural boys who have been studied might also come from families with low social status in the community.

A study which provides a partial answer to this question was not, however, specifically concerned with the problem of rural delinquency. Hollingshead in studying *Elmtown's Youth,* attempted to test the hypothesis that social behavior of adolescents is related functionally to the positions their families occupy in the social structure of the community.[25] He concluded that the lower class boys were stigmatized, held in contempt and left on their own. Drinking among class II and III boys (of good reputation) resulted in lectures by the coach who then told the superintendent of schools. No further disciplinary measures were taken because they came from families of good reputation.

As in urban areas, the total extent of hidden or unreported delinquency is likewise not known for rural areas. If the official delinquent achieves his status partially as a result of the social class of which he is a member, then a new facet is added to the definition of rural delinquency. Proof of the prevalence of deviant behavior among children of the "better families" would confirm this assumption.

Rural Delinquency and Contemporary Theory

This brief survey has given an incomplete picture of rural deviant behavior. Some of the evidence, however, serves to provide a few leads which have implications for contemporary theory. In view of some of the significant differences between rural and urban delinquents it may well be that most of the approaches based upon urban findings have limited application, or it may mean that they must be applied with considerable modification.

Certainly any of the urban theses identifying delinquent behavior with the sub-culture of delinquent gangs in areas of high delinquency have limited application to the problem of rural delinquency. The absence of a definite criminal culture in rural areas would also appear to be associated with this situation. Any approaches based primarily upon these elements, gang activity, and contacts with a criminal culture, will contribute little to a complete understanding of rural delinquency.

The Gluecks' earlier studies which culminated in their theory of maturation may apply no more to the rural delinquent than it would to so-called occasional criminals.[26] On the other hand, their more recent studies placing primary emphasis upon the influence of the family may have far more validity for rural delinquency than it has for urban groups. This tentative conclusion may be valid because of the differences noted between their urban sample and rural delinquents.[27]

Concepts concerning delinquency which pertain to differential handling and reporting would probably be fruitful if applied to studies of rural delinquency. In this connection the reckless approach of applying categoric risks would also seem to be appropriate. The most successful approach to understanding rural delinquency probably ought to give considerable weight to studying deviant behavior as a form of human behavior wherein emphasis is given to the part played by social roles and conception of self, within rural value systems.[28]

Future Study of Rural Delinquency

In the study of human behavior, one must of necessity be exceedingly humble in his approach. If this is true in studying urban juvenile delinquency, it probably applies to a greater degree to the rural situation. The vicissitudes of reporting, the dearth of studies, and even the general lack of scientific interest in rural deviant behavior make for a pessimistic view of the future.

Some shortcomings of future delinquency research appear certain. As long as continued emphasis is placed upon only the study of predominantly urban groups, we will not be able to obtain a universal theory which explains all delinquency. As information previously presented indicates, certain studies of mixed rural-urban groups will produce biased conclusions. This is particularly true of statistical studies because of some of the widely divergent characteristics of rural and urban delinquents.

Future studies, if properly designed, may provide some of the answers to the now unanswered questions concerning rural delinquency. That the ontogenetic processes of rural delinquency could be characteristic of such areas is suggested by the nature of some of the rural-urban differentials which have been demonstrated. Closer attention must be given the rural situation; we must search for significant traits which will discriminate between sub-groups of rural delinquents. The crude distinctions previously made, offer some promising leads in this direction.

Many specific studies might be suggested. An investigation of offenders belonging to favored groups or "better class" families would appear to be profitable. The existence of gangs of such youths has been suggested by some, although no study has been made of their activities. Another study might be concerned with the rural shopping center as the focal point for the property offenses of delinquent rural youths. It may also be possible to attempt replication in whole or in part of various urban studies that have been made.

Other research could be focused upon rural-urban comparisons. Ethological studies comparing rural and urban social values would probably make a significant contribution to our general understanding of delinquent behavior. The purpose of such a study would be to examine specific types of activities and attempt to determine community toleration limits. Still another comparative study could be made of rural and urban juridical systems as they affect juveniles. A thorough investigation of all of the methods and agencies handling rural deviants would also be worthwhile.

Finally, the crucial question in regard to further research in rural juvenile delinquency is not found in any of the foregoing suggestions. The crucial question is simply stated—will any studies be made? Skeptics may claim that there is not much to be learned through such efforts. Perhaps they are right but what little is known about rural deviant behavior suggests that it too must be studied before we can arrive at a more complete understanding of the whole problem of juvenile delinquency.

Selected Bibliography

Roger G. Barker and Herbert G. Wright, *Midwest and Its Children; The Psychological Ecology of an American Town* (Evanston, Ill.: Row Peterson and Company, 1955). Despite the fact that this study uses a rather anomalous term in its title "psychological ecology," it merits consideration; the daily activities of the subjects were followed closely by a group of psychologists; it was established that the youth of the town had the advantages of warm support and understanding by the adults; delinquency was not considered to be a problem.

Albert Blumenthal, *Small Town Stuff* (University of Chicago Press, 1932). This is not, nor does it pretend to be, a study of juvenile delinquency; it is, however, an analysis of informal control in a small town. The effect of gossip and the elements of sociability in it form the background against which offenses are committed; also of interest is the handling of rural law enforcement on an informal basis.

Morris Caldwell, "The Extent of Juvenile Delinquency in Wisconsin," *Journal of Criminal Law and Criminology*, XXXII, (July-August 1941), 148-157. Illustrates the differences in rural and urban incidence; also relates areal factors to rates.

Marshall B. Clinard, "The Process of Urbanization and Criminal Behavior," *American Journal of Sociology*, XLVIII

(September 1942), 202-213. Deals with a study of young adult offenders from rural areas, villages, and cities; shows that the degree of urbanization was related to criminal behavior. Networks of criminal relationships were found to vary directly with the amount of urbanization involved. This provides a basis for explaining rural-urban differences.

Marshall B. Clinard, "Rural Criminal Offenders," *American Journal of Sociology*, L (July 1944), 38-45. The distinctive characteristics of rural inmates of an Iowa reformatory are identified and studied. Although this is a study of young adults, their life histories disclosed that as adolescents they did not regard themselves as criminals, had little knowledge of criminal techniques and chose simple crimes.

August Hollingshead, *Elmtown's Youth* (New York: John Wiley and Sons, Inc., 1949). Although not specifically concerned with the general problem of rural delinquency, this study of youth in a small town does shed considerable light on the problem; the relationship of social class and the social behavior of boys and girls is investigated. Children from "across the tracks" are stigmatized and held in contempt. Boys from families of good reputation are not affected in the same way. The means of social control in a small town including the informal and formal varieties are amply illustrated.

William P. Lentz, "Rural-Urban Differentials and Juvenile Delinquency," *The Journal of Criminal Law, Criminology and Police Science*, XXXXVII, (October 1956), 331-339. Are there significant differences between rural and urban delinquency? This article attempts to answer this question in the affirmative; it reports on a study which demonstrated the existence of rural-urban differences in the offense picture, membership in gangs, and the degree of knowledge displayed in the commission of offenses; rural delinquents were also accorded differential handling. The differences noted have implications for modification of current theory and for future research.

Walter Lunden, *Social and Economic Bases of Delinquency and Dependency in Iowa* (Ames, Iowa: Iowa State College, 1952). Comparisons of juvenile delinquency and dependency rates are made for various areas. Rural areas have lower rates than the cities.

National Conference on Prevention and Control of Juvenile

Delinquency, *Report on Rural Aspects* (Washington, D. C.: U.S.G.P.O., 1947). A report such as this, although ten years old, is still timely; it considers various aspects of rural delinquency and its prevention; the need for reliable data as well as extensive research is stressed. Remedial as well as preventive programs must be available for all rural youth. The job, if it is to be done, must be done by the local community.

Mapheus Smith, "Tier Counties and Delinquency in Kansas," *Rural Sociology*, II (September 1937), 322. Introduces a unique method for illustrating the effect of urbanization upon delinquency rates. A tendency is shown for rates to vary with the size of the largest community in each county.

Sub-Commission on Causes and Effects of Crime of New York State Crime Commission, *A Study of Delinquency in Two Rural Counties* (Albany, New York, 1927). Of general historical interest, this study shows how some problems in regard to rural juvenile delinquency appeared in 1927. The role of the automobile was beginning to be a major factor in increasing the mobility of rural youth. At the time, however, rural delinquency was sporadic and not an intensive problem.

United Nations, International Review of Criminal Policy (Switzerland: January-July 1955), 7-8. The prevention of juvenile delinquency is covered in this publication; it provides an excellent review of world conditions in the field. The problem is discussed as it exists in simple cultures, in those countries undergoing rapid social change and industrialization, and in various nations which have been industrialized for many years. In part, it literally becomes a sourcebook for information concerning the relationship of social disorganization and delinquency. While rural delinquency is not discussed in detail, it offers many rural-urban comparisons.

Paul Wiers, "Can Rural and Urban Delinquency Be Measured?" *Journal of Criminal Law and Criminology*, XXX, (November-December 1940). Sophia Robeson's early question regarding the difficulties in measuring delinquency in urban areas provides the basis for raising the question in rural areas.

Paul Wiers, "Juvenile Delinquency in Rural Michigan," *Journal of Criminal Law and Criminology*, XXX, (July-August 1939) 211-222. Urban delinquency rates are higher than the rural rates. Few rural cases are dismissed and proportionately more rural than urban delinquencies are sent to correctional institutions. In Michigan, the southern non-industrial counties have the most favorable rates.

W. P. Lentz began his sociological studies in 1938 under Professor John L. Gillin; has had experience as a caseworker, employment counselor, and a vocational rehabilitation counselor; interrupted his study at the University of Wisconsin to take a position as Assistant Superintendent of the Wisconsin Child Center at Sparta, Wisconsin. Part-time study of rural-urban differentials under the supervision of Professor Marshall B. Clinard culminated in completion of his doctoral dissertation on this subject in 1954. For the past seven years he has been in charge of research for the Division for Children and Youth, State Department of Public Welfare, Madison, Wisconsin; has also served as part-time lecturer at the University of Wisconsin for courses in social disorganization and criminology; in addition, he is on the staff of the University of Wisconsin Institute for Juvenile Law Enforcement Officers.

CHAPTER 9.

ECONOMIC FACTORS IN JUVENILE DELINQUENCY

DAVID S. MILNE
San Diego State College

Consider this curious sitation: the nation which has the highest standard of living in the world also has probably the highest rate of juvenile delinquency among its young people. Despite the inadequacies of avilable statistics on juvenile delinquency, there is good reason to believe that the United States has more of its young people involved in officially recorded antisocial acts than any other modern, that is to say, Westernized, country. Why is this? What are the factors in American life which operate to bring about this alarming condition?

To begin our study of the problem, we must note that the data we have on juvenile delinquency is not very precise. Sophia Robinson has said that the statistics we have on juvenile delinquency are so imprecise and inaccurate that it is about the same as if in the field of health we had only a general illness rate for our population.[1] In the health field we have quite accurate reporting of major illnesses such as smallpox, influenza and other communicable diseases. We have no such precise figures in juvenile delinquency, hence we must recognize that our knowledge is vague and somewhat limited. We really know very little, as yet, about some of the factors which are related to the incidence of juvenile delinquency. Our situation is somewhat like the statement that Willard Waller has made about the sentiment of love, "the poet has sung his best, and the cynic has said his worst, but the scientist has said very little that is worth remembering."[2] Yet it is necessary that this little be said in order that our science may have its beginning. Therefore, we will proceed to set forth what little we know about juvenile delinquency and its presumed relationship to certain economic factors in modern life.

Poverty and Delinquency

Among the numerous writers who have considered the relation of poverty to juvenile delinquency, Cyril Burt has been one of the most insightful. Studying conditions in London shortly after 1920, Burt compared the incidence of poverty in the homes of delinquent youth with the general population of the city. Defining poverty as an income level insufficient for the maintenance of bodily health, Burt found that 19 percent of the delinquent children studied came from very poor homes, whereas only 8 percent of the total population of London belonged in this category. Also, 37 percent of the delinquents came from moderately poor homes as compared with 22 percent of the general population in this class. Altogether, over half of the total volume of delinquency in the city came from the poor or very poor families, representing less than one third of the total population.[2] This study does seem to indicate that there is a disproportionate amount of delinquency among the lower economic classes of the society.

Burt is careful to point out that poverty alone does not necessarily lead to delinquent acts. "If the majority of the delinquents are needy, the majority of the needy do not become delinquent."[3] Even in the poorest classes there are many who are quite law-abiding. Therefore, something more than poverty or low income must operate in most instances to produce delinquency.

"Poverty can only engender crime by its ultimate action, through ways more often circuitous than plain, upon the inner mental life of the potential offender. Even where its influence seems comparatively straightforward and immediate, the poverty that counts is, as a rule, not absolute poverty, but relative poverty—the ratio of available means to irresistible desires; and this relative poverty may be induced quite as much by extravagant wants as by an insufficient income."[4]

As an early financial tycoon was reported to have said when he was unsuccessfully trying to corner the market on a certain commodity, "Good heavens, Sir, you have no idea what a small sum of money a million dollars is!" Inextricably related to the matter of income then, is what is being attempted with that income, and how well or poorly one is able to live within it.

In the United States, William Healy has produced some of the most notable studies of delinquents, in which are included some observations upon poverty and delinquency. In his classic study, *The Individual Delinquent*, we find a book which, perhaps more than any other single writing, ushered in the new era of individual treatment of delinquents and criminals. Healy found poverty to be a major causative factor of delinquency in only 0.5 percent of his cases, and a minor factor in 7.1 percent.[5] In a later study with Augusta Bronner, he used a scale similar to that used by Burt, and arrived at very much the same conclusions, namely that about 27 percent of their cases came from poverty-stricken homes.[6] This is a higher proportion than in the general population, but Healy points out that even with this disproportionate representation of the poverty-level homes, there are still many cases of delinquency, nearly three-fourths of them in fact, where absolute poverty, as Burt defined it, must be ruled out as a causative factor. In another trail-blazing study by Healy and Bronner, poverty is again minimized as a causative factor except in so far as it leads to unsatisfactory human relationships which might flow from being forced to live in substandard conditions.[7] As Clifford Shaw has pointed out, a condition cannot be considered as a factor in influencing behavior until it becomes a motive.[8] Furthermore, we all recognize that some people are more easily moved to action than others who may be exposed to the same situations.

More recently, Sheldon and Eleanor Glueck and also Maude A. Merrill have made comparative studies of delinquent and non-delinquent children possessing essentially the same socio-economic characteristics.[9] Both found that the delinquent children had a higher proportion of dependent and economically marginal homes than the non-delinquent children. However, both concluded that factors other than economic conditions must be sought as an adequate explanation for delinquency, for poverty or dependency *per se* does not necessarily produce delinquency.

Social Class and Delinquency

Most of the available evidence indicates that delinquency rates are higher in the lower social classes than in the higher classes. Not too many studies have related delinquency and crime directly to social class, however, since the measurement of social class status is still rather indefinite. Warner has come closest to developing an objective system for measuring social class, and he and others using the same basic approach have produced some fairly reliable information.[10] In the first of his "Yankee City" studies, Warner found that the incidence of arrest was disproportionately high in the lower classes, and was very rare in the upper classes.[11] Hollingshead in *Elmtown's Youth* found a similar situation to exist in a small midwestern town.[12] Whether this means that the lower classes are more criminal, or simply that they are more vulnerable to arrest because of their low status and consequent lack of resources, including influential friends, is not fully determined. Reckless has advanced the idea that low social class is a "risk factor" which increases the chances of the lower classes for arrest, for conviction of offenses charged against them, and also for heavier sentences for the crimes they have been found guilty of committing.[13]

Economic Fluctuations and Delinquency

Statisticians recognize four types of fluctuations in a time series, which is a chart portraying the movements of a particular variable over a period of time. These four variations, or fluctuations, are identified as; 1) Trend, 2) Cyclical movements, 3) Seasonal Variations, and 4) Accidental, Random or Residual Variations. These may be illustrated by such economic series as stock market variations, freight car loadings, motor car sales, or many other similar time series. A chart showing the general prosperity of the country over fifty or one hundred years in the United States would probably show an upward inclination over this period. This is the trend referred to in 1) above. Trend may be shown in a time series by drawing a straight line, (although there are statistical procedures developed to deal with curvilinear trends,) following the basic movements of the data on the chart. The trend line then serves to average out the fluctuations above and below this basic general line. In fact, one such statistical trend line, the least squares trend line, can be drawn in such a manner that the squares of the variations above and below this basic line will be a minimum. This, then is the line of best fit for the data plotted on the chart.

In fitting a trend line to data plotted on a chart one of the basic requirements is having a long enough period of time in the series so that several complete cyclical variations will have been included. It would be very inaccurate to draw a trend line on the basis of just a few years, for example, for the period covered may represent only the upward, or possibly the downward, swing of a cycle. If on the upward swing, the trend line would be abnormally tilted upward, and thus would be far off the mark if projected into the future by extending the trend line. Since this is one of the basic reasons for trying to determine a trend line—to be able to make predictions for the future—it becomes very important that a long enough period of time be covered to include several cycles. It is not always easy to know just how long a period of time should be covered to get a satisfactory trend line, for the length of cycles in various situations will vary. Some data may show a seven year cycle, and others may have an eleven or even a fifteen year cycle. Hence, a twenty to thirty year period is usually the minimum that is required, and an even longer period, up to fifty years or more, is desirable.

Unfortunately, this is just what we do not have in the field of delinquency, therefore, it is impossible to make definite statements as to the trend in juvenile delinquency in the United States. The Uniform Crime Reports of the Federal Bureau of Investigation started in 1931, and are now approaching their thirtieth year. However, as far as juveniles are concerned, this series is quite incomplete. This is especially true in the earlier years of its development when only a small part of the population of the country was being covered in the arrest reports sent in to the F.B.I. Also, juvenile arrests are frequently not reported at all to the F.B.I., so this series represents only a fraction of the total number of juveniles getting into difficulty every year.

At the Juvenile Court level, the U.S. Children's Bureau has been trying to report the number of cases heard by juvenile courts in the United States. However, there are several reasons why this series is unsatisfactory: 1) Only part of the United

States juvenile courts have been reporting over the period, and only a few of these, mostly in the bigger cities, have reported continuously over the entire time. 2) The Children's Bureau has been forced to change its system of collecting the information, which has altered the courts being considered. Originally the Bureau was obtaining its data directly from the courts, but in the last few years, has switched to a system of collecting the data from the state agency responsible for juvenile court work in the particular state. As a result of this the reports since 1954 are not comparable to prior years. 3) Some juvenile courts have developed the practice of hearing certain cases on an informal or unofficial basis. This is supposed to prevent the child from having an official court record, which it probably does, but it makes it difficult to obtain any reliable data on which to measure the work of the courts.

For these reasons we have at present no reliable basis for making any statements about the trend of juvenile delinquency in the United States. In certain areas, mainly the large cities and a few states, data has been collected consistently and uniformly over a period of three or four decades, so that it is possible to make certain statements about the trend of juvenile delinquency in those areas. However, most of our reliable statistics go back only to 1940, or the early years of World War II. Since that time the trend of juvenile delinquency has been increasing, and at a rate much faster than the increase in juvenile population. New York State may be cited as an example of this trend.[14]

Cyclical fluctuations in juvenile delinquency are more readily recognizable in the available statistics, particularly those relating juvenile delinquency to the business cycle. Contrary to the general supposition, the weight of evidence indicates that juvenile delinquency is positively related to the business cycle— in other words, is high in periods of prosperity and low in periods of depression.

Lowell Carr, using data for the state of Michigan, and David Bogen, dealing with delinquency and a general business index in Los Angeles from 1925 to 1941, both found a very high correlation between the delinquency and the indices of business activity.[15] However, Reinemann in Philadelphia found a fairly high rate of delinquency for the early period of the depression,

(1930-35) while during the recovery period from 1936-40 the delinquency rate was quite low.[16] Consequently, we can come only to tentative conclusions on this matter until more complete and thorough studies have been made. Other social phenomena also vary positively with the business cycle, principally marriage, births and divorce, therefore, it may be reasonable to expect that juvenile delinquency will follow a similar path. Juvenile delinquency is intimately affected by trends in family life, and during depression periods family life appears to be strengthened somewhat. Although some families fail to bear up under the additional stress of family crises, many more seem to be more united and are able to rise to the occasion. During a depression there is less money available for outside recreation and other activities, so the parents tend to stay at home more and are able to give additional attention and more careful supervision to their children.

TABLE I
Delinquency Trends in New York State by Number of Cases and Rates
1938-1945
(Revised May 1955)

Year	Delinquency per 1000 children	
1938	5.2	
1939	5.7	
1940	4.8	
1941	5.2	
1942	5.7	
1943	7.5	World War
1944	7.2	II
1945	7.5	
1946	7.1	
1947	5.4	
1948	5.5	
1949	5.2	
1950	4.6	Korean
1951	5.3	War
1952	5.2	
1953	5.8	
1954	6.2	
17 Year Average	5.8	

In the matter of seasonal variations, there is no general conclusion which may be reached on the basis of the information available. There do seem to be rather wide variations in the monthly incidence of juvenile delinquency, whether measured by juvenile arrests or by detention or juvenile court statistics. However, the high and low points of one year seldom coincide with the high and low points of other years. Carr concludes that "concentration and thinning-out of cases in monthly periods tend, on the whole, to follow a seasonal pattern," but *this pattern is different from year to year in the same community, and different from community to community in the same year.* Wattenburg gathered evidence from several different cities which indicates that, again contrary to general expectations, delinquency appears to drop off on the whole during the summer months.[18] Another study in Philadelphia shows that in 1946 the month of December was a low point for both boys and girls.[19] On the whole, we may conclude that juvenile delinquency is seasonally affected by the school calendar, being lower in general during summer vacation and usually having another low point during Christmas vacation and holiday periods. High points often occur in the early fall, soon after the opening of school, and in the spring months.

Several reasons might explain the reduction in delinquency during the summer months.

"Many juveniles leave cities to go with parents to summer resorts or are sent to camps. Fewer complaints arise from truancy or school-connected misconduct. Since school is not in session, boys and girls do not have the same opportunities to get together to form gangs or cliques and to plan exploits. The heaviest drop in offenses charged against boys during the summer includes forms of deviant behavior that are usually committed in groups rather than by individuals alone. While these and similar conditions may explain some reductions in delinquency rates, they do not seem to be altogether valid explanations, for certain contradictory tendencies exist. At best, they would account for only a part of the reduction of delinquency in the summer season."[20]

Random, accidental, or residual fluctuations refer to those movements which occur because of unusual situations or occurrences. In economic data such instances may be due to severe droughts, floods, fires or other catastrophes. In health and related fields, unusual epidemics may occur in certain years. Juvenile delinquency is likewise affected by some of the above circumstances. For instance, in San Diego, California, in 1948, the threat of a poliomyelitis epidemic caused the cancellation of many of the usual summer activities for children. Parents were cautioned to keep their children as close to home as possible, avoiding crowds and large gatherings of other children. The polio epidemic was considerably reduced by these tactics, and so was juvenile delinquency, which hit an all-time low for San Diego during that summer.

In summary, we may say that variations in juvenile delinquency appear to be related to variations in economic areas, such as the business cycle, in several ways. Our data nationally is not yet exact enough to permit definite statements as to the relation of delinquency to the long-time trends of economic series. Our best estimate is that delinquency has been rising, just as the cost of living, or the gross national product has been rising. As to cyclical variations, it seems established that juvenile delinquency is positively related to the business cycle, being high in prosperity and low in periods of depression. Seasonally, delinquency appears to be low during the summer, a period when economic activity is high. Random and accidental fluctuations do not appear consistently enough to permit a general statement. The controlling factor in this whole matter seems to be the influence of economic fluctuations on family life. Where these economic forces tend to have a strengthening influence, causing families to do more things together, (as during depressions or summer vacations), delinquency goes down. In prosperity when more attention is given to making money and less to family activities as such, delinquency increases.

Juvenile Delinquency in Wartime

Based on the recorded experiences of many communities during World War II and thereafter, it seems clear that juvenile delinquency rises considerably in a nation at war. This seems particularly true of the younger age groups, who apparently take advantage of the absence of their elder brothers being in the military service and go on quite a spree. The Uniform

Crime Reports of the F.B.I. disclose that during the period
from 1940 to 1946 there was a drastic increase in the delinquent
activities of the young people under 18 years of age, which
more than counterbalanced the decrease in arrests for the age
groups between 19 and 22 or 23 occasioned by so many young
men being overseas. Thus, in 1945, there were more 17 year-olds
arrested than any other single-year age group. Normally, the
pattern is for each age group to show an increase over the
preceding group up to age 25, when the F.B.I. stops reporting
arrests by one-year intervals and groups the arrests into five-year
age intervals. Beginning in 1946, a sharp decrease in delinquency was recorded, reaching a low point in 1948, after which
the trend turned upward again, and increased quite rapidly in
1950 and 1951 with the outbreak of hostilities in Korea. Since
that time both police arrests and juvenile court cases have
continued to increase faster than the rate of increase in the
juvenile population.

It is interesting to note that Great Britain showed the same
pattern of juvenile delinquency as that of the United States
during World War II, with the same drop after 1946. There
was also an upward trend in Great Britain in 1950 to 1951, but
thereafter the juvenile delinquency rate turned down instead of
continuing to rise as it did in the United States. A possible explanation of this is that Great Britain was experiencing considerable difficulty in reestablishing her economy on a secure
footing. There was a long period of wartime "austerity" in Britain even after the cessation of hostilities. This may have been
the determining factor in reducing delinquency in the nation
during this period, for as noted above, delinquency seems to decrease during periods of depression. In the United States, on
the other hand, the increase in delinquency has been in line
with the steady advances in prosperity and great business
activity.

Employment and Delinquency

We have considered unemployment, as indicated by business
depressions, and its relation to delinquency, with the general
conclusion that delinquency is low during periods of economic
depression and unemployment. Conversely, delinquency rates
appear to be high during periods of prosperity and high em-

ployment. This would seem to be particularly true during periods when the employment of women is very high, as it was during World War II, and as it has seemed to be since 1950 to the present time. Recent figures indicate that as of 1952, nearly one third of all workers in the labor force were women, and that over half of these were married women.[21] Also, a very high proportion of these married women in the working force have small children, who become the charge of some person or agency other than the mother. This situation is not conducive to the type of home life established as the ideal standard for Americans. In certain European countries, particularly Sweden, where it is quite an accepted thing for married women to work, very excellent nurseries have been provided at a very nominal cost. The growth of day nurseries, private as well as publicly supported, in the United States during and since World War II has been evidence of the increased demand for such services. The matter of public support for such nurseries has been strenuously debated since the easing off of the war pressure. In California, for instance, the legislature has been threatening to cut off public support for day nurseries every year for the last six or seven years. Sufficient support has been mustered to pass appropriations continuing them, but only on a year-to-year basis and definitely not as a permanent institution to be publicly supported.

The Ecology of Delinquency

Shaw and McKay long ago observed that delinquency and crime tend to appear in certain areas of a city in high concentrations, while being very low in other areas. Sociologists have adapted the term "ecology" from biology, where it refers to the relation between organisms to their environment. The branch of sociology called "human ecology" is concerned with the spacing of people and of institutions and their resulting interdependency. Recognizing that the physical and social environment greatly influence the social life of a community, a great deal of attention has been paid to the spatial distribution of certain social phenomena, including crime, delinquency, mental illness and other so-called social pathologies.

Some of the modern leaders in the ecological approach to delinquency and other social problems have been associated

with the Department of Sociology at the University of Chicago.
Several notable studies have been published by the "Chicago
school" using data from the city of Chicago to demonstrate their
theories.[22] These studies have been guided primarily by Profes-
sors Robert E. Park and Ernest W. Burgess, who developed the
theories describing the processes governing the growth of cities.
The latest and most complete formulation of these theories is by
Clifford Shaw and Henry D. McKay. They studied the ratio of
delinquency to the differential characteristics of local communities in twenty American cities.[23] The best summary statement
of this "magnum opus" in criminology and delinquency is contained in the Introduction by Professor Burgess.

"The findings of this study establish conclusively a fact
of far-reaching significance, namely, that the distribution of
juvenile delinquency in space and time follows the pattern
of the physical structure and of the social organization of
the American city."

"For the majority of the cities studied, concentric zones
were set up by arbitrarily marking off uniform distances of
from one to two miles. Delinquency rates were calculated by
taking for each zone the ratio of official juvenile delinquents
to the population of juvenile court age."

"The findings were astonishingly uniform in every city.
The higher rates were in the inner zones, and the lower rates
were in the outer zones. Even more surprising was the
discovery that, for all the cities but three for which zonal
rates were calculated, the rates declined regularly with pro-
gression from the innermost to the outermost zone."

"The main point, of course, established by these findings
is that juvenile delinquency of the type serious enough to
appear in juvenile courts is concentrated in certain parts
of the American city and then thins out until it almost van-
ishes in the better residential districts."

"The study is important also for its refutal of the particularistic explanation of crime. Juvenile delinquency is
shown to be highly correlated with a number of presumably
separate factors, including (1) population change, (2) bad
housing, (3) poverty, (4) foreign-born and Negroes, (5) tu-
berculosis, (6) adult crime, and (7) mental disorders."

"The correlation of juvenile delinquency is so high with each of these that if any one were considered separately from the others it might be deemed the chief factor in juvenile delinquency. Since, however, juvenile delinquency is highly correlated with each of them, then all of them must be more or less intercorrelated. Therefore, all of these factors, including juvenile delinquency, may be considered manifestations of some general basic factor. The common element is social disorganization or the lack of organized community effort to deal with these conditions. If so, the solution for juvenile delinquency and these related problems lies in community organization. Juvenile delinquency, as shown in this study, follows the pattern of the physical and social structure of the city, being concentrated in areas of physical deterioration and neighborhood disorganization. Evidently, then, the basic solution of this and other problems of urban life lies in a program of the physical rehabilitation of slum areas and the development of community organization."[24]

Unlike many theories in sociology, the basic solution proposed above has been put to the test of actual application. Beginning in 1932, in several of the highest rate delinquency areas in Chicago, the so-called "Area Projects" were initiated. The aim of these projects was to restore to normal the activities and life of the "delinquency area" through the development of social organization, through which neighborhood solidarity could be developed, and more effective attacks launched on the deteriorated buildings and dwellings of the area. The area projects have been so successful that the City of Chicago has recently increased the number of areas being served by this program. The main features of the project, in outline form, include the following principles as guides: 1) The Neighborhood as the Unit of Operation, 2) Planning and management by local residents, 3) Employment of local workers, 4) Utilizing and coordinating community resources, 5) Activity programs, 6) Credit given to local residents.[25] In the areas where the project has operated it has been found that the local residents do have the talents and capabilities essential to effective participation in the planning and management of welfare activities and programs. This has tended to reorganize the community so that the destructive effects of the social ills are no longer so apparent. In short, the processes of social disorganization are being met by a program of social organization within the local area.

One of the major features of the delinquency area concept is the importance of the "delinquency traditions" which are transmitted from one generation to another living within the area. Speaking of this delinquency tradition in describing the programs of the Chicago Area projects to the National Probation Association in 1940, Mr. Fred Romano said:

> "We of the Italian community today find some consolation in the fact that the Irish, Germans, and Swedes before us experienced the problem of delinquency and crime among their children and young adults while they lived in the neighborhood. Rates of delinquency have remained relatively constant despite the successive changes in the nationality composition of the community's population. In facing our delinquency problem today we feel that we are not facing what is distinctly ours but what has confronted every group of people who ever lived in the social and economic situation of our district."
>
> "Throughout the years traditions and patterns of delinquency and crime have become established in the life of our community. These patterns and attitudes are transmitted by older boys to younger boys growing up in the district. Many children who are exposed to contacts and experiences of a delinquent nature become educated and trained in crime in the course of participating in the daily life of the neighborhood. They learned delinquency in the same fashion that children in more fortunate circumstances learn conventional forms of conduct."[26]

In stressing the importance of the delinquency tradition of an area, Shaw and McKay point out that "the fact that in Chicago the rates of delinquents for many years have remained relatively constant in the areas adjacent to centers of commerce and heavy industry, despite successive changes in the nativity and nationality composition of the population. This supports emphatically the conclusion that the delinquency-producing factors are inherent in the community."[27] It is not the deteriorated buildings themselves which lead to delinquency, for many groups, particularly Orientals, have lived in these same neighborhoods and have remained remarkably free of delinquency and crime. Shaw and McKay point out that "the dominant tradition in every community is conventional, even in those having the highest rates of delinquency. . . . Since the dominant tradition in the community is conventional, more persons pursue law-abiding careers than careers of delinquency and crime, as might be expected."[28]

However, recognizing that many factors are important in determining whether a particular child will become involved in delinquency, it is contended that "if the delinquency tradition were not present and the boys were not thus exposed to it, a preponderance of those who become delinquent in low-income areas would find their satisfactions other than in delinquency."[29] Implied herein is another point that is made more explicit when Shaw and McKay state that the youngster from such a neighborhood is not necessarily abnormal, or personally disorganized as some adherents of the psychological school may claim. "In cases of group delinquency it may be said that from the point of view of the delinquent's immediate social world, he is not necessarily disorganized, maladjusted, or antisocial. Within the limits of his social world, and in terms of its norms and expectations, he may be a highly organized and well-adjusted person."[30] Such a person may be well-integrated personally, and well adjusted in his group. The difficulty is that his particular group may be poorly adjusted to the larger society. This is true, for instance, of conscientious objectors, who may be imprisoned, and thus be considered criminal, but who are upholding standards of the group to which they feel the greatest loyalty.

"In conclusion," Shaw and McKay state, "It is not assumed that this theoretical proposition applies to all cases of officially prescribed behavior. It applies primarily to those delinquent activities which become embodied in groups and social organizations. For the most part, these are offenses against property, which comprise a very large proportion of all the cases of boys coming to the attention of the courts."[31]

The Ecology of Delinquency; Bernard Lander

One of the major tasks of a scientist is to test and to verify the hypotheses and findings of other scientists. By this means certain theories and propositions become generally established, so that they may be spoken of as "laws," and other theories are rejected. In the case of the presentation above of the main ideas developed by the social ecologists typified by Shaw and McKay, and their mentor, Burgess, it is only to be expected that other social scientists would as a matter of course subject their propositions to the test in other cities. One of the most thorough analyses of these theories that has yet been published is that by Dr. Bernard Lander, who made a very complete study of Baltimore, Maryland, to see how many of the propositions advanced by Burgess, Shaw and McKay, et al, would be confirmed in the new setting.[32] In general, he confirms some of them, but finds that others do not seem to apply to the situation in Baltimore. He criticizes the concept of social disorganization as being unsatisfactory for the development of an adequate theory for understanding juvenile delinquency in these words:

"Burgess' statement implies that social disorganization is the general basic causal factor of which juvenile delinquency and the other variables including bad housing, poverty, percentage of foreign-born and Negroes, and population change may be considered manifestations or dependent variables. The possible relationship between social disorganization and delinquency seems clear enough. The way in which poverty, the concentration of foreign-born and Negroes also become manifestations or resultants of social disorganization is not equally clear unless one views the relationship in the light of the ecological assumption of sub-social processes inherent in the process of city growth which act selectively to segregate the poor, the foreign-born and Negro groups in areas of social disorganization."

"How much this statement means is dubious in view of the fact that social disorganization itself has been defined as a complex of a group of factors in which juvenile delinquency, crime, broken homes, prostitution, truancy, etc. and other sociopathological factors are included. It is therefore circular reasoning to make a loosely defined whole the explanation of one of its own components. We should remark in this connection that the phrase social disorganization has no specific connotation and is always identified by such factors as those we have mentioned."[33]

One of the main strengths of Lander's study is his use of more refined statistical procedures, including factor analysis and multiple and partial correlation, to more fully determine the exact relationships and the interrelationships between the variables he studied. For example, with respect to housing, he found that if only housing and the juvenile delinquency rate for an area were being compared, there would be a very high correlation coefficient, approximately .70. (1.0 would represent perfect correlation.) However, the "zero order correlations" (between only two variables), conceals the fact that there may be other common factors operating which tend to produce this high correlation. If these other factors are taken into account, as may be done in multiple and partial correlation, other results may be obtained. "As a matter of fact, in this study, the indices of partial correlation between overcrowding, substandard housing, and delinquency are reduced to zero when the other variables are held constant and their influence eliminated. Despite the high zero order correlation coefficients, the partial correlations suggest that there is no *real* or substantive relationship between the delinquency rate and the physical aspects of housing as such."[34]

On the other hand, partial correlation analysis shows that the factor of home ownership is very significantly related to the juvenile delinquency rate in an area. This is one of the items which leads Lander to adopt the great French sociologist Emile Durkheim's idea of *anomie,* by which is meant the condition where the hold of social norms over an individual's conduct has broken down, as a more fundamental explanation of delinquency. Home ownership represents stability, and thus greater control over the members of a group, while poor housing as such, seems to have little fundamental relationship to group controls. In a sense, *anomie* may be related to Burgess' concept of "social disorganization," but seems preferable, in Lander's view, since it avoids the possibility of being mixed up with some of its own components.

Another factor which seemed important in the Baltimore study was the concentration of Negroes in an area as related to delinquency. Here a somewhat curvilinear relationship was found. In areas where the Negro population was less than 10%, the delinquency rate was low. As the proportion of Negroes in the area passed the 50% mark, the delinquency rates started to drop, until it became lowest in areas which were 90 to 100%

Negro. A similar pattern of delinquency frequency also characterizes the white group in relation to the proportion of Negroes. This same stiuation was found in Houston, Texas, in a study reported by the Houston Community Welfare Council, and cited in Martin H. Neumeyer.[35] Lander feels this further strengthens the concept of *anomie* since "Areas of maximum racial heterogeneity are characterized by the largest extent of social instability and *anomie*. In the areas of maximum Negro population concentration there is observable a corresponding increase of social stability and a decrease in delinquency."[35]

Lander reports that "The findings of this study do support Shaw's thesis that 'delinquent behavior is related dynamically to the community and that because of the anonymity in urban life, the individual is freed from much of the scrutiny and control which characterize life in primary group situations in small towns and rural communities.' But our findings do not support, (at least in the case of Baltimore), Shaw's hypothesis that the processes of city growth, as such provides the basic explanation of a city's wide variations in delinquency rates."[36] There is some support, although "superficial and general," for the Burgess gradient hypothesis, that delinquency rates would be highest in the center of the city and decrease as the outer limits of the city are approached. There appear to be some industrial areas on the outskirts of Baltimore which tend to upset this pattern somewhat. This may be due to the fact that the Baltimore zonal areas on which the statistics are based, are not "natural areas" as was the case in Chicago. The Baltimore zones were derived from the wards, which had a long history, and were hence important to use, but were mainly of political concern. In Chicago, the zones were drawn to follow more closely the natural limits of major streets, canals, railroads and other accepted boundaries.

Lander is not alone in finding that the Concentric Zonal theory developed by Park and Burgess to describe the processes of city growth, is not fully applicable in other areas. This theory holds that a city grows like the ripples in a pond when a stone is thrown into it—flowing outward in successive waves from the center. Chicago is a particularly good example of the theory, because even though Lake Michigan forces the circles to be semi-circles, the rectangular grid pattern of streets, (developed during days of pedestrian and street car transportation), plus the absence of natural obstacles, except for a few canals, permits the fairly even flow outward of the city from its center as it expands. One zone, therefore, tends to overflow and "invade" another, and during this process the zone being invaded, the "zone of transition" becomes characterized by the indices of social disorganization Burgess mentioned above, such as poor housing, high rates of foreign-born, population change, etc., etc.

The growth of many modern cities tends to be along certain main streets, or in sectors, rather than flowing outward evenly in all directions. This is particularly true in the west and southwest in America where large cities have grown up in the era of the motor car. When the automobile is the main means of local transportation it is quite common to see whole communities, small cities even, grow up along the major boulevards or freeways. In some of these new communities juvenile delinquency is quite prevalent, although in others it may be more under control.

In conclusion, it may be appropriate to quote Lander's summary statement:

"In our search for the understanding of the differential delinquency rate, we suggest that the nearer the explanation of this social phenomenon is to the direct motivation of behavior, the nearer it is to being an adequate explanation of the deviant behavior. We hypothesize an explanation of the differential delinquency rate in terms of the concept of *anomie*. When the *group norms* are no longer binding or valid in an area or for a population sub-group, in so far is individual behavior likely to lead to deviant behavior. Delinquency is a function of the stability and acceptance of the group norms with legal sanctions and the consequent effectiveness of the social controls in securing conforming juvenile behavior."

"A deeper understanding of the differential juvenile delinquency rate will necessitate further research on *how* community stability or instability is meaningfully and dynamically related to the differential behavior of various types of individual children. Community or situational factors ultimately influence the delinquency rate only as they affect the needs, values, goals and behavior of individual children."[37]

Conclusion: As is true of many other types of factors influencing human behavior, economic factors as such do not cause delinquency or crime. Some of these factors are related to delinquency, since they are found to be closely associated. In certain instances, as Lander found with housing in Baltimore, the relationship is indirect, and operates through other and more basic factors. Zero order correlations, or relating one variable to one other variable, may be very deceptive, although the discovery of high zero order correlations provides good leads for further study. Fundamentally it is the meaning to the person, or the interpretation given by the person of a particular situation or condition which is important in relation to possible delinquent activity. As Burt said about poverty, it is the *felt* poverty which is important in certain cases, and often one may feel poor who enjoys a very high standard of living, and vice versa. The feeling one has for his home, poor though it may be, will determine how he acts in that home and towards it as a focus of activity. If the child has internalized the standards of his parents, if he identifies with them and the larger society they represent, he is then very apt to act in accordance with those standards. If, on the other hand, the child has identified with a group or gang, which in turn has adopted the standards of predatory crime, he is very apt to become involved in criminal activities. In the few homes where the tradition itself is criminal, the child can hardly escape becoming criminal.

With the security of a family and other social groups with a law-abiding orientation, a child may come safely through exposure to what might appear to be very deleterious conditions. Our American traditions are full of the stories of poor newspaper boys living in some of the worst slums of the country who rose above their lowly start to become governors, industrial tycoons and educational leaders. Therefore, while we should continue to do all we can to remove these unfavorable and degrading conditions in our cities, we should also endeavor to build up, as our best safeguard, conditions of stability and security for the members of our society. If it is through meaningful groups such as families, school groups, recreational groups, etc. that people find their basic emotional satisfactions, then all things possible should be done to strengthen these norm-building groups and agencies in our nation. In other words, if *anomie*, (considered as the breakdown of certain controlling norms), is the underlying factor in juvenile delinquency, then efforts to strengthen these basic groups, through, what Burgess called, methods of social or community organization, should be employed to the fullest extent.

SELECTED BIBLIOGRAPHY

Milton L. Barron, *The Juvenile in Delinquent Society* (New York: Knopf, 1954). A recent text with a frankly sociological orientation as shown by the title. Good chapters on the profile and dynamics of delinquency.

Herbert A. Bloch and Frank T. Flynn, *Delinquency: The Juvenile Offender in America Today* (New York: Random House, 1956). Another recent text with particularly strong chapters on treatment agencies and institutions.

Burt, Cyril, *The Young Delinquent* (New York: D. Appleton Century, 1925). A pioneer study published in England, but containing many universally valid observations.

Lowell J. Carr, *Delinquency Control* (New York: Harpers, 1950). One of the better text books in juvenile delinquency, which also presents some original studies, particularly as to the distribution of delinquency in geographic areas. Strong emphasis on community organization for prevention.

Federal Probation Quarterly, U.S. Department of Justice, Washington, D.C. One of the leading publications in the correctional field. Presents many excellent original articles as well as speeches by leaders in the field. Also a helpful section reviewing pertinent articles in other periodicals.

Sheldon and Eleanor T. Glueck, *Unraveling Juvenile Delinquency* (New York: The Commonwealth Fund, 1950). The latest of a series of trail-blazing studies by this noted team of writers. Compares 500 delinquents with 500 non-delinquents from essentially the same neighborhoods and backgrounds.

William Healy and Augusta F. Bronner, *New Light on Delinquency and Its Treatment* (New Haven, Conn., Yale University Press, 1936). A study of delinquents and their non-delinquent siblings, including over one hundred pairs of twins. One of the really important studies of delinquency in America by highly respected authorities.

Bernard Lander, *Towards an Understanding of Juvenile*

Delinquency (New York: Columbia University Press, 1954). A fresh look at the ecological approach to juvenile delinquency using more precise statistical methods and procedures. Based on 8,464 juvenile delinquency cases in Baltimore, Maryland.

Maud A. Merrill, *Problems of Child Delinquency* (Boston: Houghton Mifflin, 1947). A ten-year study of a group of non-delinquent and delinquent children in California. Psychological orientation.

Martin H. Neumeyer, *Juvenile Delinquency in Modern Society* (New York: D. Van Nostrand Co., 1955). A good, all-around text book with very thorough documentation of research studies and other sources in crime and delinquency.

Thorsten Sellin, *Research Memorandum on Crime in the Depression* (New York: Social Science Research Council, 1947). A summary of researches on the relation of crime and delinquency to the business cycle, and also including some original studies by the author.

Clifford R. Shaw and Henry D. McKay, *Juvenile Delinquency and Urban Areas* (University of Chicago Press, 1942). The culmination of many studies of the ecological approach to delinquency, with chapters by other writers on the distribution of delinquency by areas in other American cities.

Paul Wiers, *Economic Factors in Michigan Delinquency* (New York: Columbia University Press, 1944). One of the few state-wide studies in this particular field.

David S. Milne, Professor of Sociology, and Chairman of the Division of Social Sciences at San Diego State College, San Diego, California has had literally a lifetime of experience in correctional work. His father was one of the first Juvenile Court Judges in the State of Utah, and was also Superintendent of Correctional Schools in three different western states, Utah, Nevada and California, and David was raised in the various correctional schools where his father was serving, going to school and playing with the inmates. He received his A.B. degree from the University of California at Los Angeles and then entered social work with the Los Angeles County Department of Charities, worked with the California State Relief Administration where he was Director of a Camp for Transient Boys during the winter of 1935-36, and in 1936 began work as a Parole Officer for the Whittier State School for Boys; was employed in that capacity with the California Youth Authority; next served as a Field Representative in the Delinquency Prevention Section of the Field Services Division of the California Youth Authority and in this capacity he participated in a number of community surveys of the youth-serving agencies in several counties of California. In 1946 he joined the faculty of San Diego State College. Received his Master's degree in Sociology at the University of Southern California (1939) and his doctorate from the University of Chicago (1948). In San Diego, Dr. Milne has been active in delinquency prevention work with the San Diego County Coordinating Councils; has served on the Board of Directors for a number of years, and is currently Chairman of this organization. (The Coordinating Councils are organizations of local community leaders and representatives of groups and workers in a community devoted to considerations of delinquency prevention, promotion of family and community life, and the general improvement of the social life of the community. In San Diego County this is a department of county government staffed and financed by the San Diego County Board of Supervisors.) Dr. Milne is also serving on the Board of Directors of the Mental Hygiene Association and the Juvenile Protection Committee of San Diego.

CHAPTER 10.

MASS MEDIA AND JUVENILE DELINQUENCY

DAVID J. PITTMAN
University of Rochester

Mass media, typically products of the urban society, refer to the impersonal means of communication such as the newspaper, radio, television, and motion pictures. These organs of popular culture do not provide a means for direct interaction among the consumers of the media. The mass media do present to the public the basic societal values and particularistic sub-cultural norms. For example, in the media of screen drama and television serial, homage is given to the sacred societal values of patriotism, motherhood, religiosity. Sub-cultural patterns of behavior of the business executive, the policeman, or juvenile delinquent are depicted through the media to the members of the mass society. From youth to old age, societal members are constantly bombarded by the stimuli presented in the various mass media. The pervaseness of mass media is reflected in the circulation statistics. Over five million copies of *T. V. Guide* are sold weekly, and newspapers circulate to millions of families.

With the wide dissemination of these media, both laymen and the social scientist have been interested in the consequences of the media for human behavior. Specifically parents desire to know what effect crime comic books and movie dramas have on their children. Advertisers in the mass media desire to know whether their copy sells soap or potholders to the readers of the media. Unfortunately, little scientific assessment of the specific effect of mass media on human motivation and action exists except in a tentative form. Paul Lazarsfeld, one of the most outstanding researchers on the influence of mass media on human behavior, in his testimony before the Senate Subcommittee to Investigate Juvenile Delinquency, commented that in reality we know very little concerning the permanent impact of such media as television and comic books on children or adults. His plea is for more scientific research in this area to replace the impressionistic evidence quoted by lay individuals.[1]

Despite this expert conclusion, lay observers and certain psychiatrists have stated that the content of certain forms of mass media have a deleterious effect on children and adults. A further attempt is made to causally relate juvenile delinquency and its recent increase to the content of crime, horror, sadism, and brutality found in some comic books, television programs, and motion pictures. These three forms of media have been singled out by the critics for special attention and served as a focus for the Senate Subcommittee which investigated juvenile delinquency from 1954 to 1956.

In this chapter we shall examine the evidence which has been presented by observers concerning the role of mass media in juvenile delinquency around the three major areas of (1) motion pictures, (2) television, and (3) comic books. The reader should be aware that the currently accepted theories of crime and delinquency causation in sociology place the emphasis upon explanations involving differential association and socialization within a delinquent sub-culture.

Motion Pictures and Delinquency

Motion picture films, along with other forms of mass media such as television, comic books, and radio, have been advanced as a significant factor in juvenile delinquency. The presentation of crime, horror, and brutality sequences in movies is imputed, especially by lay observers, to be partially responsible for current youthful delinquency. Some of the attention previously directed toward the influence of movies on behavior has been shifted to the newer medium of television. Consequently, the serious evaluations of the movies' effects on behavior are limited to the period, 1920-40.

Delinquency researchers, at an early period, were concerned with the impact of motion pictures on their subjects. Cyril Burt reported in 1925 that seven per cent of his delinquent boys had an all-consuming interest in films.[2] According to Burt, the film shows criminal techniques and positively advertises crime as a form of behavior. Healy and Bronner in their study of delinquents and non-delinquents in Boston, New Haven, and Detroit in the 1930's found that a larger number of delinquents exhibited regular movie attendance than non-delinquents. They reported that only a few delinquents had definitely imitated the criminal techniques which they had viewed on the screen.[3] From the treatment of movies in their work, one concludes that Healy and Bronner dismiss films as being inconsequential in the delinquencies of their sample.

The most celebrated studies of the impact of motion pictures on children's behavior occurred under the auspices of the Payne Fund during the four year period, 1929-1932. These studies conducted by university sociologists, psychologists, and educators sought to establish some basic propositions concerning the effects of motion pictures on the child's physical, psychological, and social behavior. Of particular interest to the student of delinquency is the study by the sociologists, Blumer and Hauser, entitled *Movies, Delinquency, and Crime.*

Blumer and Hauser focused on the role of films in the careers of male and female delinquents and criminals. To a lesser extent they were concerned with the impact of films on inmates of correctional institutions and non-delinquent boys and girls. Data were collected through the techniques of individual personal accounts, autobiographies, personal interviews, and questionnaires. Although the researchers maintained that their investigation was exploratory and that their statistical findings should be viewed as "rough approximations" and not as proved conclusions,[4] the tendency in social science has been to accept the study as definitive and conclusive.

Blumer and Hauser conclude that the motion picture may exert antithetical effects. For some, movies may reinforce conventional behavior but for others, films may dispose them to participation in delinquency and crime. If this point of view is acceptable, it is logical to assume that these opposing reactions are due not only to the differential content of the films but also to the differential perceptions of the individuals viewing the films. Individuals will perceive the film content and interpret its meanings in terms of their previous socialization experiences and their unique personality need-gratification system. Thus, the impact of any sequence in a film cannot be viewed in isolation from the humans who are viewing it. There is an interaction between the individuals who are viewing and the film content. Reactions to the film sequence will be contingent upon the basic personality structures of the groups and individuals viewing it. To document this point, one only need view the differential reactions of Catholic and Protestant groups to the religious film, *Martin Luther,* and the recent controversial *Baby Doll.*

Blumer and Hauser further state that films were an important factor in the criminal and delinquent careers of ten per cent of the males and twenty-five per cent of the females studied.[5] The investigators feel that these statistics are basically conservative since they only represent the cases in which the offenders were able to trace the influence of the films themselves. This assumption is not ncessarily valid since we may seriously question whether the delinquent or criminal really has the insight necessary to assess the factors which created his situation. Blumer and Hauser's assumption is analogous to a physician's accepting the patient's explanation of the reasons why he developed pneumonia. Movies, they contend, exert their deleterious influence by the presentation of the criminal pattern and role with which the pre-delinquent may establish an identification. The criminal role of the movies provides the visual imagery of techniques and styles of life along with the verbal rationalizations which offer a justification for the behavior. To their credit, Blumer and Hauser state that movies may also provide the focus for the delinquent's relearning of socially approved values and the negative social consequences of delinquent behavior.

In their concluding remarks, Blumer and Hauser observe that the children in high-delinquency areas are more sensitized to the delinquent pattern of behavior found in films than those from low delinquency areas. They assume that movies play an important role for the children who reside in the delinquency areas.[6] However, an opposing conclusion is reached by Paul Cressey in his study of the motion picture's role in a high delinquency area in New York City. After many observations under controlled conditions, Cressey concluded that movies did not have any appreciable effect on the creation of delinquency. This statement does not deny the fact that criminal techniques and rationalizations obtained from films may not be used by delinquents for filling in their repertoire, but this is quite different from assuming that movies caused delinquent behavior originally.[7]

The most serious objections concerning the validity of the Blumer-Hauser findings have been raised by Mortimer Adler in his book, *Art and Prudence*. This book is a review of the findings on the relationship of movies to human behavior and was written at the request of the representatives of producers of motion pictures. In Adler's analysis of the Blumer-Hauser study he is critical of the researchers' non-utilization of control groups with which to compare the delinquent and criminal autobiographies and questionnaires.[8]

Adler's criticism is valid since delinquent and non-delinquent boys and girls drawn from comparable socio-economic groups and interviewed under similar conditions could react to the movies in approximately the same manner. Until this basic point is clarified by the use of control groups, the conclusions of Blumer and Hauser should be accepted with reservations.

Motion pictures became a focus of the Senate Subcommittee's investigations of juvenile delinquency. Hearings held by the subcommittee in Los Angeles in 1955 were supplemented by questionnaires sent to the members of the Medical Correctional Association and the American Academy of Forensic Sciences concerning the relationship of crime and brutality in films with juvenile delinquency. The subcommittee concluded that films have increasingly emphasized brutality and crime sequences and that these negative sequences could provide the precipitating or triggering mechanisms in the anti-social and delinquent behavior of the emotionally disturbed child. Furthermore, the subcommittee felt that the continual viewing of sadistic and crime movies would have a negative impact on the normal non-delinquent child.[9] The subcommittee's conclusions were based on the returned questionnaires and testimony based chiefly on the impressions of clinicians who have been concerned with the issue. As yet no scientific study exists which shows conclusively that crime, sadistic, and horror movies have the profound deleterious effects on either emotionally disturbed or normal children which are attributed to these film types.

Comic Books and Delinquency

With the upswing in the juvenile delinquency rate in the late 1940's and the early 1950's, groups of citizens expressed alarm over this generation of teenagers and their behavior. Blame for juvenile misbehavior was diffused throughout the society; parental delinquency, working mothers, excessive television viewing, and horror and crime comics were all singled out for special examination. The role of horror and crime comics affecting juvenile behavior was placed under close scrutiny in the early 1950's by state legislative investigating committees (for example, New York), by the Senate Subcommittee to Investigate Delinquency of the Eighty-third Congress (1954), and by the formation of local groups, generally composed of parents, teachers, and character building agency representatives, to evaluate comic books and to assign ratings ranging from "no objection" to "very objectionable."

The activity of the governmental investigation committees and local citizens organizations were symptomatic of the basic alarm which these lay people had concerning the negative consequences of comic book reading for the child's personality development. Others felt that crime and horror comic books in particular were contributing causes to the increase in juvenile delinquency. In this opinion, laymen received support from the psychiatrist, Dr. Frederic Wertham, the leading crusader against the comic books.

However, there is diverse opinion in the field of human behavior concerning the precise influence which comic books exert on motivation and action. In this section we shall examine the scientific opinion of what effect, if any, crime and horror comics have on children's behavior and the relationship of this medium to juvenile misconduct.

First, a distinction should be made concerning the types of comics which are assumed to be related to juvenile misbehavior. All observers limit the area of concern to those illustrated stories which appear in pamphlet or booklet form. Newspaper comic strips such as "Steve Canyon," "Dixie Dugan," and "Little Orphan Annie," are not criticised as having negative consequences for the readers. The public's concern has been with those comic books which depict crime, horror, brutality, sadism,

or sex. Despite the presence of aggressive themes, the animal
cartoons such as "Tom and Jerry," "Mickey Mouse," and "Donald
Duck," are excluded from those which are viewed as having
deleterious effects.

Newspaper comic strips had their origin in this country
with the publication of "The Yellow Kid" in the New York
World in 1896. The Katzenjammer Kids made their appearance
in the New York *Journal* in 1897 and a new American behavior
pattern was established. Newspaper comics reach an estimated
audience of eighty million readers in this country. The origin
of the comic books was much later with *New Fun* appearing in
1935 and *Action Comics* in 1938. The decade of the 1940's witnessed a massive growth of the comic book as a popular reading pastime for children and certain types of adults. In March
1954, the Audit Bureau of Circulation noted that there were
422 different kinds of comics and comic book titles on the
newsstands. The Senate Hearings on comic books and juvenile
delinquency elicited the information that approximately 75
to 100 million copies of these booklets were circulated each
month of which one-fourth were of the crime and horror variety. This would mean that around 20 million of the crime-
horror comics were reaching the newsstands each month.[10]

Opposition to comic books by citizens groups and certain
psychiatrists has centered around the crime and horror comics.
These comics bear such titles as "Tales from the Crypt," "Lorna,
the Jungle Queen," "Beware, Terror Tales," "Forbidden Worlds,"
and "The Vault of Horror." All of the above comics were given
very objectionable ratings by the Committee on Evaluation of
Comic Books in Cincinnati, Ohio.[11]

But how significant are crime and horror comics in terms
of the total content of comic magazines? Dr. Morton Malter, an
educator, made a study of the content of comics for a two-month
period in 1951. From twenty-two comic book publishers who
were solicited, he received 185 comics from seventeen cooperative publishers. These he viewed as being a representative sample
of the comics at that time. In analyzing the content and types
of publications, he made the following classification of comic
types: Western stories, 11.1 per cent; adventure stories, 10.7
per cent; animal antics, 10.3 per cent; love stories, 10.2 per cent;
detective stories, 9.3 per cent; superman stories, 6.9 per cent;

adult antics, 6.6 per cent; adolescent antics, 5.2 per cent; jungle stories, 2.6 per cent; children's antics, 2.3 per cent; and sport stories, 0.5 per cent. Dr. Malter concludes that crime stories, as had been charged, do not dominate comics, and that the percentage of pages devoted to humor (24.4 per cent) is approximately equal to that given to crime (25.8 per cent). He further observes that neither the plates nor the drawings are erotic in the majority of the cases. His study shows that on the whole the attacks on the comic books are unwarranted; however, he would conclude that it is desirable for children to leave comic books for more sophisticated readings as they grow older.[12]

But this analysis of the content of comic books leaves unanswered the question of the comics' influence on behavior in general and juvenile delinquency in particular. Reputable opinion in the fields of sociology and psychology holds that no conclusive evidence exists that crime comic book reading is a significant factor in delinquency causation and that the full effects of comics in general on behavior have not been assessed. In opposition to this point of view is the leading crusader against crime and horror comics, Dr. Frederic Wertham, who claims that this reading material is an important contributing factor to juvenile delinquency. Briefly we shall examine both positions.

The position of sociologists and psychologists on the comic book controversy rests on the fact that no empirical study exists which shows any positive relationship between comic book reading and juvenile delinquency. Certain delinquents in interviews with psychiatrists and in hearings before juvenile court judges have blamed their crimes on ideas which were obtained from reading comic books. One should be skeptical of these stories for it is doubtful whether the delinquent fully understands why he committed the crime. Psychiatrists and laymen have at times interpreted delinquent acts as stemming directly from reading about certain forms of activity in the comic books. Thus the comic book can become a convenient and simplistic explanation for the delinquent act, and the delinquent may invoke the story to gain the sympathy of the authorities. Dr. Mandel Sherman, the educational psychologist, has stated, "In studying the causes of behavior problems of children for many years, I have never seen one instance of a child whose behavior disturbance originated in the reading of comic books nor even a case of a delinquent whose behavior was exaggerated by such readings."[13] Even if the child is an avid reader of horror and crime comics, this is no reason to assume that if a delinquent act occurs that it is the consequence of an excessive reading of these materials. A more tenable explanation would be that exaggerated concern with sex, lurid stories, or crime by children is a symptom of more fundamental disturbances in the personality structure. Remove the comic books and the child's maladjustment will find reflection in other areas of his social life space. In summary, we need to remember that not only are millions of children exposed to comics of all types without apparent harm but that juvenile delinquency existed in serious manifestations before the advent of comics.

An opposing opinion is expressed by the psychiatrist, Frederic Wertham, who maintains that crime and horror comic books are a significant contributing factor in juvenile delinquency. In his book, *Seduction of the Innocent* (1954), which Wertham maintains is based on seven years of extensive clinical observations and studies of hundreds of children and adolescents seen by him and his fellow workers in various settings (clinical and non-clinical), his position is stated in a forceful manner. He maintains that the content of comics, by their excessive presentation of horror, violence, crime, sadism, and perverted sexual material, has demoralized the egos of the children and desensitized them to normal human emotions. Since this book has received so much public attention and has been widely accepted as being valid in presenting the negative consequences of comic book reading, it is pertinent to examine his method of study and his conclusions.

Although Wertham maintains that juvenile delinquency is a consequence of a multiplicity of factors, his approach to the problem of causation is particularistic in that he singles out comic book reading as being the major factor. The field of criminology and delinquency is strewn with the wrecks of discredited particularistic explanations of anti-social behavior. At various times, physical characteristics, mental deficiency, and psychological disturbances have been advanced as the major causative explanation of crime, only to be later rejected from the results of scientific study. There is nothing in the comic book causation explanation to indicate that it will be more valid than previous particularistic explanations. In fact, as the section on the search for causes has indicated, the key to understanding juvenile delinquency is set in the interaction of the multiplicity of social and psychological factors which influence the individual's personality development.

Wertham states that his conclusions concerning the negative effects of comic book reading are based on clinical observations of children from all levels of society. However, he provides no explanation for the reader of his procedure of study; we never knew how many children were studied, how intensively they were studied, nor how normal or disturbed they were. He ignores the scientific rules for research investigations involved in the testing of one variable, comic books, on the personality of the child. If Dr. Wertham had followed the usual procedure of having experimental and control groups, one could discern the differential effects, if any, of comic books on the emotionally maladjusted child as compared to the normal child. Since Wertham is a psychiatrist, his universe of children is over-represented with those who possessed behavior disorders before they became addicted to crime and horror stories. Due to Wertham's non-differentiation between normal and disturbed children, the results are suspect.

Frederick Thrasher, a sociologist, whose research in the field of juvenile behavior has extended over more than three decades, has presented an excellent critique of Wertham's research techniques. Thrasher states:

> "Wertham's major claims rest only on a few selected and extensive cases of children's deviate behavior where it is said that comics have played an important role in producing delinquency. Although Wertham has claimed in his various writing that he and his associates have studied thousands of children, normal and deviate, rich and poor, gifted and mediocre, he presents no statistical summary of his investigations. He makes no attempt to substantiate that his illustrative cases are in any way typical of all delinquents who read comics, or that the delinquents who do not read the comics do not commit similar types of offenses."[14]

Although Thrasher's critique of Wertham's techniques appeared in 1949 before the latter's book, *The Seduction of the Innocent,* the same flaws in methodology appear along with the same unsupported assertions concerning the negative influence of comics.

Many other objections can be raised concerning the cause-effect relationships which Wertham predicates between comic books and juvenile behavior. In an extreme analysis by Wertham, the Batman stories which contain the adventures of Bruce Wayne, a socialite, and his ward, Dick Grayson, are analyzed within the framework of a homosexual syndrome of pederasty.[15] According to Wertham, this homo-erotic relationship is suggested to the child before he can read and the homosexual trend in the personality is fostered or aroused by these stories. This analysis is an excellent illustration of anthropomorphism which pervades certain types of psychoanalytical writings. Anthropomorphism is the attributing of complex adult motives, feelings, and reasoning to the infant or child. In this view, the child is constructed as a miniature adult with the same language capacity and a similar thought structure. Wertham analyzes the Batman series within the psychoanalytical frame of reference as an adult would by projecting his meanings of the relationship to the child. Of more interest to the observer is the child's perception of the Batman series and his view of the relationship of Bruce and Dick. It is doubtful whether the child sees homosexuality in the relationship for he is without the concepts or language to perceive this type of situation. It is just as plausible that the child will interpret the Wayne-Grayson situation as a positive interpersonal relationship between an older and younger male. Unfortunately, Wertham never admits the possibility that certain characters in comic stories may represent positive identification figures.

As a consequence of the Senate Subcommittee's investigation of comic books and juvenile delinquency and public pressure from citizens groups, in October, 1954, the Comics' Magazine Association of America was established with a code governing materials to be presented in these magazines. Regulations concerning the presentation of crime, sex, violence, and advertising appear to have been successful in removing the major objections of the public to comic books. The extreme crime and horror comics have been to a large extent withdrawn from the market.

In summary, no significant scientific evidence exists for the assumption by Wertham and others that comic books are a major factor in delinquency causation and are responsible for the increase in juvenile delinquency. Although comic books have changed drastically in content in the last three years, the trend of juvenile delinquency is still upward.

Television and Delinquency

The last decade in American society has seen the mass dissemination of television into the homes. According to the United States Bureau of Census, the number of households with television sets continues to increase. In 1950, 12 per cent of the households had television sets. By August, 1956, the proportion of households with one television set had increased to 72 per cent while 4 per cent of the households had two sets. The concentration of television sets is found in urban centers with a lower proportion in rural areas. The next few years will witness an almost complete saturation of homes with television sets.

As with the previously discussed media of motion pictures and comic books, the question has been posed by both researchers and lay groups of the impact of television on life activities. What effect does television have on interaction patterns within the family? What influence does television exercise on family recreational activities? What impact do television programs have on their audience, particularly the children? What relationship, if any, exists between the content of television programs and juvenile delinquency? Although many other questions have been posed concerning the impact of television on the society and individuals, we shall focus on the assumed relationships between child and adolescent television viewing and later behavioral sequences.

Examination of popular magazines and newspapers in the culture indicates that many groups are concerned with the effects that television has on the behavior of children. Civic clubs, religious organizations, women's groups, and private citizens in their statements to the press and before the Kefauver Subcommittee when it was investigating television have reflected anxiety over the imputed negative consequences of television viewing on children. These lay groups' objections to television can be listed under four areas of concern. These are:

1. Television programs are characterized by excessive violence, terror, and aggressiveness which seriously disturb the child.
2. Television programs may fail to promote respect for law and order.
3. The *modus operandi* for crimes of aggression and violence are derived from television programs.
4. Television and radio crime programs are directly responsible for the appalling increase in juvenile crime.[16]

These four lay assumptions, despite their being unsupported by scientific research, have a tenacious hold on public opinion. These lay opinions are generally supported by impressionistic articles in the lay press. For example, in the February 1953 issue of *Cosmopolitan* appeared an article by Evan Wylie entitled, "Violence on T.V.—Entertainment or Menace?" which indicted television programs through the numbers process. It was contended that during one week in one city, 852 crimes were portrayed on television programs, including 167 murders along with other violent assaultive and property crimes.[17] Wylie's implicit assumption is that this volume of crime must inevitably have a negative influence on the child's personality make-up. Unfortunately, there is no valid documentation of the mechanism by which this occurs.

Reinforcement of the layman's view is provided by the clinical observations of some psychiatrists who have qualified themselves as experts in this field. Dr. Ralph Banay, a psychiatrist who has worked in the correctional field, testified concerning television programs and their relationship to the emotionally disturbed child before the Kefauver Subcommittee investigating the causes of delinquency. From his clinical observations of delinquents and criminals, Dr. Banay testified that programs of aggression and violence on television have a profound negative effect on emotionally disturbed children and that for these individuals, television is the preparatory school for juvenile delinquency.[18] Banay's conclusions are not based on the acceptable scientific procedure of comparing the effects of television on emotionally disturbed children who are delinquent with those who are not delinquent; also no data are presented on the effect of television viewing on emotionally adjusted children. Until such evidence is available, the statement of Banay and other psychiatrists that television viewing of crime and horror programs is detrimental to the child's emotional development remains an unsupported assertion.

Unfortunately, we possess little scientific research on the effect of television viewing on children's behavior and until we do, the major questions in this area cannot be answered. One notable research project conducted by the Laboratory of Human Development at Harvard has been concerned with the role of television viewing in child socialization. This particular study was a part of a larger study concerned with identification in children. Dr. Eleanor Maccoby who participated as a member of the research team in this project reported on some of the results in her testimony before the Kefauver Subcommittee.[19] The study universe was composed of 379 mothers of the upper-middle and upper-lower classes who resided in the Greater Boston Metropolitan Area and who had a child in kindergarten. Each mother was interviewed to assess her child training methods and the amount of time the child spent watching television. Each mother was rated at the end of the interview on the degree of emotional warmth of her relationship with the child. Dr. Maccoby wanted to test the common assumption that the highly frustrated or repressed child would spend more time in television viewing than the "adjusted" child. Her conclusions do not fully support this hunch. The conclusions were: (1) In upper-middle class families, children most frustrated by their situations view television more frequently; (2) in upper-lower class families, no significant relationship was evidenced between degree of frustration and time spent in television viewing.[20]

Dr. Maccoby's study and statements before the committee indicate that more attention must be paid to the differential impact of television viewing as related to the variables of class status, emotional status and developmental level of the viewer, the situational context within which the program is viewed, and the unique content of the program. For example, to know that one television program contains two murders has little meaning unless one knows the social-psychological story context within which these events occurred. Each child, whether from television or other sources, is ultimately exposed to the fact that aggression and hostility are part of his environment. In child socialization the major problem is the channeling of these negative emotions into socially appropriate avenues of expression. The child's reaction to the television program will be cast in terms of his basic personality pattern which is largely a consequence of the interpersonal relationships in the primary group of the family. The child's personality determines his selection of certain television materials for fantasy and usage in play situations.

Most observers agree that television viewing has few if any detrimental effects on the child with a secure and well adjusted personality. Many observers, however, feel that if the child is warped in his personality development that crime and horror stories on television have a negative impact. These programs, according to this scheme, provide the content for aggressive or hostile acts and may be the precipitating or triggering mechanism in juvenile delinquency. No proof exists for the latter statement's validity. If it were valid, the child's misbehavior could be as easily triggered by the more aggressive fairy tales such as "Hansel and Gretel" and "Little Red Riding Hood." It is naive to assume that any child, emotionally disturbed or normal, can be effectively immunized from the ubiquitous aggressive-crime content of the culture. A more fruitful avenue for understanding juvenile misbehavior should be located in the context of the family and peer groups, not in television.

Are television programs then a causal factor in delinquency? Reputable opinion in the field of sociology and psychology is almost unanimous in the belief that it is not. Dr. Goldenson, a child psychologist, conducted a questionnaire survey of eighteen authorities from the fields of education, social welfare, sociology, and health on whether television programs were responsible for the problem of juvenile delinquency. The large majority of the answers were in the negative, but those who answered in the affirmative vein qualified their statements with the comment that this belief was not based on any more than impression and suspicion.[21]

In reviewing the four lay assumptions, stated earlier in this section about the negative consequences of television for behavior, it should be noted that: (1) No scientific evidence exists to validate the assumption that television programs of violence, terror, and aggressiveness disturb the child; (2) No scientific evidence exists to show that television programs fail to promote respect for law and order. The Television Code always necessitates that law and order be victorious before the program's conclusion. The criminal is always apprehended and punished which in no way reflects societal reality. In society approximately 35 per cent of the crimes known to the police are cleared by arrest. Some police officials are even complimentary about the role of television in aiding their work. Inspector Ralph Baker, Chief of the Detroit Youth Bureau, stated: "The local television stations . . . have been exceedingly helpful in carrying programs which will tend to educate parents and children alike in social behavior that will minimize our task." (3) Quite accurately the *modus operandi* for the commission of crimes of aggression and violence may be derived from television programs as from almost every aspect of the culture. Techniques of crime and delinquency are available in sources ranging from the *Encyclopedia Britannica* to the more important sources of informal contacts with peers in the clique group. (4) No scientific evidence exists that television programs of any type are responsible for the upswing in juvenile delinquency in the last decade.

The Senate Subcommittee which investigated the relationship of television and juvenile delinquency in 1954 concluded that the viewing of crime and horror television programs by children represented a calculated risk and that this risk was much greater for delinquency prone and disturbed children. The Subcommittee reached the following conclusions:

1. "Rejected all suggestions for governmental censorship.
2. Establishment of a Presidential commission to study the effects of all mass media on children's minds.
3. Establishment of 'listening councils' of 'sober, unbiased' citizens to keep a watch on children's programs in their communities.
4. Suggested stricter control of television programs by the Federal Communications Commission, which should be given the authority to levy fines and revoke licenses of stations violating the code.
5. Urged the launching of research projects by private and public foundations which would further study the effects of television on children's behavior."[22]

Conclusion

Our discussion has shown that no positive correlation can be established between the content of mass media and delinquent behavior. However, scientific information exists neither in quantity nor in depth to dismiss completely assumptions which maintain that mass media involving the presentation of crime, sadism, or brutality have a negative impact on emotionally unbalanced personalities.

Tentatively some generalizations may be stated concerning the relationship of mass media to juvenile behavior. These are:

1. Mass media do not form the entire cultural system for the juvenile; he is also exposed to the influences of the primary groups of the family and peers. Mass media are a reflection of the socio-cultural values of the society.
2. Mass media exert a differential impact on juveniles which is contingent upon factors of class, sub-culture, and unique personality configuration.
3. Mass media, as other cultural forms, do provide techniques and rationalizations for delinquent behavior.
4. No scientific evidence exists to show that mass media are primary factors in delinquency causation.

Selected Bibliography

Mortimer J. Adler, *Art and Prudence* (New York: Longmans, Green and Company), 1937. A review of the findings on the relationship of movies to human behavior. Contains a thought-provoking critique of the Blumer-Hauser study.

Herbert Blumer and Philip M. Hauser, *Movies, Delinquency and Crime* (New York: The Macmillan Company), 1933. Through personal accounts, autobiographies, personal interviews, and questionnaires, the authors attempt to measure the impact of films on inmates of correctional institutions and delinquent boys and girls.

"Juvenile Delinquency (Comic Books)," *Hearings Before the Subcommittee to Investigate Juvenile Delinquency,* April 21, 22, and June 4, 1954 (Washington: Government Printing Office), 1954. The testimony of both experts and laymen before the Kefauver Committee on the role of comic books in shaping behavior with emphasis on delinquency.

"Juvenile Delinquency (Television Programs)," *Hearings Before the Subcommittee to Investigate Juvenile Delinquency,* April 6 and 7, 1955 (Washington: Government Printing Office),

1955. The testimony of both experts and laymen before the Kefauver Committee on the role of television in influencing behavior with emphasis on delinquency.

Morton Malter, "The Content of Current Comic Magazines,"
Elementary School Journal, 52 (May, 1952), 505-510. An excellent study of the content of selected comic books for a two month
period in 1951.

Frederic Thrasher, "The Comics and Delinquency: Cause
or Scapegoat," *Journal of Educational Sociology*, 23 (December,
1949), 195-205. A scholarly critique of Wertham's position in
reference to the relationship of comic books and delinquency.

Frederic Wertham, *Seduction of the Innocent* (New York:
Rinehart and Company, Inc.), 1956. This book states the Wertham thesis that crime and horror comic books are an important
contributing factor to present-day delinquency.

Frederick Wertham, *The Circle of Guilt* (New York: Rinehart and Company, Inc.), 1956. The case of Frank "Tarzan"
Santana is analyzed in terms of Wertham's comic book causation theory of delinquency.

David J. Pittman, Assistant Professor of Sociology at the University of Rochester, obtained his B.A. and M.A. degrees in
sociology at the University of North Carolina; is the recipient of
the Ph.D. in Human Development from the University of Chicago. His major fields of research interest are crime and delinquency and demography and human ecology. He is the senior
co-author of the monograph, *The Chronic Police Case Inebriate*
(with C. Wayne Gordon) to be published by the Yale Center
of Studies on Alcohol in the summer of 1957, & has lectured on
"The Chronic Drunkenness Offender" at the Yale Summer School
of Studies on Alcohol in the summer of 1597, has lectured on
Michigan State Board on Alcoholism; also was in charge of
the delineation of the census tracts for Monroe County, New
York, in 1956.

Part III

Evaluations of Attempted Solutions

CHAPTER 11.

DELINQUENCY AND JUSTICE

CLYDE B. VEDDER
University of Arizona

The Police and Delinquent Youth

The primary function of the police is the protection and preservation of life and property. They conduct criminal investigations and apprehend violators of the law. Usually there are three categories of "children" under police supervision, (1) dependent children under ten who cannot commit a crime as in Texas, for example; (2) juveniles, ages 10-16 and (3) minor children, or all those under twenty-one. In some states, the age limit is reduced to seven in the first category, which corresponds to common law delineation.

Since the police are concerned with violations of law, this problem of law enforcement is accentuated by the fact that there are more than a billion and a half laws, including both felonies and misdemeanors, on the statute books in the United States; there are more laws than people, nearly seven for every man, woman, and child. As laws increase in number, violations tend to increase, and police make more and more juvenile arrests. Some estimates place the number of juveniles who come to the attention of the police as exceeding two million every year.

Adding to the problem of policing juveniles is the growing spirit of contempt for the law enforcement system, on both adult and juvenile levels. Parents frequently boast of evading laws in the presence of their children.

The problem of policing delinquent youth is increased due to the relative and absolute rise in the incidence of juvenile delinquency. However, juvenile statistical data is highly inaccurate due to the lack of uniform reporting, variations in court practices and community practices, the lack of compulsion in registering data pertaining to delinquents. In one state, only four out of nearly seventy counties cooperated with the Children's Bureau in Washington in supplying pertinent information. In many states, the juvenile delinquents are deliberately undercounted, so as to come "under the wire" as regards the accepted figure of two per cent of youth that are considered delinquent on the average.

Prior to World War One, the volume of delinquency was about one per cent of the 10-17 age group, but during and following World War Two, the volume has been computed at two per cent. Delinquency rose sharply from 1940 to 1945, declined to 1948, then reversed itself to score new highs. By 1953, juvenile delinquency was 29 per cent over 1948, while population increased only 6 per cent.

The police constitute the first line of defense in combating juvenile delinquency and the attitude of the police officer may determine the reaction of the juvenile perhaps for years to come. A negative or punitive approach provokes fear and hatred and revolt, yet the police must use some reasonable means to protect themselves and the community.

The police officer must make crucial decisions sometimes on a moment's notice. He must understand a child's behavior, know his community's resources, have the skill and intelligence to make the wise decision perhaps within a split second. As has been pointed out so many times in the literature, this requires the "wisdom of Solomon, the courage and strength of Sampson, the patience of Job, the leadership of Moses, the kindness of the Good Samaritan, the faith of Mary, the diplomacy of Lincoln, and the tolerance of Confucius."

It is probably safe to say that the majority of the children coming to the attention of the police have not had an opportunity to "grow up normally." Citizens who complain to the police often call back to find out why the children are home again instead of in jail. Demands are frequently made to the police that they terrify and punish the children. Should police punish children to meet the psychological needs of punitive complainants and other vengeful individuals? Citizens make the largest category of those who are sources of complaint regarding juvenile delinquents, approximately 48 per cent of total reported.

The next largest source of complaint is the Police Department itself, picking up about 30 per cent of the children in routine patrol work. Parents come in third in accounting for complaints to the police on juvenile delinquency. In Houston, Texas, parents are involved in 35 per cent of the complaints against girls, compared to only 9 per cent of the complaints against boys. Roughly 50 per cent of Houston children are released to their parents, a policy used for all first offenders. About 27 per cent are referred to Probation and 16 per cent are just "released."

Besides acquiring the facts of the case, the police officer needs information on the child himself. Facts in addition to the pertinent case aspects are often necessary to determine whether the juvenile offender should be returned home or left home with no further action, or referred to some social agency, or referred to the juvenile court. Police officers should not step out of character to do social case work and probably most police officers would rather lose a trigger finger than be forced to establish "rapport" with some recalcitrant youngster.

The number of police officers assigned to juvenile details is woefully inadequate. In a *Bulletin* on "Police Service for Juveniles" in 1954, by United States Dept. of Health, Education and Welfare, it was stated that at least five per cent of the police force should be assigned to juvenile detail, but this goal is attained in only one of six hundred communities.

Juvenile detail police officers incur considerable responsibility in the conduct of investigation and interrogation. When interrogating youngsters or talking to their parents, officers should wear a jacket and tie. An officer in shirt sleeves, with gun and handcuffs visible creates an unsuitable impression in juvenile work. Officers assigned to juvenile detail have to take a certain amount of ribbing as other personnel call them "dude undertakers," or "altar boys," or "Hey, bell boy! Front and Center. Customer for you!"[1]

The youthful offender usually has problems and the police officer may be the first one to whom the child can confide. In conducting the interview, the officer must keep in mind that the reputation of the department is at stake and which will be blemished if he uses profanity, obscenity or calls children names

such as "thief" or "liar," or loses his temper, uses physical force
or makes promises he knows he cannot keep. Should the child
suspect be caught in a lie, give him a chance to "save face." A
good technique is to furnish the excuse, such as "wasn't the
moon shining at the time," or "did you have an erection about
the time you committed the act," and many a juvenile suspect
will leap at the chance to "confess" if the blame can be attributed to some external agency or to some force beyond his
immediate control.

Questions should be put to the juvenile in simple language,
and not to encourage a Yes or No answer. Remind the child
that this is the time to make a "clean breast of it." Let the child
know you have heard worse and are not shocked by what he
is about to tell you and that you understand why young people
often violate the law. At the conclusion of the interview, it is
usually good form to say, "Is there anything else you would
like to tell me," and frequently new material may be forthcoming.

Police officers attached to juvenile detail require special
training. Pleasing personality and an even temperament is a
fundamental requirement. In-service training and recruit training is indicated on such subjects as the philosophy of child control, juvenile laws, causes of delinquency, interviewing techniques, screening, dispositions, knowledge of community resources, records, developing good relationships with the public
and programs of prevention.

As indicated above, the manner in which the police handle
juvenile offenders determines in a large degree the juvenile's
attitude toward legal authority. The National Advisory Police
Committee to the Federal Security Administrator, with approval and assistance of the United States Children's Bureau
compiled a "Manual for the Guidance of Enforcement Officers
in Dealing with Juvenile Offenders" published by the Government Printing Office, Washington, D.C. 1944. Certain procedures
were listed having to do with handling juvenile delinquents:

DO THIS:

(1) *Treat the juvenile with consideration.*

Remember that what he thinks of you and your conduct
may influence his future attitude to be in favor of, or opposed to, social and legal requirements.

(2) *Be friendly.*

Many juveniles feel that the world is against them. Do not let your conduct further the development of an anti-social attitude in the child. Many juveniles are discouraged and believe they are failures.

(3) *Be firm.*

Appeal to his intelligence, his reason, his sense of fairness.

(4) *Discover the child's problem, if you can.*

His problems are as important to him as yours are to you.

(5) *Try to gain his confidence and respect.*

In attempting to determine the child's guilt or innocence with respect to any overt act, your chances are far better if he believes in you.

(6) *Remember that the child of today is the man of tomorrow.*

A boy who hates a police officer because of the officer's abusive attitude will, as a man, have little respect for him.

(7) *Be positive in your attitude.*

Show the benefits that come from an attitude of conformity with lawful requirements rather than dwelling on the harmful effects of anti-social behavior.

DON'T DO THIS:

(1) *Don't resort to vulgarity, profanity or obscenity.*

The use of such language by a police officer is especially reprehensive and should not be tolerated under any circumstances.

(2) *Don't "brand" the juvenile.*

Epithets such as "thief," "liar," "burglar," "forger," etc., should not be used towards juveniles whether in custody or not. Such epithets give rise to justified complaints. They are rightfully resented by the parents and the use of such terms is a reflection upon the character and intelligence of an officer using them.

(3) *Don't lose your temper.*

To do so is an admission of mental inferiority to the person being interrogated.

Certainly no policeman should resort to vulgarity, profanity, or obscenity—yet such behavior on the part of the "guardians of the law" is by no means rare.

Law officers apprehend only a fraction of the juveniles they accost; they settle more violations than they take into court.

This is known as monitory justice. It is one of the factors that
lead some criminologists to believe that sincere, however misguided efforts have been in behalf of the juvenile offender.[2]
The policeman "judges" thousands of cases every year . . . such
as petty thefts, breaking windows, and starting fires on the
part of gangs in alleys. Because he is often the child's first
personal contact with the law, the policeman should conduct
himself with dignity, impartiality and competence.[3]

In keeping with this principle, the University of Southern
California's Delinquency Control Institute, known more famil-
iarly as the D.C.I. has made available courses of study to help
the police officer understand the causes, treatment, control and
prevention of juvenile delinquency. Somewhat similar courses
of instruction are given at Northwestern University's Traffic
Institute and Yale University's Bureau of Highway Traffic. Excellent courses in this type of training are to be found in the
Federal Bureau of Investigation's educational activities at the
National Police Academy and in the pre-service police training
programs pioneered by August Volmer and now regularly sched-
uled at nearly a dozen colleges and universities, including the
University of California and Michigan State, San Jose State and
Fresno State Colleges in California.

In the handling of juvenile delinquency, specialized training is indicated inasmuch as the nature and quality of juvenile
offenses frequently differ from adult crimes. Looming large
among these special areas of juvenile criminal activities is vandalism, which has been defined as the wilful destruction or de-
facement of things of beauty as works of art, literature or historical monuments. However, in the popular mind of the 1950's,
vandalism also means cutting a tire, slashing auto seats, breaking street lights, removing automobile hub caps, defacing bill
boards and the like. Most vandalism is committed by teen-agers
and has been termed by Dr. Redl as "group psychological in-
toxication."[4]

Vandalism is an outlet for aggression, a mental hygiene
problem, having its roots in the individual, home, and community.
Increasing acts of vandalism indicate a new pattern of juvenile
violence, but containing special values to teen-agers who are
expected to spend several years of life in a state of suspended
animation, awaiting their turn to be adults. Hence, wanton destruction of property lies in the opportunity to provide mean-

ingful status for youth in such sub-groups as the family, his club, or close friends. Vandalism is also an outgrowth of hostility, aggression and frustration. Children who are hostile are children difficult to accept, difficult to like and difficult to teach.

The study of vandalism has been neglected. Professional literature is silent on the subject, even in standard texts of juvenile delinquency and criminology. On the other hand, a substantial library has been built about such objects as arson, assaultive behavior, burglary, sex misconduct and truancy, which occurs with no greater frequency than vandalism in every day life.[5]

Juvenile vandalism on school property cost Chicago tax-payers around $400,000 annually; 22,082 school windows were smashed in Baltimore in one year. In Detroit kids broke into a public library branch, smashed glass cases, ripped rare books to pieces, heaped index cards on the floor and doused them with glue and stole movie projection equipment. In California a gang of boys was arrested for burning a car and running it off a cliff into the Pacific; they "wanted to see it splash." In New Bedford, Mass. five boys, aged 9-13 slashed about $15,000 worth of store windows with glass cutters, then set fire to a church, a drug-store, and an automobile. Their leader, 11, told the cops he liked the excitement when the fire engines came.[6]

The "hot-rodder" poses another problem for police officers on juvenile detail and demands understanding and insight into this modern-day phenomenon. Mechanical proficiency as "cutting down" and "souping up" demonstrate masculinity and as a sex avoidance mechanism it satisfies motives of continence, dependency and conformity. Demands for competitive prowess as in "barreling," "peeling," and "dragging" encourage hyper-masculine feats which lead directly to violations. Police coming out of training today realize that violation of traffic ordinances are not always criminal defiance but a compromise between radical lawlessness and conformity. "Teenicide" games as "chicken" is a quasi-neurotic compulsion alleviating guilt feelings. The insights supplied by psychiatry and clinical psychology are producing better police officers.[7]

An important area of controversy concerns a police prerogative of fingerprinting arrested juveniles. The juvenile offender is seldom fingerprinted or photographed by the police and his name is frequently deleted when his crime is reported by the press. However, inasmuch as the professional criminals often come from the ranks of juvenile delinquents, a reversal of this "protective" procedure might be in order. Proponents of finger-printing juvenile delinquents believe it is the best method of identification, that it helps to protect the innocent, and enables the FBI to include nation-wide juvenile delinquency statistics in their *Uniform Crime Reports*. Is fingerprinting a greater example of social stigma than going to the juvenile court? There is a greater acceptance of fingerprinting, particularly since World War Two, when military personnel and civilian workers in war plants were "printed."

According to *The New York Times* of May 30, 1948, the civilian file of the Federal Bureau of Investigation now con-sists of 65 million fingerprint cards, while the criminal file in-cludes the fingerprint cards of about 7.5 million individuals.[8]

Probably most police are in favor of fingerprinting all ar-rested offenders, juvenile or adult. However, in some states, notably Arizona, juvenile offenders who often "know their rights" cannot be questioned by police officers except in the presence of a juvenile probation officer, cannot be fingerprinted or photographed. While the juvenile court judge permits finger-printing, the permission is so hedged as to be practically worth-less. As stated by Capt. D. L. McGovney, head of the Identifi-cation Bureau of the Maricopa Sheriff's Department in Phoenix, Arizona, "I have fingerprinted five juveniles during the past year, but they were federal prisoners and were fingerprinted with the permission of the U. S. Marshal. Juveniles facing state charges can only be fingerprinted in the presence of a juvenile probation officer and the prints cannot leave his sight!"

Lack of photographs also handicaps the police, which is especially true in crimes of violence. "Not long ago, a sixteen year old girl was accosted by a teenager in a car who attempted to drag her into the vehicle. Chances are the youth had been involved before and if we had a series of pictures to show the girl, it is possible she might have identified her attacker. As it is, we're forced to rely on a general description, and this boy is still at large. The next time he may be successful in his assault, or he might even murder. In contrast, California permits both fingerprinting and photographing of boys and girls between ages 14-17 when arrested for felonies."[8a]

Some police departments have attempted to reduce juvenile

delinquency by establishing junior police systems and the youthful members assist police in traffic details near schools, churches, even down-town corners. In this way, by association with policemen, youngsters learn to respect the officer instead of thinking of him as the "boogie man," someone to be hated and feared and despised. Some studies have revealed that delinquent boys have a greater degree of hostility toward the police than toward the Juvenile Court, Probation Officers or Detention Homes.[9]

Some hostility is engendered by police surveillance that is occasioned by curfew enforcement. Strangely enough, only two articles appeared about curfew in the literature from 1896 to 1943, but in that year the National Institute of Municipal Law Officers prepared a model ordinance for minors, due to war conditions and the rising tide of juvenile delinquency. The curfew is a negative approach, not any substitute for wholesome activities. Furthermore only 14 per cent of delinquent acts by juveniles are committed after 9 P.M., the traditional curfew hour. Police are generally in favor of curfew measures for it gives them an aid in checking movements of youth as well as disrupting the congregation of gangs. However, many parents resent their children being questioned when out on a legitimate errand. Neither do parents like their children to carry "police passes" around with them. Sentiment is mixed regarding curfews for juveniles. Connecticut Juvenile Court judges are opposed to curfew laws, while the state of Arizona recently recommended a curfew on a state-wide basis. In Dade County, Florida, there are 28 municipalities contiguous to each other and some have no curfew laws, so the youngster has only to cross the street to be safe. Confusion is further indicated where four cities have curfew hour at midnight, seven cities select 11 P.M., three cities have 10:30 P.M., 23 cities have 10 P.M., 14 cities have 9 P.M. et cetera.

The City of Philadelphia passed a curfew in 1955 for those under seventeen which prohibited movement after 10:30 P.M. during weekdays and midnight on Friday and Saturdays and responsibility placed on operators of establishments catering to juveniles, with penalties provided. However, a curfew cannot change a delinquent's personal character or needs. It merely limits or circumscribes the scope of his operations. As a method of treating delinquency by the police, it can be only effective to the degree that delinquency is a disease of the night season. The most successful curfew will be the one determined by parents with an understanding on the part of the child as to why it is necessary.[10]

The popular view of the curfew in relation to the police and juvenile delinquency control is summed up by Robert Ruark in the *Miami Herald* (Florida) (August 29, 1955):

"I see nothing particularly horrifying about the nation-wide curfew for teen-agers, especially since I hear juvenile delinquency is caused by lack of sleep . . . it would seem to me that it works soundest in the big cities, where the young gangsters clot the corners in savage knots, and swagger around running people off sidewalks, and haunt the streets and parks for drunks to roll and people to beat up for fun. . . ."

Public opinion is divided on how police should treat the juvenile offender. There is a fairly large category of the public of whom it might be said, "their heart is in the right place." Stallings writes of Morris and Manny who were being detained at the police station, handcuffed to a cot in back of the sergeant's desk for public protection, since they had been picked up for robbery, and were awaiting the arrival of the Juvenile Officer. "The sergeant didn't want to place them in the tank, since it was full of drunks. It just happened that a local civic organization entered the station on some business, and seeing the handcuffed lads raised a tremendous to-do about two sweet, beautiful, cherubic children in durance vile and said, 'We'll see the mayor! We'll see the sheriff! We'll see the governor!' The sergeant, torn between duty and discretion, decided not to incur the wrath of the mayor or governor, took the cuffs off the boys. At that moment, a man drove up to the cafe next door, left his motor running and went in for cigarettes. Morris and Manny went out of the door in a flash. They dived into the car and were off. Five miles out of town, the fugitives at seventy miles an hour ran headlong into a truck loaded with oranges. Both boys were killed instantly!"[11]

Many perfectly honest people may refuse to give information that might lead to the arrest of a juvenile. Others may actually help one escape, based on the apparent feeling that a juvenile can't be a very dangerous person. A police officer in one case, was sent to transport a girl from a theater to Juvenile Hall. She was 17 years of age, but in that short time had been arrested 23 times, from prostitution to armed robbery. Sent to a state school, she escaped, and now was being held on that charge, having been identified, as she sat in the movie, by a prior victim of one of her robberies. The decision was made by the police officer and the woman deputy to forego the handcuffs since it was midday, the streets were crowded, and a break would be most difficult to make. The prisoner no sooner got on the sidewalk than she kicked off her shoes and sprinted away. The officers, who were in uniform, dashed after her but bypassers deliberately got in their way. The girl ran into the street, between two lanes of opposing cars, headed for the corner. The pursuers shouted to the traffic officer on duty to stop her, but he stood there, immobile. The girl got away. Later, the traffic man was asked why he too had failed to catch the girl and he replied, "Nuts! I work traffic."[12]

Opinion is divided in both the public and police as to the efficacy of prevention work by the police in the area of juvenile delinquency. Many people including policemen feel that they should not have the responsibility of "raising" the children of others and state it is not a true police function. Should police departments be in the recreation business?

The New York police department has been fairly successful since the early 1930's with their program of preventive activities, through the Police Athletic League (PAL). PAL's aim is to substitute wholesome recreation for antisocial activities and has more than one hundred thousand members of which 15 per cent are girls.

The addition of women to police departments, especially in juvenile work has been a progressive step. In California and in some other states the police are not permitted to transport or interrogate females between the ages of five and egihteen except in the presence of a woman. However, there still remains considerable prejudice against women in police work and in numbers account for less than one per cent of police personnel today.

The establishment of juvenile bureaus in police departments to handle juvenile delinquency cases has been disappointingly slow. Serving under various nomenclatures as Crime Prevention Bureaus, Youth Guidance Bureaus, Special Services Bureaus, they example forward-looking programs in delinquency control. Adaptation of these and similar agencies and techniques suggest a "cultural lag" in the field of law enforcement. Juvenile delinquency continues to remain a major problem to the police and shows little or no signs of abatement.

The Juvenile Court

The first juvenile court was established on July 1, 1899 in Chicago, Cook County, Illinois. The adoption of the law by the Illinois legislature on April 14, 1899, entitled "An Act to Regulate the Treatment and Control of Dependent, Neglected and Delinquent Children," blazed the trail and by 1950 every state had passed some type of juvenile court statute.

The philosophy of the juvenile court is predicated upon two premises of English common law; (1) Common law had established that children were not criminally liable if they were under seven years of age at the time of their offense. Between the ages of seven and fourteen, the capacity of the child to distinguish between right and wrong was to be determined by examination of each individual case. The juvenile court has extended this earlier age limitation of seven years to eighteen years in most jurisdictions. (2) Founded on the principle of *parens patriae*, namely that the state must exercise guardianship over a child when the parents are unable or unwilling to discharge their full responsibility to him, the juvenile court, as a court of equity, avoids any stigma for a child which a criminal court contact might place upon him.

Juvenile courts are the least understood and the most misunderstood of all the nation's tribunals. Their distinctive philosophy, procedures, and approaches are features which few people appreciate, hence have failed to measure up to the expectations of the public. Despite their existence for more than a half century, too many people still believe that juvenile courts are places where "bad" children are punished.[13]

The juvenile court is becoming "big business" as regards the increasing number of juveniles who appear before it. Prior to World War I, the volume was about one per cent of the 10-17 population which meant that the juvenile courts handled between 170,000 to 200,000 annually. Statistics on juvenile courts are not too comprehensive. In 1948, there were approximately 95,000 cases handled by 399 juvenile courts from 17 states. During World War II juvenile delinquency rates increased sharply to 1945, declined to 1948, started up again in 1949. The volume now is estimated at two per cent of all children aged 10-17. In 1952, there were 385,000 cases to appear before juvenile courts. If the trend of 1948-1952 continues, it has been estimated that nearly 600,000 children will appear before the juvenile courts by 1960.

As in adult delinquency, members of minority groups of juveniles suffer. The problem of delinquency before 1930 was the native-born child of foreign parents, but since the immigration laws of 1924, the new "migrants" are the marginal groups as the urban-drifting Negro, the Puerto Rican, and the Mexican in current juvenile delinquency statistics, due to the barriers to adjustment on social, cultural and economic levels placed in their way. Negro rates have risen, as they contribute 18 per cent of the total delinquency or almost twice their incidence in the population. In the juvenile courts in New York, Negro children appear five times as frequently as their incidence in the general population would indicate. In Los Angeles County, 4.2 per cent of the juvenile population are Negro, whereas 10.4 per cent of delinquent court cases are Negro. In Greater Los Angeles, 13.9 per cent of the juvenile population are of Spanish-speaking minority groups, but 35 per cent of all delinquents are from this group. Delinquency still appears to be a function of minority group rejection.[14]

In the *New York Times* of February 4, 1957, the statement was made that one per cent of New York's families produced 75 percent of the delinquents. These "hard core" families are not only poor but are oppressed by a "constellation" of social problems as alcoholism, drug addiction and immorality. For these and other reasons, the man in the street thinks that the lack of home training and parental neglect account for at least 70 per cent of juvenile delinquency. J. Edgar Hoover, Chief of the Federal Bureau of Investigation refers to juvenile delinquency as "the frontier of shame" and states it is up to parents and the home to do something about it.

After culling over thousands of juvenile court cases, the

Maricopa County officials of Phoenix, Arizona have some recommendations to make parents that "guarantee your child will
become delinquent and will be subsequently tried in Juvenile
Court. This formula is almost infallible."

"Don't give your son any religious or spiritual training. Just
take care of his bodily needs.

In his presence don't be respectful of womanhood or of law
and government. Belittle "Dames" and the courts, the police,
public officials, the school, the church, and business. "It's
all a racket!"

Never look for the real cause of untruthfulness in your child.
You might discover he learned the art of lying from you.

Never try to answer the endless "WHYS" and "HOWS" of
your children, because it pays to be ignorant.

Be sure to humiliate your child in the presence of his
friends. It adds to his respect for you.

If a conflict in wills arises between you and your child,
don't try to reason with him . . . just knock him down . . .
your father was boss of his home and the kids may as well
learn the "hard way."

Don't have any constructive discipline and disagree with your
wife or husband in the child's presence so that the child
will learn on whom to depend.

Be sure to criticize departed guests in the presence of your
child. He will respect your integrity.

Never give your child a reason for the commands laid upon
him; let him guess . . . it's much easier.

Don't consider his educational and emotional development
a parental responsibility. What are schools for?

Don't let him discuss his plans, problems, or pleasures with
you. Just be too busy, so he won't develop affection or security
or trust in you.

Don't teach your child to be tolerant toward people who
differ from him in race, creed or color. Teaching unfairness
in others is an excellent method for training a bad citizen.

Don't give him an allowance, because he might learn how
to save or spend. Don't ask him to give to community needs
or services. Just "dig down" yourself. That's the easiest
way.

Don't be calm or poised. Be shocked and explode when he

tells you he has done something wrong. Then he won't confide in you the next time.

Don't make a pal of him. Go alone to your sports and entertainment. He would only be in the way.

Always buy your children the most expensive games and toys because if you get them something simple they might have to use their own imagination and who wants that side of a child developed?

Never let your child forget that only for you he would not have a roof over his head. You will become a pain in the neck to your child, and he loves to hear about the many sacrifices you make for him.

Don't open your home to his companions; they will muss up the place. And don't be concerned where he spends his free time.

Be sure to keep your home from being a center of cheer. Make it a dumping ground for your grouches. Your child will love your thoughtfulness.

Be sure to forget the promises you make to your child because he will forget the promises he makes to you later, and children have no sense of appreciation.

Always accuse your daughter of being promiscuous with every date she goes out with so that she will be impressed with the fact that you were a "good woman" when you went out with the boys.

Always leave your car keys in the car. This encourages stealing, and since 98 per cent of the car thefts are caused by this method, it proves that you are doing your part to encourage delinquency.

Never praise your child for his worthwhile effort because he might take advantage of your effort and try harder to please you in the future.

Never give your child any affection, and never, never tell him how much you love him. He will get the idea you are a softy and you wouldn't want him to get that impression of you.

If you forget all the above, just remember this one. Be a poor example yourself. You know, "Do as I say, it's no one's business what I do."[15]

Although 1899 is the birth-year of the juvenile court movement, prior efforts to this end should not be overlooked. The development of probation theory by John Augustus beginning in 1841, lent itself to the spreading philosophy of the juvenile court. Also contemporary humanitarian influences made themselves felt in the reduction of capital penalties.

In 1870, Massachusetts enacted a law requiring separate hearings for children in Suffolk County. In 1877 a similar law was approved in New York. In 1892 New York provided for special trials for those under sixteen. In 1898, Rhode Island enacted legislation similar to that of New York. In 1899 Colorado under its school laws began a system of special handling of the child with the innovation that truant officers or teachers might act as his supervisors. Denver, Colorado was the next city after Chicago to create a juvenile court and the result of the efforts of a great pioneer in the juvenile court movement, Judge Benjamin Lindsey.

The underlying philosophy was sponsored by humanitarians, social scientists and a sprinkling of judges, which placed emphasis on treatment consequence, not behavior circumstance, the viewpoint of the adult criminal court. The underlying purpose of the juvenile court is to remove the child offender from criminal to equity courts, which consider the doer rather than the deed, and to have this protection extended to other children.

The Federal government entered this field much later than did the several states. In 1932, Congress provided for transfer of individuals under 21 years who violated Federal laws to state authorities willing to receive them. The Federal Juvenile Delinquency Act was passed in 1938, which permitted cases concerning youths under eighteen years to be heard before a United States District Court, using a procedure similar to that prescribed by state juvenile court laws. Frequently, Federal authorities transfer Federal offenders to local juvenile courts. Basis for this legislation harks back to a model law called a Standard Juvenile Court Act, first adopted at the annual meeting of the National Probation and Parole Association in 1925.

In most states the geographical and political area which is served by the juvenile court is the county. Only Utah, Connecticut, and Rhode Island have set up state-administered juvenile court systems.

While delinquent children challenge the attention and concern of the public, it must be noted that all children handled by the juvenile court are not necessarily delinquent. The United States Children's Bureau reported that for the year 1948, the non-delinquency cases accounted for roughly one third of the total case load of juvenile courts reporting that year. Non-delinquency cases would include the dependent, neglected, abandoned, mentally defective children falling within the general jurisdiction of the juvenile court. In addition, there are cases concerning custody, adoption, illegitimacy, marriage of minors as well as annulments, and problems of physically handicapped children. Jurisdiction may be extended to include adults where children are involved, e.g., to try an adult charged with contributing to the delinquency of a minor.

The juvenile court rests upon the principle that children under eighteen years of age have not reached that state of intellectual and emotional development which make them fully responsible for their acts. However, in actual practice this principle has been over-compromised and since the year of inception, the juvenile court has collected an inordinate number of critics.

Criticisms of the Juvenile Court

Most juvenile courts and their judges seem to be in agreement that if the juvenile's act is sufficiently repugnant, the offender should be remanded over to the adult criminal court for trial and punishment, instead of "treatment." In other words, when the juvenile offender needs the juvenile court the most, he will get it the least.

From the legal point of view, many attorneys feel that the child's constitutional rights might easily be violated, due to the informality of procedure, as testifying against himself under the guise of "talking it over." Or the judge may decide to commit the offender to the reformatory after hearing the child testify in confidence, and the child has had no trial, or for that matter the legal counsel which is his just due according to a fair interpretation of the Sixth Amendment of the Constitution of the United States which makes no distinction between adults and juveniles. It states that "the *accused* shall enjoy the right to a speedy and public trial" and a juvenile brought before the court for burglary or any other crime is an . . . accused.

Most juvenile codes specifically forbid a trial in open court, ban the use of a jury and makes no provision for the accused being represented by counsel, all of which contravenes the 6th Amendment of the Constitution which is part of the Bill of Rights.

Juvenile court codes provide that a hearing shall be held but usually it doesn't say "when." (as it does in the 6th Amendment by stating the word "speedy.") Theoretically, a child might be held in custody until he attained the age of twenty-one.

Under the Juvenile Code of Arizona, from a theoretical point of view, a child found guilty of jaywalking could be taken from its parents and placed in a foster home or be sent to the Arizona State Industrial School for Boys or the House of the Good Shepherd for girls, since Arizona has no state-owned or operated institution for juvenile delinquent females.

In Arizona, a vengeful neighbor can cause a child to be taken from its parents and placed in the juvenile detention home pending a hearing, as Section 46-122 of the code stated: . . . "the powers of the juvenile court may be exercised upon the filing of a petition by any resident of the county that a child is neglected, dependent, or delinquent" . . . without alleging the facts. Thus any resident could cause a juvenile probation officer to take a neighbor's child or any child to detention and lock him up and would not have to allege any facts to substantiate his contention the child was neglected, dependent or even delinquent.

The Juvenile Code of Arizona, which is similar to many states may violate the First Amendment which provides that . . . "no law shall be made abridging the freedom of speech, or of the press." If the framers of juvenile codes can draw a veil of secrecy about juvenile misconduct, then presumably the legislature can enact a law forbidding any mention of a public official accused of malfeasance.

Interesting questions often arise in this "twilight" zone of judicial procedure. Can the parents have right of counsel when their children are involved? In a recent case involving seventeen children taken from their parents in the 1953 polygamy raid in Arizona, the two juvenile court judges ordered the children taken from their own parents. The attorney for the parents filed a petition for a writ of habeas corpus, maintaining that he had been permitted to attend the hearing "as a matter of courtesy only" and as a consequence the parents had been deprived of legal representation. A judge in Phoenix ruled that this denial constituted a violation of the Constitution and ordered the children restored to their parents. The Attorney-General's office appealed the decision to the Arizona State Supreme Court.[17]

One of the favorite ways of reducing the power and jurisdiction of the juvenile court is to lower the ages of those to whom the philosophy of the court is available. Most jurisdictions, including 27 states, Alaska, Hawaii, and the District of Columbia have set the age at eighteen as the upper limit; in six states, the limit is age 17, and in nine states, the upper age limit is only 16. The Federal Government also set the age at 18, which is the age recommended by the National Probation and Parole Association.

Perhaps the greatest defect in juvenile court laws has been their failure to provide complete jurisdiction over children. At least twenty-one states permit either all felonies or only capital offenses to be excluded from juvenile court jurisdiction or else be shared concurrently with criminal courts, which is highly inconsistent with the original purpose of the juvenile court. Another defect is the lack of uniformity between county courts. When the original juvenile court act was passed in Illinois, there was no provision for paid probation officers and no detention home. The first paid probation officer was provided by the Chicago Woman's Club.[18]

Endeavors to curtail the functions of the juvenile court have been made and proposed by persons who believe the juvenile court tends to "coddle" youthful offenders. The Chicago *Tribune* in its May, 1939 editorial demanded that the criminal court assert its constitutional jurisdiction over young offenders, so that juveniles could be punished. In 1935, the Illinois Supreme Court decided that the criminal courts have a prior jurisdiction in criminal charges against children over ten years old, and at that time stated "it was not intended by the legislature that the juvenile court should be a haven of refuge." Federal Judge William H. Holly characterized this statement as having decided that Cook County's juvenile court had no legal status, that it existed merely by license of the county's criminal court. Ironically, this set-back to the juvenile court occurred in the county and state of its birth, the same court which has been characterized as "personalized justice," and the "greatest advance in judicial history since the Magna Charta."

It appears that juvenile courts are set up on the theory that children have not reached the state of intellectual and emotional development making them fully responsible for their acts, but, if the act is reprehensible enough, it is suddenly decided that the child is responsible after all and not a "fit subject" for the juvenile court, so he is sent over to the adult criminal court.

What can happen to a juvenile offender was dramatically brought out in the case of William Cook, Jr., charged with six murders. Psychiatrists for both defence and prosecution studied the young defendant. Three psychiatrists stated he was sane enough to stand trial, and four psychiatrists said he wasn't sane enough. Confronted with such guidance, Judge Chandler decided Cook was sane enough to plead guilty, but not sane enough to be given the death sentence, so he sentenced him to serve five consecutive sixty year terms in Alcatraz, or a total of 300 years. The prosecutor had demanded the death penalty and left the courtroom snapping, "the goddamdest travesty on justice, ever." The Dept. of Justice, also dissatisfied with the judge's decision agreed to surrender Cook to Imperial County, California where he eventually did get the death sentence, the gas chamber at San Quentin.[19]

On balance, the evidence would seem to favor the continuation of the juvenile court, provided the philosophy of the juvenile court is adhered to, rather than the almost universal system of compromising that obtains today. The juvenile court is an integral part of every community program of services to children. It is an administrative treatment agency as well as a judicial agency.

According to Dr. Harrison A. Dobbs, the juvenile court is a unique institution. Some essential characteristics include a charter, own personnel, maternal apparatus, activities, and goals. The juvenile court's constitutionality has been determined and sustained. The state has long acted *in loco parentis* for destitute and needy children, but excluded many boys and girls from the prerequisites of criminal law. In extending the old principle of *parens patriae*, a courageous step was taken.

The juvenile court is in a unique position of pressing for support of child guidance clinics, mother's pensions and juvenile detention. Because of its specialized interests and methods, the juvenile court has focused up successfully the necessity of attacking social and psychological problems where and when they start. It is not unreasonable to claim for the juvenile court movement much of the credit for mental hygiene programs.

Too often, the juvenile court is used as a community scapegoat. There isn't a court in the country prepared to cure socially ill children with the precision and efficiency of the pediatrics ward of first-class hospitals. There is much community neglect and part of the blame lies on the public. The great achievement of the juvenile court has been founding of a social institution which respects the dignity and potentialities of children and adolescents. Best of all, from the standpoint of progress in civilization, it represents justice for youth.[20]

The Juvenile Court Judge

Juvenile court judges are either elected or appointed by state or federal executives. In either system of selection, political influences often determine the outcome, and there appears to be an enormous variety in the qualifications considered for the assignment, from possessing a "high moral character" to qualifying under the "Missouri Plan," in which the appointee is virtually "on probation" for twelve months. Under this plan, the judge is appointed by the governor from three names submitted to him by a commission and after twelve months "internship," he runs for election for a full term, his success dependent upon popular vote.

No juvenile court can rise above its judge, who may be solicitous or vindictive; he may be as impersonal as law itself or he may be highly personal. This great latitude calls for men and women of professional training and judgment.

The work of a juvenile judge can be disappointing, depressing, or rewarding and inevitably situations will arise beyond judicial skill to help and beyond judicial skill to solve. The short tenure of office in many jurisdictions often discourages qualified men and women from seeking the job, and the juvenile court judge is sometimes thought of as the "low man on the totem pole." This is more a reflection of the importance of this position in the popular mind because the judge occupies and fulfills a role of dispenser of justice with those of chief administrator, policy maker, and public relations official.

Judge Charles H. Boswell lists a series of "Don'ts" for juvenile court judges which may be telescoped by saying DON'T

. . . delay court hearings, be too formal, unpleasant or impressive; play politics in courts; permit derogatory testimony on parents be made by children; be hostile; make unreasonable probation conditions; relie on a mere scolding to do much for an immature, unhappy youngster; make threats; make probation recommend a reformatory sentence then continue the juvenile on probation; or expect probation officers to be able to accomplish a full and adequate social investigation overnight.[21]

Walter H. Beckham, Judge, Juvenile and Domestic Relations Court, Miami, Florida adds a few more "Don'ts": . . . have the juvenile court look or act like a regular court; have hard and uncomfortable chairs; make distant officers testify last; permit officers to carry guns, billy clubs; fail to compliment offenders' personal appearance if at all possible; forget to let others have their say; tear down respect, love, and faith the child has in his own parents; let the child have all the "dirt" or tell him "he's adopted"; threatens anyone with jail or punishment; encourage disloyalty to religious beliefs; use filthy, vulgar or obscene language; address the juvenile as "kid," "brat,"; fail to operate the court for convenience of parents and children; and forget to be active in all community and civic affairs.[22]

The judge should offer to shake hands with youthful defendant, according to the 1945 *Yearbook* of the National Probation and Parole Association. One boy blurted out, "I thought I'd see some old sourpuss." The handshake is often unexpected, and many boys have lifted their hands impulsively as though to ward off a blow. One boy remarked: "I thought no one would shake hands with me." His own father hadn't spoken to him in months.

Judge Bowdoin Hunt of the juvenile court of Bartow, Florida suggests that much good can be accomplished when parents and children appear seeking advice, to let them talk and talk and many times they will think of their own solution. The judge should listen, as well as advise. Every child coming to the juvenile court is helped, and many for the first time see democracy in action . . . for he has been heard.[23]

In no jurisdiction is the juvenile court judge empowered to impose a death penalty on any child under its authority. If the juvenile court has exclusive and original jurisdiction over a child and has no power to transfer it to a criminal court, this child cannot be sentenced to death.

The Interstate Compact on Juveniles, endorsed by the Council of State Governments may be utilized by and for the juvenile court. The Compact provides the parents of the runaway child means of applying to the juvenile court for a requisition to return the juvenile which is directed to the juvenile court in the state where he went to or to the Compact Administrator in that state. A corresponding procedure is set forth for escapees and absconders who cross state lines. In each case of a child returned, the state of residence is responsible for probation costs.[24]

Sir Basil Henriques, Chairman of the East London Juvenile Court criticizes our techniques:

"I sat in courts all over the country. On almost every occasion there was at least one case more serious than I ever had to deal with in England during 33 years on the bench.

It should not be left to the discretion of a policeman whether to make an arrest or let the child go. In England, if a boy is caught, he must come before the court. That is better, both for society and the boy. Juvenile delinquency is a moral disease. In England, the delinquent goes direct to the "Doctor." Here, he goes to a quack . . . by the time the boy reaches the doctor, he's got double pneumonia."[25]

The juvenile court judge is by no means the only potential weak spot in the juvenile court system. Perhaps of equal importance are the problems resulting from the failure of state and county agencies to provide the facilities necessary for carrying out the functions of the court efficiently.

Modern-day trends in the juvenile court idea may be discerned on every hand. Juvenile courts are still in the process of evolution and new procedures and techniques are continually being developed.

Due to the great increase in courts to about 3,000 in number and the daily increasing offenses and offenders which come under the purview of the court, the appearance of the child guidance clinic and the counselor is almost a foregone conclusion in the large city juvenile courts. The clinic makes a diagnosis of the offender, while the counselor serves as an assistant to the judge, as he does the preliminary work of interviewing the juvenile offender, and contacting all persons concerned in the case. His recommendations are usually accepted by the judge. Frequently, parents appear unwilling or unable to understand the function of the clinic and may, along with the children, think of the clinic as part of the punishment.

The juvenile court idea is being extended into areas which include adolescents' courts, youth corrective authorities, and family courts. The pervasive influence of the juvenile court is reflected in the procedures of some of the criminal courts. Public Law 865, the Federal Youth Corrections Act . . . "to provide a system for the treatment and rehabilitation of youth offenders" and "to improve the administration of criminal justice" . . . was enacted by the Eighty-First Congress and approved by the President on September 30, 1950. This Act has been called the most forward step in law enforcement history. The Act defines a youth as a person under twenty-two years of age, and gives the courts greater discretion and new alternatives for dealing with him.

The juvenile court idea has been expanded to include youth of older years, has influenced the treatment of many kinds of "family" cases, such as those pertaining to domestic relations, legal custody, adoption, illegitimacy, and related problems. Such are the implications ahead for other courts which might "adopt" some juvenile court characteristics such as the lack of formalism, the by-passing of "crime" and "convict" labels, and more utilization of social science.

As Tappan has indicated there has been a tendency to exaggerate the contrasts between juvenile court procedures and those of the criminal court systems, in favor of the former. There is great variation in the juvenile courts' conduct, much more so than in criminal courts, due to the lack of consensus as to desirable goals in dealing with children and adolescents.[26] These problems will ultimately be solved and today, more than ever, citizens are concerned about the improvement of an institution so important in the area of justice for youth.

Probation

Probation has as its primary objective the protection of society against crime. It is post-judicial treatment. It begins when the court has heard the defendant's case and found him guilty. The court extends its powers over the future behavior and destiny of the defendant for as long a period as it sees fit, or as is prescribed by law.

The term "probation" is derived from the Latin *probare,* meaning to "test on approval." The "inventor" of probation was John Augustus, a Boston shoemaker, who took compassion on a drunken man in a court room in 1841. Yet, after a century of experimentation, probation still continues to suffer from "growing pains." It is still the unusual thing to be granted to defendants, with tremendous variation ranging from about 12 per cent in North Dakota to about 70 per cent in Rhode Island. There is great variation even between the counties within the same state. It has been estimated that an increase of only ten per cent of probation in California would keep one thousand men out of prison each year.

There are no "grounds" for probation, rather it is a matter of grace, not right, even to co-defendants. Not too long ago, probation was impossible *with venereal* disease in one state, while in another state, probation was impossible *without* venereal disease.

Legislation may stupidly handicap a judge as "no probation granted when a deadly weapon is used," and as a result, hundreds of first offenders are sent to prison yearly when they could have adjusted well on probation.

Approximately one third of the nation's population is without probation service and another third is handicapped by case loads of over two hundred and the utilization of ex-officio officers. New Mexico, Mississippi, Nevada, South Dakota and Texas are still without adult probation service.

There still remains continuing obstacles to successful probation techniques, such as isolation from community resources, lack of diagnostic facilities, rigidity and inflexibility of probation conditions, arbitrary terms of probation, lack of individualized programs, unqualified personnel, restrictive statutes, and the general misconception of the public who "picks up the tab."

There is virtually no probation system in the United States. There are many systems, very few alike, and with extreme administrative differences, state by state, and county by county. The general public are not too familiar with the processes and techniques of probation. Not too many years ago, a legislator was asked his opinion as to the possibility of probation being adopted in the state and he replied: "Oh, it's bound to come, either that or local option."

Probation has many positive values. It is the most individualistic form of treatment and it uses the constructive values of authority. Because it is not considered punitive, it is relatively free of social stigma. Workers in the field of probation were heartened to learn recently that a Sub-Committee on Probation of the Division of Social Activities of the United Nations noted that probation, both in juvenile and adult levels, had progressed farthest in the United States of America.

Probation is approximately 19 times cheaper than incarceration. Once the public is aware of this cheaper way to handle offenders, perhaps the public's tradition of punitive reprisal will tend to disappear.

Probation for the juvenile delinquent is a form of court-disposition, once his guilt has been established. Although it is a nonpunitive method of treating delinquents, it should not be interpreted as leniency or mercy.

Probation's social principle is to keep juveniles out of reformatories and with their families at home. It is not punishment and it is for this reason that many officials, and even a large part of the public, oppose probation. Probation is a counseling service which emphasizes friendship, helpfulness and sympathy. As Sanford Bates expressed it, "Probation may be regarded as an investment in humanity . . . it encourages rather than embitters. It builds up rather than degrades. It is an investment in community protection."[28]

Probation may be simply defined as the suspension of the sentence, conditioned upon good behavior, during a period of liberty in the community. This action may be either a suspension of the *imposition* or the *execution* of the sentence and is generally considered a substitute for imprisonment.

Probation is less expensive than incarceration even for juvenile offenders. It has been estimated that it takes about three years to rehabilitate a serious child offender at a cost of several thousand dollars. It will cost society much more to retain the juvenile in a reformatory or a prison, from which he is likely to emerge, not a reformed person, but an enemy of society, more eager than ever to "get even."

Probation may not be the answer for some juveniles in

trouble. To return to his home and neighborhood may actually be a disservice to the individual himself, to society, and to the cause of probation as well. To return to his home and neighborhood an individual of any age who has become habituated to criminal practices or who has deep-seated maladjustments, or whose delinquent behavior springs from brutality or immorality at home, or from membership in a neighborhood gang may be the worst solution possible.[29]

The way probation is practiced throughout the United States makes it virtually impossible to calculate the number of juveniles who are on probation at any one-given time. The number must be several times the number of correctional school graduates, which approximate thirty thousand a year. Estimates range from sixty-five thousand to one hundred thousand juveniles who are placed on probation each year, with even the latter figure erring on the side of conservatism.

The Probation Officer

Recent years have brought considerable improvement in the standards of probation officers, but the need for trained specialists in this area remains a serious problem. Too often, political considerations influence the selection of the personnel of probation offices and there is little general agreement concerning appropriate qualifications for the probation officer, on either adult or juvenile level.

The term itself, "probation officer" connotes the criminal court and punitive treatment and it does not suggest the social casework done with children in juvenile courts. Many individuals tend to shy away from any "officer," lest the child concerned gets a "record." And countless others are convinced that any child that needs to be supervised by a probation officer must have committed at least a high misdemeanor, if not a felony. This is especially true if the title is "chief probation officer." Some states have "called a rose by another name," such as "probation counselor," or "youth counselor" in Rhode Island, or "director" in Mississippi, and in the cities of Toledo and Cleveland, Ohio, "supervisor," and in the District of Columbia, "director of social work."

A case load of fifty boys or forty girls is the maximum number recommended, but in some counties the probation officer may have from two hundred to three hundred juveniles at any one time to counsel and supervise. While probation is treatment, not all probationers can or will respond. Hence probation officers must continually strive to develop and refine current methods, and keep abreast of today's research.

The general public have but little conception of the manifold duties and obligations of the probation officer. To complete a typical pre-sentence investigation, the probation officer must secure information relative to the present offense, the status of co-defendants and accomplices, statements of the defendant, and attitudes of the complainant, any aggravating and mitigating circumstances, any prior criminal history, the offender's antecedents and family background, a developmental history of the defendant, residence arrangements, religion, mental and physical health, as well as the character, habits and associations of the youthful offender.[30]

Authorities, such as Walter Reckless have pointed out that a schism exists today in the field of delinquency control, between social work training and correctional work training. Perhaps the delinquent should not receive case work primarily. Certainly, the public and not a few professionals are confused if not confounded by some of the pre-sentence prose. One of the not uncommon occupational diseases of report writers seems to be an incapacity to credit their readers with any imagination or any critical faculty at all. Instead of marshaling and presenting the facts in such a manner that they speak for themselves, some have a compulsion to spell out laboriously the conclusions—even the obvious ones—to be derived from the facts. Worse still, they do so in the dreadful idiom of the social casework textbooks instead of in English. For example, one student doing his field work in an Eastern court, offered this "diagnosis" of a 45-year-old defendant who had assaulted a cop and who had been in no real trouble since his parents and the police stopped "picking on him" twenty-five years before:

> "Internalizing, integrating and building upon a series of frustrating infantile and early adolescent life experiences in which his delinquent ventures were invariably met with a rigidly structured parental opposition and with quick apprehension act punishment, the memory of which appears to be reviving with the onset of the involutional phase of his life,

the defendant has reverted to an initial pattern of viewing all authority figures with suspicion. His present offense clearly demonstrates an evolving or re-evolving antisocial *affect,* featured by a need for ego enhancement, as represented by the status achieved in thinking of himself as a "big shot" who will not be dominated by the police."

There is of course the possibility that the writer of it wished to do a little judicial jaw-breaking in the event His Honor might be rash enough to read the effusion aloud.[31]

The main prerequisite of a well-functioning probation program is an adequate staff. In the juvenile court, more than in any other judicial branch, the judge must rely on the work of court aides; the probation officers, juvenile officers or the probation counselors. In the majority of instances they are appointed by the juvenile court judge. On January 1, 1947, there were 3,681 probation officers for juveniles in the United States appointed locally or as state employees. This number has not been substantially increased since then. Many of these probation officers functioned in juvenile *and* adult cases, and in juvenile delinquency as well as child dependency and neglect situations. Not included in the above figure were 267 Federal probation officers whose work is overwhelmingly concerned with adult offenders, since Federal offenders of juvenile court age are often supervised by local juvenile court probation officers. Not all of the 3,681 probation officers are employed full time in this capacity; the other duties of part-time probation officers may include those of sheriff, bailiff, welfare worker, clerk of the court, attendance officer, or other.[32]

The qualifications of the probation officer according to the "Standards" of the National Probation and Parole Association would include a B.A. or equivalent; one year of paid fulltime experience under competent supervision in an approved social agency; and possess good character and balanced personality. Some states have little to ask in regard to qualifications and others are so vague that "discreet person of reputable character" could qualify. The "Standards" suggest appointments made from eligibility lists resulting from competitive examinations and the appointees should have reasonable tenure since the judges who appoint them often have to run for re-election, and may lose.

The "Standards" state that the best training for probation

and parole work is in a graduate school of social work. As mentioned before, Walter Reckless inclines to the belief that training in the field of corrections, such as criminology, penology, police work is more important than "case work," and more and more individuals working in the field are tending to agree with him. While there is considerable overlapping between delinquency and cases of neglect and abandonment, there are different techniques available and which are not necessarily interchangeable.

In length and termination of probation, the minimum suggested is from six months to one year. A violation automatically terminates probation and technically, probation with a juvenile offender can last until he reaches the age of twenty-one, regardless of the juvenile court age limits of 16, 17, or 18.

Probation conditions for both juveniles and adults are full of "negatives" and "don'ts." The probation officer should conceive his task as that of a counselor, an adult friend and strive to win the confidence of the child, to be accepted by the parents and other family members as he may be reconstructing all of them. Some officers report that 75 per cent of their time is with the juvenile offender's family.

According to L. J. Carr, the curse of probation work is that it is not recognized as requiring professional training. Probation is still a "new" method of dealing with delinquency, since only six states had permissive legislation by 1900. Too often, only lip service is given to probation standards; the selling job concerns probation officers to the public and unless professionally wide standards for staff recruitment are put into practice, the public will believe that no special skills, aptitudes, or techniques are needed for probation officer. What is called "individual treatment" is frequently having the probationer submit written reports or perfunctory "check-off" office calls. No wonder the public is loath to support better salaries and higher standards. To attain goals, probation supervision must be sustained, affirmative, and positive.[33]

Probation officers should be interested in their charges, and exhaust every effort to ascertain the truth, particularly in making the pre-investigation report. In the case of J.B. who pleaded guilty to armed robbery of a postoffice, he stated he was only 17 and requested a hearing under the Federal Juvenile Delinquency Act, but the official birth record said he was 18, which made it mandatory upon the court to impose a sentence of

25 years against a possible minority commitment of three years, seven months and 27 days. Such is the absurd difference one year makes. Because of this important fact and its consequences, every effort was made to verify the boy's story, and after much laborious investigation and checking, it was learned that the boy was only 17 so for $316 received in the robbery, he served the minimum sentence of over three years. However, the interest and concern in the boy apparently was wasted, for after obtaining his freedom at the end of three years, he committed another armed robbery within two months of his release, and this time got a 5-10 year sentence, and two months later committed suicide.[34]

The major contribution by a probation officer is forming a strong, friendly bond to the delinquent, but it is difficult to get a juvenile offender to accept an adult as an ally. Many juveniles have no respect for the officer they can outwit. The interview is the chief tool of the probation officer and it requires considerable practice to conduct a meaningful session. It takes practice to relax and to get the juvenile to relax too. Many juveniles in trouble with the law are suffering from feelings of inferiority from failure in school, or rejection from the home or his community. This imposes an additional burden on the probation officer because most of them do not have the assistance of a child guidance clinic or an out-patient psychiatric dept.[35]

The family being the basic unit of society is involved in probation. In family casework, the client has the right to accept or reject service, but the probation officer is symbolic of the law and authority. Occasionally a father will ask for aid by saying, "Scare the pants off him. I've tried it but it doesn't work; maybe he'll listen to you. I can't do anything with him." Here the pathology is not localized in the boy, but elsewhere. The family must understand that the probation officer is neither mother, father, brother or sister, but a *person* invited in or required by law to work on the problem. The family climate when he first arrives will range from torrid temperature to cold hostility and to some families, the probation officer often appears to be the executioner, or the delinquent thinks the family has rejected him and adopted the probation officer as the adequate, responsible son. Such a mantle must be gently and patiently removed.[36]

The average layman knows little about probation or parole. Even judges use these terms incorrectly or synonymously, as when they speak of paroling defendants (possible only after incarceration in prison) when they mean placing them on probation. Everyone is interested in delinquency, but most people are given a distorted or inadequate picture of probation, parole or reformatories. The good probation officer "must see, listen, learn, labor, join, meet, and speak; do everything except smell!"

Probation officers ought to make the best public relations men in the world for the very qualities necessary for their success as common sense, patience, even temper and a co-operative spirit are the very qualities needed for good public relations.[37]

Probation was first thought of as a means of saving defendants from prison and that the more decent offender would appreciate another chance. Today, probation assumes a more positive approach, introducing him to a better way of life. The basic principles of treatment are based upon the consent of the offender, the plans thought out for him which he accepts and which concern his own situation, in an effort to redirect the offender's emotions and the necessary parts or roles that are played by his relatives and friends. Some delinquents have bad friends, some have no friends, and a few are solitary, lonely people, detached from reality. The aim of the probation officer is to build up the probationer's self-respect. Thus probation is more than a matter of devising plans of recovery and handing them out to a compliant probationer. The probation officer learns to listen and the lonely ones who have never had an audience before, often warm up to their adult friend. This is a training in responsibility to others.[38]

Juvenile offenders against federal law have presented a special problem because there is no provision for their handling in the penal structure of the federal government. In 1932, legislation authorized United States Attorneys to divert those under 21 to state or local courts. The Federal Juvenile Delinquency Act became a law on June 16, 1938, provided a person under 18 can be prosecuted on information rather than indictment, if he consents in writing. In January, 1946 the Attorney General authorized all U.S. attorneys to make use of the "deferred prosecution" procedure sometimes referred to as the "Brooklyn

Plan." Here, prosecution is deferred and the probation officer exercises supervision over the youth and who submits progress reports to the U.S. Attorney, and if they continue favorable, the original complaint against the offender is dropped, thus protecting the youth against the stigma of an official criminal record. Of two hundred cases supervised in Brooklyn on this deferred prosecution plan, only two violators had to be referred to the court by due process of law.[39]

It should be noted in conclusion that probation, both in conception and development, is America's distinctive contribution to progressive penology and its origins do not go back to British common law or even "the received ideals" of Continental legal systems. The development of probation has been entirely statutory, certainly so insofar as the system is an expression of *planned state policy*. Probation in the United States is characterized principally not by affinities with, but by deliberate divergencies from, the common law and European precedents in general.[40]

The success of the Brooklyn Plan and numerous other recent advances in the probation system in the United States are encouraging signs in the treatment of juvenile delinquency. Once the press, and in turn the general public are made aware of the socially therapeutic value of probation for the vast majority of youthful offenders, the general area of probation will acquire the status and prestige of a dignified profession.

Parole

The term "parole" is derived from the French word *parole* and is used in the sense of "word of honor."—*parole d'honneur.* Although the initial parole legislation was enacted in Mass. in 1837, New York in 1877 was the first state to include the word "parole" in the statute.

Parole is an administrative act . . . a form of release granted to an inmate after he has served a portion of his sentence in a penal institution. When he is paroled he finishes serving his "time" outside reformatory walls.

The roots of parole extend back to the time of Capt. Maconochie, who headed the penal colony on Norfolk Island, East of Australia in the 1840's and who developed a plan whereby the convicts passed through a series of stages, with graded degrees of freedom. First there was strict imprisonment, then labor in chain gangs, then freedom in a limited area, the ticket-of-leave (some states today have this term imprinted on the parole papers), conditional pardon, and finally complete freedom. A system of marks governed promotion from one stage to another. This marks system was borrowed by Sir Walter Crofton and became known as the Irish System and its influence is still strong in our juvenile training schools. Parole as a full-fledged, working system was first introduced with the opening of the Elmira Reformatory in 1876, since both parole and the reformatory idea were built on the philosophy of rehabilitation and readjustment to normal living. Parole was first extended to the prisons in 1884 in Ohio. The last state to grant parole to inmates was Mississippi in 1944.

Parole, in principle, is neither mercy nor leniency, but rather an extension of the punishment. It does not imply forgiveness and is not designed as a reward for good conduct in the institution. No inmate has the *right* to parole, and the public doesn't have a *right* to parole him. The individual inmate does not achieve *eligibility* for parole by his own efforts because all inmates become eligible for parole. Although most inmates make "good" records, not more than 30 percent are paroled from a reformatory or prison.

The first elements of parole began in the United States in colonial times as a system of indenture for juvenile delinquents when young prisoners were released and placed in the employment of private citizens to whom they were legally bound. The juvenile offender was then permitted to earn his final discharge from the employer. Later, state visiting agents were appointed to supervise the children so indentured and to prevent their exploitation by employers and this system was adopted by the New York House of Refuge founded in 1825.

Juvenile parole, sometimes called "after care" has for many years constituted a neglected field in the child welfare program. Many institutions for juvenile delinquents are private or semi-private and not subject to state regulation and supervision in any significant manner. The growing policy governing adult supervising on a state level has not been adopted in the juvenile field. Since one of the most important phases of the training program involved in institutional experience is the inmate's parole into the community, the need to improve parole procedures on a juvenile level is evident.

In large part, because of this rapid development of the philosophy of parole among the forty-eight states, the various parole systems present a mixed picture. Some states have central boards vested with the power to grant parole to inmates of prisons and reformatories; in other states the sole power to grant parole is vested in the governor while still other states utilize institutional parole agencies.[41]

Where institutions serve a rather large territory and cannot let their staff members travel to outlying counties for purposes of investigation, the granting of parole and its supervision may be in the hands of the committing juvenile court. State agencies, such as the Youth Authority in California, the Youth Service Commission in Wisconsin, the Youth Service Board in Massachusetts, and the Division of Juvenile Parole Services of the Illinois Department of Welfare, are charged with the preparation and the supervision of parole of those committed to institutions in these states.

The crux of the parole system is the supervisory process, which is often hampered by inadequate staffing, lack of funds, inefficient planning, large case loads, and inflexibility of legal and administrative rules. On the adult level the prerequisites of parole are—a job, and no detainer on file against the inmate.

Parole staffs are often of poor quality due to low salary scales and competent men may not remain very long for that reason. Civil Service examinations are not necessarily the best method recruitment for such examinations do not always measure their alleged goals. It is not always possible to determine from a written test whether an applicant has the temperament, the ability and personal integrity so desirable in a parole officer. For example, in one Civil Service examination, an applicant passed the test with flying colors only to go to prison subsequently for dishonesty; another, at the bottom of the list, barely managed to get appointed but became one of the most valuable members of the parole staff.[42]

Authorities frequently require a sponsor if the youth is to be released on parole. The sponsor may be a family friend, a clergyman or other interested citizen. The sponsor is no substitute for the parole officer who officially supervises the boy. In juvenile parole, the sponsor cooperates with the parole officer

and seeks his advice. Since the sponsor is responsible for one
individual only, he can more readily concentrate his efforts
and available time than an over-burdened parole officer.

Civic organizations in recent years have volunteered as
sponsors for delinquent youth as the Philadelphia Junior Chamber of Commerce sponsoring released boys from the Pennsylvania Industrial School. The Kiwanis Club of Pueblo, Colorado,
(The Pueblo Plan) was started to substitute "foster homes for
reformatories" and the Club is paying out $400 monthly. It all
began when Judge Hubert Glover discovered that of 124 youths
committed to the State Industrial School prior to 1948, that
42 graduated into reformatories, 15 went to state's prison, 13
to federal prisons and nine to insane asylums. Out of the original 124, only 44 did not recidivate. Thus far the Kiwanis Club
has handled 37 children and have rehabilitated 34 of them. They
started with two children, and now care for ten each month.

In selecting the sponsor, certain principles are to be kept
in mind such as picking men who will have enough time, match
the right sponsor with the right boy, select men who understand human behavior, reject the "perfectionist," and the moral-
izer, avoid the "Caspar Milquetoast" type and pass over the
"lonely soul." Select men with a reputation for following through,
who will stay with it when the going gets rough and particularly for the men who will "accept" the boy right from the
start.[43]

Sponsoring a delinquent is simply an art by which an adult
works out a constructive relationship with a youngster who has
been or who is in trouble to the mutual benefit of both the
youngster and the adult. It has been called "the art of disin-
terested friendship." In selecting sponsors, one must beware of
the "do-gooders" who wander around seeking victims for their
predatory kind of altruism. Also pass by the "gentleman and
lady bountiful type" as they lavish entertainment that is inappropriate, bewildering, and destructive. The sponsor must be
willing to seek guidance of a professional nature, since the
sponsor may be a lawyer, physician, business man, but still a
layman as far as correctional work is concerned. Incidentally,
don't be disturbed when the boy inquires what your racket
is as he may assume crooked means were partially responsible
for your success.[44]

Parole rules are not easy to obey. The parolee may not associate with anyone who has a police record, may not write to anyone incarcerated in any institution, or carry weapons, use narcotics, commit immoral acts, drive a car, take a drink. The parolee must get permission from his parole officer to move, change jobs, take an auto ride, leave the city, county, or state, or to get married, and usually must retire by 10:00 P.M. Any violations means a return to the reformatory with no hearing or trial. The parolee has to report to the parole office once a month, on a certain date, or certain hour, but the parole officer can visit him unexpectedly at any time, day or night.

Occasionally a parolee may be annoyed by another parolee. One young man released from an Illinois Reformatory, got a job driving a small truck for a Chicago factory, whose owner knew nothing about the employee's parole status. The parolee made interstate hauls, often collected much money for his employer. Another former inmate found out about this job and because he was unable to borrow money from the employed parolee, informed the employer that he had an ex-con working for him. The employer at once phoned the Milwaukee consignee telling him to take delivery but not to pay his driver, "because he's an ex-con from the reformatory and I'm going to fire him."[45]

Much still remains to be accomplished in the area of parole. In general the parole system in correctional institutions for juvenile delinquents is decentralized, with parole service directly connected with the institution from which the youthful offender is released. At the present time, a majority of the institutions are without psychiatric counsel, a lack that increases the work and responsibility of the parole authorities in selecting those inmates eligible for parole. The authorities are especially handicapped in dealing with psychopathic delinquents, the mentally retarded, and habitual "sex" cases without psychiatric aid.

Decentralization is indicated because the number of juvenile delinquents is comparatively small, and does not require the complex, statewide systems as are necessary to handle the many thousands of adults released on parole each year.

Parole is also an area in need of help of scientific knowledge. A long-range program of research could be initiated, for example, to study the behavior of released inmates over a prolonged period of time, supplementing the important research activities by the Gluecks in this area. In general, the important fact about parolee selection is not why, or where, or even who, but *when* should the inmate be released. Continued research is recommended, to shed light on a field still comparatively unknown.

Selected Bibliography

J. M. Braude, "Boys' Court: Individualized Justice for the Youthful Offender," *Federal Probation*, XII, (June, 1948), 9-14. Much is rightly made of the paradox of the social order that permits a youth to die on the battlefield or gallows, yet is not considered socially mature enough to vote. Judge Braude illustrates discriminatory and contradictory aspects of civil and criminal laws.

Charles L. Chute, *Yearbook*, (New York: National Probation and Parole Association, 1941), "The Development of Probation," 29-40. An authority on probation traces the early growth of probation in the United States.

Lowell Juilliard Carr, *Delinquency Control* (New York: Harper, 1941), Chapter 7: "Finding the Children Who Need Help." In any plan of rehabilitation, the physical, emotional, social and vocational needs of an individual must be met in order to produce a socially adjusted member of society.

F. James Davis, "The Iowa Juvenile Court Judge," *Journal of Criminal Law and Criminology*, XLII (September-October, 1951). The result of a survey conducted to test the attitudes of juvenile court judges regarding the cases appearing before them. Only a few judges retained the bias of the "criminal court" approach.

John R. Ellingston, *Protecting Our Children from Criminal Careers*, (New York: Prentice-Hall, 1948), Chapter 2: "The pervasive influence of a lawless society partially explains much of the unlawful behavior of youth including the major role played by the area of delinquency."

John R. Ellingston, *Protecting Our Children from Criminal Careers*, (New York: Prentice-Hall, 1948), Chapter 21: "New Police Methods with Children." An excellent discussion relative to the role of the policewoman in handling juvenile delinquency. In addition, various types of juvenile bureaus specializing in juvenile cases are also presented.

Frank W. Grinnel, *Yearbook* (New York: National Probation and Parole Association, 1941), "The Common Law Background of Probation," 23-29. This selected reading is worthy of the attention of those who are interested in the legal background that made the concept of probation a living reality today.

Frank W. Haggerty, *Yearbook* (New York: National Probation and Parole Association, 1944), "Classification and Parole Success," 196-209. The many imponderables that enter a parole-risk situation place a heavy burden on classification committees. Some failure appears to be inevitable, but such techniques represent a vast improvement over the guesses and hunches of parole boards.

Samuel W. Hartwell, "The Guidance Clinic and the Court," *Federal Probation*, XII (September, 1948), 22-29. An excellent summary of the various relationships of the clinic officials and various juvenile court judges are presented.

Frederick W. Killian, "The Juvenile Court as an Institution," *The Annals* of The American Academy of Political and Social Science, 261 (January, 1949). An excellent treatment of the origin, growth, and development of the juvenile court.

Donald E. J. McNamara, "Police Training in Prevention of Crime and Delinquency," *Journal of Criminal Law and Criminology*, XLII (July-August, 1951) 263-269.

Sol Rubin, "The Legal Character of Juvenile Delinquency," *The Annals* of The American Academy of Political and Social Science, 261, (January, 1949). This summary points up the fact that despite more than half a century of practice and progress, there still remains a sizable gap between theory and practice in the juvenile court.

Frank A. Ross, "A Lawyer Looks at Probation," *Federal Probation*, XV (December, 1951). A provocative analysis of probation from the legal point of view.

Paul W. Tappan, *Juvenile Delinquency* (New York: McGraw-Hill Book Co., 1949), Chapter Thirteen: *"Probation."* A first-rate discussion of probation. Tappan makes a detailed analysis of the specific tasks of probation as well as professionalization in probation.

Clyde B. Vedder, Samuel Koenig and Robert E. Clark, *Criminology: A Book of Readings* (New York: Dryden Press, 1953), Chapter 20: "Parole." For the student interested in the parole process on both adult and juvenile levels, this chapter contains five articles reflecting informed opinion on the subject.

Randolph Wise, *Yearbook* (New York: National Probation and Parole Association, 1950) "Parole Progress," 19-26. The various meanings and uses of the concept "parole" are exemplified by Wise as well as the progress made in the past twenty-five years.

Clyde B. Vedder acquired his terminal degree at the University of Southern California (June, 1947), taught at this institution, and also at the University of Michigan and the University of Florida, and was formerly Chairman of the Department of Sociology at the Houston University; is now Chairman of the Program in Corrections, University of Arizona and Professor of Sociology. Has edited and contributed to *Criminology: Book of Readings* (New York: Dryden Press, 1953), *The Juvenile Offender, Perspective and Readings* (New York: Random House, 1955), *Social Problems* (New York: Thomas Y. Crowell, 1955), and contributed articles to such periodicals as the *Proceedings* of the American Prison Association, *Social Forces, Journal of Criminal Law, Criminology and Police Science, Social Therapy,* etc.

CHAPTER 12.

EXPERIMENTS IN DELINQUENCY PREVENTION
AND CORRECTION

GARNETT LARSON
University of Nebraska

It is difficult to prepare a chapter on experiments in delinquency prevention and correction in view of the widespread concern with delinquency among various professional and lay groups and the number of experiments now in progress. Literature concerned with delinquency prevention and its treatment appears in a variety of fields, including those of education psychology, psychiatry, mental health, public health, public welfare, social work, community planning, civic clubs, citizens' committees, governor's committees, religion, law, sociology, law enforcement, corrections, special education, physical education, agricultural extension work, philosophy, and the special therapies such as occupational, physical, and art.

Various Concepts of Delinquency

Delinquency is, strictly speaking, an adjudicated determination, but the term is so loosely used that it has often a social meaning. Although the delinquent child is one who, because of his behavior, has received the attention, concern and planning of the courts, more frequently he is regarded as any child whose behavior has elicited the disapproval or the troubled concern of an adult. He is usually regarded as a pre-delinquent when, in the judgment of an adult and in light of his past behavior, it is believed that he will become unacceptable to a social group.

The delinquent child is purported not to be regarded as one who has committed a crime but whose unacceptable behavior is an indication of parental failure in affording him supervision and training. Delinquent acts are, then, an open accusation that the adults who have responsibility for the child have been derelict or incompetent in the pursuit of their responsibility toward him. He usually reflects his relationships with his teachers as well as his parents, with those who provide him with religious instruction and with opportunities for recreation. The behavior may serve as an index to the quality of his relationship with adults who have responsibility for his experiences and the meeting of his emotional and physical needs. Almost every adult, then, has some personal stake in the general rate and type of delinquency existing in the social group where he identifies, for if he has no direct responsibility to a child he reflects the culture with which he identifies and in which the child lives.

Delinquency—Everybody's Business

In most instances, the child is unaware that his unacceptable behavior challenges the competency, if not the self-image, not only of the adults with whom he has primary relationship but also those with whom he has no actual contact. He may by some behavioral expression, perhaps lack of obedience and inattentiveness, not only challenge the adequacy of his parents as parents, but also that of his teachers as teachers, of his priest or minister as a spiritual guardian, of the policeman in his attempt to enforce the law, of the group worker in the use of his professional skill, of his neighbor who wishes him to respect his property, even of the contributor to the Community Chest in his support of community agencies. To find himself in trouble with all those adults, he may (although he frequently does not) present to them all the same type of behavior but pile up for himself a rather impressive accumulation of adult hostility. But he may also arouse the uneasiness and often the guilt of numerous individuals whom he does not know and about whom he does not care. If he becomes a statistic, or if his disobedience is headlined in the paper, he may awaken in other parents, other teachers, other policemen, other priests and ministers, and other neighbors a guilty awareness of defective fulfillment of their responsibility either to their own children or to the children who are members of the social group to which they belong. If the child has been found loitering or stealing, or had been injured while hooking a ride on the back of a truck or bus in place of using the recreational and agency facilities provided him through the Community Chest for his pleasure, the adults who contributed to the Chest may feel personally piqued and unappreciated by his choice of fun. Or if they had not contributed so he might have opportunities for more acceptable enjoyment, they may feel guilt and anger at the child who apparently became injured because of their own lack of responsibility. It is possible, then, that a number of adults, both known and unknown to him, might be baffled and disgruntled if not angry that he had not used other means of enjoyment. Not all the hostility of these adults may be directed to him as a person, for some may be directed at the group of children or youth whom this particular child represents.

The consequences of such delinquent behavior may unite certain persons or groups of persons in their interest to provide for his welfare according to his needs. But he may also unite certain adults against other adults and consequently against him. Parents often regard the school as a corrective for their own inadequacy, just as the school frequently regards the parents as basically responsible for all untoward behavior of their child, or a priest or minister may feel that the parents of the child should be more remindful of his religious duties and the parents may feel that the pastor is lacking either in concern and ability when he does not bring about a wanted change in the child's behavior or attitude. The policeman who returns the child to his home may be met with the anger of the parents and the accusation that he is picking on the child since he must have someone to pick on. In turn, the policeman may order the parents to become better parents under threat of arrest for neglect. Even the man who contributed to the Community Chest, or who offered his services as a recreational leader for a boys' group, may find himself angry at this unknown boy because he did not make use of the Center to which he has contributed and who disassociated himself from the program designed to help him.

As a result, the adult in the community is often impervious to the need or condition of the child in his hunt for a scapegoat among other adults to bear the onus of his defection. Although not as frequently as formerly, there is still heard the common cliché, "There are no bad children; only bad parents," or the question asked about teachers, "What do they teach anyway?" or the remark, "You know how the police are; they mark a child and then they lay for him," or "What can you expect from religious persons who know nothing about the ways of the world?" In the same way, judges who are designated by law to act in place of parents for a child so in need may advocate fining parents of delinquent children, frequently scolding them before the child and reminding them of their responsibilities to him, and occasionally writing articles to point publicly an accusatory and derogatory finger at their defection. Curfew laws may require that children under a designated age be off the streets by a certain hour unless accompanied by their parents or the child so found on the street will be returned to his home under police escort, this with a hope that it may have salutory effect upon the parents. Where such ordinances have appeared to be successful, delinquency usually was not a real problem and for the most part the ordinance has fallen into disuse. But in communities where delinquency is of grave concern, the implementation of such an ordinance frequently has resulted in parents pitting themselves against the police department in order to maintain their self-respect and to retaliate against other adults who by use of the official prerogative so publicly remind them of their responsibility to their child. In at least one city known to the author, both parents and children by tacit consent made such a curfew ordinance unworkable, for children with the knowledge of their parents appeared in greater number on the streets after the designated hours. When the police returned them to their homes, they were berated by the parents who defended their right to allow their child to loiter and to keep late hours.

This is not to say that the child loitering and keeping late hours is not in need of another means of satisfaction, or that many children who appear in court are not those whose parents have little control over them. In fact, parents frequently acknowledge their lack of control of a child by signing the petition that brings the child into the court and by requesting that their parental responsibilities be removed and that the court assume responsibility for his behavior. There is little reason to assume that many parents become better parents simply by becoming aware of the disapproval of other adults, for had they needed only hostility to inject quality into their parenthood, they would already have been paragons of parental ability.

The child may well be the legitimate object of the court's interest, of the school's concern, or of the community's demand that in view of his behavior he can no longer be regarded as an acceptable member of the community. Even when this is patently true, he may be of secondary interest to those adults who seek to point a finger of guilt at other adults. Some children are adept at using the propensity of adults to accuse each other to escape being the primary object of their concern. Other children are aware that adults disapprove of them, but regard them as phonies and have little respect for them, for they know that adult behavior has in it the same elements as their own. Or a child may be puzzled, frightened of these adults who accuse each other of having been derelict in their duty toward him, and emotionally immersed in fear that his badness has resulted in the adult anger that pours against him and yet shows no awareness of him.

The persistent publicity given to what appears to be rising delinquency rates and to an increase in acts of senseless and sometimes guiltless violence has resulted in widespread concern about how to prevent children and youth from performing these delinquent and criminal acts. Delinquency prevention has become everybody's business. Less widespread is the concern over how to deal with the personality pattern of the youth or child who has committed a delinquent offense in convictive but non-punitive way.

Confusion in the Concept of "Delinquency Prevention"

A great deal of confusion has resulted from the use of the term "delinquency prevention." It often expresses the uneasiness of adults in their relationship with children. It is sometimes difficult to distinguish between programs for children in general and those specifically designed to aid the child whose personality and behavior pattern is such that if unchanged he may later be at variance with the law. Schools may provide day care centers for children whose parent or parents work as a means of delinquency prevention. Slums may be cleared for the same reason, sanitation improved, recreation programs provided, health programs instituted, Boy and Girl Scouts troops formed, teen-canteens organized, drag strips permitted, all in the name of prevention. For the same reason, civic organizations have been known to provide pigs and calves for rural children to raise or to pay for camp scholarships for city children. Occasionally these things are done for the simple reason that children have a right to such adult consideration, whether they are potential delinquents or because they are children. As Fritz Redl has indicated, it is difficult to produce a delinquent and there are many children who will never be delinquents regardless of their experiences. Yet these children, too, have as much right to opportunities for enjoyment and for satisfying, creative living as do those who may later challenge the social order.

In fact, many of these programs indicated as contributing to the reduction of juvenile delinquency tolerate only the child whose behavior meets with the approval of the leader and who submits to his discipline and structure, not the delinquent or pre-delinquent. Particularly is this true of certain national groups who sponsor children and youth programs but define narrowly the child who may belong. In some instances, the type of experience that the child shall have is also defined as well as the achievements that are expected of him if he continues to be a member in good standing. For example, one program excludes the boy whose parents or parent cannot or will not engage in defined activities with him, at the same time encouraging its members to wearing the uniform. The child who is excluded for whatever reason thus becomes obvious and is easily identified as one whose parents either will not or cannot act as do the parents of his peers. One cannot say that a child so excluded is consequently in danger of becoming a delinquent, but neither can one assume that he who does not wear the cloth has not experienced a keen feeling of rejection, real or fancied, often of inferiority, and has had demonstrated to him that adults may take away from his pleasures or prestige by requiring things not of himself but of his parents whose decisions he cannot control but whose rejection he can feel.

In like manner, recreational facilities provided children to help "prevent juvenile delinquency" is an expression of adult distrust and uneasiness about their relations with children, yet usually no effort is made in such programs to help the child whose behavior is disturbing, rebellious, destructive, sometimes obnoxious, who refuses to conform to rules or persists in being a disrupting member of the group. It apparently is difficult for an adult to "pleasure a child" simply because a child needs pleasure. For the most part, the same program may serve both the child who is in need of outlets for his healthy interests and energies and for the child who needs opportunities to achieve healthy social relationships and acceptable, rewarding activities. To be able to distinguish the noisiness, aggression, withdrawal, non-conformity, and demands of a healthy child from those of the unhealthy child is often a matter of professional skill.

The same confusion of purpose, and the same reluctance to provide certain experiences for children simply because they are good for children is sometimes seen in youth programs. This was true of two groups known to the author who were instrumental in the establishment of a Youth Employment Bureau. In both instances the publicity for the Bureau leaned heavily on its value to the "prevention of juvenile delinquency," even though it would only serve youth from 16 to 21. Both Bureaus have been effectively and efficiently managed by persons all under 21 years of age. But so persistent is the delinquency prevention motif that the "Introduction" of both Annual Reports written by the adults serving on the Advisory Board, indicates the primary achievement of the Bureau as effective delinquency prevention. Both cities had low rates of delinquency prior to the establishment of the Bureaus and apparently these did not increase during their operation. Neither was there indication that the rates decreased. Since the success of the Bureaus' operation can be demonstrated in almost every area other than that of delinquency prevention, the claim of the Advisory Boards may be significant as it reflects the need and fears of the adults who must measure their success in terms of their lack of failures. It is not enough to provide for all children, healthy, adjusted, capable ones included, according to the diversity of their needs.

Certainly Employment Bureaus should have facilities to

help those whose personal difficulties and behavior patterns affect their employment and should give guidance and help in how to use an employment experience for growth and maturation. This, however, is the right of every youth, including the delinquent, for just as the delinquent has his growth problems, so does the non-delinquent. It is well, then, to distinguish between the "preventive" program which actually serves children in general and the ones which have features primarily to help those apt-to-be delinquent programs which will be discussed later.

The term "pre-delinquent" has a somewhat more specific meaning than "delinquency prevention." It connotes presumptive delinquency or the near certainty that were the child brought to the attention of the court he would be adjudicated as delinquent. It does not indicate a type of behavior distinguishable from delinquent behavior, nor does it usually indicate the degree of seriousness of the behavior.

The Work of Social Agencies

For the most part the same social agencies provide services for the "predelinquent" child as for any other child with a problem. The specific nature of such services is usually determined according to the need of the child. This may include planning with the parent and exploring with him the parent-child relationship, casework treatment with the child himself, arranging for substitute home care and supervision if needed, planning for group experiences, helping him acquire a capacity to form and use relationships, helping him achieve a sense of personal worth and status, and in many instances providing him an adult to whom he can relate with corrective results. If it seems indicated, request can be made to the court to consider whether the child can best be helped by declaring him delinquent and structuring a situation within a legal framework that has meaning for him.

Voluntary agencies are often referred to as private agencies in that their source of support is not from public funds and they operate under a Board representing the community which they serve. In order to provide services to children, many of them require that one or both parents voluntarily request services as an indication of their willingness to assume some responsibility for their child's difficulty and its amelioration. These agencies are for the most part staffed by highly trained, experienced personnel and usually have available medical, psychiatric, and psychological consultative services to aid them in diagnostic evaluation and differential treatment planning. They may be Family Agencies which accept cases dealing with almost every phase of inter-personal problems, including parent-child relationship, or children's agencies, such as Child Guidance Clinics which accept cases only if children are involved, or Psychiatric and Mental Health Clinics with out-patient facilities and which give service to those having neurotic and psychotic difficulties and, in some instances, to those with character disorders. Most of these agencies exclude from treatment children whose parents for some reason refuse personal involvement. They see no need for it or for reality reasons, such as work schedules, transportation time, or small children at home, cannot make satisfactory arrangements to become a client also. Although certainly the premise that the child is mainly the product of his parents is sound and that the best service that can be provided the child is to help establish a healthy parent-child relationship, the policy excludes the child whose need may be even greater than the one whose parents exhibit concern, for he is excluded not because of his need but because of that of his parents.

Public Welfare services are provided by the State Divisions of Child Welfare through the County Welfare Agencies. In most states, these include services to the child whose social behavior has gotten him into trouble and the child on probation or parole. Intake of these agencies cannot be restricted, for they carry statutory responsibility for children in need of care, protection, and special services if not otherwise provided. In much of the United States, services through the County Welfare Agency are the only community ones available to the child and their quality differs drastically from excellent, differential services to those of almost non-existent quality and those of questionable purpose. Several State Divisions of Child Welfare, however, in cooperation with County Welfare Agencies are foremost in experimenting with programs both for the prevention and the control of the incidence of delinquency and in effective methods of treatment of the already delinquent. Some states have separate divisions or departments dealing only with corrections, including probation and parole, while others have located such responsibility within a larger already existent division. In many states, however, services to the delinquent child are still catch-as-catch can in each community and are dependent upon the accident of who in the community calls the shots. By basic philosophy, there is no child so deprived, so bad, or so dependent that he loses his right to the concern of the state. Actually, this is frequently in concept only, for, to return to my original observations, the child holds the key to the success of the adult who undertakes responsibility for him. Responsive and rewarding children are easily protected and cared for; children who resist the efforts, the philosophies, the personal desires of the adult, who arouse in him all the angers of his own childhood and the emotional impacts of the insecurities of his environment, or who energize anew adult hostilities or the latent delinquent desires usually concealed in the adult unconscious, are ones whose simple need of service is not enough to insure them of adult understanding and regard. And delinquent children are able to accomplish these things. This is one reason why no child should not become everybody's child or everybody's concern. Public or private services, whether representing the concern of churches, the state as a whole, teachers, parents, or the desires of any specific community should be provided only by those who have become knowing people in the ways of themselves as well as in the ways of children.

The School and Delinquency

The delinquent child must, by definition, exhibit unacceptable social behavior to some adult in some place. Some areas of a child's life are more frequently used for this purpose than are others to demonstrate his rebellion against, his indifference toward, or his response to the social group within whose structure he is requested to walk. It is almost axiomatic that if he is in school, much of his behavior regarded as delinquent will already have been expressed there. Every school requires of a child some degree of identification with the school, some demonstrated response to the requirements of the teacher regardless how indirectly or directly extracted, some adherence to rules imposed upon the group, and some submergence of the individual ego into the group.

Most delinquents find difficulty meeting these requirements and exhibit their protests in discernible ways. These ways often are similar in type and seriousness to the protests and reluctance of normal children. It is often only when the child's history or behavior has been reviewed that it can clearly be seen that he wrote his diagnosis in bold letters on the days of his schooling. Some schools use delinquency predictive scales, although such scales have low forecasting accuracy for individual pupils, for the multiplicity of variables that impinge on the behavior of any individual qualify the value of using any testing procedure to predict his delinquency potential.[1] It may well be that for the present time the final discerning procedure that can be applied to the sum total of what is known about the child is that of human judgment and humane response to what is believed.

In many ways schools have perverted their educative function by attempting to be all things to all children. In preparing the child for "life," they have frequently failed to give proper respect to knowledge and its use, and have become chary of sharing any portion of their students during school time with other professions whose major interest is the adequate functioning of the child.

It has long been noted that a disturbingly large number of delinquent children have difficulty in reading or are non-readers, although their determinable intelligence potential is of such a quality as to warrant the belief that they are capable of learning to read. Much more study is needed in this area, for reading is a means of communication, of extending the horizons of the reader's world, of introducing him to new and sometimes contradictory ideas or facts that force him to consider a possibility if not the fact of his error. It might well be that the child who finds his immediate world unsatisfactory or frightening is unwilling to enter another one which may be worse than the one he is in as long as he holds the power to keep it closed. Or that having achieved satisfactory explanations he is not going to expose them to the impact of other ideas and so threaten them with error and a return of anxiety about himself in relation to what is known. Or that the frightened and insecure child might not deliberately refuse to achieve in an area where such a beginning would bring more and more demands. This is not a question of reading methods, for if motivated most children will learn to read, but of the services selected for children capable of reading who for some reason cannot read.

To a young child of the middle and upper classes, learning to read is frequently the reward for attending school. Usually a child looks forward to reading the books the adult has read to him. Ability to read often is a promise to parents that their child shall accomplish more by the use of his mind than by use of his body. It is a means of becoming aware of the continuum, of identifying with the past, and of becoming a responsive creative part of the future. It is, for many, the constant and renewable means of attaching the present to what may appear to them as infinity. So vital is reading to our self-concepts that we deride being a "brain" or an "egghead" lest we find ourselves wanting. A child may be complimented upon his interest in things other than books, but he will be punished for a lack of accomplishment in gaining knowledge from books. The lower class child has less need of reading accomplishment, for he lives physically and in the present, with yesterday behind him and little reason for courting tomorrow. His narrow frame for living is his gang, the fellows in the pool hall, the street corner, under the stairs, or on the roof. He is engaged in conflicts with the law, with teachers, with other adults, with girls, with members of rival gangs, or with anyone who has not stilled his suspicion. It is a narrow frame. It needs little from the printed page.[2]

By the very nature of the school curriculum, however, not learning to read at the proper time results in years of constantly demonstrated inadequacy, of predictable hostility from teachers and sometimes from parents and probation officers, for the child has so many hours, so many days, so many months and so many years he must endure the consequence of his early failure. By law he cannot escape without punishment, yet he either must endure the humiliation of remaining with an increasingly younger group or, if he continues with his peer group, he must achieve status through other means. He frequently responds with truancy or in-school rebellions. As his body and natural capacities mature, he must seek a society where reading and the consequent knowledge is not of importance, for only here can he belong. Even a healthy desire to correct his reading deficiency cannot mitigate the need to keep firm hold on that part of him that is already known adequate or protective. Remedial reading classes usually do not serve this child for the primary need is to be accepted as he is. He then may be able to become something different. Experiments are now being conducted where the social worker or the school counsellor by use of his relationship with the child, helps him take whatever direction he wishes in pushing back the reading boundaries of his world. The purpose of using relationship is not "insight giving" but of walking with him into a world that frightens him, for every frightened person clings to what he knows he can handle.

Many urban schools include on their staff social workers (sometimes known as visiting teachers), psychologists, and sometimes a consulting psychiatrist. The school social worker works only with those students, referred through the principal, who have problems of a personal nature that hinder their school achievement or adjustment. Such referrals include many students who exhibit a delinquent-like behavior, who are truants or who may already have been in trouble with the police or have been known to the court. The social worker, in consultation with the classroom teacher, the principal, the parents, and when indicated, the psychologist, attempts to determine the factors contributing to the child's behavior and, in the light of this knowledge, help him with his difficulties, whether they are situational, environmental, inter-personal, parent-child, school pressures and conflicts, or hostility breeding feelings of inadequacy. He may be referred to an agency for specific types of service that the school does not give, such as the need of the family for financial assistance, the need for medical care, a disruptive home situation or protection from physical abuse, but his specific difficulty in school is handled by a service provided him by the school.

Some schools have also undertaken employment counselling, job placement, and work-study programs to help students who need to make the transition from dependent childhood into responsible, productive adulthood. They particularly provide help for the confused, impatient, insecure student who is not so upset by trying to decide what he is going to be as his fear that he may not be anything, the student who must contribute to his own and the support of others and either must or wishes to remain in school, and the student who finds waiting until he is 16 before dropping out of school unpalatable. Often such employment programs bring together the student and the employer at a time when the experience has considerable appeal to the student and is rewarding both to him and his employer. I have seen no convincing evidence that such school programs have any significant effect upon the rate of delinquency, for the statistics are mostly those of activity. This does not mean that the programs are not defensible but it remains to be demonstrated that they have salutory effect upon the child who wishes to move in an undemanding and unstructured society that complements his own lack of purpose and structure and who has a firm faith that when the future comes, he shall be able to handle it.

Another experiment in both delinquency prevention and correction has been the establishment of Boys' Towns, Ranches, or Villages patterned after Boys' Town founded by Father Flanagan at Omaha, Nebraska. Many of these homes are under sectarian auspices but provide for boys without regard for religion or race. A large number of the boys have elicited some agency, court, or general community concern and a few have been placed in the home as a part of a court plan for rehabilitation. Although these boys may have committed delinquent acts, they are usually believed capable of establishing sound peer relationships and of becoming responsible members of the community. Usually they have basically strong personality patterns and respond well to a change of environment, to a lightening of pressures and a separation from situations causing anxiety. Their need is not for a child-parent experience but an acceptable self-expression among peers and relationship with a limited number of adults under conditions of physical freedom. Many of the Towns, however, are neither staffed nor philosophically equipped to handle the continuingly difficult boy, the one who persists in lying, stealing, who runs away or engages in sex practices, who continues disobedient or whose aggressiveness takes a destructive form, or who incites others to rebellion or is persistently rebellious himself.

New Perspectives For Research

So far, we have given primary consideration to programs or experiments designed for helping children achieve satisfaction, adjustment and growth but not specifically directed toward delinquents in spite of the claims of their sponsors. It has long been known that certain areas have an accumulation of children whose group patterns of delinquency often suggest that such behavior might be regarded as a norm. There is a growing speculation that the theory of *anomie* might explain in a defensible manner the inadequate balance between the culture and the supporting social structuer that appears to result in a breakdown in the normative structure of the society in which these children live. In "New Perspectives for Research on Juvenile Delinquency," Robert Merton raises the question that if delinquency under certain circumstances, as suggested by Isidor Chein, might reflect the emergence of a new norm, and given "a state of relative breakdown in the shared standards of a group (the cultural or normative aspect), what is the impact on further social relations between the members of the group who are experiencing this normative breakdown? Do social relations become changed with mutual distrust? Or does one observe progressive social isolation as a phase response to normlessness?"[3] I insert this briefly, for although it will have no direct bearing on this paper, I have a feeling that discussions like these will have a vital impact upon much of our thinking, both about the individual who becomes a delinquent because he cannot identify with norms of his social group, the one who is a delinquent because he does, and the one whose social group provides him no norms and he responds to his own desires or his immediate associates. This is an over simplification, but its implication for those engaged in the handling and treatment of children regarded as delinquent is considerably less easily stated.

About twenty-five years ago, Clifford Shaw demonstrated that the rate of delinquency was inordinately high in areas where people crowded together and shared the problems produced by common poverty, slum housing, inadequate schools, sub-standard health and recreation faciilties, and erratic employment opportunities.[4]

He attributed much of this to the lack of neighborhood cohesiveness with consequent lack of concern for the welfare of the children of the area. He and his associates formulated what became known as the Chicago Area Project that had as its purpose the encouraging of self-help enterprises through developing a sense of neighborliness and mutual responsibility. He believed that if this could be accomplished there would result a change in the character of neighborhood life resulting in a wholesome environment that would enhance the responsibility, self-respect, and social as well as personal expression of the adults who, in turn, would become more responsive for the welfare of their children. Emphasis was placed on recreational activities, summer camps, discussion groups and social action. Natural leadership was stressed. Both children and adults were engaged in group activities, and persons with "status" or who "rated" were asked to pay special attention to the youngsters who were on probation or on parole from the training schools. Although no full scale evaluative study has been made of the results of the Project in the areas chosen for demonstration, it was believed that there is evidence that changes occurred, although their relationship to the delinquency rates has not been fully demonstrated.

It had also been observed that in areas of high delinquency, recreation facilities were usually meager or lacking, and when available, either as playgrounds or within Settlement or Neighborhood Houses, they are used largely by the non-delinquent children. Several experimental attempts were made to engage the delinquent and apt-to-be delinquent youngsters, usually boys, in recreational and club activities. Studies of these attempts, all somewhat different in character, were made by Shanas and Dunning,[5] Frederic M. Thrasher,[6] and Ellery Reed,[7] all of whom were engaged in at least one such club or group project activity. According to these studies, the success of these projects was somewhat disappointing both in the fact that the gains were not great and in some instances did not continue over a long period of time. There was considerable evidence that group work agencies were serving a selected group of children who, although they had a defensible claim for such activities, could not be regarded as delinquent or potentially delinquent. Neither Thrasher nor Reed rule out that the hypothesis of the potential and actual delinquency rate of an area might be affected by club and other group activities, for certainly the method of group projects might have a large number of variations. These experiments provided more evidence that the delinquent and the apt-to-be delinquent do not easily experience satisfaction from the same type of group activity as does the non-delinquent. He is not incapable of satisfaction but his satisfactions are apparently essentially different from those of the non-delinquent. It may also be assumed that for the most part, the apt-to-be delinquent children who reside in an area of high delinquency incidence may well show less neurosis or emotional disturbance about their behavior than the delinquent children who have no in-group with which they can identify.

It would be possible to refer to many other similar experiments, many of them less carefully handled, but the above lends weight to the hypothesis indicated in the first part of the chapter, that providing a community of children with programs normally used by and satisfying to non-delinquent children may serve no purpose as a measure for juvenile delinquency prevention. For that reason, reports of the volume of use made of the programs by a large number of undifferentiated children have but dubious value in demonstrating effective delinquency prevention, particularly when previous rates of incidence and other pertinent variables are not taken into account.

Police Experiments

An interesting variation in the experimental use of recreation for delinquency control was the formation of Police Athletic Leagues, Junior Deputy Sheriffs Organizations, and in at least one community, a Police-Gun Club.[8] This movement, less widespread now than a decade or so ago, was based on the assumption that if the delinquent or apt-to-be delinquent would relate in a friendly manner to his traditional enemy, the law enforcement officer, and take as his mentor the upholder of the law, he might as a consequence also feel some need to uphold the law.

For the most part, however, it is now believed the police are probably more effective in their function of helping people maintain a respect for and adherence to the law, but in so doing may need new methods. Police have been late in adopting the philosophy that was responsible for the establishment of the juvenile court, that children, regardless of their behavior, are not adults and should not be treated as adults. In many places the traditional role of the police who have contact with children has changed, not only their approaches to the child, but in their concern with the prevention of juvenile delinquency. Certainly the police force of any city deals with more delinquent children than does any other community agency with the exception of the schools. The manner in which a child is handled when he experiences the limits put upon him by society may well influence his response to such restrictions in his future social behavior. Important decisions regarding the individual delinquent are made by the police, since they initially determine whether the act of the child is of a serious nature, whether he should be released to his parents without referral, released with referral to a social agency, referred to the juvenile court but left in the custody of his parents, or referred to the juvenile court and placed in detention. From available statistics it would appear that for the most part the juvenile police refer but a small part of the children with whom they have some contact. The quality of the contact between child and police is thus important. Many communities are establishing special juvenile units in their police force, variously known as Youth Aid Bureaus, Juvenile Bureaus, Juvenile Divisions, Juvenile Aid Bureaus, Juvenile Units, or Juvenile Control Bureaus and attempting to staff them with persons who are known to have a liking for youngsters and can tolerate without verbal or physical retaliation the provocations of the frightened or brash adolescent. The question of the extent of their responsibility and their relationship to other community agencies still looms large.[9]

Because more importance is being attached to the work of the police with juveniles, there is a growing feeling that persons serving in this capacity should have special knowledges and skills that would contribute to their effectiveness in dealing with juveniles. To this purpose some universities and schools of social work have conducted special institutes and training workshops, usually including other persons working with the delinquent child, since the work of the police, if well done, cannot be divorced from that of other community agencies.

The Use of Psychiatry

Social agencies have in the past offered the major part of their service to parents and children who have economic and environmental needs they are unable to meet and who, like the alcoholic, have come to realize that in order to solve interpersonal problems, particularly those of their child-parent relationship, they need help in exploring the facets of the situation, and in achieving a better understanding of their reactions to each other and of themselves as individuals. Also commonly provided are services to children who need protection from the neglect or abuse of their parents, who need substitute or foster home care, medical care for their handicaps, or special institutional services which otherwise would not be provided.

Because of this major focus, social workers have leaned heavily upon the psychiatric understandings of human behavior and of the emotional growth and development of the child as well as the factors that prevented full, satisfying, and responsible parenthood. The psychiatrist and the clinical psychologist contributed their knowledges of human behavior and familial interrelationships to the purpose and the interpretations of the social worker. Although the profession gained greatly from such dependence, it also paid its toll in tending to providing its services principally for a selected group of people who undertook enough responsibility for their problem through their recognition that it existed to come to the agency voluntarily to request help and in interviews, to talk through the content of their situation and increase their ability to make a solution. For the most part studies of behavior have been made using those people who exhibited this pattern of facing and solving a problem and who exhibited neurotic and psychotic patterns if unable to do so. They represented a definable group of people, but not a cross-section of the universe. It becomes, therefore, widely assumed that any expression not tending to help the individual appropriately adjust to the social norms was the result of emotional conflict resulting from his wish to conform and his hostile rebellion or retaliation for some early experience in not doing so. Again, this is an over-simplified statement of complex and demonstrable knowledge and theory.

Social workers, psychiatrists, and psychologists became more and more skilled in working with people to whom this body of knowledge was applicable but much less successful in applying their methods to those groups who had not been represented among those known to clinicians. Among these were parents who had a different concept of the responsibility of parents towards their children and of parenthood in general. Their children exhibited a disturbing freedom from striving for what was considered "normal" parental approval. They frequently appeared to have incorporated no parental ego-image on which to pattern their own ideas of themselves and no guilt for anti-social behavior.

The explanations for the characteristic behavior known to the psychiatrist, the clinical psychologist, and the social worker as symptomatic of parental rejection or of child conflict-demand for parental approval with the usual resulting hostility and compensating behavior often do apply to delinquent children and their parents. These parents and children may exhibit the same type of overt behavior as do those who respond to the usual therapeutic methods, but this behavior apparently has a different meaning. In fact, as Bernard Lander's study[10] indicates and as presented by Robert Merton in his discussion on the social and cultural environment and *anomie* at a conference on juvenile delinquency sponsored by the Children's Bureau,[11] there appear to be great numbers of people about whom adjustments in theoretical knowledge and consequently in methods of modifying behavior patterns will have to be made. Certainly great numbers of parents of delinquents do not display the kind of guilt that results in their seeking out social agencies and psychiatric clinics. They do not regard their parent-child relationship as the type of a problem to explore with a professional person, nor do they see value in attempting to resolve a type of guilt they do not currently have. Their parenthood may have a normlessness that is an adaptation to the normlessness of the society in which they live.

Just how much this contributes to the knowledge of delinquency and its prevention or correction is not known, but certain things are known that tend to support the hypothesis that a different approach must be made to this type of delinquent and his parents.

The Use of "Detached Workers"

It is not unusual for children to become members of a youthful gang that stakes out a claim to sacred territory and creates a peculiar type of street-life of its own, has its own hierarchy of power with highly protected loyalties, and often adopts a livery of distinctive jackets, haircuts, and style of suits. The activity of the gang may be predatory or desultory and carries a quiet but dangerous challenge. Acceptance by the gang is a core of its members' existence. Members submit to a loss of individuality. The gang frequently operates with wariness against the prevailing social order. These youngsters do not come to group work agencies or neighborhood houses. They frequently serve their time in institutions and live to do so again. They do not benefit from the usual probationary and parole procedures, for they form few relationships with persons other than the members of their gang. Their world is small and vulnerable.

Several organizations (among them the Commission on Community Relationships of the American Jewish Congress, the Welfare Council of New York City and in its Harlem Street Group Project, the Los Angeles Youth Project and the Brooklyn Council for Social Planning) have tried to penetrate the imperviousness of these street groups to the appeals of ordinary youth activities by the use of "detached workers."[12] These workers represent no particular agency or already existing programs and allow themselves to be observed and studied during what might be termed a period of judicious and ubiquitous presence. They locate boy gangs in their usual hangouts, establish contacts with them by just being around, remain on the periphery of their world with an appropriate and natural knowledge of their terminology, their type of music, and their ability to shoot pool, and are willing to keep their hours. The worker's purpose is first to become a familiar figure and as the gang accepts him, to form relationships, particularly with the natural leaders.

The workers attempt to maintain subtly their own social norms without challenging the behavior of the gang. When the members of the club have arrived at cautious trust and will talk about their problems before the worker, he uses his relationship to suggest other means of solution which, if accepted, will move the club closer to his own type of behavior. In the preliminary reports of these projects, there is enough evidence to assume that they may have some demonstrable value. How much a single worker can accomplish remains to be determined as well as how effective the method is and under what circumstances or conditions, the type of person who can so carefully balance between a culture and a sub-culture and still pull others into his own culture, and the permanence of the results.

"Aggressive Social Casework"

Another attempt at "reaching the unreached" is that of "aggressive social casework."[13] The first full scale experiment was by the New York City Youth Board and the Department of Welfare which acted on the assumption that a community not only has the right but also the responsibility to protect its children and to take action in their behalf when their behavior may result in serious consequences. They instituted a project to "reach out" to these parents rather than waiting for the parents to come to them. Formerly, if parents were not themselves concerned with the anti-social behavior of their children, this neglect was principally a matter for law enforcement and in many instances social services were provided only after the children had become court wards.

The Youth Board–Board of Education project established referral units in eleven schools in an attempt to locate children with serious behavior problems who came under a two-part definition, that there was a clear danger to the child because of his anti-social behavior or that evident damage was resulting to him because his parents did not attempt to seek help in order to modify his situation. The Youth Board discovered that at least one-third of the families whose children were a cause of concern to the schools or other reporting sources had not sought agency service for what the units regarded as their "problem." Many others who had contacted such agencies had not continued with them. When the families to be included in the project had been selected, the social worker wrote the parents the time she planned to visit. If her first attempt to see them was not successful, she returned as many times as was necessary to make the contact. The problem of the child as seen by the community was stated specifically to the parents. Although the worker often was met by hostility and resistance, the worker maintained a respect for the parent, a firmness of interest in the child's situation and behavior, and an alertness to his physical and environmental as well as emotional needs. Services were largely those of ameliorating environmental pressures, but frequently changes also occurred in the parental relationship with the consequent modification of the child's behavior. Here, too, more evaluative study needs to be done. The effectiveness of the project on delinquency rates has not been fully explored. Although there is the danger in this type of "reaching out" of not respecting the right of privacy of individuals and the inherent relationship of parent and child, there is increasing awareness that corrective services to the delinquently behaving child may be more effective if provided the child while still in his family by other than a court procedure. Although this philosophy has consistently been a part of social work principles, many agencies have been reluctant to be "judgmental" or to use "authority," for the terms have been too closely associated with law enforcement or carry the semantics of psycho-analysis. That the term has many meanings is being recognized with salutary effect upon the type and extent of services social agencies are increasingly willing to provide.

Another but earlier project was one sponsored by the Children's Bureau, the St. Paul Experiment in Child Welfare instituted in 1937.[14] It had a three-fold purpose, to study the problems in identifying and providing treatment to children presenting personality and behavior problems, to learn what is involved in the development and integration of services provided by agencies and organizations concerned with children, and to study the ways of interpreting to the community the needs of these children. The area chosen for intensive work was one of high delinquency incidence. Children with incipient behavior and personality difficulties were located both through a community educational program and through the schools and the police. Whatever services were given were provided by the staff of a newly instituted Child Guidance Clinic.

The oldest of such child guidance clinics is the Judge Baker Guidance Center of Boston which for years was headed by Dr. William Healy who worked closely with the juvenile court, primarily providing diagnostic and planning services. Dr. Healy was a proponent of research dealing with delinquency and much of the early work of Sheldon and Eleanor T. Glueck was done here. It was their finding, and one frequently overlooked, that the boys for whom the court had received no diagnostic and planning services from the Clinic had no better record of staying out of later trouble than those who did, but when the Clinic provided treatment as well as diagnostic services, much better results were obtained. Much more is needed to be known about types of children who respond to child guidance services and those who do not as well as the best source of such services, for it would appear that a service provided by one agency, such as the court, and the same service provided by another agency, such as a child guidance clinic, may have different results. In both experiments, the St. Paul and the Judge Baker Clinic, services to children with exceptional personality disorders or who lived under gross social pathology were highly unsuccessful.

An attempt to integrate school and police facilities for the study and treatment of children was made by the Passaic (New Jersey) Children's Bureau, also established in 1937. The New York City Youth Board was established ten years later and, using schools as referral units, tried three different approaches, that of working with street clubs through a Council of Social and Athletic Groups, of having a group psychotherapy project administered by the Girls' League of New York City, and of going out to families to offer casework services by professional social workers for hard-to-reach families and children. (See above.) Here too an evaluative study should be made of the methods used and characteristics of the children that these methods served successfully or unsuccessfully.

Many other experiments should be mentioned, such as Fritz Redl's work at the National Institute of Mental Health with a small group of highly aggressive children and Mazie F. Rappaport's effective work with prostitutes through the Division of Protective Services of the Baltimore Department of Public Welfare and her demonstrated success with parents of delinquent children who had been ordered by the court to accept service from the Division. Edwin Powers and Helen L. Witmer completed an "action-research" study, known as the Cambridge-Somerville Youth Study, testing the hypothesis of the late Dr. Richard Clarke Cabot that the impact of personality upon personality, guided by good will and maturity of judgment, would have beneficial results.[15] The most general conclusion from this study seemed to show that none of the evaluative methods employed indicated any degree of success. It was, however, a bold, pioneering study, particularly in its approach of including the consideration of values.

Related Experiments

Too space consuming for consideration in this chapter is the use of detention, institutions and their correctional programs, use of cottages and grounds, forestry camps, parole and probation camps, the use of minimum security, institutional operation contributing to making the institution a "therapeutic community," the use of special skills as group therapy, group work, social casework, vocational and employment training and counselling, and methods for helping the educationally retarded child. In all of these areas new knowledges are emerging with consequent changes in method. Mention should also be made of the Youth Commissions or Youth Authority existent in a few states and of the work and willingness of some State Departments of Youth Services and Corrections to finance and undertake experiments.

There is also a rising interest in services for older delinquent children, those from the ages of 16 to 21 commonly known as "youthful offenders."[16] Usually the youthful offender has not been distinguished from the juvenile when programs and services have been discussed, but in most states he has a different legal status. The decision whether he will be regarded as a juvenile and handled by the juvenile court or as an adult and tried by the criminal court is a matter that may be determined by a number of things, such as the right of a judge to make such a decision (oftentimes the judge decides which court he will use to hear the case since he acts in the capacity of both the juvenile and the district court judge), the seriousness of the act, whether the child has been previously known to the court and for what reason, the traditional procedure of that particular court, and the provisions of the state law concerning the age determining court assignment. This, too, is an area needing much study and experimentation, for the late adolescent is neither child nor adult.

Oftentimes the quality and amount of change that has

taken place within an already existing program is hard to determine, for some programs seem merely to have adopted a name more in keeping with current terminology but have neither expanded their service nor arrived at a new philosophy for working with the delinquent. Sometimes they have expanded the scope of their functions or have gained new respect for the importance of their contact with the delinquent, but have been reluctant to re-think either the methods and the reasons for the methods they use or the content and type of the academic and field training that would be most valuable. For example, law schools have done little or nothing in preparing a body of knowledge dealing with the juvenile court or in recognition of the wealth of information that is available to those who will serve children in so vital a way as does a juvenile court judge. Juvenile court judges, for the most part, still learn by experience and the child is dependent upon the personal qualities and philosophies of the particular judge he appears before. Courts themselves have given recognition to their need for services other than of a legal nature and have assumed quasi-social agency functions for judicial decision in the cases of those children whose behavior is of such a nature as to warrant consideration of commitment to a correctional institution or removal of custody from his parents or legal guardian. In these courts, a referee system is used. A staff usually composed of social workers and sociologists make unofficial dispositions of the majority of cases after a study of the child's situation, contact with him and his parents, the use of special services as psychological testing, medical and psychiatric examinations, and school evaluations. In other courts the staff is directly responsible to the judge and all plans are either reviewed by him or, upon the basis of a social history provided him without recommendation, he plans for the child. This has many of the elements of a "social court," a term that may well suggest some essential contradictions. In much the same way, schools often close their staffs to services that might be provided by members of other professions in their insistence that the teacher be equipped to be all things to all students or that every service provided within its walls must be done so by a professional teacher. Yet for twelve years of a child's life only his own home provides a larger part of his living experience, and sometimes the school sees him for longer periods of time than do his parents and may have greater influence upon him. The primary function of the school is to provide its pupils education in the field of knowledge and its use, still one of the most respected and important of purposes, with a secondary purpose of giving him a positive living experience. The classroom teacher cannot be expected to minister to his environmental needs or to help him with the deepness of his emotional problems along with her educative function, even though the manner by which she educates is of vital importance. So also social workers may narrowly define their function as well as the therapeutic method they use, often crowding out the delinquent who does not respond to the traditional casework methods or whose parents do not willingly enter into casework planning and treatment. Many schools of social work are, however, becoming aware that the field of corrections is also a part of professional responsibility and that the child whose situation is complicated by lack of parental concern is one perhaps more in need of social work services than the one who has the benefit of parents who recognize their problems and desire to change for the child's benefit as well as their own. Police for the most part still maintain their traditional function but there is evidence that they are slowly becoming aware of the fact that they probably have contact with more delinquents than any of the other services and that their decisions impede or contribute to the continuing delinquency or the means of the rehabilitation of this particular child. In spite of this increasing awareness, many police still resist any change in their concept of themselves or in what should be their preparation to best fit them for the sensitive position that they hold. Kvaraceus has indicated, "Existing facilities are seldom the result of any prior community planning and organization. Usually they represent an aggregate of services—the sum of single approaches arising out of special interests. . . . The result is an overlapping of services, agency rivalry for funds and for clients, the preservation of agencies that have outlived their usefulness, and a lack of coordination of youth services."

Signs of Progress

Nevertheless, progress is being made. Schools of Social Work are cooperating with the Children's Bureau, the National Probation and Parole Association, Sociology Departments of Universities, and other lay and professional groups directly concerned with working with the delinquent and the youthful offender in conducting short term training programs, institutes and workshops for the exchange of experiences, thinking, and methods in the field of prevention and correction. Although some of these early attempts at communication and achieving the mutual respect and understanding have been difficult and sometimes tortuous, the increasing number of such group meetings being held and the increase in their attendance suggest that there is progress in inter-communication.

It remains to be seen if these and other experiments contribute significantly to the ways of dealing with delinquents by placing more responsibility upon integrated services provided by the community agencies for the child who by the nature of his actions might be regarded as non-adjudicated delinquent as well as redefining the correctional services to the adjudicated delinquent. It is also important that as children are identified these services are tailored to their normlessness as well as their conflict with the norms of society.

Certainly jurisdictional disputes either between adults, programs, or agencies can serve no purpose to the child. It is a difficult thing to share knowledge and the secrets of methods as long as members of any group achieve status through professional or lay exclusion of all but the chosen. It is sometimes doubly difficult to recognize the competence of others who differ in motivation, training, or experience. Because the delinquent child goes his way through the community and is acceptable to so little of it, he becomes everybody's child. He is exposed to little safety and many dangers as he arouses the angers or the protective instincts of adults. He has great need that adults learn much about him, that they do not use him as their possession, or regard him as too difficult and unrewarding for their attention and effort. He has great potentials, for it is the nature of the child to change; change is the labor of the adult.

Selected Bibliography

Herbert A. Bloch, & Frank Flynn, *Delinquency, The Juvenile Offender in America Today* (New York: Random House, 1956). A critical analysis of the latest developments in the field of delinquency, including new approaches for sociological investigation, new methods of treatment, and the most recent improvements in probation techniques and policies.

James J. Brennan, *The Prevention and Control of Juvenile Delinquency by Police Departments* (New York, Juvenile Aid Bureau of New York City, 1952). An abridgement of a dissertation submitted to New York University dealing with the activities of police departments in the field of delinquency prevention and control, the first part establishing frame of reference for the analysis and the second, the analysis and some suggestions to help improve the areas considered.

California Children in Detention and Shelter Care (Los Angeles, California, Committee on Temporary Child Care, 1955). A study to determine the type and extent of detention and shelter care in California and what is being done through protective services to prevent separation of children and youth from their families.

Alfred J. Kahn, *Police and Children* (New York: Citizens' Committee on Children of New York City, Inc., 1951). A study of the Juvenile Aid Bureau of the New York City Police Department to clarify the nature of the difficulties which bring children to the police, to evaluate the procedures and operation of the various sections of the Bureau, and to determine how police working with children might be strengthened by the long range program of protective services for children in New York City.

William T. Kvaraceus, *Juvenile Delinquency and the School* (New York: World Book Company, 1954). A study of the Passaic Children's Bureau project of combining the facilities of the school system and the police department for the study and treatment of problem children.

Bernard Lander, *Towards an Understanding of Juvenile Delinquency* (New York, Columbia University Press, 1954). A study correlating delinquency rates by race and sex with socioeconomic variables by the use of the techniques of factor analysis, indicating that slum communities fail to produce social conformity because inter-group conflicts prevent the development of any sense of togetherness, referred to as "anomie," a concept of the French sociologist Emile Durkheim.

Robert K. Merton, *Social Theory and Social Structure* (Glencoe, Ill.: The Free Press, 1949). Presents the theory that an unknown but substantial proportion of deviant behavior represents socially induced deviations which the culture and the social organization conjoin to produce.

New Perspectives for Research on Juvenile Delinquency, edited by Helen L. Witmer and Ruth Kotinsky, (Washington, D. C.; U. S. Department of Health, Education, and Welfare, Children's Bureau, U. S. Government Printing Office, 1956). A report of a conference held May 6-7, 1955, on the relevance and inter-relation of certain concepts from sociology and psychiatry for delinquency, particularly dealing with ego identity as presented by Erik H. Erikson and with social and cultural environment and *anomie* as presented by Robert K. Merton.

Harris B. Peck, M.D. & Virginia Bellsmith, *Treatment of the Delinquent Adolescent* (New York: Family Service Association of America, 1954). A presentation of treatment practices and processes considered to be especially useful in group and individual therapy with parent and child.

Police Services for Juveniles, (Washington, D. C.: U. S. Department of Health, Education, and Welfare, Children's Bureau, U. S. Government Printing Office, 1954). A review of some current opinion and infomation about police services for juveniles, including a report on the East Lansing Conference, August 3-4, 1953, sponsored by the Children's Bureau in cooperation with the International Association of Chiefs of Police and the Special Juvenile Delinquency Project.

Edwin Powers & Helen Witmer, *An Experiment in the Prevention of Delinquency* (New York: Columbia University Press, 1951). A report on the Cambridge-Somerville Study, originally instituted and financed by Dr. Richard Cabot of Harvard, to test the hypothesis that delinquency might be presented or the delinquent aided by the continued friendship of an adult deeply interested in him who could also secure for him the community services he needs.

Reaching the Unreached (New York: New York Youth Board, 1952). Fundamental aspects of the program of the New York City Youth Board, including the philosophy upon which development of the Youth Board was founded, and the special projects of directing teen-age gangs, casework with families who do not voluntarily accept social agency services, and psychotherapy with a selected group.

Ellery Reed, "How Effective are Group Work Agencies in Preventing Delinquency?" *Social Service Review,* XXII (1948),

340-348. A report on the children using group work programs in Cincinnati.

Clifford R. Shaw, *"Methods, Accomplishments, and Problems of the Chicago Area Project,"* 1944 (Mimeo). A review of the Chicago Area Project started in 1934 in ten deteriorated neighborhoods as an experiment in reducing delinquency rates and in rehabilitating the delinquent through organization of neighborhood committees who by self-help undertook improvements through committee and recreational work.

Sybil A. Stone, Elsa Castendyck, & Harold B. Hanson, *Children in the Community: the St. Paul Experiment in Child Welfare* (Children's Bureau, Washington, D. C., 1946). A report of a project in St. Paul in 1937 by the U. S. Children's Bureau to study the problems confronted in the identification and treatment of children presenting problems, the integration and development of agencies providing services to children, and the ways of interpreting the needs in services to children to the community.

Clyde B. Vedder, ed., *The Juvenile Offender* (Garden City, New York, Doubleday and Company, Inc., 1954). A collection of readings arranged to reflect the principal divisions of the field of juvenile delinquency, including readings on etiology, extent and causes, apprehension and detention, and corrective programs.

Helen L. Witmer & Edith Tufts, *The Effectiveness of Delinquency Prevention Programs* (U. S. Department of Health, Education and Welfare, Children's Bureau, Washington, D. C., U. S. Government Printing Office, 1954). A review of the research literature to determine what has been learned about the effectiveness of various delinquency prevention measures that have already been tried, with the purpose of discovering what has not been evaluated as well as how adequate or inadequate the evaluative studies are that have been done.

Garnet Larson received her B.S. degree in Education (1929) and a Master of Arts in English (1930) from the University of Nebraska; taught as an Instructor in English at the University of Kansas (1930-1935) and received her Ph.D. in English and Philosophy from the University of Kansas (1935); taught English at the Nebraska State Teachers College, Chadron (1935-1944). Attended the University of Pittsburgh (1944-1946), receiving her

Masters Degree in Social Work. Associated with the North
Dakota Public Welfare Board (1946-1949), working on a special
medical research project and later with the Division of Field
Services. Since 1949 associated with the Graduate School of
Social Work of the University of Nebraska; has also served as a
Special Consultant to the Division for Children and Youth of
the North Dakota Public Welfare Board and on a Field Foundation Grant (held by the Elizabeth McCormick Memorial Fund
of Chicago), and is the author of numerous publications in the
field of Social Work.

Part IV

International Trends

CHAPTER 13.

INTERNATIONAL TRENDS
IN JUVENILE DELINQUENCY*

MARTIN H. NEUMEYER
University of Southern California

Juvenile delinquency is an old problem, a problem which has increased in extent and intensity during the past two decades. The world upheaval caused by World War II and subsequent international disturbances, coupled with the dynamic conditions of modern society, have produced noticeable increases in both juvenile delinquency and adult crime. But it is exceedingly difficult to ascertain with any degree of accuracy the major international trends in juvenile delinquency, owing to the variations in criminal laws and the extent of law violation, the methods of dealing with offenders, the systems of reporting crime, and the effectiveness of preventive measures.

The interest in the spread of delinquency is evidenced by the number of studies that have been made of the problem and the volume of published material on the subject. The Division of Social Welfare, Department of Social Affairs, of the United Nations has sponsored studies of delinquency and has conducted regional consultative conferences which have produced important information relative to certain phases of the problem of juvenile delinquency. The reports of these studies and conferences are used chiefly as the basic data regarding international trends reported in this article. Well-known experts were invited to prepare five regional reports on North America, Europe, Latin America, Asia and the Far East, and the Middle East, using as their material the government replies to the United Nations questionnaire on the treatment of juvenile delinquents and various other official sources.[1] The International Review of Criminal Policy has been published since January 1952. The articles and reports in this publication are primarily devoted to the methods employed in the treatment of offenders and in the prevention of crime, which may be appropriately described as "applied criminological science." These types of publications have been supplemented by documents on probation and related measures and on child and youth welfare programs.

The topical bibliographies of current literature on crime and delinquency, published in the earlier issues of the *International Review of Criminal Policy*, indicate the extent of publications in this field.[2] Even though it is not possible to obtain a complete list of publications on various phases of crime and delinquency, the bibliographies that have been published by the United Nations contain more than 1,800 technical or semitechnical publications per year; at least this seems to have been the production rate during the first three years of the present decade.

Attempts to achieve international cooperation with respect to the treatment of offenders and the prevention of crime preceded the work of the United Nations, which was mainly the by-product of the growth of a more scientific approach to the problem of crime. A number of international nongovernmental organizations and world conferences on crime have stimulated interest in various phases of the problem of crime and have also aided in doing something about the spread of crime.

When the Social Commission of the United Nations considered that the constructive handling of the problem of young delinquents and of neglected children who are likely to develop criminal tendencies unless properly dealt with at an early stage was an important function assigned to the United Nations in the field of social defense, the efforts in delinquency prevention received a new impetus. The Secretariat considered that

international action in the field of juvenile delinquency necessarily implied: (a) a dynamic programme in which a balance should be maintained as much as possible between other social policies such as those dealing with social services; research and practical action; (b) co-ordination between housing, community development and social defense policy; and (c) co-operation between the United Nations and the specialized agencies and non-governmental organizations interested in the problem of juvenile delinquency.[3]

This policy accounts for the extent of information assembled on specific measures of prevention of delinquency, treatment of offenders, courts and agencies with jurisdiction over juveniles, changes in legislation and the variations in criminal laws, and related matters. Limited data on the causes of juvenile delinquency, and the relation between causation and the prediction of delinquent behavior, are presented.

The concepts in the field of delinquency are undergoing marked changes and vary considerably in accordance with national and regional differences in backgrounds. They often vary considerably in different parts of the same country. However, two broad criteria which make up the main conception of delinquency are (a) the nonadult status of the person concerned and (b) that the act on the part of such a person is regarded as delinquent behavior according to the laws of the country. But the discussions in the seminars which were held in Europe, Latin America, Middle East, and Asia and the Far East, under the auspices of the United Nations, revealed considerable divergencies of views with respect to such matters as the lower and upper age limits of persons who may be regarded as delinquents, the specific acts which are defined by criminal law as delinquencies, and the inclusiveness of the term "delinquency."

Where English legal precedents prevail, the lower age limit of discernment is usually fixed at either seven or eight years of age, but the Latin American Seminar (Rio de Janeiro, 1953) recommended that "States should fix a uniform age of minority (which should in no case be less than the age of fourteen years) for the purpose of criminal law below which a minor would not be capable of incurring liability."[4] The Middle East Seminar (Cairo, 1953) expressed a tendency to do away with the lower age limit altogether, thus dispensing with the concept of criminal responsibility.

The upper age limit is the dividing line below which a person is regarded as a juvenile. The range of the upper limits is from fourteen years in Haiti and Dominica to twenty-one years in Chile, the states of Arkansas, California, and Wyoming (female) in the United States, and the British Solomon Islands. The most common upper age limits range from fifteen to eighteen years. There is a noticeable trend to raise the upper age limit of juvenile court jurisdiction. Some countries designate several age groups, each with different emphasis of discernment and methods of treatment. For instance, in France, juveniles between the ages of 13 and 16 receive less severe treatment than thoes between ages 16 and 18 for the same kind of offense. In Sweden, juveniles are subdivided into two age groups: from 15 to 18 and from 18 to 21, the treatment of offenders in each group being governed by somewhat different provisions.

Originally, the term "juvenile delinquency" referred exclusively to minors having committed offenses defined by criminal codes. There is a trend in different countries in favor of placing under the jurisdiction of juvenile courts and related administrative agencies not only the violators of criminal codes but the predelinquent (or potentially delinquent) juveniles who are in need of special forms of treatment, even though their deviant behavior is not specifically designated by law as constituting delinquency. Children in need of care and protection by reason of unfavorable circumstances over which they have little or no control are likewise placed under the jurisdiction of legally constituted authorities in various countries. There is no unanimity of opinion regarding the inclusiveness of the concept "delinquency" or of the jurisdiction of courts. The salient feature of the divergent and often controversial views is that juveniles who have committed acts in violation of criminal laws should be regarded as offenders and not as ordinary criminals.

The passage of new legislation on juvenile delinquency and the change or discontinuance of old laws have grown out of the changing conception of what constitutes delinquency and the functions of juvenile courts and other administrative bodies. Changes in legislation have affected the methods of treatment of delinquent or maladjusted children and the statistics of the extent of juvenile delinquency.

The increase of juvenile delinquency has been stressed as a problem affecting, with few exceptions, all countries; but the available statistics are inadequate to substantiate the contention that a veritable epidemic of law violation has swept over the entire world. In some areas of the world, such as parts of Latin America, Asia and the Far East, the Middle East, and Africa, juvenile delinquency has only recently become a problem of concern. In countries where statistics of delinquency are to be found, great caution must be used in drawing conclusions from them. Comparative statistics of different countries have little value because of the variation in legislation, in methods of treatment, and in reporting cases. Crime is not regarded at the same stage in the statistics of the countries concerned. Statistics are valid only in perspective of a country's total correctional system and must be assessed chiefly in relation to the stage of legislation and of the correctional system. They refer only to figures which have been reported. However, those who deal professionally with delinquents seem to be in agreement that law violation among juveniles has become a serious problem.

The information on causal factors of juvenile delinquency is limited to specific studies. In some countries very little has been done to ascertain the reasons for the increase of law violation. It is pointed out that the problem becomes a matter of special concern in those countries where industrialization and urbanization have increased and where there has been a disintegration of the traditional way of life. In some areas the problem is confined to the great centers of population; rural and sparsely settled territories have fewer delinquents. In societies where the tribe or clan still plays a powerful role or where the handling of deviants is entrusted to the family or clan, there is little need for more formal machinery of law enforcement.

The trend is to emphasize multiple causes and the interrelationship of causal factors. This calls for an interdisciplinary approach and emphasis.[5] Even those who stress primarily one approach, using data from different parts of the world, recognize other types of conditioning factors.[6] Whatever the methods used to ascertain the etiology of crime and delinquency, they must be appropriate to the conditions and problems inherent in a given area.

Among the numerous variables that may be directly or indirectly related to juvenile delinquency, the following are noted as of considerable significance: age factor (delinquency increases with age), sex differences (law violation is more common among males than among females), mental backwardness and lack of education, family organization, growth of industrialization and urbanization, unpleasant and unhygienic living quarters in urban areas, economic distress, and general conditions of social disorganization in the area. In some instances improvement in standards of living has added to disorganization, but usually children of the lower economic and social classes have the highest rates of delinquency. Offenses against property always predominate, which seems to indicate that necessity is an important causative factor. Delinquency is less frequent among indigenous minors than among minors of other ethnic groups (more of the former live in rural areas). Ethnic differences influence irregular conduct in exceptional cases. Illegitimate birth is not as decisive a factor in delinquency as may be assumed.

The material on the treatment of juvenile offenders is extensive, especially with respect to juvenile courts and other agencies with jurisdiction over juveniles, the treatment in freedom (probation and foster-home care), treatment in institutions (public and private), and procedures of release and after-care. Even though great variations exist in different parts of the world in stages or degrees of advancement of modern methods of dealing with offenders, progress is being made in nearly all advanced countries in certain aspects of the treatment processes. The progress that has been made in England and Wales, and in some of the countries of the British Commonwealth, notably the Borstal System of training young offenders, is especially noteworthy. The role of juvenile courts is not uniformly recognized, but improvements have been made in the organization and functions of courts, the conduct of court proceedings, and in jurisdictions. Improvements have likewise been made in detection, police protection, observation and case studies, probation, detention services, long-term institutional care and after-care, and the training of personnel in the agencies that deal with juveniles. It is broadly true that nearly all countries have enacted the necessary legislation and regulations for the treatment of juvenile offenders.

The need for preventive policies and programs is increasingly being recognized. Direct measures of prevention include programs for the detection and subsequent treatment of juveniles showing marked tendencies toward crime (commonly known as potential or predelinquent juveniles) and more efficient methods of treating offenders that are designed to prevent recidivism. Indirect measures are attempts to improve the social environment of juveniles, particularly living conditions, and the development of nondelinquent patterns of behavior. During recent years the indirect measures have received more attention on the assumption that the general improvement of living conditions should reduce delinquency.

The approaches to prevention vary in accordance with the conception of causation. The role of the State in the preventive program is not clearly defined, but the seminars that were held in the different areas of the world summarized the functions under the following headings: (1) coordination, (2) technical aid and setting standards, (3) finance, (4) control and supervision of services and institutions, (5) state organized services, (6) legislation, and (7) research.

The role of the police in both the treatment of offenders and the prevention of delinquency has been expanded considerably during recent years. The regional reports of the United Nations (*Comparative Survey on Juvenile Delinquency*) indicate that while police officers are generally regarded as responsible for the detection and arrest of delinquents, there is a growing tendency in many countries to use special police in this respect and to expand their functions to include the treatment of the young or less serious offenders, to act as liaison officers in dealing with parents and teachers, also various types of community agencies, and to participate in preventive programs.

The role of the school in relation to the prevention of delinquency differs from region to region, but the general trend is for the school authorities to assume increasing responsibility for the detection of delinquent tendencies, to provide a more flexible curriculum adapted to the multifarious interests of pupils, and to provide special schools or classes for maladjusted children. Schools are key institutions in communities to spearhead preventive programs.

The role of the community in delinquency prevention is in certain respects analogous to that of the State, except that community action is basically the planning and organizing of services on the local level. More systematic planning, whether on the local or on a broader basis, is particularly needed in an effective preventive program. It is here that the various government and private service agencies can render their most useful services.[7] Recreation centers, youth serving agencies, and churches are of particular significance in providing wholesome and constructive activities for children and young people.

The family is one of the major institutions in any delinquency prevention program. It provides the immediate environment for the socialization of human beings from infancy to maturity. It is in the family that most children learn the norms and values of the social world in which they live.

From the point of view of the social scientists, the most significant trend in delinquency prevention is the growth of research. The volume of literature referred to earlier in this article is an indication of the extent of interest in conducting studies of the problem. An examination of research on the subject of juvenile delinquency indicates two broad categories under which many of the studies may be classified: namely, (1) the studies that deal with the etiology of delinquency behavior and (2) those which evaluate treatment and preventive programs instituted on the basis of the findings of research.

Martin H. Neumeyer, B.A. degree (De Pauw University, 1919), B.D. (Garrett Biblical Institute, 1921), M.A. (Northwestern University, 1922), and Ph.D. (University of Chicago, 1929), was public school teacher and student minister (1914-1915 and 1917-23), Instructor in Sociology, Chicago Training School (1923-1927), Assistant, Associate, and Full Professor, University of Southern California (1927 to the present time). Now Professor of Sociology & Head of the Department of Sociology, University of Southern California. Is also President of the United Chapters of Alpha Kappa Delta, National Sociology Honor Society and Managing Editor, *Sociology and Social Research;* Chairman of the Special Committee of Crime and Delinquency, Society for the Study of Social Problems, and Joint Chairman of Criminology Section, American Sociological Society (1956-1957); also served one term as President of the Pacific Sociology Society. Has written numerous articles and book reviews, and is the author of *Community and Society* (with L. D. Osborn, 1933); *Leisure and Recreation* (with Mrs. Neumeyer, 1936, 1949, 1958); *Juvenile Delinquency in Modern Society* (1949, 1955); and *Social Problems in a Changing Society* (1953).

CHAPTER 14.

YOUTH CRIME AS A PROBLEM AROUND THE WORLD*

ROBERT ALDEN
New York *Times*

The problem of juvenile crime casts a long shadow that reaches every part of the globe.

A world-wide survey by New York Times correspondents reveals that much of today's juvenile crime was spawned in the wake of the chaos created by World War II. Juvenile crime was rampant in the first of the post-war years.

Since then the situation has improved markedly in many cities abroad. But in some large urban areas in the United States, such as New York, it has grown worse. Three murders were committed here recently within a week.

The menace of juvenile crime can be depicted partly in terms of statistics. In most of the cities surveyed juveniles were responsible for a considerable percentage of all crime committed.

For example, in New York, persons under 21 years of age constituted 14.9 per cent of those arrested for all crimes. Youths in the same age group made up 50 per cent of those arrested for robbery and 61.3 per cent of those arrested for burglary.

But, as one social worker put it, statistics do not tell the story of delinquency as it should be told. Juvenile crime, particularly in the United States is often unprovoked and without reason.

In each of the cities surveyed, the problem was recognized as a menace that required special treatment. Each city has taken some action to fight juvenile delinquency.

Abroad all the cities but London feel they have gained the upper hand.

However, in the United States, the situation appears to be growing worse.

Only Chicago reported that it was holding its own in the battle against the delinquent. But even there, where the number of arrests remained the same, the crimes committed by youths were becoming more serious in nature.

Those who have studied the problem of juvenile delinquency, both here and overseas, have come to the conclusion that youngsters usually go wrong when they do not have a suitable home environment.

Law enforcement agencies in all the cities surveyed are approaching the solution of the problem from that point of view. Special police units are formed and trained and these units work in close cooperation with social agencies.

Paris Shows Success

Paris is a good example of a city successfully fighting its delinquency problem. It has found that between 80 and 90 per cent of the juveniles who find themselves in the toils of the law come from broken homes.

Few of these children go to jail. They are handled by a special police squad. When the youths are arrested they are sent to a center for two months of physiological and psychological testing.

A children's court then decides what kind of rehabilitative center is most suitable in the case. Vocational training is frequently given. Where the home environment is very bad the children are often placed in more wholesome surroundings.

There are divergencies, however, in the handling of youth crime. New York and San Francisco have fundamentally opposite views as far as juvenile gangs are concerned.

In San Francisco juvenile gangs are broken up as soon as they are uncovered. In New York social workers try to rechannel the activities of the gangs along socially acceptable lines.

In San Francisco there is a curfew forbidding youths under 18 to be on the streets after 11 P.M. New York has no curfew.

The Moscow Bureau of The New York Times reported that there was a shortage of statistics and information on juvenile crime in that city. There have been, however, many reports of late hooliganism and other evidences of juvenile delinquency in Moscow.

Anxiety in London

London, Aug. 13—Increases in teen-age crime in London in the last two years have become "a cause for anxiety," according to Sir John Nott-Bower, Commissioner of Police.

The number of persons under 21 years old who have been arrested has risen in the last two years, reversing a downward trend that started after 1951.

Gang activity has been on a much smaller scale than in New York, but it has resulted in the death of at least two gang members in recent years.

Arrests of youths between the ages of 8 and 21 increased by 12.6 per cent in 1956 over the previous year and by 9.3 per cent in 1955 over 1954. Crimes of violence committed in 1956 by persons under 21 were 25.3 per cent of the year's total crime.

Nearly two-thirds of the persons under 21 who committed crimes last year, the Police Commissioner noted, acted in company with other persons. The groups ranged in size from two to eight persons.

London has its so-called "Teddy Boys" who affect exaggerated Edwardian dress of long jackets and pipestem trousers similar to the American zoot suits. Some have formed gangs with names such as the Skeletons, the Battersea Boys and the Tooting Boys. They engage in vandalism and rowdyism and occasionally fight each other.

Social workers and the police attribute juvenile delinquency here to a multitude of causes that include broken homes, lack of parental supervision, a need by the young to be identified in some way and to feel important, and feelings of insecurity.

There is an elaborate system for rehabilitating offenders. Great reliance is placed in carefully supervised probation. Offenders guilty of less serious crimes are required to give up two hours every Saturday afternoon to police-supervised training, particularly in discipline. For those who have committed more serious offenses there are detention centers where young toughs are submitted to "a short, sharp shock" of three months of rigid discipline.

Paris Stresses Correction

Paris, Aug. 13—This city of 2,850,000 people has its trouble-making juveniles like any other large urban center. But its officials are able to sit back with relative complacency and react with long-distance shock to adolescent crime in New York.

After a spate of juvenile delinquency just after the war, crimes by youths from 8 to 18 years old dropped by 50 per cent between 1949 and 1952.

The rate of youth crime remained stable until 1955, when an increase of 2.4 per cent was noted. But officials point out the juvenile population rose by 6 per cent so no cause for alarm was seen. There has been no appreciable change since 1955.

What bothers officials here the most is not the juvenile crime rate, but how to deal with the young people who get into trouble. A great deal of attention is paid to corrective treatment, both physiological and psychological.

A young offender goes to an observation center for two months, and receives medical and psychological examinations. The children's court then decides on what kind of rehabilitation center would best suit him.

Vocational training in private or state-run institutions where his associates are of his own age is the general rule. A prison term is the rare exception.

Special Brigade Aids Youths.

In Paris, a special section of the police called the Brigade for the Protection of Minors is devoted exclusively to adolescent problems. It consists of fifty women police assistants and thirty police officers.

Between 80 and 90 per cent of the young people who have brushes with the law come from families that are broken or abnormal in some way.

A close watch is kept on families where alcoholism—a serious problem in France—neglect or brutal treatment of children has been reported. Bad housing, which still plagues Paris, is also conducive to trouble-making. Children are often separated from alcoholic, neglectful or brutal parents and placed in more wholesome surroundings.

Paris does not have neighborhood gangs. Occasionally, youths will join together to steal a car or rob cellar bins of apartment houses, but there is little gang warfare.

Only a minority of the juvenile crimes or misdemeanors are against persons. But the theft of scooters, motorcycles and cars is a big item on children's court agendas.

The biggest item of all is what is called "vagabondage," cases of teen-agers who have left home and are found wandering in Paris. French law provides no punishment for this, but the children must be taken in and rehabilitated before they turn to crime.

Berlin Isn't Worried

Berlin, Aug. 13—The generation of toddlers who picked rags and scraps of food from the wreckage of defeated Berlin today constitutes its teen-age crime problem. However, civic authorities are not worried about the threat to public order.

The police of both East and West sectors of Berlin agree on this.

West Berlin police statistics show that one of five law violators who are caught are in the 14-to-21-year-old group. The police say that adult criminals are much better at escaping, so teen-agers probably commit only one-seventh of all violations.

A police official said that serious crime by teen-agers in West Berlin showed a downward trend. Traffic violations make up the bulk of youthful breaches of the law.

Little Gang Crime.

Social workers of the West Berlin administration record more cases of juvenile mischief than do the police. This is because they go beyond cases where a breach of law is established.

They express some concern about the rowdy behavior of youthful groups in the evening. However, they say there is comparatively little gang crime.

There are occasional shocking cases of small gangs attacking couples who are spooning in parks. Women walking alone in parks are also the prey of youth gangs occasionally.

Another type of gang goes in for stealing cars, breaking into closed shops and willfully damaging gardens and other property.

Social workers, as well as the police, say that a basic cause of teen-age crime in West Berlin is that corporal punishment is no longer widely used in homes and schools.

Materialism Growing

While the police are likely to stress such a diagnosis, social workers say also that youngsters are affected by the ideas of the time. The conceptions of freedom and individual activity are often distorted into excuses for wild behavior. The growth of materialism is said to have created an intellectual vacuum. Planless violence often follows.

The number of children born in Berlin during World War II and in the first years afterward was greatly reduced by heavy casualties among adults. Many of the frictions faced by youngsters in other overpopulated metropolitan areas are absent here.

Social workers and the police try earnestly to cut youthful delinquency by getting teen-agers off the streets and into clubs and cultural centers. The authorities condemn the effects of violent films and periodicals and are distressed about the increasing use of alcohol by teen-agers. But the city in general feels juvenile delinquency is not a really serious problem.

Rome Has No Gang Problem

Rome, Aug. 13—Rome has no teen-age crime problem. The gang as understood in New York and other great American cities is unknown or almost unknown here. Minors are responsible for only a small part of the total crime in Rome and for almost no crime of violence.

Immediately after World War II, juvenile delinquency flared and educators and law enforcement agencies worried for some years. A particularly disquieting feature about it was that teen-age criminals who specialized in hold-ups and crimes of violence came mostly from good middle-class and even from well-to-do families. The flare-up subsided about ten years ago, and the police report that since then juvenile delinquency has constantly declined.

Under Italian law, wrongdoers under 14 go unpunished because they are not considered responsible. Minors between 14 and 21 get special treatment if found guilty of a crime. Statistics on juvenile delinquency in Italy refer to the 14-21 age bracket.

In Rome, juvenile crime accounts for about 2 per cent of the total, according to the police. Last year, an estimated total of 1,300 minors had charges brought against them. Rome has a population of 1,800,000.

The 1,300 youthful lawbreakers were petty thieves and crooks. About one-third were booked for misdemeanors, the remainder for more serious offenses. Cases of violence were few.

Singapore Relatively Free

Singapore, Aug. 13—Juvenile crime in this city of 1,250,000 is almost negligible. Offenses by juveniles, those under 16 years old, are more of a problem for social welfare workers than for the police.

Police authorities say that the only problem involving youths —including the 16-to-20-year age group—is that of secret societies. These secret society gangs make use of unemployed ignorant youths merely as informers and collectors for "protection fees."

These youngsters sometimes branch out into groups of their own, coining names such as Yankee Gang to match the tight-fitting jeans they wear; and Tony Curtis Gang for the hair styles they sport.

The crimes prevalent in these groups mostly include petty thefts and small-scale protection rackets among street hawkers, prostitutes and small retail shops. Their demands are usually small, and victims pay up to be rid of the nuisance. Gang fights occur occasionally with the main weapons being bicycle chains and bottles. But the moment a police car is sighted, the fight is ended and the participants scramble into hiding.

Political Activity Feared

Teen-age delinquency along political lines is a latent danger in the Chinese middle schools. In fact, the Government classifies such activity as subversion.

In May, 1956, and October of last year, explosive situations arose when Communist-led students instigated bloody riots that paralyzed the entire city for several days. The students rioted in a protest against legislation affecting them and in support of industrial strikes.

The Government has admitted that Communist cells exist in Chinese high schools, mostly led by older students. Documents that have been seized have shown that these cells were linked to the Malayan Communist party, but the acutal number of party members in the schools is unknown.

The police point out that in 1955 there were 9,240 arrests of delinquents and 838 convictions. Last year there were 583 arrests and 543 convictions.

The juvenile court operates for two hours twice a week. Upon conviction the delinquents are sent to approved schools or remanded to homes and "places of safety" where they are regarded as youngsters who need protection.

Social welfare workers regard these institutions as of a high standard comparable to those of the United Kingdom. Of the number of probations last year only 17 per cent were failures compared to 25 per cent in Great Britain.

Few Gangs in Melbourne

Melbourne, Australia, Aug. 13—Apart from automobile thefts and joy riding, teen-age crime is not regarded as a major problem in this city of 1,500,000 population.

Melbourne has very little traffic in narcotics, and there is no evidence that juveniles use drugs. There are very few organized teen-age gangs.

Police figures show a light increase in the numbre of sex and prostitution cases in the last few years but not noticeably among teen-agers.

On the other hand, the police and the state regard auto stealing as a major problem. Last year more than 4,000 automobiles were stolen in Melbourne. Eighty-four per cent of the joy riders and thieves arrested were juveniles.

Stiff Penalties Set

The state recently passed legislation providing much stiffer penalties for joy riding. Youths can now be fined $225 and sent to jail for a first offense. The maximum jail term for a second offense is five years.

Last year the Government appointed a special committee to inquire into and report on juvenile delinquency.

The committee recommended the establishment of a special police unit to detect and prevent teen-age crime and to advise youths and parents.

Further, it proposed the use of school buildings after hours as youth clubs, the creation of state training establishments for wayward and problem children, the building up of municipal recreational and social outlets for children and adequate Government support for youth clubs.

Robert Alden, a member of the *New York Times*, has followed a familiar American pattern of working himself up through the ranks of his profession. A native of Huntington, Long Island, he attended the College of the City of New York; while attending the college, he worked part-time for the *New York Times* as a messenger. He served in the Army (1942-1946) and came out a Captain, returned to the *New York Times* and started as an office boy, moved up the ladder until he joined the News Staff in 1949; in 1952 became a foreign correspondent covering the Korean War, later was assigned to a vast area of Southern Asia and has covered a large number of countries from Singapore down to Australia.

Reprinted by permission of The New York *Times, CVI,* 363 (August 15, 1957).

NOTES—*Chapter 1.*

1. 23 *Illinois Revised Statutes* 190.

2. August Aichhorn, *Wayward Youth* New York: (Viking Press, 1935), 3-5.

3. Cf., Kurt Eissler, Ed., *Searchlights on Delinquency* (New York: International Universities Press, 1949), 3-25.

4. Cf., S. Kirson Weinberg, *Society and Personality Disorders* (New York: Prentice-Hall, 1952), Cr. 12.

5. This classification of factors is based, in part, on the studies of Prof. N. Goldman of Syracuse University, as reported in an unpublished paper presented at the Annual Meeting of the Society for the Study of Social Problems, 1956.

6. Cf., S. Axelrad, "Negro and White Institutionalized Delinquents," *American Journal of Sociology*, LVII (May 1952), 569-74.

7. Cf., Daniel Bell, "What Crime Wave?", *Fortune* (January 1955), 96-99, 154-156.

8. Cf., Edward E. Schwartz, "A Community Experience in the Measurement of Juvenile Delinquency," *National Probation Association Yearbook 1945* (New York: National Probation Association, 1946), 157-181.

9. Fred J. Murphy, Mary M. Shirley and Helen L. Witmer, "The Incidence of Hidden Delinquency," *American Journal of Orthopsychiatry*, XVI (October, 1946), 686-696.

10. E.g., J. S. Wallerstein and C. J. Wyle, "Our Law-Abiding Law-Breakers," *Probation*, XXV (April 1947), 107-112; A. L. Porterfield, *Youth in Trouble* (Fort Worth: Leo Potishman Foundation, 1946), Ch. 2.

11. James F. Short, Jr., "The Study of Juvenile Delinquency by Reported Behavior" (Unpublished paper presented at the Annual Meeting of the American Sociological Society, 1955).

12. Mimeographed summaries prepared by Sociological Services, Institute for Juvenile Research, Chicago, and personal correspondence from Mr. Henry D. McKay dated October 16, 1956.

13. See Clifford R. Shaw and Henry D. McKay, *Juvenile Delinquency and Urban Areas* (University of Chicago Press, 1942).

14. Quoted in Helen L. Witmer and Ruth Kotinsky, *New Perspectives for Research on Juvenile Delinquency* (Washington: U.S. Children's Bureau Publication No. 356, 1956), 27.

15. L. E. Hewitt and R. L. Jenkins, *Fundamental Patterns of Maladjustment* (Springfield, Illinois: Department of Public Welfare, 1946).

16. See: Frank Tannenbaum, *Crime and the Community* (Boston: Ginn and Co., 1938), especially Chapters I and III; Albert K. Cohen, *Delinquent Boys* (Glencoe, Ill.: Free Press, 1955).

17. Robert K. Merton, *Social Theory and Social Structure* (Glencoe, Ill.: Free Press, 1949), Chapter 7.

18. Cf., Solomon Kobrin, "The Conflict of Values in Delinquency Areas," *American Sociological Review*, XVI (October, 1951), 653-662; Daniel Glaser, "Criminality Theories and Behavioral Images," *American Journal of Sociology*, LXI (March, 1956), 433-444.

NOTES—*Chapter 2.*

1. William H. Sheldon & Associates, *Varieties of Delinquent Youth* (New York: Harper, 1949), 822.

2. Paul W. Tappan. *Comparative Survey of Juvenile Delinquency*, Part I: *North America* (New York: UN Division of Social Welfare, 1952), 3.

3. *New York Penal Laws* (1892) Section 817. Also cited in Mabel A. Elliott, *Conflicting Penal Theory in Statutory Law* (University of Chicago Press, 1931), 34.

4. See: Frederick B. Sussman, *Law of Juvenile Delinquency: The Laws of the Forty-Eight States* (New York Oceana, 1950), Appendix I, 67-79; see also: Sol Rubin, "The Legal Character of Juvenile Delinquency," *The Annals of The American Academy of Political and Social Science*, 261 (January, 1949), 6.

5. For a concise summary of state by state variations in concurrent jurisdiction practices, see: William C. Kvaraceus, *The Community and the Delinquent* (New York: World Book Co., 1954), 65-74.

6. Sir William Blackstone, *Commentaries on the Law of England* (12th ed.), Book IV, Chap. 2 (London, 1795), 23.

7. *Commonwealth v. Trippi*, 268 Mass. 227, 167 N.E. 354 (1929), 148.

8. Roscoe Pounds, *Interpretations of Legal History* (New York: The Macmillan Co., 1923), 134-135. Pound believes that the courts came first and the philosophy of equity was later seized upon to defend them.

9. Herbert H. Lou, *Juvenile Courts in the United States* (Chapel Hill, N. C.: University of North Carolina Press, 1927), 8; for a decision in this matter see: *Nugent V. Powell*, 4, Wyo. 173 (1893) and a conflicting decision in, however, a non-delinquency matter, see: *In re Hudson*, 126 Pacific (20) 765 (1942).

10. State of Connecticut, *Annual Report of the Juvenile Court, 1949*, 4; cited also in Herbert A. Bloch & F. T. Flynn, *Delinquency: The Juvenile Offender in America Today* (New York: Random House, 1956), 346.

11. Alfred J. Kahn, *A Court for Children: A Study of the New York City Children's Court* (New York: Columbia University Press, 1953) 149-171.

12. *Commonwealth v. Fisher*, 213 Pa. 48 (1905); see also: *Lindsay v. Lindsay*, 255 Ill. 332 (1913) and *Cinque v. Boyd*, 121 Atl. 678 (1923).

13. *People v. Lewis* (Matter of Arthur Lewis) 260 N. Y. 171 (1933).

14. Paul W. Tappan, *Juvenile Delinquency* (New York: McGraw-Hill Book Co., 1949), 179-180.

15. *A Standard Juvenile Court Act.* rev. draft (New York: National Probation and Parole Association, 1949), 34.

16. Gilbert Geis & Robert Talley, "Cameras in the Courtroom," *Journal of Criminal Law, Criminology and Police Science,* XLVII, 5 (January-February, 1957), 559-560.

17. *Hills v. Pierce,* 113 Ore. 386 (1924), *Kelsey v. Carroll,* 22 Wyo. 85 (1913), and *In re Hill,* 247 Pac. 591 (1926).

18. Lou, *op. cit.,* 141.

19. *Ibid.,* 141.

20. Tappan, *Juvenile Delinquency, op. cit.,* 208.

21. Walter Reckless, *The Crime Problem* (New York: Appleton-Century-Crofts, 2nd ed., 1955), 232-235.

22. *People v. Bergotini,* 172 Cal. 717 (1916).

23. There are conflicting decisions on this issue, but this seems to be the weight of authority; for a discussion of this and other features of contributing causes see: Lou, *op. cit.,* 55-60.

24. *State v. Lehman,* 125 Wash. 617 (1923).

25. *State v. Taylor,* 209 N.W. 287 (1926).

26. See: Austin L. Porterfield, *Youth in Trouble* (Austin, Texas: Leo Potishman Foundation, 1946), *passim,* and Kahn, *op. cit.,* 46-47.

27. For a list of various delinquency descriptions state by state, see: Sussman, *op. cit.,* 20-21.

28. Herbert A. Bloch & Frank T. Flynn, *Delinquency: The Juvenile Offender in America Today* (New York: Random House, 1956), 8-9.

29. Tappan, *Juvenile Delinquency, op. cit.,* 210.

30. *Ibid.,* 205.

31. American Law Institute, *The Youth Correction Authority Act* (1940), Sections 8, 30, 33, especially.

NOTES—*Chapter* 3.

1. In a recent longitudinal study, it was found that 65 percent of delinquents "reform" as they enter early manhood. See William and Joan McCord, *The Genesis of Crime* (in preparation).

2. Richard Dugdale, *The Jukes* (New York: Putnam's, 1877).

3. Henry H. Goddard, *The Kallikaks* (New York: Macmillan, 1912).

4. See William McCord and Joan McCord, *Psychopathy and Delinquency* (New York: Grune and Stratton, 1956), Chapter IV, for further discussion and specific references.

5. Johannes Lange, *Crime and Destiny* (New York: C. C. Boni, 1930), translated by Charlotte Haldane.

6. See H. Barnes and N. Teeters, *New Horizons in Criminology* (New York: Prentice-Hall, 1943), Chapter VIII for discussion and specific references.

7. A. J. Rosanoff, et. al., "Criminality and Delinquency in Twins,"

Journal of Criminal Law and Criminology, (January-February, 1934), 923-934.

8. A. J. Rosanoff, "The Etiology of Child Behavior Difficulties," *Psychiatric Monographs,* 1, (1943).

9. F. J. Kallman, *The Genetics of Schizophrenia* (New York: J. J. Augustin, 1939).

10. Henry H. Goddard, *Feeble-Mindedness: Its Causes and Consequences* (New York: Macmillan, 1914).

11. Charles Goring, *The English Convict* (London: 1913).

12. Edwin H. Sutherland, "Mental Deficiency and Crime," in *Social Attitudes,* ed. by Kimball Young (New York: Henry Holt, 1931), 357-375.

13. William McCord, Joan McCord, and Irving Zola, *The Genesis of Crime* (in preparation).

14. Cesare Lombroso, *Crime: Its Causes and Remedies* (Boston: Little, Brown and Co., 1911).

15. Ernst Hooten, *Crime and the Man* (Cambridge: Harvard University Press, 1939).

16. William H. Sheldon, *Varieties of Delinquent Youth* (New York: Harpers, 1949).

17. Sheldon and Eleanor Glueck, *Unraveling Juvenile Delinquency* (Cambridge: Harvard University Press, 1950), *Physique and Delinquency* (New York: Harpers, 1956).

18. Sheldon and Eleanor Glueck, *Physique and Delinquency, op. cit.,* page 35.

19. See William McCord and Joan McCord, *Psychopathy and Delinquency, op. cit.,* for a further discussion of these studies.

20. M. Ostrow and M. Ostrow, "Bilaterally Synchronous Paroxysmal Slow Activity in the Encephalograms of Non-Epileptics," *Journal of Nervous and Mental Disease, III* (1946), 346-358.

21. R. Sessions-Hodges, "The Impulsive Psychopath: a Clinical and Electro-physiological Study," *Journal of Mental Science,* XCI (1945), 476-482.

22. Sheldon and Eleanor Glueck, *Unraveling Juvenile Delinquency, op. cit.,* Chapter XIV.

23. William and Joan McCord, *Psychopathy and Delinquency, op. cit.,* Chapter IV.

NOTES—*Chapter 4.*

1. S. M. Strong, review of S. R. Slavson, *Re-educating the Delinquent Through Group and Community Participation,* in *American Journal of Sociology,* LXII (July, 1956), 125.

2. Donald R. Cressey, "Changing Criminals: The Application of the Theory of Differential Association," *American Journal of Sociology,* LXI (September, 1955), 116-117.

3. Michael Balint, "On Punishing Offenders," in George B. Wilbur and Warner Muensterberger, eds., *Psychoanalysis and Culture: Essays in Honor of Géza Róheim* (New York: International Universities Press, 1951), 266.

4. David Abrahamsen, *Who Are the Guilty? A Study of Education and Crime* (New York: Rinehart, 1952), 125.

5. Ben Karpman, "Criminal Psychodynamics: A Platform," *Archives of Criminal Psychodynamics*, I (Winter, 1955), 96.

6. Eugene Davidoff and Elinor S. Noetzel, *The Child Guidance Approach to Juvenile Delinquency* (New York: Child Care Publications, 1951), 150.

7. Hertha Tarrasch, "Delinquency Is Normal Behavior," *Focus*, XXIX (July, 1950), 101. The title of this article is belied by most of its content.

8. Henry A. Segal, "Searchlights on Delinquency: A Critical Synthesis," *Archives of Criminal Psychodynamics*, I (Summer, 1955), 585.

9. Leontine R. Young, "We Call Them Delinquents," *Federal Probation*, XV (December, 1951), 8.

10. Herschel Alt and Hyman Grossbard, "Professional Issues in the Institutional Treatment of Delinquent Children," *American Journal of Orthopsychiatry*, XIX (April, 1949), 280.

11. *Ibid.*, 279.

12. *Ibid.*, 280.

13. Desmond Curran, "Psychiatry Ltd.," (Abridged), *Proceedings of the Royal Society of Medicine*, XLV (March, 1952), 105-108.

14. Leon Eisenberg, "Social Law and Social Medicine: Some Comments by Lawyers and Psychiatrists," *NPPA Journal* (published by the National Probation and Parole Association), I (October, 1955), 138.

15. Benjamin Pasamanick, "The Epidemiology of Behavior Disorders of Childhood," in *Neurology and Psychiatry in Childhood*, Proceedings of the Association for Research in Nervous and Mental Disease (Baltimore: William & Wilkins, 1956), Vol. XXXIV, p. 398.

16. Forrest N. Anderson and Helen C. Dean, *Some Aspects of Child Guidance Clinic Intake Policy and Practices: A Study of 500 Cases at the Los Angeles Child Guidance Clinic, Los Angeles, California*, Public Health Service, Department of Health, Education, and Welfare (Washington, D.C.: Government Printing Office, 1956), 9.

17. An interesting attempt to introduce sociological concepts into the practices of a child guidance clinic is described in the following works: Otto Pollak and others, *Social Science and Psychotherapy for Children: Contributions of the Behavior Sciences to Practice in a Psychoanalytically Oriented Child Guidance Clinic* (New York: Russell Sage Foundation, 1952); Otto Pollak, *Integrating Sociological and Psychoanalytic Concepts: An Exploration in Child Psychotherapy* (New York: Russell Sage Foundation, 1956).

18. Ausubel, who is both a psychologist and a psychiatrist, says, "For all practical purposes the data of social psychology, experimental psychology, child development, etc., are nonexistent for the psychiatrist." See: David P. Ausubel, "Relationships Between Psychology and Psychiatry: The Hidden Issues," *American Psychologist*, XI (February, 1956), 101. Anthropology and sociology can certainly be added to this list.

19. Harris B. Peck, "New Approaches to the Treatment of the Delinquent

Adolescent," in *Casework Papers, 1955* (New York: Family Service Association of America, 1955), 21. Incidentally, to explain a term occurring in the excerpt, psychiatrists use the expression, "acting out," to refer to delinquency or other aggressive behavior regarded as the overt manifestation of certain mental illnesses or personality disturbances. In contrast, some mental illnesses are said to result in "inner conflict" and do not result in "acting out." To turn to the last sentence in the excerpt, while there is room for argument on the meaning of the words "few" and "definitive," most sociologists would doubtlessly be in agreement that research has conclusively established the point which "some" psychiatrists "have begun to suspect." They would also be in agreement that for several decades now there have been in existence a number of "definitive" studies which validate the point.

20. One clinic did not diagnose any delinquent as "normal" for the reason that "normality is a vague concept because everybody simply projects his own ideal of perfection into it." Pierre Rubé, "Psychiatric Clinic for Adolescent Delinquents," *Quarterly Journal of Child Behavior*, IV (1952), 43.

21. The overwhelming bulk of this research has been done by sociologists, psychologists, and others. An insignificant amount of it has been done by psychiatrists.

22. Karl F. Schuessler and Donald R. Cressey, "Personality Characteristics of Criminals," *American Journal of Sociology*, LV (March, 1950), 476-484.

23. Starke R. Hathaway and Elio D. Monachesi, eds., *Analyzing and Predicting Juvenile Delinquency with the MMPI* (Minneapolis: University of Minnesota Press, 1953).

24. This is made clear in Schrag's review of the book by Hathaway and Monachesi. See *American Sociological Review*, XIX (August, 1954), 490-491.

25. The psychologists, as distinguished from psychiatrists, have made some notable contributions in the direction of developing such means. They have probably come nearest to being truly scientific in their approach.

26. *Juvenile Delinquency (Comic Books)*, Hearings Before the Subcommittee to Investigate Juvenile Delinquency of the Committee on the Judiciary United States Senate, 83rd Congress, 2nd Session, April 21, 22, and June 4, 1954, (Washington, D.C.: Government Printing Office 1954), 159.

27. Many more psychiatrists, however, do not show awareness of the scientific issues involved, ignore, or are not familiar with, conflicting or contradictory views and evidence, object to criticism, and are bent, at all costs, on getting a favorable reception for their profession.

28. Nathan W. Ackerman, "Psychiatric Disorders in Children—Diagnosis and Etiology in Our Time," in *Current Problems in Psychiatric Diagnosis*, Proceedings of the Forty-first Annual Meeting of the American Psychopathological Association (New York: Grune & Stratton, 1953), 220-221.

29. Henry H. W. Miles, "Part Two: Discussion I," *ibid.*, 108-109.

30. Nathan W. Ackerman, *op. cit.*, 221.

31. *Ibid.*, 222.

32. "The New Nomenclature," (Comment), *American Journal of Psychiatry*, CIX (January, 1953), 548.

33. Pierre Rubé, *op. cit.*, 54. Percentages not in the original table.

34. Annual Report of the Cuyahoga County (Cleveland) Juvenile Court for 1952, p. 51, Table 15. Percentages not in the original table.

35. Sheldon and Eleanor Glueck, *Unraveling Juvenile Delinquency* (New York: The Commonwealth Fund, 1950), 245, Table XIX-1.

36. Ronald Taft, "The Ability to Judge People," *Psychological Bulletin,* LII (January, 1955), 1-23.

37. It is customary, in textbooks on juvenile delinquency, to discuss mental deficiency in the chapter dealing with psychological factors. However, the role of mental deficiency in the causation of delinquency is no longer a controversial issue. A vast amount of research by sociologists and psychologists has demonstrated that mental deficiency is a negligible factor in this connection. An excellent review of this research is presented in the following article: Mary Woodward, "The Role of Low Intelligence in Delinquency," *British Journal of Delinquency,* V (April, 1955), 281-303. With the exception of a small minority, psychiatrists have gone along with these findings.

Mental deficiency is no longer the psychological factor commonly implicated in the causation of delinquency. It has been superseded by other psychological factors in the thinking of psychiatrists and others. These are the ones it is important to discuss.

38. John Dollard and others, *Frustration and Aggression* (New Haven: Yale University Press, 1939).

39. William I. Thomas, *The Unadjusted Girl* (Boston: Little, Brown, 1923).

40. William Healy and Augusta F. Bronner, *New Light on Delinquency and Its Treatment* (New Haven: Yale University Press, 1936).

41. *Ibid.,* 122.

42. *Ibid.,* 128-129.

43. *Ibid.,* Chaps. 1 and 9.

44. Herbert A. Bloch and Frank T. Flynn, *Delinquency: The Juvenile Offender in America Today* (New York: Random, 1956), 82.

45. Edwin H. Sutherland, rev. by Donald R. Cressey, *Principles of Criminology,* 5th ed. (Chicago: J. B. Lippincott, 1955), 129-130.

46. Almost invariably, for example, psychiatrists testifying for the defense and those testifying for the prosecution in criminal trials take diametrically opposed positions regarding the mental condition of the defendant.

47. For example, the American Medical Association, after deliberations among representatives of medicine, psychiatry, and law, went on record as early as 1930 in support of the view that a diagnosis of mental disease is permissible "even when the criminal has shown no evidence of mental disease other than his criminal behavior." See "Psychiatry in Relation to Crime," (Editorial), *Journal of the American Medical Association,* XCV (August 2, 1930), 346.

48. Ernest Jones, *The Life and Work of Sigmund Freud,* Vol. II, *Years of Maturity, 1901-1919* (New York: Basic Books, 1955), 127.

49. John Bowlby, *Maternal Care and Mental Health* (Geneva: World Health Organization, Monograph Series, No. 2, 1951), 11.

50. Lauretta Bender, *Aggression, Hostility and Anxiety in Children* (Springfield, Ill.: Thomas, 1953), 152.

51. Margaret A. Ribble, *The Rights of Infants: Early Psychological Needs and Their Satisfaction* (New York: Columbia University Press, 1943), 4.

52. John Bowlby, *op. cit.,* 22.

53. *Ibid.,* 48-49.

54. *Ibid.*, 28.

55. *Ibid.*, 47.

56. J. M. Tanner and Bärbel Inhelder, eds., *Discussions on Child Development*, Proceedings of the Second Meeting of the World Health Organization Study Group on the Psychobiological Development of the Child (New York: International Universities Press, 1957), 213-234.

57. John Bowlby, *op. cit.*, 23.

58. *Ibid.*, 49.

59. *Ibid.*

60. Lauretta Bender, "Psychopathic Behavior Disorders in Children," in Robert M. Lindner and Robert V. Seliger, eds., *Handbook of Correctional Psychology* (New York: Philosophical Library, 1947), 375, 377.

61. John Bowlby, *Forty-four Juvenile Thieves: Their Character and Home-Life* (London: Bailliere, Tindall & Cox, 1946).

62. *Ibid*, 41.

63. *Ibid.*, 6-7.

64. John Bowlby, *Maternal Care and Mental Health* (Geneva: World Health Organization, Monograph Series, No. 2, 1951), 15.

65. Samuel R. Pinneau, "The Infantile Disorders of Hospitalism and Anaclitic Depression," *Psychological Bulletin*, LII (September, 1955), 429-452.

66. Samuel R. Pinneau, "A Critique on the Articles by Margaret Ribble," *Child Development*, XXI (December, 1950), 222.

67. Hilda Lewis, *Deprived Children—The Mersham Experiment: A Social and Clinical Study* (London: Oxford University Press, 1954), 76-77. Lewis' figures were actually more adequate than Bowlby's.

For an excellent criticism of Bowlby's work, and for a discussion of other studies, habitually ignored by him, which contradict his position, see N. O'Connor, "The Evidence for the Permanently Disturbing Effects of Mother Child Separation," *Acta Psychologica*, XII (No. 3, 1956), 174-191.

68. John Bowlby, *Maternal Care and Mental Health* (Geneva: World Health Organization, Monograph Series, No. 2, 1951), 46.

69. John Bowlby and others, "The Effects of Mother-Child Separation: A Follow-up Study," *British Journal of Medical Psychology*, XXIX (September, 1956), 233.

70. Adelaide M. Johnson and S. A. Szurek, "Etiology of Antisocial Behavior in Delinquents and Psychopaths," *Journal of the American Medical Association*, CLIX (March 6, 1954), 814-817.

71. *Ibid.*, 814.

72. Adelaide M. Johnson, "Sanctions for Superego Lacunae of Adolescents," in K. R. Eissler, ed., *Searchlights on Delinquency: New Psychoanalytic Studies* (New York: International Universities Press, 1949), 225-245.

73. Mary E. Griffin, Adelaide M. Johnson, and Edward M. Litin, "Specific Factors Determining Antisocial Acting Out," *American Journal of Orthopsychiatry*, XXIV (October, 1954), 673.

74. Adelaide M. Johnson and S. A. Szurek, *op. cit.*, 816.

75. Adelaide M. Johnson, *op. cit.*, 227.

76. Ruth S. Eissler, "Scapegoats of Society," in K. R. Eissler, ed., *Searchlights on Delinquency: New Psychoanalytic Studies* (New York: International Universities Press, 1949), 288-305.

77. *Ibid.*, 289.

78. *Ibid.*, 295.

79. *Ibid.*, 297.

80. *Ibid.*, 303-4.

81. For a cogent review of the evidence leading to the rejection of the concept of the unconscious, see Robert E. L. Faris, *Social Psychology* (New York: Ronald, 1952), Chap. 6. Kubie, a psychoanalyst, says: "There are plenty of 'licensed,' esteemed and even distinguished practitioners of psychoanalysis who do not really believe in unconscious or preconscious processes, although they talk about them all the time and this despite one or two or even three so-called training analyses." See Franz Alexander, *Psychoanalysis and Psychotherapy: Developments in Theory, Technique, and Training* (New York: Norton, 1956), 234. This statement was made by Kubie in answer to a query by Alexander.

82. O. Spurgeon English and Constance J. Foster, *Fathers Are Parents Too: A Constructive Guide to Successful Fatherhood* (New York: G. P. Putnam's Sons, 1951), 64.

83. Harry Joseph and Gordon Zern, *The Emotional Problems of Children: A Guide for Parents* (New York: Crown, 1954), 119; Frances L. Ilg and Louise Bates Ames, *Child Behavior* (New York: Harper, 1955), 165.

84. Flanders Dunbar, *Your Child's Mind and Body: A Practical Guide for Parents* (New York: Random, 1949), 111-112.

85. Benjamin Spock, *The Pocket Book of Baby and Child Care* (New York: Pocket Books, 1946), 241.

86. Michael Balint, *op. cit.*, 266.

87. Oscar Sternbach, "The Dynamics of Psychotherapy in the Group," *Journal of Child Psychiatry*, Vol. I, Part I, 1947, cited in S. H. Foulkes, *Introduction to Group-Analytic Psychotherapy: Studies in the Social Integration of Individuals and Groups* (New York: Grune & Stratton, 1949), 58-59.

88. Melitta Schmideberg, "The Psychoanalysis of Delinquents," *American Journal of Orthopsychiatry*, XXIII (January, 1953), 14.

89. David Abrahamsen, "Evaluation of the Treatment of Criminals," in *Failures in Psychiatric Treatment*, Proceedings of the Thirty-seventh Annual Meeting of the American Psychopathological Association (New York: Grune & Stratton, 1948), 59.

90. Henry A. Davidson, "Psychiatrists in Administration of Criminal Justice," *Journal of Criminal Law, Criminology, and Police Science*, XLV (May-June, 1954), 18.

91. Brian Bird, "Antisocial Acting Out: 3. Discussion," *American Journal of Orthopsychiatry*, XXIV (October, 1954), 687.

92. K. R. Eissler, "Some Problems of Delinquency," in K. R. Eissler, ed., *Searchlights on Delinquency: New Psychoanalytic Studies* (New York: International Universities Press, 1949), 18-20.

93. Adelaide M. Johnson, "Collaborative Psychotherapy: Team Setting," in Marcel Heiman, ed., *Psychoanalysis and Social Work* (New York: International Universities Press, 1953), 84.

94. Annette Garrett, "Historical Survey of the Evolution of Casework," in Cora Kasius, ed., *Principles and Techniques in Social Casework: Selected Articles, 1940-1950* (New York: Family Service Association of America, 1950). 393.

95. John G. Watkins, "Psychotherapy: An Overview," in L. A. Penning-

ton and Irwin A. Berg, eds., *An Introduction to Clinical Psychology*, 2nd ed. (New York: Ronald Press, 1954), 493.

96. Franz Alexander, *op. cit.*, 211. This statement was made by Karl Bowman in answer to a query by Alexander.

97. Clifford J. Sager, "The Clinic Team in Adult Treatment," *American Journal of Psychotherapy*, XI (January, 1957), 9-10.

98. Karl M. Bowman and Milton Rose, "Do Our Medical Colleagues Know What to Expect from Psychotherapy?" *American Journal of Psychiatry*, CXI (December, 1954), 401-409.

99. Mary E. Giffin, Adelaide M. Johnson, and Edward M. Litin, *op. cit.*, 676.

100. Beatrice R. Simcox and Irving Kaufman, "Treatment of Character Disorders in Parents of Delinquents," *Social Casework*, XXXVII (October, 1956), 388-395. This article is very mystifying. Although it was supported, in part, by a research grant from the National Institute of Mental Health, it is completely devoid of any evidence that it is based on research. There is not even a control group of parents of nondelinquents. It would have been well to compare the group of parents described, for example, with a group of social workers who are parents of nondelinquents. The anal and oral conditions of the social workers could then have been compared with those of the parents of delinquents. In the absence of a control group, it is impossible to tell whether the traits characterizing the group studied are peculiar to them or are more characteristic of them than of other groups. In this study, for example, one of the characteristics attributed to a person having an anal character is that "he sees things only in terms of opposites. . . ." (p. 393). Yet, one psychiatrist has reported that this very trait characterizes almost all psychotherapists. See Jurgen Ruesch, "The Trouble with Psychiatric Research," *Archives of Neurology and Psychiatry*, XLVII (January, 1957), 96.

101. Sheldon Glueck and Eleanor T. Glueck, *One Thousand Juvenile Delinquents: Their Treatment by Court and Clinic* (Cambridge: Harvard University Press, 1934).

102. *Ibid.*, 169.

103. H. Warren Dunham and Mary E. Knauer, "The Juvenile Court in Its Relationship to Adult Criminality," *Social Forces*, XXXII (March, 1954), 290-296.

104. LaMay Adamson and H. Warren Dunham, "Clinical Treatment of Male Delinquents: A Case Study in Effort and Result," *American Sociological Review*, XXI (June, 1956), 312-320.

105. *Ibid.*, 320.

106. Edwin Powers and Helen Witmer, *Experiment in the Prevention of Delinquency: The Cambridge-Somerville Study* (New York: Columbia University Press, 1951).

107. *Ibid.*, x.

108. *Ibid.*, 379.

NOTES—*Chapter 5.*

1. See Richard Wright, *Black Boy.*

2. William Poster, " 'Twas A Dark Night In Brownsville," *Commentary,* IX (May, 1950), 461.

3. Solomon Kobrin, "The Conflict of Values In Delinquency Areas," *American Sociological Review,* XVI (October, 1951), 653-61.

4. William Healy and Augusta Bronner, *New Light On Delinquency And Its Treatment* (New Haven: Yale University Press, 1936), 88.

5. Case Study No. 6 in Author's file.

6. Clifford R. Shaw and Henry D. McKay, *Delinquency and Urban Areas* (University of Chicago Press, 1942).

7. S. Kirson Weinberg, "Theories of Criminality and Problems of Prediction," *Journal of Criminal Law and Criminology* XLV (1955), 88.

8. Sophia M. Robison, *Can Delinquency Be Measured?* (New York: Columbia University Press, 1936).

9. Christian T. Jonassen, "A Re-evaluation and Critique of the Logic and Some Methods of Shaw and McKay," *American Sociological Review,* XIV (1949), 608-17.

10. Robert K. Merton, *Social Theory and Social Structure* (Glencoe, Ill.: Free Press, 1949).

11. Albert K. Cohen, *Delinquent Boys: The Culture of the Gang* (Glencoe, Ill.: Free Press, 1955), 134.

12. Albert K. Cohen, *Delinquent Boys: The Culture Of The Gang* (Glencoe, Illinois: The Free Press, 1955), 134.

13. Clifford R. Shaw and Henry D. McKay, "Social Factors In Juvenile Delinquency," *Causes of Crime* (Washington, D.C., U. S. Government Printing Office), 249.

14. Clifford R. Shaw and Henry D. McKay, "Social Factors In Juvenile Delinquency," *op. cit.,* 65-75.

15. See Arnold M. Rose and Caroline Rose, *America Divided* (New York: Alfred Knopf Co., 1948), 246.

16. See Herbert A. Bloch and Frank T. Flynn, *Delinquency: The Juvenile Offender in America Today* (New York: Random House, 1956), 44-47.

17. Sidney Axelrad, "Negro and White Institutionalized Delinquents," *American Journal of Sociology,* LVII (May, 1952), 569-74.

18. Sheldon and Eleanor Glueck, *Unraveling Juvenile Delinquency* (Cambridge, Mass., Harvard University Press, 1950), 83-85.

19. *Ibid.,* 83-85.

20. Charles W. Coulter, "Family Disorganization as a Causal Factor in Delinquency and Crime," *Federal Probation,* XII (September, 1948), 13-17.

21. Clifford Shaw and Henry D. McKay, "Are Broken Homes A Causative Factor in Juvenile Delinquency?" *Social Forces* (1932), 514-24.

22. John Slavson, *The Delinquent Boy: A Socio-Psychological Study* (Boston: Badger Co., 1926).

23. Ruth S. Cavan, *Criminology* (New York: Thomas Y. Crowell Co., 1948), 97.

24. M. G. Caldwell, "Home Conditions of Institutional Delinquents,"

Social Forces, VIII (1929-30), 390; H. Ashley Weeks, "Male and Female Broken Home Rates by Types of Delinquency," *American Sociological Review,* V (1940), 603; Sheldon and Eleanor T. Glueck, *Five Hundred Delinquent Women* (New York: Alfred A. Knopf & Co., 1941); Sheldon and Eleanor T. Glueck, *Five Hundred Criminal Careers* (New York: Alfred A. Knopf and Co., 1930), 116.

25. Clifford R. Shaw and Henry D. McKay, "Social Factors In Juvenile Delinquency," *National Commission On Law Observance And Enforcement* (Washington: Government Printing Office, 1931).

26. Ruth S. Cavan, *Criminology* (New York: Thomas Y. Crowell, 1948), 26.

27. *Ibid.,* 97.

28. See: Clifford R. Shaw and Associates, *Brothers In Crime* (University of Chicago Press, 1938), 49-75.

29. Sheldon and Eleanor Glueck, *Juvenile Delinquents Grown Up* (New York: The Commonwealth Fund, 1940), 8.

30. Judge Paul W. Alexander, "What's This About Punishing Parents?" *Federal Probation,* XII (Marc, 1948), 23-28.

31. Stanislaus Szurek, "Genesis of Psychopathic Personality Trends," *Psychiatry* V (1942), 1-3.

32. Adelaide M. Johnson, "Sanctions For Super-ego Lacunae," *Searchlights on Delinquency,* edited by R. R. Eisler, (New York: International University Press, 1949), 227.

33. Sheldon and Eleanor Glueck, *Unraveling Juvenile Delinquency* (Cambridge University Press, 1900), 127-31.

34 *Ibid.,* 127-31.

35. William Healy and Augusta Bronner, *New Light on Delinquency and Its Treatment* (New Haven: Yale University Press, 1936), 48-49.

36. Sheldon and Eleanor Glueck, *Unraveling Juvenile Delinquency* (Cabridge, Mass., Harvard University Press, 1950), 114-16.

37. Clifford Shaw, Editor, *Brothers In Crime* (University of Chicago Press 1938), 56.

38. Cyril Burt, *The Young Delinquent* (New York: Appleton-Century-Crofts Co., 1925), 42.

39. Sheldon and Eleanor Glueck, *Unraveling Juvenile Delinquency* (Cambridge: Harvard University Press, 1951), 120.

40. Raymond Sletto, "Delinquency and the Only Child," *Sociology and Social Research,* XVIII (1934), 519-29; Raymond Sletto, "Sibling Position and Juvenile Delinquency," *American Journal of Sociology,* XXXIX (1934), 657-69.

41. William W. Wattenberg, "Delinquency and Only Children: A Study of a Category," *Journal of Abnormal and Social Psychology,* XLIV (July, 1949), 356-366.

42. Henry H. Hart and Sidney Axelrad, "The Only-Child Delinquent Contrasted With Delinquents In Large Families," *Journal of Criminal Law and Criminology,* XXXIII (1941), 42-66.

43. Raymond Sletto, "Sibling Position and Juvenile Delinquency," *American Journal of Sociology,* III (1934), 657-669.

NOTES—*Chapter 6.*

1. See Harry E. Barnes and Negley K. Teeters, *New Horizons in Criminology* (New York: Prentice-Hall, 1946), 6.

2. Robert K. Merton, "Social Structure and Anomie," *American Sociological Review*, III (October, 1938), 672-682.

3. Herbert A. Bloch and Frank T. Flynn, *Delinquency, The Juvenile Offender in America Today* (New York: Random House, 1956), 189.

4. *Ibid.*, 190.

5. See: T. Lynn Smith and C. A. McMahan, *The Sociology of Urban Life* (New York: The Dryden Press, 1951), 292.

6. Bureau of the Census, *Current Population Reports: Population Characteristics*, "Mobility of the Population of the United States: April 1954 to April 1955," Series P—20, No. 61 (October 28, 1955) 1.

7. See: for example, Calvin Schmid, "Minneapolis and St. Paul, Minnesota" in Clifford Shaw and Henry D. McKay, *Juvenile Delinquency and Urban Areas* (University of Chicago Press, 1942), 431; see, also, Sheldon and Eleanor Glueck, *Unraveling Juvenile Delinquency* (New York: The Commonwealth Fund, 1950), 155-156.

8. Erich Fromm, *Escape From Freedom* (New York: Rinehart, 1941).

9. Albert K. Cohen, *Delinquent Boys* (Glencoe: The Free Press, 1955), 25.

10. See Ronald R. Taft, *Criminology* (New York: The MacMillan Company, 1950), 232.

11. Merton, *op. cit.*

12. *Third Interim Report of the Special Committee to Investigate Crime In Interstate Commerce*, S. Res 202, 81st Congress (Washington: U.S. Government Printing Office, 1951).

13. "Bureau of the Census, 1950 United States Census of Population," "Number of Inhabitants: United States Summary, Totals for Regions, States, Cities, Metropolitan Areas," Report P—A1, Reprint of Vol. 1, Chapter 1, 1952., Table 4, 1-5.

14. *Ibid.*

15. See: Louis Wirth, "Urbanism As A Way of Life," *American Journal of Sociology*, XLIV (July, 1938), 1.

16. Taft, *op. cit.*, 233.

17. Pitirim A. Sorokin, *Contemporary Sociological Theories* (New York: Harper and Brothers, 1928), 99-101.

18. Robert E. Park, Ernest W. Burgess and R. McKenzie, *The City* (University of Chicago Press, 1925).

19. Clifford Shaw, *et. al.*, *Delinquency Areas* (University of Chicago Press, 1929); Clifford Shaw, Henry McKay *et al.*, *Juvenile Delinquency and Urban Areas* (University of Chicago Press, 1942).

20. Ernest W. Burgess, "The Growth of the City," in Park, Burgess & McKenzie, *op. cit.*, 51.

21. Shaw and McKay, *op. cit.*

22. See Schmid *op. cit.*, 431.

23. Glueck, *op. cit.*, 5.

24. See, for example, Glueck, *op. cit.*, 167; see, also, William Lentz, "Rural Urban Differentials and Juvenile Delinquency," *The Journal of Criminal Law, Criminology and Police Science*, XLVII (Sept.-Oct., 1956), 335.

25. Frederick M. Thrasher, *The Gang* (University of Chicago Press, 1927); see, also, Sam Glane, "Juvenile Gangs in East Los Angeles," *Focus*, XXIX (September, 1950), 136-141.

26. Cohen, *op. cit.*, 24-32.

27. *Ibid.*, 32-36.

28. *Ibid.*, 33.

29. *Ibid.*, 33-34.

30. *Ibid.*

31. *Ibid.*, 35.

32. *Ibid.*, 121-136.

33. *Ibid.*, 135.

34. Fritz Redl, "The Psychology of Gang Formation and The Treatment of Juvenile Delinquents," *The Psychoanalytic Study of the Child*, I (1945), 371.

35. Cohen, *op. cit.*, 137.

36. For an impressionistic and somewhat sensational account of youthful vice particularly as it relates to commercialized recreation, see Courtney R. Cooper, *Designs In Scarlet* (Boston: Little, Brown and Co., 1939).

37. Glueck, *op. cit.*, 163.

NOTES—*Chapter 7.*

1. See P. F. Valentine, Chapter IX, "Education," in Joseph S. Roucek and Associates, *Social Control* (New York: D. Van Nostrand, 1947), 131-138; also H. C. Brearly, Chapter 12, "Problems in Education," in T. Lynn Smith and Associates, *Social Problems* (New York: Thomas Y. Crowell Co., 1955), 335-362.

2. Cf. William J. Gnagey, "Do Our Schools Prevent or Promote Delinquency?", *Journal of Educational Research*, L (November, 1956), 215-219.

3. Philip M. Smith, "Antisocial Aspects of Conventional Grading," *The Educational Forum*, XIV (March, 1950), 357-362.

4. Cf. Max Kramer, "The Teacher Who Taught Me to Hate," *McCall's Magazine*, LXXXIV (February, 1957), 71-74.

5. Martin H. Neumeyer, *Juvenile Delinquency in Modern Society* (New York: D. Van Nostrand, rev. ed., 1955), 230.

6. Lowell J. Carr, *Delinquency Control* (New York: Harper & Bros., rev. ed., 1950), 489.

7. Elizabeth R. Roby, "Blackboard Jungle, Jr.," *Ladies' Home Journal*, LXXIII (September, 1956), 85, 192, 193; cf. Robert C. Lloyd, "I Teach Big-City Teenagers," *NEA Journal*, XLV (October, 1956), 412-13.

8. Sheldon and Eleanor Glueck, *Delinquents in the Making: Paths to Prevention* (New York: Harper, 1952), 80.

9. *Ibid.,* 71.

10. William C. Kvaraceus, *Juvenile Delinquency and the School* (New York: World Book Co., 1945), 144-145.

11. *Ibid.,* 141.

12. Bertram M. Beck, "Delinquents in the Classroom," *NEA Journal,* XLV (November, 1956), 485-487; see also "The School and Delinquency Control," by the same author, in *Annals of the American Academy of Political and Social Science,* CCCH (November, 1955), 61-65. Book credits Dr. Richard L. Jenkins with identifying the social, asocial, and neurotic types in an article written in 1944.

13. Cited by *NPPA News,* XXV, 5 (November, 1956), 7 (published by the National Probation and Parole Association, New York, N. Y.); the original report, published by the NEA, is entitled, *Teacher Opinion on Pupil Behavior, 1955-56.*

14. E. K. Wickman, *Children's Behavior and Teachers' Attitudes* (New York: The Commonwealth Fund, 1928); for a good summary of the findings of this study, see Paul H. Landis, *Social Policies in the Making* (Boston: D. C. Heath and Co., 1952), 174-175.

15. George A. W. Stouffer, Jr., "The Attitude of Secondary-School Teachers Toward Certain Behavior Problems of Children," *The School Review,* LXIV (November, 1956), 358-362.

16. Gilbert J. Rich, "Childhood as a Preparation for Delinquency," *Journal of Educational Sociology,* XXVII (May, 1954), 409.

17. Darrel J. Mase, "Emotionally Insecure and Disturbed Children," *Childhood Education, XXXII* (January, 1956), 220.

18. See *Juvenile Delinquency and the Schools, Forty-Seventh Yearbook of the National Society for the Study of Education* (University of Chicago Press, 1948).

19. Cf. Sidney L. Green, M.D., and Alan B. Rothenberg, "If Your Child Plays Hooky," *Parents' Magazine,* XXXI (Jan., 1956), 38-39.

20. Philip M. Smith, "The Schools and Juvenile Delinquency," *Sociology and Social Research,* XXXVII (November-December, 1952), 90.

21. Warren Stromberg, "School Dropouts in State High," Detroit *Free Press,* February 10, 1957.

22. From an article by Irmengard Pohrt in the Detroit *Times,* February 10, 1957. The terms "suspension" and "expulsion" are sometimes used in such a way as to mean the same things. A suspension that becomes permanent is tantamount to expulsion.

23. Ann Miller, "Modifying the Antisocial Behavior of Mentally Retarded Children," *The School Review,* LXII (February, 1954), 99.

24. See: Allison Davis, *Social-Class Influences Upon Learning* (Cambridge: Harvard University Press, 1950); W. L. Warner, R. J. Havighurst, and W. J. Loeb, *Who Shall Be Educated?* (New York: Harper and Bros., 1944); A. B. Hollingshead, *Elmstown's Youth* (New York: John Wiley & Sons, 1949).

25. Howard S. Becker, "Social-Class Variations in the Teacher-Pupil Relationship," *Journal of Educational Sociology,* XXIII (April, 1952), 458.

26. *Ibid.,* 461.

27. *Ibid.,* 462.

28. *Ibid.,* 463.

29. Stephen Abrahamson, "Our Status System and Scholastic Rewards," *Journal of Educational Sociology,* XXV (April, 1952), 441-450.

30. *Ibid.,* 444.

31. *Ibid.,* 445.

32. *Ibid.,* 446.

33. *Ibid.,* 447.

34. Some teachers do not realize that lower-class children may feel embarrassed, and even ashamed, when asked to state their father's occupation in the presence of middle-class children.

35. It must not be supposed that child guidance facilities in this country are anywhere near adequate. Only the largest school systems can provide clinics of their own, and in many parts of the nation only one clinic may be available in an area covering several counties.

36. From the Foreword, "Three Schools Project, Bronx," (Mira Talbot, Issue Editor), *The Journal of Educational Sociology,* XXV (November, 1951), 132.

37. *Ibid.,* 134.

38. *Ibid.,* 135.

39. Ellen Cohen, Mary Lou Xelowski, and Staff of the Elementary School, "The Modern School Clinic is a Community-Oriented Clinic," *op. cit.,* p. 157.

40. *Ibid.,* p. 163.

41. See: Sheldon and Eleanor Glueck, *Unraveling Juvenile Delinquency* (New York: The Commonwealth Fund, 1950), Chapter XX.

42. Ralph W. Whelan, "An Experiment in Predicting Delinquency by the New York City Youth Board," *The Journal of Criminal Law, Criminology and Police Science,* XLV (November-December, 1954), 6-7. (mimeographed reprint)

43. *Reducing Juvenile Delinquency: What New York State Schools Can Do* (Albany: New York State Youth Commission, 1952), 31, 33; the report was made by Ralph B. Spence, J. Gordon Crowe directed the original study, and Leo C. Dowling is Director of the Commission.

44. Philip M. Smith, "The Prevention of Delinquency," *Sociology and Social Research,* XXIX (July-August, 1945), 442-448.

NOTES—*Chapter 8.*

1. National Conference on Prevention and Control of Juvenile Delinquency, *Report on Rural Aspects* (Washington, D.C.: Government Printing Office, 1947), 74.

2. A few decades ago rural-urban differences in crime and delinquency formed an extensive literature. See especially: Sorokin, P. Zimmerman, Carle, and Galpin, Charles, *A Systematic Sourcebook in Rural Sociology* (Minneapolis, University of Minnesota Press, 1930), 27-52. Almost all texts in rural

and urban sociology deal with some of the various rural-urban differences. The field is broad when one takes stock of the specific kinds of variables described. Rural-urban differences have been noted in regard to fertility, intelligence, education, welfare agencies, marriage, sanitation, health, social organization, value systems, community life, religion and many other categories.

3. For more detailed information on matters covered in this section see: United Nations, *International Review of Criminal Policy*, Numbers 7-8 (Switzerland, January-July 1955), 20-37.

4. Children's Bureau Statistical Series No. 37, *Juvenile Court Statistics 1955* (Washington, D.C., Children's Bureau Statistical Series No. 37, Government Printing Office, 1955).

5. F.B.I., *Uniform Crime Reports,* Annual Bulletin XXVI, (Washington, DC., 1955), 84.

6. For a review of this see Adolph Tomars, "Rural Survivals in American Urban Life," *Rural Sociology,* VIII (December 1943), 379.

7. Marshall B. Clinard, "The Process of Urbanization and Criminal Behavior," *American Journal of Sociology,* XLIII (September 1942), 202-213.

8. See the following representative studies: Morris Caldwell, "The Extent of Juvenile Delinquency in Wisconsin," *Journal of Criminal Law and Criminology,* XXXII No. 2, 148-157; Paul Wiers, "Juvenile Delinquency in Rural Michigan," *Journal of Criminal Law and Criminology,* XXX (July-August 1939), 211-222; Walter Lunden, *Social and Economic Bases of Delinquency and Dependency in Iowa* (Ames, Iowa: Iowa State College, 1952); Mapheus Smith, "Tier Counties and Delinquency in Kansas," *Rural Sociology,* II (September 1937), 310-322.

9. Lunden, *op. cit.*

10. Barker, Roger G. and Wright, Herbert G., *Midwest and Its Children; the Psychological Ecology of An American Town,* (Evanston, Illinois: Row Peterson & Co., 1955), *passim.*

11. William P. Lentz, "Rural Urban Differentials and Juvenile Delinquency," *Journal of Criminal Law, Criminology, and Police Science,* XXXXIII (October 1956), 331-339.

12. Kathryn Eddy and Johnny Wood, *A Study of Commitments to the South Carolina Industrial Schools,* (Columbia, South Carolina, State Department of Public Welfare, 1954), 32.

13. Clinard, Marshall B., "Rural Criminal Offenders," *American Journal of Sociology,* L (July 1944), 38-45.

14. Lentz, *op. cit.,* Chapter V.

15. Clinard, *op cit.,* 40.

16. Lentz, *op. cit.,* Chapter VI.

17. Sub Commission on the Causes and Effects of Crime of New York Crime State Commission, *A Study of Delinquency in Two Rural Counties* (Albany, N. Y., 1927).

18. Lowell J. Carr, "Most Courts Have to Be Substandard!," *Federal Probation,* XIII No. 3, (September 1949), 29-31.

19. Starke Hathaway and Elio Monachesi, *Analyzing and Predicting Juvenile Delinquency with the M.M.P.I.* (Minneapolis: University of Minnesota Press, 1953), 49-50.

20. *Ibid.*

21. Bernard Greenblatt and Ernest Harburg, Disposition Study, *Juvenile Court Report 1955*, Division for Children and Youth, State Department of Public Welfare (Madison, Wisconsin 1955), 7-20.

22. Lentz, *op. cit.*, 336-337.

23. Lentz, *op. cit.*, Chapter VII.

24. Albert R. Cohen, *Delinquent Boys: The Culture of the Gang* (Glencoe, Ill.: Free Press, 1955), *passim.*

25. August B. Hollingshead, *Elmtown's Youth* (New York: John Wiley, 1949), 439.

26. Glueck, Sheldon and Glueck, Eleanor, *Juvenile Delinquents Grown Up* (New York: The Commonwealth Fund, 1940), Chapter 7.

27. The urban group studied in the Gluecks' *Unraveling Juvenile Delinquency*, was much like the urban group studied in Wisconsin. In view of the significant differences previously noted, the Gluecks' group would also differ from the rural group.

28. For an elaboration of this approach, see Clinard, Marshall B. *The Sociology of Deviant Behavior* (New York: Rinehart & Co., 1957).

NOTES—*Chapter 9.*

1. In a textbook on Juvenile Delinquency to be published in 1957 by Dryden Press, New York.

2. Willard Waller and Reuben Hill, *The Family; A Dynamic Interpretation* (New York: the Dryden Press, 1951), 107.

2. Cyril Burt, *The Young Delinquent* (New York, D. Appleton & Co., 1929), 65-66.

3. *Ibid.*, 89.

4. *Ibid.*, 89.

5. William Healy, *The Individual Delinquent* (Boston, Little, Brown & Co., 1918), 134.

6. William Healy and Augusta F. Bronner, *Delinquents and Criminals: Their Making and Unmaking* (New York, The Macmillan Co., 1928), 121.

7. William Healy and Augusta F. Bronner, *New Light On Delinquency and Its Treatment* (New Haven: Yale Univ. Press, 1936), 34 and 201.

8. Quoted by Paul Tappan, *Juvenile Delinquency* (New York: McGraw-Hill, 1949), 61.

9. Sheldon and Eleanor Glueck, *Unraveling Juvenile Delinquency* (New York: The Commonwealth Fund, 1950); Maude A. Merrill, *Problems of Child Delinquency* (Boston: Houghton Mifflin Co., 1927), 77-78.

10. W. Lloyd Warner, Marchia Meeker and Kenneth Eels, *Social Class in America* (Chicago: Science Research Association, 1949).

11. W. Lloyd Warner and Paul S. Lewt, *The Social Life of A Modern Community* (New Haven: Yale University Press, 1941), 376.

12. August B. Hollingshead, *Elmtown's Youth* (New York: Wiley & Sons, 1949), 411-12.

13. Walter C. Reckless, *The Crime Problem* (New York: Appleton-Century-Crofts, 1950), 60.

14. "Children in Trouble," *Youth Service News* (December, 1955), 10 (New York State Youth Commission).

15. Lowell J. Carr, *Delinquency Control* (New York: Harpers, 1950), 83-33.

16. Cited in Negley, Teeters and John O. Reinemann, *The Challenge of Delinquency* (New York: Prentice-Hall, 1950), 133.

17. Carr, *op. cit.* 82 (italics in original).

18. William W. Wattenburg, "Delinquency During Summer Months," *Journal of Educational Research,* (December, 1948), 253-267.

19. Cited by Martin H. Neumeyer, *Juvenile Delinquency In Modern Society* (New York: D. Van Nostrand Co., 1955), 64.

20. Neumeyer, *loc. cit.*

21. Women's Bureau, *Handbook of Facts on Women Workers* (Bulletin 242, 1952), 1 & 17; cited in Paul B. Horton and Gerald B. Leslie, *The Sociology of Social Problems* (New York: Appleton-Century-Crofts, 1955), 148-149.

22. Robert E. Park & E. W. Burgess, *The City* (University of Chicago Press, 1925); F. M. Thrasher, *The Gang: A Study of 1313 Gangs in Chicago* (University of Chicago Press, 1936); Clifford Shaw, *Delinquency Areas* (University of Chicago Press, 1929).

23. Clifford Shaw and Henry D. McKay, et al., *Juvenile Delinquency and Urban Areas* (Chicago, Univ. of Chicago Press, 1942).

24. *Ibid.,* pp. ix, x, xi (from introduction).

25. *Ibid.,* 442-444.

26. Fred A. Romano, "Organizing a Community for Delinquency Prevention," National Probation Association Yearbook, *Dealing with Delinquency* (New York: National Probation Association, 1940), 2.

27. Shaw & McKay, *op. cit.,* 435.

28. *Ibid.,* 440.

29. *Ibid.,* 441.

30. *Ibid.,* 436.

31. *Ibid.,* 441.

32. Bernard Lander, *Towards an Understanding of Juvenile Delinquency* (New York, Columbia University Press, 1954).

33. *Ibid.,* 9-10.

34. *Ibid.,* 79-80.

35. Neumeyer, *op. cit.,* 45.

35. Lander, *op. cit.,* 83.

36. *Ibid.,* 86.

37. Lander, *op. cit.,* 89-90.

NOTES—*Chapter* 10.

1. "Juvenile Delinquency (Television Programs)", *Hearings Before the Subcommittee to Investigate Juvenile Delinquency,* April 6 and 7, 1955 (Washington: Government Printing Office), 99-103.

2. Cyril Burt, *The Young Delinquent* (New York: D. Appleton-Century Co., Inc.), 137.

3. William Healy and Augusta Bronner, *New Light on Delinquency and Its Treatment* (New Haven: Yale University Press), 72.

4. Herbert Blumer and Philip Hauser, *Movies, Delinquency, and Crime* (New York: The Macmillan Company), 1-3.

5. *Ibid.,* 198.

6. *Ibid.,* 202.

7. Frederic Thrasher, "The Comics and Delinquency: Cause or Scapegoat," *Journal of Educational Sociology,* XXIII (December 1949), 199.

8. Mortimer J. Adler, *Art and Prudence* (New York: Longmans, Green, and Co.), 280.

9. "Notes of the Senate Subcommittee to Investigate Juvenile Delinquency," April 25, 1956 (Washington: Committee on the Judiciary), 1-2.

10. "Juvenile Delinquency (Comic Books)," *Hearings Before the Subcommittee to Investigate Juvenile Delinquency,* April 21, 22, and June 4, 1954 (Washington: Government Printing Office), 4.

11. *Ibid.,* 43.

12. Morton Malter, "The Content of Current Comic Magazines," *Elementary School Journal,* LII (May, 1952), 505-510.

13. "Juvenile Delinquency (Comic Books)," *op. cit.,* 18.

14. Frederic Thrasher, *op. cit.,* 203.

15. Frederic Wertham, *The Seduction of the Innocent* (New York: Rinehart and Co.), 190-192.

16. "Juvenile Delinquency (Television Programs)," *op. cit.,* 1-3.

17. Evan M. Wylie, "Violence on T.V.—Entertainment or Menace?" *Cosmopolitan,* CIIIV (February, 1953), 34-39.

18. "Juvenile Delinquency (Television Programs)," *op. cit.,* 83-84.

19. *Ibid.,* 4-23.

20. *Ibid.,* 20-23.

21. *Ibid.,* 54.

22. "Notes of the Senate Subcommittee to Investigate Juvenile Delinquency," November 10, 1955 (Washington: Committee on the Judiciary), 2.

NOTES—*Chapter* 11.

1. Harold L. Stallings, with David Dressler, *Juvenile Officer* (New York: Thomas Y. Crowell Company, 1954), 35.

2. Clyde B. Vedder and Louis J. Maloof, *Social Problems,* Edited by T. Lynn Smith (New York; Thomas Y. Crowell Co., 1955), 168.

3. Clyde B. Vedder, *The Juvenile Offender: Perspective and Readings* (New York: Random House, Inc., 1955), 193.

4. Martha M. Eliot, "What is Vandalism," *Federal Probation,* XVIII, No. 1 (March-April, 1954), 3.

5. *Ibid.,* 16.

6. "Editorial," *Life* (March 15, 1954).

7. Paper read at *American Sociological Society* annual Meeting, (September, 1953, Berkeley, California), by A. N. Cousins.

8. For the "pro" and "con" of this question, see: Warden L. Clark Schilder, "Juvenile Offenders Should be Fingerprinted," and Judge Victor B. Wylegala, "Juvenile Offenders Should Not be Fingerprinted," *Federal Probation,* (January-March, 1947), 44-48.

8 (a). W. R. Harrod, *Arizona Republic* (Phoenix), (December, 29, 1955), 1.

9. Ames W. Chapman, "Legal Attitudes of Juveniles," *Sociology and Social Research,* XL, 3 (January-February, 1956), 173.

10. Frank L. Manella, *Florida's Children's Commission Report* (1956 series, 59-A Caldwell Bldg., Tallahassee, Florida).

11. Harold L. Stallings, *op. cit.,* 82.

12. *Ibid.,* 83-84.

13. Clyde B. Vedder, *op. cit.,* 230.

14. Herbert A. Bloch & Frank T. Flynn, *Delinquency, The Juvenile Offender in America Today* (New York: Random House, 1956), 51.

15. From *Reprint* (courtesy of Philip B. Gilliam, Judge, Juvenile Court, Denver, Colorado).

17. The *Arizona Republic* (Phoenix) (December 30, 1955), 1.

18. Charles L. Chute, *Federal Probation,* XIII (September, 1949), 4.

19. *Time* (April 2, 1951), 19.

20. Harrison Allen Dobbs, "In Defense of Juvenile Courts," *Federal Probation,* XIII, 3 (September-October, 1949), 24-29.

21. *Federal Probation,* XV (March, 1951), 26-30.

22. *Federal Probation,* XIII (June, 1949), 10-14.

23. Speech made by Judge Hunt, Juvenile Delinquency Institute, University of Florida, Gainesville, May 1, 1953.

24. "Interstate Compact on Juveniles," Current Notes (V. A. Leonard, Ed.), *Journal of Criminology, Criminal Law and Police Science,* XXXXVI, 3 (September-October, 1955), 367.

25. *Time* (March 5, 1956), 82.

26. *Juvenile Delinquency* (New York: McGraw-Hill Book Co., 1949), 179-180.

28. Reported in J. Howard McGrath, "The Role of the Federal Probation Officer in Criminal Justice," *Federal Probation,* XIV (December 1950), 5.

29. John R. Ellingston, *Protecting Our Children from Criminal Careers* (New York: Prentice-Hall, 1948), 83.

30. Edmond Fitzgerald, "The Presentence Investigation," *NPPA Journal*, II, 4 (October, 1956), 334-335.

31. *Ibid.*, 330.

32. John Otto Reinemann, "Probation and the Juvenile Delinquent," *The Annals* of The American Academy of Political and Social Science, CCLXV (January 1949), 116.

33. James N. York, "Evaluating the Everyday Work of a Probation Officer," *Federal Probation*, XII (September, 1948), 27.

34. Robert L. Noble, "What a Difference a Year Makes," *Federal Probation*, XIII (June, 1949), 49.

35. Hyman S. Lippman, "The Role of the Probation Officer in the Treatment of Delinquency in Children," *Federal Probation*, XII (June 1948), 37.

36. David Crystal, "Family Casework in Probation," *Federal Probation*, XIII (December, 1949), 51.

37. William C. Nau, "Let Them Know About It," *Federal Probation*, XV (September 1951), 36.

38. Elizabeth R. Glover, "Probation: The Art of Introducing the Probationer to a Better Way of Life," (*Federal Probation, XV, September*, 1951), 11.

39. Charles H. Z. Meyer, "A Half Century of Federal Probation and Parole," *Journal of Criminal Law and Criminology*, XLII (March-April, 1952).

40. Edmond Fitzgerald, *op. cit.*, 321.

41. George G. Killinger in Paul W. Tappan, ed., *Contemporary Correction* (New York: McGraw-Hill Book Company, 1951), 362.

42. David Dressler, *Parole Chief* (New York: The Viking Press, 1951), 309.

43. Harr E. Brager and Richard A. Chappell, "Jim, Mr. Brown and You," *Federal Probation*, XIII (June, 1949), 47.

44. G. Howland Shaw, "Sponsoring a Delinquent," *Federal Probation*, XII (December, 1948), 15.

45. John R. Ellingston, *Protecting Our Children from Criminal Careers*, (New York: Prentice-Hall, 1948), 161.

NOTES—*Chapter* 12.

1. Melvin Roman, Joseph B. Margolin, and Carmi Harari, "Reading Retardation and Delinquency," *NPPA Journal*, I (July, 1955), 1-7.

2. *Loc. cit.*

3. *New Perspectives for Research on Juvenile Delinquency*, ed. by Helen L. Witmer and Ruth Kotinsky (Washington, D.C.: U. S. Department of Health, Education and Welfare, 1956).

4. Clifford R. Shaw, *Methods, Accomplishments, and Problems of the Chicago Area Project,* 1944 (Mimeo).

5. Ethel Shanas and Catherine E. Dunning, *Recreation and Delinquency* (Chicago Recreation Commission, 1942).

6. Frederic M. Thrasher, "The Boys' Club and Juvenile Delinquency," *American Journal of Sociology,* XLII (1936), 66-80.

7. Ellery Reed, "How Effective are Group Work Agencies in Preventing Delinquency," *Social Service Review,* XXII (1948), 340-348.

8. Alfred J. Kahn, *Police and Children* (Citizens' Committee on Children of New York City, Inc., 1951); also *Police Services for Juveniles* (Washington, D.C.: U. S. Department of Health, Education and Welfare, 1954).

9. *Loc. cit.*

10. Bernard Lander, *Towards an Understanding of Juvenile Delinquency* (New York: Columbia University Press, 1955).

11. *New Perspectives for Research on Juvenile Delinquency, op. cit.*

12. *Reaching the Unreached* (New York City Youth Board, 1952), 98-127.

13. *Ibid.,* 51-62.

14. Sybil A. Stone, Elsa Castendyck, and Harold B. Hanson, *Children in the Community: The St. Paul Experiment in Child Welfare,* Children's Bureau, 1946.

15. Helen L. Witmer and Edith Tufts, *The Effectiveness of Delinquency Prevention Programs,* (Washington: U. S. Department of Health, Education, and Welfare, U. S. Government Printing Office, 1954).

16. See *NPPA Journal,* April 1956, entire issue.

NOTES—*Chapter* 13.

* Reprinted from *Sociology and Social Research,* XLI, 2 (November-December, 1956), pp. 93-99, by permission of the author and the editor of this periodical.

1. The publications are entitled *Comparative Survey on Juvenile Delinquency:* Part I. *North America* (1952), Part II. *Europe* (1952); Part III. *Latin America* (1953); Part IV. *Asia and the Far East* (1953); and Part V. *Middle East* (1953).

2. No. 1 (January 1952) lists 1,992 articles which were published from January 1950 to June 1951, compiled from 124 periodicals directly or indirectly concerned with various phases of crime and 195 secondary references. No. 2 (July 1952) gives a topical bibliography of 979 publications other than periodical literature (books, pamphlets, etc.), including significant and analytical reviews of these publications. No. 3 (January 1953) contains a limited bibliography of 86 references (approximate period, January 1948 to June 1952) on medico-psychological and social examination of offenders. No. 4 (July 1953) has a list of 1,227 references (books, pamphlets, and periodical articles),

delimited somewhat more narrowly in scope than the earlier bibliographies. No. 6 (July 1954) has a similar topical bibliography of 1,248 references to technical publications. No. 5 (1954) and No. 7-8 (1955) do not have bibliographies. For other publications on crime, delinquency, probation, and related subjects, published by the United Nations, see "A Selection of Social Publications of the United Nations," New York, 1956.

3. Cf. *International Review of Criminal Policy*, United Nations, No. 7-8, (January-July 1955), p. 6.

4. Cf. *International Review of Criminal Policy*, United Nations, No. 7-8 (January-July 1955), p. 13. For fuller discussion of this point, consult *Comparative Survey on Juvenile Delinquency*, Part III. *Latin America*, 1953. Part IV. *Asia and the Far East*, 1953, and Part V. *Middle East* (1953), indicate wide ranges of both the lower and upper age limits in the countries of these regions with respect to juvenile court jurisdiction.

5. Cf. Sheldon and Eleanor Glueck, *Unraveling Juvenile Delinquency* (Cambridge, Massachusetts: Harvard University Press, 1950).

6. Cf. L. Bovet, *Psychiatric Aspects of Juvenile Delinquency* (Palais Des Nations, Geneva, Switzerland: World Health Organization, 1951); *International Review of Criminal Policy* (No. 3, January 1953). The first reference deals chiefly with psychiatric causes and the second with medicopsychological factors, but both give certain social data.

7. Cf. Helen L. Witmer and Edith Tufts, *The Effectiveness of Delinquency Prevention Programs* (United States Department of Health, Education and Welfare, Children's Bureau, 1954).

INDEX